Technologies for Children

Third edition

Technologies for Children is a comprehensive guide to teaching design and digital technologies to children from birth to 12 years. Aligned with the Early Years Learning Framework and the Australian Curriculum: Technologies, this book provides practical ideas for teaching infants, toddlers, preschoolers and primary-aged children.

The third edition includes expanded content on teaching digital technologies, with a new chapter on computational thinking. Key topics covered include food and fibre production, engineering principles and systems, and computational thinking. The content goes beyond discussing the curriculum to consider technology pedagogies, planning, assessment and evaluation. Case studies drawn from Australian primary classrooms and early childhood centres demonstrate the transition from theory to practice. Each chapter is supported by pedagogical reflections, research activities and spotlights, as well as extensive online student resources.

Written by Marilyn Fleer, this book presents innovative, engaging and student-centred approaches to integrating technologies in the classroom.

Marilyn Fleer is an Australian Research Council Kathleen Fitzpatrick Laureate Fellow, and holds the Foundation Chair of Early Childhood Education and Development in the Faculty of Education, Monash University.

Cambridge University Press acknowledges the Australian Aboriginal and Torres Strait Islander peoples of this nation. We acknowledge the traditional custodians of the lands on which our company is located and where we conduct our business. We pay our respects to ancestors and Elders, past and present. Cambridge University Press is committed to honouring Australian Aboriginal and Torres Strait Islander peoples' unique cultural and spiritual relationships to the land, waters and seas and their rich contribution to society.

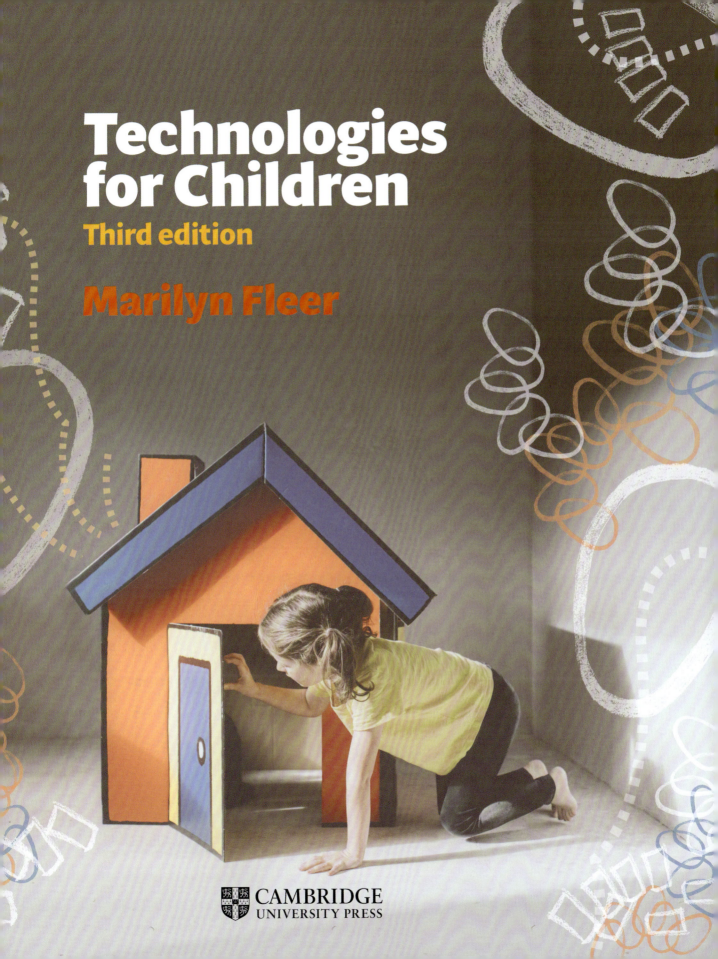

Shaftesbury Road, Cambridge CB2 8EA, United Kingdom

One Liberty Plaza, 20th Floor, New York, NY 10006, USA

477 Williamstown Road, Port Melbourne, VIC 3207, Australia

314–321, 3rd Floor, Plot 3, Splendor Forum, Jasola District Centre, New Delhi – 110025, India

103 Penang Road, #05–06/07, Visioncrest Commercial, Singapore 238467

Cambridge University Press is part of Cambridge University Press & Assessment, a department of the University of Cambridge.

We share the University's mission to contribute to society through the pursuit of education, learning and research at the highest international levels of excellence.

www.cambridge.org
Information on this title: www.cambridge.org/highereducation/isbn/9781009229593

© Cambridge University Press & Assessment 2016, 2019, 2023

This publication is copyright. Subject to statutory exception and to the provisions of relevant collective licensing agreements, no reproduction of any part may take place without the written permission of Cambridge University Press & Assessment.

First published as *Technology for Children* by Prentice Hall 1999
Second edition published by Pearson Education 2004
Third edition published as *Design and Technology for Children* by Pearson Education 2011
First published by Cambridge University Press 2016
Second edition 2019
Third edition 2023

Cover designed by Tanya De Silva
Typeset by Integra Software Services Pvt. Ltd
Printed in China by C & C Offset Printing Co., Ltd, May 2023

A catalogue record for this publication is available from the British Library

A catalogue record for this book is available from the National Library of Australia

ISBN 978-1-009-22959-3 Paperback

Additional resources for this publication at www.cambridge.org/highereducation/isbn/9781009229593/resources

Reproduction and communication for educational purposes
The Australian *Copyright Act 1968* (the Act) allows a maximum of one chapter or 10% of the pages of this work, whichever is the greater, to be reproduced and/or communicated by any educational institution for its educational purposes provided that the educational institution (or the body that administers it) has given a remuneration notice to Copyright Agency Limited (CAL) under the Act.

For details of the CAL licence for educational institutions contact:

Copyright Agency Limited
Level 12, 66 Goulburn Street
Sydney NSW 2000
Telephone: (02) 9394 7600
Facsimile: (02) 9394 7601
E-mail: memberservices@copyright.com.au

Cambridge University Press & Assessment has no responsibility for the persistence or accuracy of URLs for external or third-party internet websites referred to in this publication and does not guarantee that any content on such websites is, or will remain, accurate or appropriate.

Please be aware that this publication may contain several variations of Aboriginal and Torres Strait Islander terms and spellings; no disrespect is intended. Please note that the terms 'Indigenous Australians', 'Aboriginal and Torres Strait Islander peoples' and 'First Nations peoples' may be used interchangeably in this publication.

Contents

About the author ... ix
Acknowledgements ... x
Guide to online resources ... xi

PART 1 RESEARCHING TECHNOLOGY AND TECHNOLOGIES EDUCATION ... 1

1 What is technologies education? ... 2
Introduction ... 2
The people behind the technology ... 3
What do children think about technology? ... 9
Technacy ... 13
Technology transfer ... 16
Sustainable technologies ... 17
Technological knowledge ... 21
Teaching technology to children ... 29
Summary ... 29
Acknowledgements ... 30

2 Key ideas in the technologies curriculum ... 31
Introduction ... 31
What is unique about technologies education? ... 32
Looking inside a classroom: Making the content of the Australian Curriculum: Technologies visible in the teaching program ... 33
Generating designs ... 42
Case study: Evaluating design briefs ... 43
Analysing design briefs ... 51
Looking inside an early childhood setting: Engaging with the Early Years Learning Framework ... 56
Looking inside a classroom: Investigating, making, evaluating and designing paper planes ... 60
Summary ... 69
Acknowledgements ... 70

3 Designing and creating preferred futures ... 71
Introduction ... 71
Children conceptualising futures ... 73
Children's views of the future ... 76
Drawing about the future ... 79
Looking inside a classroom: Year 6 children planning for the design and creation of preferred futures ... 80

Looking inside a classroom: Year 1 and 2 children planning for the design and creation of preferred futures ... 82
Looking inside an early childhood setting: Planning for the future is about young children learning to plan ... 86
Summary ... 90
Acknowledgements ... 90

4 Creativity in design ... 91

Introduction ... 91
Design and technologies: Imagination and creativity in design ... 91
Digital technologies: Imagining and creating digital environments ... 92
Questioning the created environment ... 93
A framework for stimulating quality design questions ... 96
Case study: Practices and content suitable for preschool and Foundation to Year 2 ... 99
How do designers in the community work? ... 102
Creativity and imagination ... 107
Play as foundational to design thinking ... 110
Looking inside an early childhood centre: Toddler play as creative design ... 111
Looking inside a classroom: Primary children's play as creative design – architect's studio ... 113
Summary ... 117
Acknowledgements ... 117

PART 2 THE CURRICULUM IN ACTION ... 119

5 The curriculum in action: Digital technologies in everyday life, the community and the classroom/centre ... 121

Introduction ... 121
Digital technologies in everyday life ... 121
Ethics and digital technologies ... 123
Understanding the Australian Curriculum – Digital Technologies ... 129
Looking inside a classroom: A snapshot of teaching programs ... 131
Looking inside a classroom: Years 3 and 4 ... 134
Looking inside a classroom: Foundation level ... 139
Summary ... 143
Acknowledgements ... 143

6 The curriculum in action: Digital technologies – computational thinking ... 144

Introduction ... 144
What is computational thinking? ... 145

Looking inside a classroom: Year 6 computational thinking Conceptual PlayWorld	155
Looking inside a classroom: Years 5 and 6	160
Looking inside an early childhood centre: Preschoolers	165
Looking inside an early childhood centre: Toddlers	167
Summary	171
Acknowledgements	171

7 Technologies contexts: Food and fibre production and food specialisations — 172

Introduction	172
Approaches to technologies education	173
Approaches to technological contexts: Background information on fibre and fashion	175
Looking inside a classroom: The fashion industry under the microscope for Year 6 students	184
Looking inside a classroom: Fibre production in Year 3 – knitting	185
Looking inside an early childhood setting: Fibre production in early childhood	187
Approaches to technological contexts: Background information on food specialisations	187
Looking inside a classroom: Food specialisations – starting with children's everyday experiences with food	192
Looking inside a classroom: Years 5 and 6 designing and setting up their own café	194
Looking inside a classroom: Food specialisations – a snapshot of Year 3 and 4 children	196
Looking inside a classroom: Food specialisations – a snapshot of Foundation to Year 2 children	198
Summary	200
Acknowledgements	200

8 Technologies contexts: Engineering principles and systems, and materials and technologies specialisations — 201

Introduction	201
There are many types of engineers	202
Knowledge and approaches to learning in engineering contexts	204
Engineering design principles	207
Looking inside a classroom: Designing a city for Year 6	214
Looking inside a classroom: Engineering principles and systems when looking at human movement for Foundation and Years 1 to 4	218
Looking inside a classroom: Learning about materials and technologies specialisations through bridge-building for Years 1 to 4	221
Looking inside an early childhood setting: Materials and technologies specialisations using blocks	226
Summary	230
Acknowledgements	230

CONTENTS   vii

9 The curriculum in action: Project management — 231

- Introduction — 231
- The community project approach in technology — 232
- Looking inside an early childhood setting: Project management — 236
- Looking inside a classroom: Project management — 239
- Progression in project management — 241
- Project management: Setting up a class newspaper — 242
- Project management: Setting up and curating an art gallery — 244
- Project managing mini-enterprises — 246
- Engaging children holistically — 250
- Summary — 251
- Acknowledgements — 251

PART 3 PEDAGOGICAL PRACTICES FOR TECHNOLOGIES — 253

10 Planning, assessment and evaluation in technologies — 254

- Introduction — 254
- Finding out what children know — 254
- Setting up the learning environment — 268
- Designing spaces and interactions for assessment and planning — 271
- Organising learning environments to support creativity and imagination — 276
- Tinkering activities designed to enhance girls' technological capabilities — 285
- Summary — 292
- Acknowledgements — 292

11 Planning for teaching technologies: Analysing the pedagogical approaches — 293

- Introduction — 293
- Designing for pedagogical diversity — 294
- Summary — 305
- A final word — 305
- Acknowledgements — 306

References — 307

Index — 318

About the author

Laureate Professor Marilyn Fleer holds the Foundation Chair of Early Childhood Education and Development at Monash University, Australia. She was awarded the 2018 Kathleen Fitzpatrick Laureate Fellowship by the Australian Research Council and was a former President of the International Society of Cultural-historical Activity Research (ISCAR). Additionally, she holds the positions of an honorary Research Fellow in the Department of Education, University of Oxford, and a second professor position in the KINDKNOW Centre, Western Norway University of Applied Sciences, and has been bestowed the title of Honorary Professor at the Danish School of Education, Aarhus University, Denmark. She was presented with the 2019 Ashley Goldsworthy Award for Outstanding leadership in university-business collaboration, and was recently elected as a fellow of the Australian Academy of Social Sciences and inducted into the Honour Roll of Women in Victoria as a change agent.

Acknowledgements

Marilyn acknowledges the valuable contributions and support provided by Susan Jarvis (copy editor) and the staff at Cambridge University Press, Alison Dean (Content Manager), Rose Albiston (Publisher), Lauren Magee (Senior Development Editor) and Jodie Fitzsimmons (Assistant Director, Content Operations).

Marilyn recognises the Australian Research Council Laureate Fellowship Scheme (FL 180100161) and the PlayLab team.

The author and Cambridge University Press would like to thank the following for permission to reproduce material this book.

ACARA material: © Australian Curriculum, Assessment and Reporting Authority (ACARA) 2010 to present, unless otherwise indicated. This material was downloaded from the Australian Curriculum website (www.australiancurriculum.edu.au) (accessed July 2022) and was not modified. The material is licensed under CC BY 4.0 (https://creativecommons.org/licenses/by/4.0). Version updates are tracked in the 'Curriculum version history' section on the 'About the Australian Curriculum' page (http://australiancurriculum.edu.au/about-the-australian-curriculum/) of the Australian Curriculum website. ACARA does not endorse any product that uses the Australian Curriculum or make any representations as to the quality of such products. Any product that uses material published on this website should not be taken to be affiliated with ACARA or have the sponsorship or approval of ACARA. It is up to each person to make their own assessment of the product, taking into account matters including, but not limited to, the version number and the degree to which the materials align with the content descriptions and achievement standards (where relevant). Where there is a claim of alignment, it is important to check that the materials align with the content descriptions and achievement standards (endorsed by all education Ministers), not the elaborations (examples provided by ACARA).

Tables 1.5, 4.4 and **6.6:** Extracts from the *Early Years Learning Framework for Australia V2.0* (AGDE, 2022) are © Australian Government Department of Education for the Ministerial Council and reproduced under a CC by 4.0 International licence, https://creativecommons.org/licenses/by/4.0/.

Every effort has been made to trace and acknowledge copyright. The publisher apologises for any accidental infringement and welcomes information that would redress this situation.

Guide to online resources

The student online resources for *Technologies for Children* are available online at: www.cambridge.org/highereducation/isbn/9781009229593/resources. Visit the site to explore a variety of resources, including weblinks, activities, videos and downloadable templates.

 This margin icon is used throughout the book to indicate that a resource relating to the content under discussion is available online. The icon's descriptor can be used to help you easily identify each resource in the chapter's downloadable document.

Chapter 1 What is technologies education?

Video activity 1.1 Inventor Hedy Lamarr: Foundational technologies

View these three short videos to catch a small part of Hedy Lamarr's important work.

- Hedy Lamarr: Scientist and Actress (MSNBC)
- Meet Hedy Lamarr – Hollywood Star and Inventor of Wi-fi (Hiscox UK)
- Hedy Lamarr and Howard Hughes' Relationship (American Masters PBS)

Hedy Lamarr also designed new aerodynamic planes that could travel faster than previous planes. Conceptualised through the study of the aerodynamics of birds and a close examination of fish, a synthesis of form, shape and science resulted in the design.

PART 1

Researching technology and technologies education

This book is designed to be interactive. That means you are invited to replicate the research presented in the following chapters, as it is through documenting research evidence that greater understandings will be gained about the nature of technologies education.

You are also encouraged to consider the questions posed throughout the chapters in the Pedagogical Reflections, Spotlights and Activities sections. Try not to read on unless you have at least thought about your views on the questions raised. If you do this, the text that follows will be more meaningful and will position you as someone who is contributing to building, rather than just receiving, knowledge about the curriculum area of technologies. Through this process, you will be able to gain insights into what it means to be a researcher and teacher of technologies education for children from birth to 12 years. Although explicit reference is made to the Australian Curriculum: Technologies, this book seeks to go beyond just this particular interpretation of technologies. As will be shown throughout the book, views on what technology is, and therefore how to teach technologies education, are constantly changing. The key is to be part of this journey and to join the search for better conceptualisations and approaches to the teaching of technologies. This book seeks to support you in this important endeavour.

CHAPTER 1

What is technologies education?

Introduction

The terms 'technology' and 'technological literacy' are heard in many different forums (e.g. Seery et al., 2018). Newspapers often feature articles relating to technology and many politicians associate economic success with technological products and capabilities. Yet what do we really mean when we talk about technology, and what constitutes knowledge in technology education? This book brings together research on technologies education. You are invited to reflect critically upon this research by recording your reactions to the examples of teaching practices, children's comments and work samples, as well as the research, presented in each chapter.

This chapter aims to encourage you to clarify the meaning of technology, to think about the people behind various technologies and to broaden your perspective on how global issues relate to technology. Armed with this knowledge, you are invited to think about how you might challenge children through planning activities that are set in purposeful technological contexts (Figures 1.1 and 1.2). This is in keeping with the international evidence, which says that the most successful countries in Science, Technology, Engineering and Mathematics (STEM) are those that have made learning 'more engaging and practical, through problem-based and inquiry-based learning, and [with] emphases on creativity and critical thinking' (Freeman, Marginson and Tytler, 2015, p. 10).

PEDAGOGICAL REFLECTION 1.1

What is technology?

What do you understand by the term 'technology'? What are your images, concepts and feelings about technology in general, and how does technology fit in with your life and society as a whole? Record one key idea.

Following are some responses from student teachers to this question:

- Technology is everything we use around us – construction, clothing, tools, computers, machines, medicines and so on.
- We couldn't function as efficiently without technology, and probably wouldn't have as much leisure time.
- I have negative feelings about the impact new technologies have had on the environment.

- Technologies have contributed to the emancipation of women.
- Technology feels challenging and overwhelming when you don't know how to use it.

Are your views similar? How are they different/the same?

Thinking about the nature of technology and technologies education is important for building your own personal approach to teaching this important curriculum area (Xu, Williams and Gu, 2021). To broaden your thinking about the nature of technology, this chapter begins by exploring the people behind technology, considering societal views about technology and contemplating the cultural dimensions of technology. The chapter will conclude with an overview of the Australian Curriculum: Technologies (ACARA, 2023).

Figure 1.1 Engaging children in exploring digital technologies through a social purpose: the wild robot needs help. How do we code a robot to navigate around the bushland near the school?
Source: Monash University PlayLab and Redeemer Lutheran College.

Figure 1.2 Is this technology? Exploring digital technologies when explaining the program needed to help the wild robot navigate the school grounds.
Source: Monash University PlayLab and Redeemer Lutheran College.

The people behind the technology

Researchers have been interested in the connections between science, technology, engineering and mathematics for quite some time, linking them together in a range of ways over the years. These include a **silo approach** (keeping the subjects separate), an **embedded approach**

Silo approach: Keeping the subjects separate.

Embedded approach: One subject, such as maths, is taught through another subject, such as technologies.

Integrated approach: An approach where a problem is posed and knowledge of the subject areas is used in the service of solving the common problem.

(one subject, such as maths, is taught through another subject, such as technologies) and an **integrated approach**, where a problem is posed and the knowledges of the subject areas are in service of solving the common problem (García Terceño et al., 2021). Connection of these discipline areas is often highlighted in the work of technologists. The following narratives about technologists shed light on how inventions come about and how technological products can be developed in an integrated way that encourages a common passion and community of inquiry to emerge (O'Connor, Seery and Canty, 2018).

Knowing about technologists, their passions and their career milestones is relevant today because technology is in a state of constant change. We can learn a great deal from reflecting on the past and looking at the individuals who made a difference in their particular sphere. Teachers of technologies can highlight the people behind the technology and how they came up with cutting-edge technologies. Several narratives follow.

Foundational technologies

Hedy Lamarr was one of Hollywood's greatest stars in the 1940s. At the same time, she was an ingenious inventor. She could imagine technological solutions to complex problems through a series of inventions – many of which the world was not yet ready to understand or appreciate in terms of their power and significance to change life conditions. In her early childhood, she recalls many moments spent with her father discussing and looking at everyday objects in relation to 'how things work'.

Later in life, Hedy Lamarr invented 'frequency-hopping', which laid the foundation for wireless technology; this enabled the development of the internet, GPS, email and Wi-Fi.

SPOTLIGHT 1.1

Frequency-hopping spread spectrum (FHSS): A method of transmitting radio signals which rapidly switch from one frequency channel to another.

Inventor Hedy Lamarr conceptualises frequency-hopping

The term **frequency-hopping spread spectrum (FHSS)** is defined as a method of transmitting radio signals, which rapidly switch from one frequency channel to another. The pattern of switching frequency channels is identical for both the transmitter and the receiver.

Video activity 1.1 Inventor Hedy Lamarr: Foundational technologies

The concept of frequency-hopping arose during World War II. Hedy Lamarr was worried about the loss of life on ships and boats as a result of torpedo attacks at sea and wanted to keep marine vessels and their passengers safe. Inspired by an incident in which a boatload of children was attacked at sea by a torpedo, and not one child or crew member survived, she set about designing a method of signalling that was resistant to jamming and could act as a secure system of communication.

Computer technologies

In 1976, Steve Wozniak and Steve Jobs successfully launched Apple Computer I (or Apple I), yet neither of them had a university degree. They began a business in Jobs' garage, bringing the computer to market. Wozniak has described himself as a natural risk-taker and 'just a good engineer, doing what I was meant to do in life' (Wozniak, cited in Leyden 2008, p. 101).

Since leaving the company in 1987, Wozniak has taught for eight years in primary schools, written an autobiography, developed and brought to market the first universal TV remote control and helped to float a technology-development company. He says he is only interested in technology for the masses and believes that anyone can be a technologist. However, he advises would-be entrepreneurs not to start a company with just a good idea because the ability to build the technology is equally important.

Because of Bill Gates' vision for the personal computer, Microsoft became a leading computer and software company, making him one of the richest men in the world almost overnight. Gates also imagined what was to become the internet revolution, and in 1996 he radically reinvented his company around the internet.

During Gates' time as a student at Lakeside School in Seattle, the Mothers' Club did some fundraising to provide a computer terminal and computer time for students. Gates wrote his first software program, for playing tic-tac-toe, when he was 13 years old. The computer was huge and cumbersome, and writing the program was slow because the computer terminal had no screen. After typing the moves on a typewriter-style keyboard, Gates and his friends had to wait until the results sluggishly emerged from a printer before they could decide on the next move. Gates recalls:

> A game of tic-tac-toe that would take thirty seconds with a pencil and paper might eat up most of a lunch period. But who cared? There was just something neat about the machine. I realized later that part of the appeal must have been that here was an enormous, expensive, grown-up machine and we, the kids, could control it. We were too young to drive or do any of the other things adults could have fun at, but we could give this big machine orders and it would always obey. (Gates, 1996, pp. 1–2)

Games technologies

Game pioneer Allan Alcorn, the designer of the world's first popular video game (in 1972), was a junior engineer at Atari and his first task was meant merely to test his skills. However, the result was 'Pong', an electronic table-tennis game that led the way for modern video games. In contrast to coin-operated pinball machines, Pong was a social game that required two players, and it was the first game that appealed to young females. Alcorn said:

> I enjoy talking about the early days of video games and the fun we had. Perhaps I can inspire a young person to get involved in science and technology. Video games are part of a worldwide culture and as such we need to understand where it came from and where it is going. I hope that as a medium for entertainment it will add to the public good. (Alcorn, cited in Parker and King, 2008, p. 29)

Video activity 1.2
Game and animation technologies

Although the videos in the online resources activity relate to *information technology*, it is possible to notice that science, technology and engineering are needed, and in the real world these often overlap. We can also see that different types of STEM professionals are needed in information technology development (Figure 1.3), and these professionals work together when testing devices and materials to determine which are most suitable for the realisation of their designs (Lo, 2021). Some further examples follow.

Video activity 1.3
Biometrics

Biomimetics: Velcro® technology

One of the context areas in the Australian Curriculum – Technologies (ACARA, 2023) is fibre production, where technologies associated with fabrics are presented (see also Chapter 7). Within this context, have you ever wondered how technological innovation moves from research and into everyday life? Biomimetics is one fun fact to read about. The narrative of the founder of the product Velcro®, George de Mestral, provides a good starting point for a discussion of biomimetics, where design mimics naturally occurring phenomena. He trained as an electrical engineer and was fond of hunting in the lower slopes of the Jura Mountains in Switzerland. De Mestral's grandson said, 'Everyone remarked that he was often lost in his own world. In that "own world" of his he was on the lookout for fasteners' (Forbes, 2006, p. 94). At the time, De Mestral was motivated by the frustration of trying to fasten the hooks and eyes on his wife's evening dresses. Not wanting to be late for social functions, he thought there must be a better method of fastening garments. In 1948, after one of his hikes, he was examining the burrs that he had plucked from his pants and his dog's coat, and found that their spines were tipped with tiny hooks. This observation sparked his invention of Velcro® (Mueller, 2008).

Figure 1.3 Digital technologies increase access to new ways of thinking, being and working.

Fashion designers did not adopt his product until later, when nylon became available after the end of World War II (although it had been invented in 1937). Early applications of Velcro® were used in the first artificial heart surgery. Another early user of the hook-and-loop construction that grips instantly, but lets go with a tug, was NASA, which incorporated Velcro® into the space boots worn by its astronauts in the moon exploration missions. The *Apollo* astronauts also wore gloves with Velcro® tabs so they could latch down loose items when in zero gravity. The original patent was filed in 1951 and the product came onto the market in 1955.

The progression from the hook-and-loop or hook-and-eye fastener to gecko adhesion shows the size reduction in nanostructures. Designers have used the unique features of the gecko's toes, each of which has 6.5 million spatula-tipped hairs that adhere to surfaces. A product known as Geckskin was developed. This adhesive product allows for a draping action in the adhesion – that this, the product draws upon a gecko's gravity-defying locomotion across walls and ceilings.

Link 1.1 Geckskin

The team took the original research forward and developed Stickybot, a 500-gram robot, using a shape deposition manufacturing (SDM) process (Figure 1.4). The team comprised Mark Cutkosky (roboticist), Sangbae Kim (designer), Bob Fuller (expert in animal locomotion) and Kellar Autumn (a world authority on gecko adhesion). Bringing human stories into technologies offers another way of conceptualising the curriculum content. There will be other everyday contexts that humanise the Australian Curriculum: Technologies.

Designers argue that Stickybot has search-and-rescue applications suitable for collapsed buildings. Cutkosky said:

> I'm trying to get robots to go places where they've never gone before. I would like to see Stickybot have a real-world function, whether it's a toy or another application. Sure, it would be great if it eventually has a lifesaving or humanitarian role ... (Cutkosky, cited in Mueller, 2008, p. 86)

Figure 1.4 Stickybot
Source: Linda A. Cicero/Stanford News Service.

Biomimetics: Multidisciplinary teams for solving technological problems

The narrative of Andrew Parker, an evolutionary biologist and leading proponent of biomimetics, shows how he is applying designs from nature to solve problems in engineering, materials science and medicine. For example, Parker investigated iridescence in butterflies and beetles, and anti-reflective coatings in moth eyes, and his research led to brighter screens for cellular phones (Mueller, 2008). 'Biomimetics brings in a whole different set of tools and ideas you wouldn't otherwise have,' says materials scientist Michael Rubner of Massachusetts Institute of Technology (MIT), where biomimetics has entered the curriculum (Mueller, 2008, p. 74).

Biomimetics: Inclusive technologies

A further example of biomimetics can be seen in the work of bio-inspirationist Joanna Aizenberg with the microfabrication of crystal structures that has resulted in technical products. Aizenberg has different skills from those researchers who analyse natural structures. Her expertise in biomineralisation (the science of how mineral lattices are formed) was utilised at Bell Laboratories in New Jersey in the United States. In 2003, she discovered that at the base of the sea sponge Venus flower basket (*Euplectella aspergillum*) there are fine spines or whiskers that are made of optical fibres of superior quality. She is also working with the brittle star lens system and has shown that it is made from a single crystal of calcium carbonate. She found that each lens is engineered to bring the light to a focus according to the same principle as that first devised by Descartes and Huygens in the seventeenth century (Forbes, 2006). The lens array focuses the light at a point where there is a nerve receptor, 4 to 7 micrometres below the surface of the lens. Aizenberg is aiming to create technical equivalents to generate a new type of lens system that could help people who suffer from blindness. She is seeking to understand the modulating factors that affect crystal growth patterns and to produce crystal structures similar to those in nature.

These vignettes reveal the people behind the technologies, how they were inspired, what led to their breakthrough discoveries and how they worked. Technologists often work in multidisciplinary teams, testing materials and designing useful products to make life easier and to improve the general quality of life for everyone. Technologies work in real contexts, and this is something that teachers should consider when thinking about creating learning opportunities for children.

PEDAGOGICAL REFLECTION 1.2

What are the technological contexts in our society?

What other professions do you associate with technology? Make a list of the professions in a table similar to Table 1.1, give a reason for why you have selected the professions and illustrate your thinking with an example of the technology with which they work. Consider what might be all the technological contexts in our society. You will come back to your response in Activity 1.2.

Download 1.1 Professions in technology template

Table 1.1 Professions in technology

Profession (context)	Rationale	Technology use	Possible example of working as a multidisciplinary team

The points you included in Table 1.1 may have named other common 'high' technologies (digital devices) or the development of simple technologies (e.g. hook and eye). Technological processes such as cattle breeding, simple technologies such as the paper clip or traditional technologies like digging sticks are often not considered. Studies of student teachers, children and many Australian teachers have shown that they too only associate high technologies with the term 'technology' (Robbins and Babaeff, 2012). For this reason, only part of society is represented when high technologies are considered. The Australian Curriculum: Technologies (ACARA, 2023) redresses this by covering two subjects:

Design and Technologies: Using design thinking and technologies to generate and produce designed solutions for authentic needs and opportunities.

Digital Technologies: Using computational thinking and information systems to define, design and implement digital solutions for authentic problems.

- **Design and Technologies**, in which students use design thinking and technologies to generate and produce designed solutions for authentic needs and opportunities
- **Digital Technologies**, in which students use computational thinking and information systems to define, design and implement digital solutions for authentic problems.

The unique aspect of the Australian Curriculum: Technologies is that technologies enrich and impact on the lives of people and societies globally. They can play an important role in transforming, restoring and sustaining societies and natural, managed and constructed environments (ACARA, 2023). The following technological concepts are provided, broadening our thinking about the professions associated with technologies (ACARA, 2023). Perhaps some of the following came up in your list:

- engineering principles and systems
- food and fibre production
- food specialisations
- materials and technologies specialisations.

These contexts shown in the Australian Curriculum: Technologies are represented in our society as recognised fields in engineering, food technologies, digital technologies and more. But do children think about technologies in this way? We now turn our attention to what children think about technologies.

What do children think about technology?

As part of the journey of thinking about what is and is not technology, the perspectives that children bring should be considered. This has been a long-standing concern of researchers globally because children's attitudes shape how they engage in technologies education (Chiang et al., 2020). For instance, children's thinking about technology is important to consider because their technological questions create engaging contexts for organising learning. Children want to know the answers to their questions – they want to know how their world works. But how can children engage with, and contribute to, their designed environment? For instance, in Figure 1.5 a child asks some important questions about an everyday object – a sticky tape dispenser. What about everyday fun things that children do, such as blowing up balloons or applying face paint – could they be considered as technology (Figure 1.6)?

> How does sticky tape work?
> What is sticky tape made from?
> I think it is made of a piece of paper.
> Why is one side sticky and the other side not sticky? And the other side is slippery?

Figure 1.5 How does sticky tape work?

Jarvis and Rennie (1994) used a picture quiz to identify Australian and British children's perceptions of the term 'technology'. The researchers asked children (aged 7 and 11) to identify, from the following list of 28 items, which items had something to do with technology. Although this study was done some time ago, it still has relevance today. The list of items was:

- computer
- statue
- aeroplane
- factory
- volcano
- rose
- poodle
- gun
- bridge
- book
- advertisement
- telephone
- clock
- windmill
- cup
- platypus/fox
- cheese
- plan of house
- bedroom
- playground
- microwave oven
- sheet of music
- Stone Age axe
- gum tree/oak tree
- jeans
- cough medicine
- fish and chip shop
- mine.

Figure 1.6 Could balloons, face paint, the fabrics in jumpers and party preparation also be considered as technology?
Source: Kelly-Ann Allen.

The most frequently listed item was the computer (high technology) and the least frequent was the poodle (technological process). Do you think children's thinking in your community would be different now? Surprisingly, similar results have also been noted by Robbins and Babaeff (2012) in their study of teachers in Singapore and Australia.

More recently, a whole-school approach to finding the technologies in children's everyday lives was undertaken under the name of the 'Hastings–Monash School–Community Science and Technology Challenge'. In this project, the children were positioned as researchers investigating their community for the technologies and science they could find in everyday life – and things about which they were curious. The children wore a badge that said 'researcher'. This gave them the status and role of being someone who is in the process of investigating their technological environment. Wearing their researcher badges, the children undertook an environmental walk. They took photographs of what they were curious about. The children asked many questions about their designed environment, including:

- (photograph of neon lights) Where does light come from and where does it go?
- (photograph of houses being constructed – different stages) What are houses made from?
- (photographs of bicycles, cars, electric scooters) How do they move?
- (photographs of wind turbines) How do they move? How do they help us?

These and similar questions show that children want to know how things work. The children, with the support of their teachers and community volunteers, turned their questions and photographs into postcards – both e-cards and printed paper cards – that they sent to others in the community. They also set about investigating the answers to their questions through a series of in-school activities in their classrooms, but also investigated these questions in their after-school tinkering club. The tinkering club was an important space and place for children to answer their questions through pulling apart machinery, and also for inviting community members to work alongside them as they dismantled and often repaired everyday equipment (lawnmowers), used materials (sticky-tape and dispenser) and went on environmental walks to better understand the technologies that supported them (e.g. following pipelines, going to building sites).

Very young children also ask questions about their environment – questions that are meaningful to them (Figure 1.7). For example, in a project where families took photos at home of the everyday technologies that interested their children, 3-year-old Tommy asked his mother about a running tap: 'Where does the water go?' Tommy also showed the same interest in the flow of water and the mechanisms in the system in the toilet. His mother

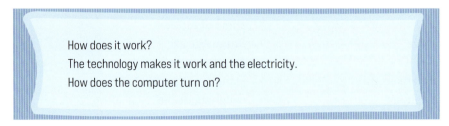

Figure 1.7 How does it work?

and teacher commented that he explored these everyday technologies through his play. For instance, he often used discarded pipes to build an array of channels in his sandpit, and frequently connected these up to a garden hose and observed the flow of the water.

ACTIVITY 1.1

Children's thinking about technology

Prepare a set of cards that show pictures or words relating to a broad range of technologies, such as those listed earlier. Invite a small group of children (an equal number of boys and girls) to sort the cards into piles of what they think is 'technology' and 'not technology'. Ask the children to explain their reasons for their decisions. If you don't have access to children, try this activity with a family member or a peer. Record your result and compare it with a colleague. What did you find? Do young children still associate technology with high technology? Do they think of technology as evidence of some form of societal advancement?

In Figure 1.8, a student sorts cards into what she associates with technology and what she believes is not technology.

Figure 1.8 What I associate with technology and what is not technology

There is a myth that technology is synonymous with progress, and this is reinforced by the belief that technology is advanced (Williams, Jones and Buntting, 2015). It has been argued that much of the popular literature presents a 'linear continuum between high and low technology' and this is seen also in the context of other binaries, such as 'inferior and superior technologies', or 'primitive and advanced civilisations and their technologies' (Williams, Jones and Buntting, 2015). What is often considered is how 'high' technology means some form of new technical invention, a labour-saving device, and frequently in the context of

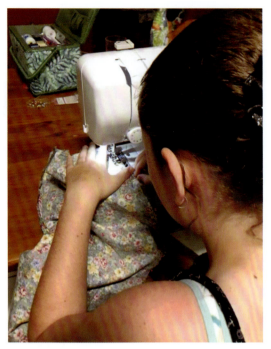

Figure 1.9 Could sewing be considered technology?
Source: Trisha Gleeson and Lani.

high consumption of resources (Figure 1.9). Only recently have some societies taken seriously the idea of using resources in technological inventions that can easily be recycled (Conway, Leahy and McMahon, 2021). For instance, laws in Sweden regarding the production of technologies such as TVs, mobile phones and refrigerators only allow for the use of components that can easily be recycled. In Denmark, plastic water bottles are now no longer available.

Stereotypes still exist that new or recently invented technologies suggest a measure of social and cultural development that positions old and traditional technologies as somehow inferior. It is argued by some that communities may equate technologies with the idea of advancement or sophistication. For instance, there has been a strong association between technology and advancement in Western cultures. Technologies are thought to be value free, but in fact they are value laden. Some technologies are positioned as having a higher social value than others. In Activity 1.2, you are invited to find out what people in your community think about technology.

ACTIVITY 1.2

What does the community think about technology?

In order to gain insight into what others in your community think about the term 'technology', interview the following people:

- a friend the same age as you
- a person from an older generation (e.g. a grandparent)
- a colleague who comes from a cultural heritage different from your own
- a farmer (if possible)
- a business person
- a person who works in some form of industry (e.g. manufacturing)
- a tradesperson (if possible)
- a person who works from home (e.g. domestic and/or home office).

Ask your interviewees to comment on:

- what comes to mind when they hear the word 'technology'
- the forms of technology they use
- their general thoughts or feelings about technologies
- technologies that they recall from their childhood
- how technologies have changed.

Invite interviewees to give examples of technologies as part of their responses. Analyse the responses. What do you notice? How were the comments similar to or different from the responses you gave in Pedagogical Reflections 1.1 and 1.2?

The research suggests that people think about technologies in a broad range of ways – for example:

- Technologies in most instances are viewed as stable and applied consistently to specific contexts in people's everyday lives.
- Different age groups think about technologies in different ways.
- Technology is immediate, often embodied in machinery and appliances, and thought about as representing some form of advancement.
- Technologies have been segregated by gender – domestic technologies (women); outdoor or work-related technologies (men).
- Technologies induce relatively strong feelings – for example, when digital technologies fail to work or are slow.

One of the ways in which technology has been conceptualised and defined is through the concept of **technacy**. The naming of technacy fits with the tradition of liter*acy* and numer*acy*, thus validating technologies as a key learning area. As you read the next section, consider whether the term 'technacy' captures a broader and more holistic view of technologies than the term 'technology'.

Technacy: Like liter*acy* and numer*acy*, technacy is 'the main art, skill and knowledge of appropriate technologists' (Seemann, 2000).

Technacy

The term 'technacy' was first introduced in 2000 by Kurt Seemann (2000, p. 68), who called for students to become competent in holistic technology practice, arguing the case for value-laden 'technacy', defining it as 'holistic technological problem solving, communication and practice. Technacy is the main art, skill and knowledge of appropriate technologists.' He refined the meaning of technacy education by using spotlight case study examples of technological solutions to problems faced by Aboriginal people in the remote Australian outback (see details in Spotlights 1.1 to 1.4). Seemann (2003, p. 252) also illustrated the interconnectedness of humans, tools and environmental settings, contending that a holistic or interconnected understanding of technology teaching and learning for any culture or gender setting is referred to as 'technacy education'.

Seemann (2022) questioned the relevance of studying technology disconnected from its social and cultural contexts. He argued that the social embeddedness of technologies is so important that it cannot be removed from technological learning, and he cited two examples to illustrate this social embeddedness: the introduction of the steel axe into remote Aboriginal communities and the construction of pandanus baskets by Aboriginal women. The examples are reproduced in part here in Spotlight 1.3 and Spotlight 1.4, respectively.

Web activity 1.1
Technacy and Kurt Seemann

These case studies highlight not only how artefacts and systems are socially embedded, but also that isolating them from their social context in technology education renders the experience invalid. Consequently, limiting children's learning to segments of reality – however contextualised they may be in the classroom (e.g. making a bird-feeder) – is a narrow and disembedded approach to technology education. Seemann (2022) argues that, as much of Western technical education is modularised and taught in relation to technical skills only, the meaning of the technology is lost. Gumbo (2020) argues that highlighting or integrating local Aboriginal and Torres Strait Islander technologies into the children's curriculum pushes against misconceptions about traditional technologies being less advanced. He suggests that integrating Aboriginal and Torres Strait Islander technology into the curriculum will also bridge the gap between home and school, particularly when disjunctions can create polarity, contradictions, distance and discontinuity. Both Seemann and Gumbo maintain that technologies must always be studied within the social and environmental contexts from which the particular technology emerged in the first place. Gumbo (2020) suggests that collaborations between Aboriginal and Torres Strait Islander learners and other students on design projects can support a broader view of what constitutes technology for a particular community. Specifically, he notes the riches of everyday technologies that can be found and drawn upon to show the resourcefulness of communities (Gumbo, 2020).

SPOTLIGHT 1.2

Rich design contexts for supporting the study of technologies education in poorly resourced communities

There is variability across communities around the world in terms of the availability of resources for technologies education. But often poorly resourced communities are thought to have few opportunities to support technologies education. In contrast, Gumbo (2020) argues that nature and the designed surroundings can provide a rich context for studying technologies. For example, Gumbo (2020, p. 296) has introduced a scenario for the study of food technologies whereby

> the idea of *morogo wa lerotho* is presented as part of processing products. This brings forward the idea of something not being thoroughly washed from dust. Products are laid on an iron sheet in the sun dry so that it can be preserved. However, this also makes the products susceptible to stealing or being vandalised by an animal.

How might this scenario be used to build a unit or project on design and technologies to support food technologies?

SPOTLIGHT 1.3

The steel axe

Most traditional Aboriginal and Torres Strait Islander communities today use the short-handled steel axe for hunting and gathering, and for crafting goods for the tourism market. However, when missionaries first handed out the axes to encourage church patronage, a ripple effect disrupted long-standing social structures – the axe was traditionally a man's tool. The prized smooth stones of traditional axes were tradable items, linking local groups with trade lines across the country. For groups in the far north, the hardwood axe handle had to be traded from desert groups to the south as local woods were less suitable. Some men held particular status because of acquired skills as trade negotiators, and because they had established friendships across vast lines of trade. Skills of diplomacy in trade gave rights to men to regulate use of the axe. To gain a traditional education in the production of axes was to develop social trading skills, technical knowledge and techniques in assembly and selective extraction of local natural resources.

For a school to teach a module that leads to the fabrication of a traditional stone axe without genuinely developing skills in trade negotiation, and in the selective extraction of raw timber from the environment in a socially acceptable way [disembeds the technology from real life].

Source: Seemann (2000, p. 63).

SPOTLIGHT 1.4

Pandanus basket construction

For women in island communities, learning the technical skills of basket construction is necessarily a social event deeply embedded in sustainable human and environmental relationships. The whole exercise necessarily integrates social, technical and environmental knowledge and skills. To represent the pandanus 'curriculum' in a series of parts would be to misrepresent the quality of the integrated knowledge these women have developed. A disintegrated curriculum simply produces disintegrated judgements, and hence inadequate solutions to the project or problem at hand.

Source: Seemann (2000, p. 66).

SPOTLIGHT 1.5

Zulu Mama Chair

Also drawing upon the concept of technacy, Gumbo (2015) examined the significance of integrating Indigenous technology into the Technology curriculum, arguing that this systematically validates a broader set of views about what technology is – especially Indigenous technologies. He cited the example of the iconic Zulu Mama Chair, which integrates both valued Indigenous Zulu basket weaving and recently developed plastic materials to form a comfortable chair that is rich in meaning. Gumbo (2015, p. 72) states that 'the basket seat expresses the archetypal feminine activity of gathering, an appropriate gesture for indoor and outdoor café seating'. In addition, the weaving activity supports the economy of the community, provides economic independence and has resulted in additional industries being formed because the woven plastic is made from recycled factory waste.

Web activity 1.2 Zulu Mama Chair revisited

Seemann's introduction of the word 'technacy' in the context of his research into local Aboriginal and Torres Strait Islander technologies illustrates the complexity of naming technologies, and the need for considerably more thought to be given to capturing the social embeddedness of technology when teaching programs are being developed. Technacy suggests that the technological practices and artefacts are part of the cultural practices of a community; therefore, culture and technology are interwoven. Despite these insights into how to frame technologies in education, there is still a serious gap in the research literature regarding how to successfully integrate Indigenous technologies into technology education (Gumbo, 2015). For instance, Miller (2014, p. 71) states that in the context of sustainability, educators must be mindful of not:

- trivialising the richness and diversity of Indigenous peoples through simplistic talk, images and resources (of their technologies)

- romanticising aspects of Indigenous cultures and relying on overt cultural symbols – for example, art, dance, music and food – that objectify Indigenous peoples and practices
- accessing support and engagement as a reactive step, including educators making contact only when gaps in their own knowledge become apparent or in response to a new policy direction
- failing to demonstrate preparedness – for example, listening, learning, unlearning, self-analysis – in partnership with Indigenous people to support reciprocity and long-term engagement.

Serious problems have arisen from technologies being misappropriated and transferred across cultures where the technological contexts are very different (see also Chapter 2, Table 2.1).

Technology transfer

In a global world, we often see the transfer of technologies from one culture to another; however, some technology transfers are likely to yield long-term problems – for example, the Lapps or Laplander people from Nordic regions have adopted new technologies into their traditional cultural practices. Technology is constructed within a particular culture to meet the needs of that culture, and therefore cannot be transferred easily, as described in Spotlight 1.6.

SPOTLIGHT 1.6

Technology transfer – the snowmobile

When they [the snowmobiles] were purchased for use in reindeer herding in Lapland, the owners found they needed to carry ample supplies of fuel and spare parts, and to acquire new skills to accomplish emergency repairs when breakdowns occurred. The social impact of the snowmobile was, however, much more profound than this. The initial costs associated with buying the snow-mobiles and the ongoing maintenance costs meant that only a small number of families could herd cattle with the new technology. In addition, it was determined that it would be uneconomical for small herders and farmers to buy snowmobiles. As such, only the farmers from the big farms bought them. This had the effect of farmers from small holdings being bought out, and these farmers in turn became labourers or were unemployed. The net effect was that a predominantly egalitarian society, where all owned and worked their own farms, was transformed into a dual society, inegalitarian and hierarchical. Indigenous industries associated with previous methods of herding, involving sledges, skis and dogs, were adversely affected by the change, and an increase in dependency on foreign sources of snowmobiles followed.

Source: Layton (1992, p. 42), cited in Siraj-Blatchford (1997, p. 29).

PEDAGOGICAL REFLECTION 1.3

Does technology transfer really occur?

Can you think of other technologies that have been transferred from one culture to another? What were the results?

In the past, many aid programs operating in countries in which the majority of the people were poor caused long-term problems and disruptions to the fabric of the community. Deliberate attempts are now made to develop technological solutions from within the context of the community in which the need arises, using local resources, skills and technologies.

A further consideration in the analysis of culture and technology is the exploitation of some poor, under-developed countries by richer nations. There are many examples of natural resources (e.g. genetic material) that are scarce or no longer in existence in rich, developed countries. This is often the result of a country's over-consumption and the eventual depletion of resources (e.g. plants, variety rights), land abuse and mass production (e.g. a few varieties of wheat being taken from poor, under-developed countries, patented and sold back to them at exorbitant prices). The extensive development and over-consumption of resources in rich minority countries have also led to environmental problems (Engstrom, 2018), which is raised as a concern by teachers (Svensson and von Otter, 2018).

Similar arguments can be directed towards rich, developed countries such as Australia, where goods from some countries can be purchased at very low prices. In some cases, the low prices reflect the sub-standard conditions in which young girls and women work to produce goods for sale overseas. From time to time, there are discussions in the media about unsafe working environments and the need for countries to make decisions about what is imported. The ethics of purchasing is foregrounded (Svensson and von Otter, 2018). It is often suggested that legislation should be enacted to prevent the purchase of goods from companies that exploit their workers.

PEDAGOGICAL REFLECTION 1.4

Exploitation and technology

Can you think of other ways Australians can change their practices so as not to endanger or encourage the exploitation of people in poor majority countries? How can these issues be raised with young children? Write down three key ideas and share these with a colleague.

Sustainable technologies

Eco-development, which makes use of natural contexts and natural resources, has seen a shift away from 'economic' fitness to 'ecological' fitness, such as integrated agro-industrial ecosystems that use environmentally responsible methods to produce food, energy and chemicals.

In Australia, the Centre for Appropriate Technology in Alice Springs is actively involved in developing technological solutions for Aboriginal communities and isolated settlements.

Eco-development: Using natural contexts and natural resources, such as integrated agro-industrial ecosystems that use environmentally responsible methods to produce food, energy and chemicals.

Figure 1.10 Is a cup of coffee a technology? Where was the coffee grown? Is it Fair Trade coffee? Is it organic? What might its footprint be?

A two-way relationship has developed, with both researchers and teachers applying and learning from Aboriginal problem-solving in technology. Sustainability requires everyone to rethink the way technology is assessed, chosen and used, but how can we decide what might be a sustainable and appropriate technology? The following list of criteria can be used with children, first to explain the concept of appropriate technology, then to evaluate whether the technology is sustainable and therefore appropriate. Children can also be encouraged to produce their own list of criteria for evaluating whether or not technologies are appropriate. Three types of questions are introduced, relating to sustainability, economics, and power and agency (Figure 1.10).

Sustainability questions:

- Do we need it?
- What is the footprint of the resources? Can we draw upon local skills?
- Does it use renewable energy?

Economic questions:

- Can we afford it?
- Will it make money?
- Can we market it to create a demand?

Power and agency questions:

- Who is in control – the user, the designer or the producer?
- Is it culturally acceptable?
- Does it increase self-reliance?

Download 1.2 Checklist: 'Is it an appropriate technology for us?'

PEDAGOGICAL REFLECTION 1.5

Evaluating the appropriateness of technologies

Use the checklist in Table 1.2 as a guide to evaluate your own design work and that of other designers from a similar culture. Evaluate the appropriateness of the technologies listed by placing a tick or a cross in each box. Add your own examples of technology and check these against the criteria.

Table 1.2 Checklist: 'Is it an appropriate technology for us?'

Technology	Do we need it?	What is the footprint?	Does it use renewable energy?	Cost	Can we create market demand?	Who is in control?	Is it culturally appropriate?
1 Plastic chopstick							
2 Child's shoe with Velcro® strap							

Table 1.2 (cont.)

Technology	Do we need it?	What is the footprint?	Does it use renewable energy?	Cost	Can we create market demand?	Who is in control?	Is it culturally appropriate?
3 Robotic doll							
4 Remote-controlled vehicle							
5 Egg carton							
6 New rose variety							
7 Digital device							
8 Sunscreen							
9 Commercially produced snack							
10 Cup of coffee							
11 Leather bag							
12 Water bottle							
13							
14							
15							

These are important activities to engage in when working with others, and when reflecting upon the appropriateness of particular technologies. Young and Cutter-Mackenzie (2014, p. 147) suggest that in the context of early childhood sustainability, staff and families should come together and undertake the following critique of their programs:

- Examine the practice of sustainable education (including appropriate technologies) with a focus on educators' experiences in the development and implementation of sustainable education programs.
- Examine whether community engagement informs and influences sustainable education (including appropriate technologies) and how this enables young children to participate in community life as active and informed environmental citizens.
- Examine how sustainable education (including appropriate technologies) is incorporated into the curriculum and how this enables young children to construct environmental world-views.
- Identify the barriers and drivers to the emergence of sustainable education (including appropriate technologies) with a focus on systems thinking and ethics.

Svensson and von Otter (2018) have studied teachers' views on sustainability, asking: 'What is sustainable development for you? What do you think about the relationship between technology and sustainable development?' They found that teachers perceived sustainable development in relation to technology education in terms of three themes:

1. recycling thinking
2. consequence thinking
3. systems thinking.

Recycling thinking includes considering raw materials to recycling (footprint), recycling from a social perspective (impact on other countries of not being sustainable) and recycling from a global perspective (how it affects the entire Earth).

Consequence thinking involves the impact of the technology and its consequences on the environment, the potential of technology to solve environmental problems and the ethical dilemmas related to whether the technology is perceived as good or bad, or right or wrong, in relation to the environment.

Finally, Svensson and von Otter (2018) note that in **systems thinking**, the teachers in their study used a life-cycle analysis, such as the product's life-cycle (where the resources come from, where the product goes). They also drew upon a material analysis approach, where they examined the flow of materials within a system. In studying the technological system as a whole in the environment itself, such as transport systems or energy systems, teachers argued that then it becomes possible to focus on particular components of a system in relation to the whole environment as a system. The positive and agentic approach of the teachers suggests that a relationship between technologies and the environment affords the potential to act for change.

A further agentic approach is presented by Young and Cutter-Mackenzie (2014, pp. 145–6), who identify a series of steps as an action plan for supporting local attention on sustainability that is useful for thinking about how to institutionalise localised **sustainable technologies**:

1. whole-school commitment
2. establishment of committee (including parents)
3. policy development
4. setting goals and targets
5. baseline data collection
6. assessment and audit practices, infrastructure and operations
7. community partnership
8. development of action plan
9. development of curriculum plan
10. implementation of action plan
11. monitoring and evaluation.

Although action in local communities may influence institutional change, there must also be national policies and expenditures that encourage the innovative use of sustainable technologies.

The previous section examined beliefs about technology, and looked at some of the people behind the technology to give a human quality to thinking about technologies. These ideas have been taken further in this section by examining technology as embedded in society and as part of people's cultural practices. This section has also considered the ideas of technological transfer, and the development and use of sustainable and appropriate

---

Recycling thinking: Considering raw materials to recycling (footprint), recycling from a social perspective (impact on other countries of not being sustainable) and recycling from a global perspective (how it affects the entire Earth).

Consequence thinking: Considering the impact of technology and its consequences on the environment, the potential of technology to solve environmental problems and the ethical dilemmas related to technology.

Systems thinking: Studying a technological system as a whole in the environment itself, such as transport systems and energy systems.

Sustainable technologies: A series of steps as an action plan for supporting local attention on sustainability.

technologies to support human needs. The next section looks at the research evidence that has provided this broad conception of technology, and that has shaped thinking about the nature of technological knowledge.

ACTIVITY **1.3**

Government resources

Go to your local government website.

Consider how you might use the material on this website as a resource to investigate from a sustainability perspective. How might you work together with a group of children to develop an action plan? Draw on Young and Cutter-Mackenzie's (2014) action plan to help you.

Technological knowledge

In the context of technological knowledge, Gumbo (2020) asks whose knowledge gets legitimised in the school curriculum. Gumbo suggests that Indigenous technological knowledge is vast and deep, and includes a body of knowledge that has been developed by a culture to serve their needs and improve their lives. For instance, he has shown how Indigenous technology includes looms and textiles; jewellery and brass-work manufacture; and technological knowledge about agriculture, fishing, forestry, resource exploitation, atmospheric management techniques, knowledge-transmission systems, architecture, medicine and pharmacy. Gumbo supports the idea of Indigenous technological content knowledge being conceptualised as:

- technology as it relates to multiple contexts
- epistemological issues surrounding the concept of technology
- end-users' cultural values versus designers' cultural values
- technologies and designs that include Indigenous contexts, including case studies
- technological resources and materials that include those in Indigenous contexts
- principles of technological applications that embrace those in Indigenous contexts
- profiles of prominent innovators and technologists, including those from Indigenous contexts
- trade value of the technologies, including those from Indigenous contexts (Gumbo 2020).

In line with Gumbo (2020) and Seemann (2022), Fox-Turnbull (2015, p. 116) makes the point that both context and concepts are integral because the context acts as a 'vehicle' through which the learning of the concepts occurs, and this is key to technology education. However, she makes the distinction between context and concepts when thinking about teacher planning. Fox-Turnbull (2015, p. 116) suggests that while context and concepts should always be integrated, in planning for learning it is useful to separate these out to enable teachers to notice the 'key technological concepts and ideas to be taught'. An example is provided in Table 1.3.

Table 1.3 Learning outcomes with context separated

Learning intention	Context
Children's learning involves:	
Engaging in making a mock-up and noticing that this improves quality	Dolls' clothing
Technological planning, which involves everyone and maximises team members' input	Preparing a school birthday party or other celebration
Engaging with the physical and functional aspects of equipment and noticing how they support performance	Outdoor play equipment
Examining environmental issues and their impact	Smartphones
Representing ideas in 3D plans using software programs	Cubby houses
Working with clients to produce a product	Web pages

Source: Adapted from Fox-Turnbull (2015).

The issue of what constitutes the content knowledge of technologies education has also been examined by Barlex (2015), who argues that it is useful to conceptualise ideas *about* technology and ideas *of* technology. He gives the following examples.

Ideas *about* technology:

- People develop technologies to change the natural world.
- Technologists use a broad range of knowledge from other disciplines, such as science and mathematics.
- There are multiple solutions to technological problems.
- The worth of a technology is always a value judgement.
- Technologies will often have unintended outcomes, which cannot be predicted in advance.

Ideas *of* technology include:

- knowledge of materials (sources, properties, longevity, footprint)
- knowledge of manufacturing (subtraction, addition, forming assembly finishing)
- knowledge of functionality (powering, controlling, structuring)
- knowledge of design (identifying needs and wants; seeking market opportunities, generating, developing and evaluating design ideas)
- knowledge of critique with regard to impact (for justice and stewardship).

Barlex (2015) argues that most of the made and modified natural environment comes into existence through design, and this is based on human needs and a strong element of critiquing and evaluating impact. Manufacturing, for instance, has been conceptualised around human needs in the context of market forces (supply and demand).

Barlex (2015) cites the example of the automobile industry as a disruptive innovation because initially car technology was expensive and so did not disrupt the horse-drawn transport industry until the Model T Ford was introduced in 1908. Henry Ford specifically sought to design and manufacture a car that could be assembled cheaply from good-quality materials in order to make it affordable for most families. The final car design had to go through the production line efficiently so it could be produced cheaply. It had to be painted black because this colour would dry fastest and not hold up production along the assembly line. In this example, the knowledge of manufacturing is clearly linked to a strong knowledge of critique – of how the technology might deliberately disrupt established technologies.

Williams (2012) argues that there is no common view of what constitutes technological knowledge across countries. There is a diversity of views and a diversity of cultural practices and beliefs associated with technologies and technology education. At this early stage of considering what might be included in a definition of technologies, and what might constitute content knowledge of this area, document your thoughts about the key ideas you believe are important following the key prompts in Table 1.4.

Table 1.4 Technological concepts

Topic	Key idea 1	Key idea 2	Key idea 3
What do you intend the students to learn about this idea?			
Why is it important for the students to know this?			
What are some difficulties/limitations connected with teaching this idea?			
What other factors influence your teaching of this idea?			
What are some specific ways of ascertaining student understanding or confusion about the idea?			

Source: Adapted from Williams (2012).

Download 1.3
Technological concepts

PEDAGOGICAL REFLECTION 1.6

What might be content knowledge of technologies?

Williams (2012), working with colleagues, examined what teachers thought were important aspects of technologies education. He asked what professional knowledge might be needed to determine what content knowledge formed technologies, and how this content might be taught successfully. Table 1.4 presents the matrix he used to solicit teacher views. In drawing upon what you have read in this section, record your one key idea. Don't worry if you leave some lines blank, as your ideas are still forming and will continue to do so as you read through this book. You will return to this table and this pedagogical reflection later in the book.

Williams (2012, p. 171) found that teachers needed to have a context within which to discuss the key ideas – that is, they needed to contextualise content knowledge in technology in relation to a 'project which permitted the application of the content'. This finding supports the arguments put forward by Barlex (2015), Fox-Turnbull (2015), Gumbo (2020) and Seemann (2022) about the integration of context and concepts for authentic and engaging learning in technologies for all children – but particularly Aboriginal and Torres Strait Islander children.

What has emerged in the literature is a model that foregrounds pedagogical content knowledge of technology, known as **TPACK** (previously known as TPCK). TPACK stands for Technological Pedagogical Content Knowledge (see www.matt-koehler.com/tpack-101). Integrating this as the context for the teaching and learning of technologies focuses on:

- content knowledge (CK)
- pedagogical knowledge (PK)
- pedagogical content knowledge (PCK)
- technology knowledge (TK)
- technological content knowledge (TCK)
- technological pedagogical knowledge (TPK)
- technological pedagogical content knowledge (TPCK).

> **TPACK**: Technological Pedagogical Content Knowledge.

In Figure 1.11, we can see how TPACK brings together content, pedagogy and technological knowledge. This framework suggests that the key to technologies is understanding their *concepts*. Pedagogical content knowledge is about knowing what kind of pedagogy best helps children to learn technologies. Knowing students' prior ideas is important. When using this framework, it is important to gain insights into what ideas children might have about technologies and to create the pedagogical conditions that allow children a range of ways of looking at the same common problem or idea.

What does this mean for teachers of technologies when looking closely at the concepts put forward in curriculum documents? Most curriculum documents outline explicit concept statements, but do not necessarily outline the pedagogy or the context within which these take place (Doyle et al., 2018). A curriculum details those concepts that a particular society has agreed are the concepts to be learned and the order in which they should be learned.

As a teacher of technologies, you will also need to find out how technology is defined in the Australian Curriculum: Technologies (ACARA, 2023) and/or the Early Years Learning Framework (AGDE, 2022). The term 'technologies' is used to help bring together these *two subject areas of Digital Technologies and Design Technologies* into *one learning area*.

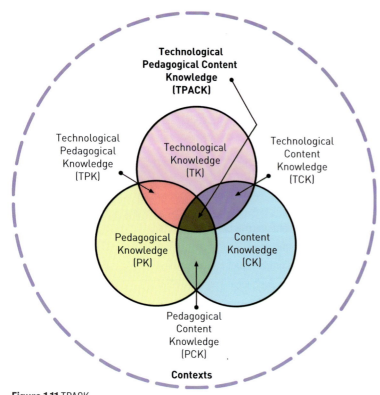

Figure 1.11 TPACK
Source: Reproduced by permission of the publisher, © 2012 by tpack.org.

Design and Technologies is thought about as a subject where children use design thinking and digital technologies to generate and produce solutions. These solutions are designed for authentic needs and opportunities, such as designing a new lunch-ordering system so that the children's lunches arrive hot.

Digital Technologies involves students using computational thinking and information systems to define, design and implement digital solutions (Fox-Turnbull, 2018). For example, after going on an excursion where numerous photos were taken, the children might use a digital platform to store, organise and retrieve a series of photos to put into their digital book to capture and discuss the event. We see this (and more) also represented in the subject area of Digital Technologies:

- *Digital systems:* processing data in binary, made up of hardware, controlled by software, and connected to form networks.
- *Data representation:* data being represented and structured symbolically for storage, use and communication, by people and in digital systems.
- *Data acquisition:* numerical, categorical or structured values acquired or calculated to create information.
- *Data interpretation:* extracting meaning from data.
- *Abstraction:* reducing complexity by hiding details so that the main idea, problem or solution can be defined and focus can be on a manageable number of aspects.
- *Specification:* defining a problem precisely and clearly, identifying the requirements, and breaking the problem into manageable pieces.
- *Algorithms:* the precise sequences of steps and decisions needed to solve a problem, often involving iterative (repeated) processes.
- *Implementation:* the automation of an algorithm, typically by writing a computer program or using appropriate software.
- *Privacy and security:* the protection of data when it is stored or transmitted through digital systems. (ACARA, 2023)

Video activity 1.4 Digital Technologies F–7

Design and Technologies and Digital Technologies are clearly interrelated. For instance, children can investigate an existing lunch-ordering system by digitally photographing existing practices, gathering data in a digital survey on what people think about it or ideas they may have to improve the system, then put forward a design solution for the class to consider and vote on.

The two subject areas support the aims of the Australian Curriculum: Technologies. The curriculum focuses on developing the knowledge, understanding and skills of individuals and collaborative groups of children, so that children:

- investigate, design, plan, manage, create and evaluate solutions
- are creative, innovative and enterprising when using traditional, contemporary and emerging technologies, and understand how technologies have developed over time
- make informed and ethical decisions about the role, impact and use of technologies in their own lives, the economy, environment and society for a sustainable future
- engage confidently with and responsibly select and manipulate appropriate technologies – tools, equipment, processes, materials, data, systems and components – when designing and creating solutions
- analyse and evaluate needs, opportunities or problems to identify and create solutions. (ACARA, 2023)

These aims capture much of what is already known about the nature of technology and technology education previously introduced in this chapter; however, it is important to note that the curriculum introduces this important content through two interrelated *strands*:

- Knowledge and Understanding
- Processes and Production Skills.

Figure 1.12 shows the digital content structure for Digital Technologies, and Figure 1.13 shows the content structure for Design and Technologies. The figures show how the learning areas are structured into strands and sub-strands.

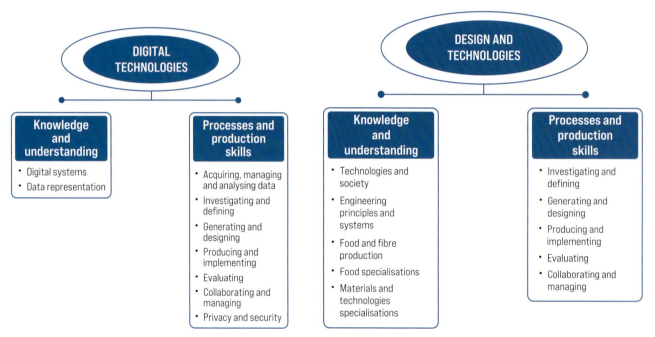

Figure 1.12 Digital Technologies content structure
Source: ACARA (2023).

Figure 1.13 Design and Technologies content structure
Source: ACARA (2023).

When you jump onto the website for the Australian Curriculum, you will see that the platform provides a common introductory section for each learning area, which includes:

- *Introduction:* specifies which year levels are provided in this curriculum.
- *Rationale:* describes the importance of the learning area, and how students will benefit from its study.
- *Aims:* identify the learning that students demonstrate as a result of being taught the content of the learning area.
- *Structure:* describes how the learning area is structured into strands and sub-strands.
- *Key considerations:* provides important information to help teachers gain a deeper understanding of the learning area and plan for teaching and learning.
- *Key connections:* identifies the relationship of the learning area to general capabilities, cross-curriculum priorities and other learning areas (ACARA, 2023).

As you dive deeper into the website, you will see that each learning area or subject of the Australian Curriculum gives a sequence of learning from Foundation to Year 10. The

Technologies learning areas (Design and Technologies and Digital Technologies) present the curriculum for Foundation year and then in two-year bands up to Year 10.

When navigating your way around the website, you will come across some key terms and labels:

- *Year or band level descriptions:* provide an overview of the learning that students should experience in each year or two-year band.
- *Achievement standards:* describe the expected quality of learning that students should typically demonstrate by the end of each year or two-year band. Achievement standards are accompanied by annotated work samples to assist teachers to make judgements about the extent to which the achievement standard has been met.
- *descriptions:* specify the essential knowledge, understanding and skills that students are expected to learn, and teachers are expected to teach, in each year or two-year band. Content descriptions are organised into strands and, in some learning areas, are further organised into sub-strands. They are accompanied by content elaborations.
- *Content elaborations:* provide teachers with suggestions for and illustrations of ways to teach the content descriptions. They are optional material only; they are not a set of complete or comprehensive content points that all students need to be taught. They illustrate and exemplify content descriptions with a diverse range of examples (ACARA, 2023).

The introduction of this new version of the Australian Curriculum: Technologies on a web platform means that the elaborations and working examples will continue to be updated – keep looking over time as new content becomes available to support your planning for learning in the subject areas of Design and Technologies and Digital Technologies.

The Early Years Learning Framework

As teachers, you will also need to examine the Early Years Learning Framework (EYLF) for the birth to 5 years sector. How might you engage infants, toddlers and preschool-aged children in technologies education (Figure 1.14)? What does the study of technologies look like in the EYLF? Why might it be important to study technologies in the birth to 5 years area? We invite you to think about these questions by preparing a mind map, where you constantly add to your existing thoughts what you learn as you progress through the chapters in this book.

Where is technologies education in the EYLF? Examination of the EYLF (AGDE, 2022, p. 58) shows that technologies are included. For instance, Outcome 5 focuses on children becoming effective communicators, where digital technologies are highlighted: 'Children use digital technologies and media to access information, investigate ideas and represent their thinking.'

Figure 1.14 How might you teach the technologies curriculum to infants?

Video activity 1.5 Digital Technologies: The Early Years Learning Framework

A strong rationale is given in the EYLF (AGDE, 2022, p. 57):

> Children live in a digital world. They are digitally connected through many devices. Digital technologies offer possibilities for learning, engagement, wellbeing and social connection. Children learn about, and how to use, digital technologies in their relationships with other children and adults. Valuable learning opportunities can be found in children's everyday activities that support shared engagement and learning. All children benefit from opportunities to explore their world using technologies and to develop confidence in using digital technologies and media.

The EYLF suggests that educators should integrate technologies into children's play. This might be apparent when children learn how to operate a digital camera and upload photos to make a digital book or animation (e.g. a movie) or when they use blocks or digital tools to design a theatre for their puppets (see Figure 1.15). It might also mean giving children a smart device to document their play, to share with a child who may be absent, thus providing continuity for children's play across days.

Using everyday technologies, such as non-representative materials like icy pole sticks, pipe cleaners and bottle tops, also enriches children's play (see Robbins and Babaeff, 2012) is also seen in the EYLF (AGDE, 2022). This is also seen when everyday real technologies, such as chopsticks, knives and forks, and replica and miniature household items, are made available to children in the home corner. For instance, the EYLF (AGDE, 2022, p. 56) recognises in Outcome 4 (Children are confident and involved learners) the place of materials technologies. Table 1.5 shows extracts from 'Children resource their own learning through connecting with people, place, technologies and natural and processed materials'.

Figure 1.15 Children use technologies to enrich their play

Table 1.5 Children resource their own learning through connecting with people, place, technologies, and natural and processed materials

This is evident when children, for example:	Educators promote this learning for all children when they, for example:
• use their senses and body movements to explore natural and built materials and environments • explore the purpose and function of a range of tools, media, sounds and graphics • manipulate natural and manufactured materials and resources to investigate, take apart, assemble, invent and construct • experiment with different technologies • explore 2D and 3D forms of expression to develop understandings of different artforms and elements.	• provide sensory and exploratory experiences with a wide variety of open-ended natural and processed materials • select and introduce appropriate tools, technologies and media and provide the skills, knowledge and techniques to enhance children's learning • provide opportunities for children to both construct and take apart materials as a strategy for learning

Source: ADGE (2022, p. 56).

The Australian Curriculum: Technologies and the EYLF both provide educators with perspectives on what might constitute the nature of technology and technologies education. The key features of these curriculum documents in action are shown through a series of case studies in later chapters in this book.

Teaching technology to children

Technology education for early childhood and primary education in Australia has continued to change over the years. What have been your experiences as a technological learner in school? How do you feel about teaching this area of the curriculum to young children?

> **PEDAGOGICAL REFLECTION 1.7**
>
> **What are your feelings about teaching the curriculum area of technologies?**
>
> Record what you think technologies education should involve. Add to this your thoughts that you have already documented in your mind map of where and why technologies appears in the EYLF. How should this learning area be taught to children? Draw an image of yourself teaching children technologies education. Now consider what might be the important learning outcomes that come under the umbrella of technologies education. Record your ideas.

An example of a student teacher's response to 'drawing themselves teaching technology' is shown in Figure 1.16 (before). This image was made at the beginning of the student teacher's time learning about technologies. Figure 1.17 (after) shows her follow-up drawing in the final tutorial for the unit. Look carefully at the first drawing (Figure 1.16) and notice that the children are facing the teacher, who is in an authoritative, explaining mode. In the second drawing (Figure 1.17), the focus is on a range of different technological activities and reveals the student teacher's understanding of technology in the curriculum. The student teacher recognises that her perceptions of technology have changed throughout the semester. Keep the drawing you prepared for this pedagogical reflection tucked away in your book. You will be invited to repeat this activity in Chapter 10 so you can self-reflect about your learning regarding the teaching of the technologies curriculum area.

Summary

This chapter has brought together key points from the research literature about the nature of technology, technological knowledge and the work of technologists. After reading this chapter, you will be in a good position to revisit your definition of technology (Pedagogical Reflection 1.1), particularly from the perspective of Design and Technologies, but also your emerging ideas about Digital Technologies. As teacher researchers, it is important to continue to examine the literature and to reappraise your views in light of the evidence presented.

Figure 1.16 Pre-service teacher's initial drawing

Figure 1.17 Pre-service teacher's final drawing of her teaching technologies

The pedagogical reflections, literature and case examples presented in later chapters are designed to support a thoughtful critique of the teaching–learning process in technologies education. For a more detailed discussion of digital technologies, see Chapters 5 and 6.

Acknowledgements

Special thanks to my colleagues Dr Liang Li for providing the infant photo in this chapter, and to Associate Professor Kelly-Ann Allen for the photo of Florence. Also thanks to Bob Greaves for his work on technologies education captured in some of the photos in the chapter, to Bas Gerald for photos of the Wild Robot and Charina Pumpa from Redeemer Lutheran Primary School who taught the Conceptual PlayWorld. Finally, thanks to Yuwen Ma for support with updating the references for this chapter.

Key ideas in the technologies curriculum

CHAPTER 2

Introduction

Chapter 1 examined technology, exploring a range of perspectives. The chapter also introduced an overview of the Australian Curriculum: Technologies and the Early Years Learning Framework. This chapter discusses what is unique about the nature of technologies education and unpacks some of the key ideas found in the Australian Curriculum: Technologies. Examples of creating preferred futures, and engaging with project management, systems thinking, design thinking and computational thinking, are all considered unique to technologies education (Hallström and Klasander, 2019). This chapter focuses specifically on the most obvious of these ideas: generating designs (see Figure 2.1). Through a series of case studies, it explores the various features of a design brief and the design process in action (Figure 2.2).

> Allie: You sord design thesing 1st so you now wear the parts go.
> Tui: You shoud follow your plan because then you will know what your doing. Then you won't make a mistake.
> Sam: Designs should be done because you know what you're doing and because it would turn out good. If you think it wouldn't turn out good you can change it.

Figure 2.1 Tui says, 'You should follow your plan because then you will know what you are doing.'

PEDAGOGICAL REFLECTION 2.1

What makes technologies different from other learning areas?

Why should there be a separate learning area in the Australian Curriculum called 'Technologies'? To answer this, think about what could be unique about this learning area, and what resources or practices might already exist in the classroom or centre that could come under this learning area. Record three key ideas about what makes technologies different from other areas, such as mathematics, literacy or the arts:

Idea 1:_____
Idea 2:_____
Idea 3:_____

Figure 2.2 Year 6 students develop and modify digital solutions
Source: Monash University PlayLab and Laburnum Primary School.

What is unique about technologies education?

Thinking about what makes technologies different from the other curriculum learning areas is challenging because early childhood and primary teachers do not necessarily think and plan in discrete areas (Hanson and Lucas, 2020). Rather, learning is planned in an integrated way to mirror how children think and work. For example, in preparing a school newsletter or making a box construction, literacy can be discussed in relation to the content of the newsletter, and mathematics in terms of the spatial knowledge needed to prepare a box construction. The design and layout of the newsletter can also be considered to make it more attractive, efficient and digital in order to increase its circulation. These are clearly technological processes and skills. Similarly, when a preschool or Foundation level child works with box-construction materials, joining different shapes and surfaces, technological production skills are being developed. So what is unique about technologies? How might you foreground the key ideas in technologies in your classroom or early childhood centre so valued forms of technological processes and thinking still feature? The following case study looks at a teacher who sought to specifically research her own classroom practices in order to explicitly build into her existing practices a more visible approach to learning in technologies.

Looking inside a classroom: Making the content of the Australian Curriculum: Technologies visible in the teaching program

With the introduction of the new version of the Australian Curriculum: Technologies (see Chapter 1 for structure), new ways of thinking and working became evident to Karina. She decided to look at what she was already doing with her children in her Year 4/5 classroom before preparing a technologies program for them. She determined that a great deal of technological activity was taking place:

> A favourite activity for the children is making new inventions, making houses for pets and creating a variety of items from junk materials or construction kits. It won't be hard to tap into this existing activity and make the technological element of it more specific.

Karina had already organised her classroom so the daily program provided many opportunities for self-directed and self-chosen activities through what she called 'learning centres'. Her classroom contained a number of physically defined curriculum areas housing different resources and equipment. Children planned their activities for the session, carried out their plans and, at the end of each day, reflected on what they had achieved and learned. At the end of each week, individuals and small groups then presented their work to the whole group.

In this classroom environment, it was very easy for Karina to focus on technologies education. She was able to explicitly involve her children in thinking about the processes involved in technologies education, particularly design thinking. The children were creating designed solutions by investigating, generating, producing, evaluating, collaborating and managing. However, Karina noted that these processes and production skills were interrelated. She and the children developed a number of key statements that reflected the technological processes and production skills. These were made into wall charts by the children. The content of the charts is shown in Figures 2.3–2.5.

Production processes – begin with playing with the materials

When we evaluate, investigate, generate designs, generate project plans and make/produce, we:

1. collaboratively play (investigate) with the materials
2. evaluate the materials and think about how they could be used
3. generate designs and create a project plan for making the item
4. produce or make the item
5. evaluate the item
6. write about the item and talk with others
7. display the item.

Figure 2.3 Processes and production skills poster – investigate, generate designs, generate project plans and make/produce

> **Production processes – begin with making something**
>
> When we make/produce, evaluate, investigate, and generate designs and project plans, we:
>
> 1. collaboratively produce or make the item
> 2. write and talk about the item and how it was produced, then read about it
> 3. talk to the teacher about ways the item could be improved or changed, and include these ideas in the written explanation and evaluations
> 4. make a design of the item or the evaluated item and develop a project plan for making the item
> 5. display the item, the design and the project plan, and talk about them.

Figure 2.4 Processes and production skills poster – make/produce, evaluate, investigate, and generate designs and project plans

> **Production processes – begin with the design**
>
> When we generate designs, plan projects, make/produce and evaluate, we:
>
> 1. draw a design of what we plan to make and share it with the teacher
> 2. plan out our project
> 3. produce the item, following the design and the project plan
> 4. write about the item so that others can read about it
> 5. talk to the teacher about ways the item could be improved or changed and include these ideas in the written explanation
> 6. display the item in the classroom or school, together with the written explanation.

Web activity 2.1
Production processes and the Australian Curriculum: Technologies

Figure 2.5 Processes and production skills poster – generate designs, plan projects, make/produce and evaluate

PEDAGOGICAL REFLECTION 2.2

Wall charts

If you were to bring digital technologies into Karina's classroom, how would these charts look? Prepare your own charts to showcase the processes and production skills for the subject area of Digital Technologies, featuring the sub-strands:

Investigating and defining:_____
Generating and designing:_____
Evaluating:_____
Collaborating and managing:_____
Privacy and security:_____

How are they the same as or different from those shown in Figures 2.3 to 2.5?

The children found that they could begin the processes and production skills by making something, evaluating what they had made, then drawing a design of the finished product and finally producing a project plan. The children's chart in Figure 2.4 indicates this process.

The process did not finish there for the children. They also had the chart shown in Figure 2.5 in their room. Return to Figures 1.12 and 1.13 in Chapter 1 and note how Karina's charts (Figures 2.3–2.5) relate to Design and Technologies. Also consider how Karina's charts could be improved in relation to Digital Technologies.

As can be seen from the children's wall charts, technologies education is not a static or linear set of processes and production skills. For these children, it can begin as an idea from the class, from the materials themselves or from problems encountered – real-life problems for the children, such as how to organise an engaging system for a class fire drill so children take notice. An equivalent example for adults is the Air New Zealand-designed safety demonstration on its jets, where it draws upon the narratives and costumes of *The Lord of the Rings* and *The Hobbit*.

One of the important elements of Karina's program was the sharing sessions she organised for the children at the end of each week. These provided an opportunity for children to share what they were doing, thus building common knowledge and cohesion across the group (and a range of technological activities), as well as providing a forum in which children could ask for assistance.

Video activity 2.1
Real-life problems: Designing systems to keep people safe

> One group of children had been making a farm and wanted to put a pond in the yard. They had been experimenting all week with ways to make it work. Their comments during the session as we discussed their items were:
> 'We used plasticine to make a waterproof thing for the pond but it didn't work.'
> 'Yeah, all the water leaked away overnight.'
> 'Then we tried putting cling wrap over the plasticine and that was better but still some of the water leaked away.'
> 'Has anyone got any other ideas?'

Karina's diary provides some insight into how teachers can integrate technologies learning into the things that are already happening in the classroom. She demonstrates how children can explicitly discuss the process of generating designs, planning projects, producing and evaluating, and shows how children can begin designing, making or playing with materials. Her work illustrates how the evaluation process is an important part of each stage of the process. The terms used by the children reflected the terminology of the Technologies curriculum upon which Karina was drawing. Technologies education for Karina's children provided them with another way of thinking about the different technologies: food and fibre; food and nutrition; home economics; information and communication technology; and multimedia (Balme et al., 2022; Miles-Pearson, 2020; Rutland, 2018).

Since the children organised themselves into small groups or acted independently, the charts displayed around the room (which had been jointly constructed by the children and the teacher) provided explicit steps they could use as they worked. Through Karina's technologies program, the children had a valuable thinking tool to use as they worked. Learning opportunities were broadened as a result of introducing technologies education into this classroom. The important aspect for the children's learning was that Karina had analysed the essence of what constituted the processes and production skills of investigating and defining, generating and designing, producing and implementing, evaluating, and collaborating and managing. These technological processes and skills were explicit for the children, but the nature of their introduction was integrated meaningfully into the existing classroom and teaching program (Hanson and Lucas, 2020). Table 2.1 presents extracts from the Australian Curriculum: Technologies that show the nature of the technologies content with which Karina was working for Design and Technologies.

Had Karina also analysed the digital technologies dimensions of the activities occurring in her classroom, she would have featured the content shown in Table 2.2.

The key to technologies is understanding that creating designed solutions does not follow a specific linear process (Grobler and Ankiewicz, 2021; Svärd, Schönborn and Hallström, 2018).

It is possible to see from the diary and the curriculum content in Table 2.1 that the children were exploring different materials (investigating and defining) when they experimented with a range of joining techniques while producing working models and using a range of tools (producing and implementing). The example of the children inviting help from their peers about how to stop the pond from leaking also links with the development of processes and production skills (collaborating and managing). Karina's diary shows that it is possible to analyse existing practices in the classroom and, with the support of the Australian Curriculum: Technologies, to foreground the development of children's design and technological processes and production skills. This can also be supported through use of digital tools. For example, in Figure 2.6 students select and use appropriate digital tools effectively to plan, create, locate and share content.

Figure 2.6 Selecting and using appropriate digital tools effectively to plan, create, locate and share content
Source: Monash University PlayLab and Laburnum Primary School.

Table 2.1 Australian Curriculum: Technologies content descriptions for Design and Technologies (Processes and Production Skills)

Sub-strands	Years 3 and 4	Elaborations
Investigating and defining	explore needs or opportunities for designing, and test materials, components, tools, equipment and processes needed to create designed solutions AC9TDE4P01	• exploring the designs and performance of models of First Nations Australians' watercraft, and the opportunities for their designs to inform the design of a floating toy • examining the production of local products, services and environments to enhance their own design ideas, for example discussing the processes and systems that might be used to distribute hot food to a large number of people at a community event • selecting and making judgements about appropriate joining techniques for materials to produce designs, prototypes, structures or working models, for example joining fabric, paper or cardboard in various ways • exploring and testing a range of materials under different conditions for suitability including sustainability considerations, for example the compostability of paper-based materials or the strength and durability of natural materials • exploring the different uses of materials in a range of products, including those from a country in Asia, to inform design decisions, for example in shelters, boats, handmade tools, baskets, wooden items, musical instruments, clothing and fabric
Generating and designing	generate and communicate design ideas and decisions using appropriate attributions, technical terms and graphical representation techniques, including using digital tools AC9TDE4P02	• visualising innovative design ideas by producing thumbnail sketches, models and labelled drawings to explain features and modifications, for example drawing one or more designs for a machine to collect waste, and including labels and descriptions to explain materials used, their properties and the intended function of components or the whole system • planning, sharing and documenting creative designs, ideas and processes using digital tools and appropriate terms and privacy considerations, for example a class blog or collaborative document that has been selectively shared with peers • communicating design ideas using annotated diagrams, for example labelling a diagram for a pushcart with technical terms and explanations about components such as the chassis, axle, wheels and steering • generating design ideas for solutions using Safety by Design principles, for example designing communication that is accessible for all parents and carers

Table 2.1 (cont.)

Sub-strands	Years 3 and 4	Elaborations
Producing and implementing	select and use materials, components, tools, equipment and techniques to safely make designed solutions AC9TDE4P03	• exploring ways of joining, connecting and assembling components that ensure success including the impact digital tools have on these processes, for example using virtual reality or simulations to experience assembling materials or using tools • using tools and equipment accurately when measuring, marking and cutting, for example when creating a template or pattern, measuring ingredients in a recipe or preparing a garden bed for sowing seeds • explaining the importance of safe, responsible, inclusive and cooperative work practices when designing and making, for example when handling sharp equipment such as knives and scissors • selecting and using materials, components, tools, equipment and processes with consideration of the environmental impact at each stage of the production process, for example considering how packaging and offcuts could be recycled or used for other purposes before choosing materials for a project • using appropriate technologies terms to describe and share with other students the procedures and techniques for making, for example how to safely make an engineered solution such as a robotic device
Evaluating	use given or co-developed design criteria including sustainability to evaluate design ideas and solutions AC9TDE4P04	• developing design criteria with others including considering universal design principles to address social sustainability, for example a criterion that specifies flexible or intuitive use or low physical effort • using design criteria to evaluate, revise and select design ideas, for example when designing an e-textile toy for a young child to ensure it will be safe • comparing the amount of waste that would be produced from different design ideas and the potential for recycling waste, for example exploring the choice of materials to construct a toy and whether these materials are repairable or able to be recycled once the toy breaks or is no longer wanted • reflecting on how well their designed solution meets design criteria, such as ensuring safety and wellbeing of users and meeting the needs of communities or different cultures, for example reviewing and discussing the choice of fabrics used to make re-usable bags and how they could be made more appealing to all cultural groups by considering modifications to style
Collaborating and managing	sequence steps to individually and collaboratively make designed solutions AC9TDE4P05	• determining planning processes as a class, for example recording when parts of a project need to be completed on a timeline, in a spreadsheet, calendar or list • discussing the importance of managing time and resource allocation throughout production, for example discussing the roles different people might take in a team and identifying the tasks they will complete and the resources they will each need • identifying the steps in a mass production process, for example drawing a flowchart or making a video recording of a procedure for packing identical boxes of food for community members in need, where each student in a group has a separate task as part of the production process

Source: ACARA (2023).

Table 2.2 Australian Curriculum: Technologies content descriptions for Digital Technologies (Processes and Production Skills)

Sub-strands	Years 3 and 4	Elaborations
Investigating and defining	define problems with given design criteria and by co-creating user stories AC9TDI4P01	• recognising a range of familiar problems and defining achievable solutions using given design criteria, for example buying presents for family members within a specified budget • using responses to guiding questions to write a user story, for example a family member wants a way of entertaining their puppy when they are at school to stop it digging holes • co-creating a user story using a template such as "A <type of user> has <some goal> so that <some reason>", for example "a sports team wants to access league rankings online so that they can see their progress" • developing a problem statement for collecting and managing information, for example how First Nations Australian rangers could monitor animal populations, such as local marine turtles, using global positioning systems (GPS) • co-creating user stories about exploring hard-to-reach locations, for example a school student wants to explore neighbouring countries or communities classified as remote to compare how people live
Generating and designing	follow and describe algorithms involving sequencing, comparison operators (branching) and iteration AC9TDI4P02	• following the steps and decisions of algorithms and knowing what step they are up to, for example following rules to form the past tense of regular verbs such as 'create' to 'created', 'try' to 'tried' and 'cook' to 'cooked' and checking off items on a list as they are completed • describing algorithms using representations such as a list of steps or a diagram, for example drawing a diagram of a recipe involving decisions • understanding there can be more than one sequence of steps to solve a problem, some are better than others, and the steps should be unambiguous, for example describing 2 different ways to get to the same location • describing the decisions needed to solve a problem, including numerical and text comparisons, for example if the UV index is above 3, put on sunscreen and a hat • describing algorithms that repeat steps a fixed number of times, for example calculating multiplication using repeated addition, where the sum changes in each iteration • brainstorming possible design ideas and discussing these with their peers, for example sketching different ideas for a computer game • discussing whether the needs identified from the user story are met by generated design ideas, for example comparing design ideas in pairs for encouraging people to recycle • ideating multiple design ideas and comparing them against user stories, for example as a class, discussing the needs identified from the user story and brainstorming multiple design ideas (accepting all suggestions as possibilities)

Table 2.2 (cont.)

Sub-strands	Years 3 and 4	Elaborations
Producing and implementing	implement simple algorithms as visual programs involving control structures and input AC9TDI4P04	• writing and editing programs to solve simple problems using branching and simple iteration in a visual programming environment, for example helping a user understand multiplication by displaying the repeated addition in order • writing programs that take input from the user or environment, for example asking the user for their name and displaying it or sensing the temperature from the environment to make a decision • writing programs that make decisions involving comparison, for example comparing whether the temperature is above 25 degrees Celsius to label the weather hot or cold • writing programs that repeat one or more steps a fixed number of times, for example writing a program that displays repetitive song lyrics, such as in 'Ten in the bed' • running and testing a program to check it performs as expected, for example a character: 1. moves forward 2. turns left 3. moves forward • implementing a program that demonstrates the strict routines and techniques followed by First Nations Australian ranger groups when caring for or handling specific native animals, for example using IF and THEN statements to create a training manual, such as: IF <insert animal name> is injured THEN the ranger will <insert action>
Evaluating	use the core features of common digital tools to create, locate and communicate content, following agreed conventions AC9TDI4P06	• describing the way familiar digital systems allow the user to perform tasks, for example discussing how a family member could place an order online for something they cannot buy locally • discussing how a digital solution meets the different needs of users, for example how maps help people to locate places in the community or interactive store directories help shoppers to find a particular store in a shopping centre • making judgements on their digital solutions against the design criteria and user stories, for example how high their friends score in the game they created to help them learn what is recyclable • reflecting on how the systems in the school help it run, for example how the librarian keeps track of books borrowed
Collaborating and managing	use the core features of common digital tools to create, locate and communicate content, following agreed conventions AC9TDI4P06	• discussing and creating as a class a set of steps they need to follow to safely find information online • using an online search engine to find suitable sources to create and communicate information, following agreed steps, for example creating a presentation on life cycles • grouping, naming and itemising objects using a logical hierarchy, for example creating a section of a virtual library or virtual supermarket using folders and files

	use the core features of common digital tools to share content, plan tasks, and collaborate, following agreed behaviours, supported by trusted adults AC9TDI4P07	• using an agreed folder to make it easy for students to collaborate on shared content in a group project • demonstrating safe sharing of content with a select audience, for example sharing a holiday adventure without revealing exact dates, specific names or other personal information • listening to others when participating in online environments to share content, for example respecting the rights of others by taking turns to suggest and add words or images to a factual slide deck to share with the teacher • interacting cooperatively in a group in an online environment to plan and complete a task, for example writing and responding to others' views on canteen products • using digital tools to plan an event as a class, for example jointly creating a class survey to help plan an end-of-year party, where responses conform to the class's accepted behavioural expectations
Privacy and security	access their school account using a memorised password and explain why it should be easy to remember, but hard for others to guess AC9TDI4P08	• recalling their school username and password from memory to login to a school laptop or desktop • explaining how keeping a password secret prevents others from accessing their data, for example how their work is saved in their account and can only be accessed using their secret password • exploring techniques to create an easy to remember and hard to guess password, for example creating a password using 3 unrelated but easy to remember words
	identify what personal data is stored and shared in their online accounts and discuss any associated risks AC9TDI4P09	• identifying the personal data stored in accounts they use at school and at home and who has access to it, for example documents in their school cloud storage are accessible by the teacher, or their nickname in their online gaming accounts is visible to all players • discussing how personal data stored in online accounts forms a person's digital identity and can reveal detailed information about people, for example looking at photographs of themselves, friends or fictional characters that reveal details about a person's location, habits or home

Source: ACARA (2023).

SPOTLIGHT 2.1

Research into design

Design involves distinct elements and phases, and when interrelated they result in innovation (Meinel and Thienen, 2022; Svärd, Schönborn and Hallström, 2018). Leahy (2018) demonstrates that there are multiple design representations at play – for example, idea sketches, client ideas, sketch model, referential sketch, operational model, design development model, operational model, pre-production prototype and production. In her research, Leahy asked students to identify and discuss the following questions:

- What function does the design serve?
- Where did the idea come from?

Through this process, she observed whether and how students modified their designs and/or prototypes (as an iterative process of design development) and determined that multiple idea generation led to greater levels of creative and innovative solutions to the design challenge and a superior final result.

Generating designs

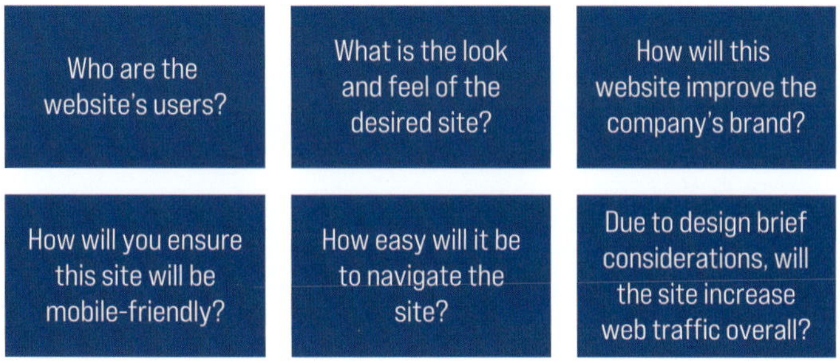

| Who are the website's users? | What is the look and feel of the desired site? | How will this website improve the company's brand? |
| How will you ensure this site will be mobile-friendly? | How easy will it be to navigate the site? | Due to design brief considerations, will the site increase web traffic overall? |

Figure 2.7 Design brief for website design
Source: Weller (2020).

Contextual challenge: Students can explore public spaces to enhance a person's or community's experiences. Conceptualised as the 'S' approach, this includes designing something for someone and for a particular situation.

Link 2.1 How to write a design brief

Generating designs is a specific cultural practice that children need opportunities to learn to do. Most teachers in Australia implement a design approach to technologies by setting challenges for their children in the form of design briefs for group activities. Design briefs outline the activity and provide the children with specifications with which they need to comply where a great deal of certainty is evident, but these can also be situated within a context that allows for different possible approaches (Barlex and Steeg, 2018). For example, Figure 2.7 provides a digital solution and Figure 2.8 a general description of the components of a design brief.

Barlex and Steeg (2018) researched the idea of the nature and role of **contextual challenge**. Specifically, students can explore public spaces to enhance a person's or community's experiences. Conceptualised as the 'S' approach, this includes designing something for someone and for a particular situation. Design decisions found were:

- conceptual – What does it do?
- technical – How does it work?
- aesthetic – What does it look like?
- marketing – Who is it for?
- constructional – How does it fit together?

Barlex and Steeg (2018) suggest that there are three phases involved in setting up contextual design challenges:

1. Explore the situation; identify the need and wants of people in the situation; develop design ideas to meet needs and wants.
2. Identify the most promising or feasible idea; develop and refine that design idea; realise that design idea.
3. Evaluate the outcome.

Title of project

Introduction
Introduces children to the context or problem and asks them to help solve it.

Brief
Sets out what the children have to do by explaining what they are to design and construct.

Generating designs
Invites children to generate a series of designs as potential solutions to their problem or challenge.

Project specifications
Sets out the constraints placed on the children with respect to their design, and lists the materials that may be used and the special features that must be included.

Project management
Details the steps and processes involved in bringing a design to production.

Evaluation
Sets out evaluation criteria for children to consider or test out in relation to their product.

Presentation
Explains to children how they are to present their design and associated materials when completed.

Time
Suggests a time allotment for the activity.

Download 2.1 A design brief

Figure 2.8 A design brief

Phase 1 represents a lot of uncertainty, Phase 2 represents less uncertainty and in Phase 3 there is little or no uncertainty.

Design briefs that are introduced to children can be open or tightly framed. In order to gain insights into the differences between design briefs, the following case study looks at student teachers who participated in two very different design briefs.

Video activity 2.2 Detectives at work

Case study: Evaluating design briefs

PEDAGOGICAL REFLECTION 2.3

What are the differences between the design briefs?

A group of university students who were studying to become primary and early childhood teachers participated in a closed design brief where they made popcorn, followed by a more elaborate design brief where they were asked to design and demonstrate their creation on a catwalk. The students then compared their experiences and evaluated the strengths and limitations of each type of design brief. Their experiences and evaluations are presented below. As you read these case examples, reflect upon the following questions:

- What level of creativity does each of the design briefs promote?
- Can students work individually or collaboratively? What might be the strengths and limitations of each approach?
- What level of autonomy is afforded – that is, do the children need a lot of help or can they work without teacher support?
- How long does the activity take? How much time would you need to allow?
- What level of teacher preparation is needed?
- What prior skills might children need to successfully generate design briefs, and produce and evaluate their product?
- What are the outcomes of successfully responding to the design brief?
- What level of engagement in learning is promoted through the design brief?
- What design brief do you prefer, and why?

Closed design briefs: Making popcorn – what the student teachers did

The student teachers were greeted by the smell of popcorn as they entered their classroom. The classroom was made up of groupings of tables that seated approximately five students, with a long walkway between them. At each set of tables was a bowl of popcorn and a design brief on a sheet of A4 paper. The design brief is shown in Figure 2.9.

Make your own popcorn holder to collect your free popcorn

Design context

Free popcorn is being given away by the local cinema. All you have to do is take your popcorn holder to the counter to collect your popcorn.

Design criteria

Your task is to turn this single A4 size sheet of paper into a popcorn holder. You cannot use any adhesive to make the popcorn holder. You must be able to hold the popcorn holder in one hand. Once you have successfully made your popcorn holder, fill your holder.

Evaluating the product and processes

From all the designs produced, which popcorn holder holds the most popcorn?

Download 2.2 Design brief: Make your own popcorn holder

Figure 2.9 Design brief for making your own popcorn holder

Once the student teachers had made their popcorn holders (see Figures 2.10–2.12), and had held a competition and declared the winner, they ate their popcorn and reflected upon their experiences:

Figure 2.10 Making popcorn holders

Figure 2.11 Weighing the popcorn

Alita: That was so much fun. I couldn't believe how many different types of popcorn holders could be invented with just one piece of paper!

Mayur: I thought it was really hard to make a holder without using sticky tape. You had to really think about the folds, and the consequences.

Shelley: Once we got the idea of folding the paper in particular ways to strengthen the sides, it was relatively quick to make the popcorn holder without using sticky tape.

Alex: It was only when we turned the activity into a competition that we had to think again about the design, and had to change the design so it would hold more popcorn.

Figure 2.12 Different designs of popcorn holder – which will hold the most popcorn?

Alita: We tried out many different designs and eventually worked out that the flat holders held the most popcorn.

The activity lasted for approximately 20 minutes, including eating the popcorn and reflection from the small groups and whole group. The student teachers were then invited to participate in the next technological challenge, the wardrobe wonder, which lasted for an hour and a half.

Open design briefs: Wardrobe wonder – what the student teachers did

The student teachers had been asked to bring into university an item from their wardrobe that they were happy to discard. It could be a hat, shoes, a bag, a t-shirt, a dress, trousers and so on. The student teachers were asked to share their item with their small group and to discuss:

- the history of their item from the wardrobe
- why they were happy to discard the item

- why they had once liked it
- the kinds of materials (manufactured materials, natural materials) and technological tools (e.g. buttons) they could see in the item
- the kinds of technological processes or systems that had been used to create the item.

The student teachers were then asked to use all of the items at their table as 'source material' for the creation of a new item they would exhibit on the 'catwalk' that would form between the cluster of tables in the room. The student teachers were given two possible design ideas (Figures 2.13 and 2.14) to choose from, or they could create their own.

Design idea: Wardrobe wonder – you are what you wear

Design context

You have been invited to a dress-up party. The invitation invites you to wear a wacky creation.

Design criteria

Your costume must be made from discarded items of clothing. The base piece of clothing must be decorated. The materials can be joined together using sewing, a hot glue gun, staples or pins. The design creation must be able to withstand the wear and tear of the catwalk.

Evaluating the product and processes

Prior to the catwalk parade, field test the creation. Check it for wearability and durability. During the catwalk, note how well received your creation is by the critics in attendance.

Teacher evaluation criteria

Could the students:
- assess their creation
- modify their creation, design or model in light of new ideas or problems encountered
- create something from all the materials gathered together from the group's discarded wardrobe items
- join the materials together for the desired result
- plan or generate a model of their creation prior to making the full-size version?

Download 2.3 Design idea: Wardrobe wonder – you are what you wear

Figure 2.13 Party accessories design brief

Superhero catwalk: Exhibiting the technological creation

The student teachers were asked to develop a script for introducing their technological creation. They were also invited to generate an engaging narrative that they could present as their creation was exhibited. The student teachers worked in groups and each person had a specific role:

- model
- narrator

Design idea: Superhero catwalk

Create a new superhero character. Design the costume your character will wear. Generate a comic strip of actions around a story that your superhero will perform.

Investigations

Go onto the internet and search for cartoon characters, taking note of the dress of each character. Download examples that reflect design ideas you like or that create particular qualities that you desire to have in your creation. Note the kind of accessories that the character wears or uses – masks, helmets, swords and so on.

Design criteria

The costume and the comic strip must be complementary. The accessories must be relevant to the storyline you create.

Evaluating the product and processes

Prior to the catwalk parade, field test your creation. Check it for wearability and durability. Do the costume and design ideas and film strip match? During the catwalk, note how well received your creation is by the critics in attendance.

Teacher evaluation criteria

Could they:

- assess their creation
- modify their creation, design or model in light of new ideas or problems encountered
- create something from all the materials gathered together from the group's discarded wardrobe items
- join the materials together for the desired result
- plan or generate a model or film strip of their creation prior to making the full-size version?

Download 2.4 Design idea: Superhero catwalk

Figure 2.14 Media characters design brief

- scriptwriter
- designer
- materials production
- project manager.

Although not necessary for adult learners, the student teachers were provided with name tags for each of these roles to pin to their tops. This signalled the specific role they were to take in the team and gave them a pedagogical strategy for supporting cooperative learning in groups when later teaching on their field placement.

Comparing design briefs: What the students found

At the conclusion of the catwalk, the student teachers discussed their experiences of the two design briefs. (See also Figure 2.15, in which the students evaluate their popcorn holders.)

Mayur: We laughed so hard during the process of making our creation, and again when we were on the catwalk. But we also laughed at the other groups' creations too.

Alita: It was good we had access to glue guns because it meant that what we wanted to create could be done quickly and easily – but there was a drawback: the final product was not really that durable or wearable. It was rather stiff and uncomfortable to wear.

Alex: I really like the idea of using name tags to give specific roles to each member of the group, even if the model had to also act as the project manager! We didn't have enough people in our group.

Alita: Yes, it meant we had to think about specific features of design and technologies as well as digital technologies. We did a quick search of the curriculum document to check what we had to do – for example, the role of project manager was very new for us.

This is what the students found out:

> **Project management skills**: Successfully and efficiently planning, managing and completing projects to meet identified design criteria.

- **Project management skills** help people to successfully and efficiently plan, manage and complete projects to meet identified design criteria.
- **Personal and social capability:**

    Students develop personal and social capability as they engage in project management and design and production activities in a collaborative workspace. They direct their own learning, plan and carry out investigations, and become independent learners who can apply design thinking, and technologies understanding and skills when making decisions. They develop social skills through working cooperatively in teams, sharing resources and processes, making group decisions, resolving conflict and showing leadership. Designing and innovation involve a degree of risk-taking, and as students work with the uncertainty of sharing new ideas, they develop resilience. (ACARA, 2023)

Alita Even though we found a design to follow, we didn't actually generate any designs. We got so carried away with the materials we had brought that our design process was mostly done concretely as we played with the materials and moved them about for a range of effects. I think what we did was make a model rather than a design. We later discussed the limitations of doing this – we thought we might have been more systematic and efficient if we had done a design. We certainly would have been more focused on the evaluation criteria!

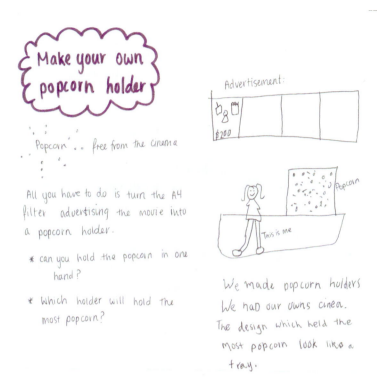

Figure 2.15 The students evaluate their popcorn holders

The students looked at the Australian Curriculum: Technologies to see what it suggested about design briefs, and they found the concept of design is nuanced:

- **Design brief:** A statement clarifying a project task and defining the need or opportunity to be resolved. It usually identifies the users, design criteria, constraints, resources and timeframe.
- **Design criteria:** Criteria used to determine if the proposed solution meets the requirements. They are drawn from the solutions requirements, user stories, if appropriate, and constraints.
- **Design process:** A process that involves investigating and defining; generating and designing; producing and implementing; evaluating; and collaborating and managing to create designed solutions that meet needs.
- **Design thinking:** An approach which helps people to empathise and understand needs, opportunities and problems; generate, iterate and represent innovative, user-centred ideas; and analyse and evaluate those ideas.
- **Designed solutions:** The products, services or environments that have been created for a specific purpose or intention as a result of design thinking, design processes and production processes. (ACARA, 2023)

The student teachers then turned their attention to comparing the two different types of design briefs:

Alex: I think the popcorn design brief is really very tightly framed when compared with the wardrobe wonder design brief. This was reflected also in how long each took. We spent over one hour on designing both our product and designing our presentation.

Alita: I really enjoyed both approaches. But I learned way more in the open-ended design brief because it allowed me to really explore materials in a meaningful way. That is, I really thought about how much waste there is when we don't recycle things. I also was able to study a broader range of materials and consider more closely different approaches and techniques for joining them. I think I would cover more of the curriculum in this open-ended design approach.

Alex: What was really helpful about the popcorn holder is that it was simple. It would be a really good way to begin teaching technologies to children. I could really see myself using a tightly framed design brief the first time I teach technologies, as the steps are really clear. I think if the children have not yet worked with design briefs, then it would also be a good introduction. But I don't think I would only use this approach. In the long run it would be really limiting and wouldn't necessarily allow me to get into big-ticket items, such as values, ethics and sustainability.

When you reflect back on what you recorded in Pedagogical Reflection 2.3, did you come up with similar ideas to the student teachers? The level of teacher preparation for each of the design briefs is quite different. Inviting children to bring in resources from home is one way a teacher can gain support in providing a rich materials base for technologies. Teachers can also organise a 'collection point' for children and families to bring in materials to use, perhaps making specific what is needed by positioning a box at the door to the classroom or early childhood setting with a sign – for example, 'Wanted – old birthday cards, Christmas cards, Diwali cards, Hannukah cards'.

When you reflect upon your other responses, did you reach a position about which design brief you preferred? This question is examined further in the next section.

ACTIVITY 2.1

Design briefs for preschool children – envelopes and Diwali cards

Create your own design briefs for decorated envelopes and a card for the Hindu festival of Diwali suitable for: (1) preschool children; (2) Year 6 children.

Now compare your design briefs and consider:
- What is the same?
- What is different?
- How might progression be considered?

PEDAGOGICAL REFLECTION 2.4

Open-ended design briefs

Figures 2.16–2.18 are examples of a range of design briefs. Examine each of the design briefs closely to see how open-ended they are. Plot the design briefs on a continuum from open-ended design briefs to tightly framed briefs.

What might be the advantages of an open-ended design brief? What might be the disadvantages? When would you use a tightly framed design brief? How might you use these design briefs in early childhood settings?

Analysing design briefs

Following are examples of open-ended design briefs that are suitable for both early childhood and primary children. Children can:

- refurbish the doll's house
- design a new home corner
- design a new classroom arrangement
- redesign the playground
- design and record their own songs
- design a stage set for a play
- design their own LEGO programs
- develop their own newspaper
- design their own dance
- use construction materials to design a range of artefacts
- use children's literature to create their own children's books
- construct their own cards (using flaps)
- make their own jack-in-a-box
- construct their own games, including board games
- design their own musical instruments
- design their own dolls' clothes
- design and make decorations for festivals.

Some of these possibilities are elaborated on below.

Generating designs

Generating designs for producing greeting cards

Design brief

There is a very special occasion coming up. Design a card that you think your friend will like.

To make a very special card, you will need to follow the process of investigating, generating, producing, evaluating, and collaborating and managing.

Investigating

You will need to interview your partner. You are to ask: 'What kinds of things are special about this day?' Write down three things that your friend finds special about this day.

Generating

From the information you have written down, design at least two greeting cards. These designs are a mock-up of what the card might look like. You should aim to:

- have one moveable part
- use the materials available.

Look at your designs. Which do you like best, and why?

Producing

Using the materials, follow your preferred design, and make your greeting card.

Evaluating

Write down three questions that could be used to evaluate your greeting card. Your questions could be asked of the person to whom you will give the card, or you could ask other children in your class. Write down what people say about your card. From these responses, decide how effective your card is.

Collaborating and managing

Think about how you might change your card so that more than one card could be made. How might you effectively make sets of cards in your class? How could you work with others to produce a set of cards? Find five friends and together plan out how you would make five cards quickly. Test out your plan. Did it work? Why did it work or why did it not work?

Download 2.5
Generating designs for producing greeting cards

Figure 2.16 Designing, producing and evaluating a greeting card

Generating designs for producing hats

Design brief

It is the first day of summer and almost everyone has forgotten to bring in their hats. But everyone wants to play outside at playtime. In groups of five, design and make a summer hat for each member of your team.

What you need to think about:
- How can you tell one hat from another?
- Make sure that each hat is designed for the particular person – make it special for them.
- The hat must provide enough shade that it passes the 'sun smart hat guidelines'.
- How to use the available material.
- Can the hat can be worn while playing? Find out what games each child is likely to play and include that as an important criterion for hat design.

Investigating

You will need to interview each person in the team. You are to ask: 'What do you usually play at playtime?' Write down one thing that each friend does at playtime. Using a digital device, take photos of the children at playtime to see what they like to do.

Generating

From the photos you have taken, analyse what the children do. Design at least two hats. Think about what their play might mean for a hat design that won't fall off when they are playing. You should aim to have a hat that:
- is comfortable
- is unique enough that it can be identified easily by the wearer
- shades the face
- stays on easily during play.

Look at your designs. Which do you like best, and why?

Producing

Using the materials, follow your preferred design, and make your hat.

Evaluating

Write down three questions that could be used to evaluate your hat. For example: Is the hat comfortable? Is it unique enough that it can be identified easily by the wearer? Does it shade the face well? Does it stay on easily during play? Your questions could be asked of the person to whom you will give the hat, or you could ask other children in your class. Write down what people say about your hat. From these responses, decide how effective your hat is.

Collaborating and managing

Think about how you might change your hat design so more than one hat could be made. How might you effectively make lots of hats for your class? How could you work with others to make 'spare hats'? In your team, plan how you would make five hats quickly. Test your plan. Did it work? Why did it work or why did it not work?

Download 2.6
Generating designs for producing hats

Figure 2.17 Designing hats

Generating designs for producing musical instruments

Design brief

You have been asked to design and make some musical instruments for a children's party. To determine the most appropriate materials to use and possible instruments to make, you are going to need to investigate materials and then think about the different sounds that materials can make.

Follow all of the technological processes of investigating, generating, producing, and collaborating and managing.

Collaborating and managing

Set up working groups of about four people. Think about how you will use just the materials available in the room. There is not much time! How will you manage the project? You will need to adhere strictly to the times outlined for each phase below.

Investigating (about 20 minutes)

Do the following:
1. In your groups, brainstorm what you know about musical instruments and the sounds they make. Consider how the materials affect the sound.
2. Develop two materials tests to help you find out information for your designs.
3. Draw some designs for musical instruments on a sheet of paper. You will select one of them to share with the whole group in your oral presentation at the end of the project.

Generating (about 20 minutes)

Look at the available materials. As a group, design at least two musical instruments that you could make using these materials. You will then need to annotate your drawings, showing:

- the materials you would use
- why you would choose these materials.

As a group, select the instrument you wish to make, and indicate on your drawing why you have selected that option.

Producing (about 25 minutes)

The group is to make the selected product, using the available tools safely and appropriately.

Evaluating (about three minutes per group)

The evaluation of the product will be in the form of a three-minute oral presentation. The presentation needs to cover:

- an explanation of one of the materials tests and the results of the test
- an explanation of the instrument and a demonstration of how it works
- a display of the original drawing and a discussion on any changes made, and why
- a reflection on the success of the product in terms of its function, its aesthetics and the tools and processes used throughout the project.

Download 2.7
Generating designs for producing musical instruments

Figure 2.18 Making musical instruments

Analysing design briefs

ACTIVITY 2.2

Analyse the design briefs in Figures 2.16–2.18 and answer the following questions:
1. Are they open-ended or closed?
2. How could the design briefs be adjusted so that they can be open-ended?
3. How could the design briefs be adjusted so that they are closed?
4. When might you use open-ended design briefs?
5. When might you use closed design briefs?

In the examples of design briefs given in Figures 2.16–2.18, some are open-ended, such as the wardrobe wonder design brief, and some are very tightly framed, such as the popcorn holder design brief. Do you think the design briefs – open and closed – support children to achieve the aims shown below from the Australian Curriculum: Technologies, namely:

- develop confidence as critical users of technologies and designers and producers of designed solutions
- investigate, generate, iterate and analyse ethical and innovative designed solutions for sustainable futures
- use design and systems thinking to generate design ideas and communicate these to a range of audiences
- produce designed solutions suitable for a range of technologies contexts by selecting and manipulating a range of tools, equipment, materials, systems and components creatively, competently and safely; and managing processes
- evaluate processes and designed solutions and transfer knowledge and skills to new situations
- understand the roles and responsibilities of people in design and technologies occupations and how they contribute to society. (ACARA, 2023)

You may have noticed that some high-level questions, such as issues of sustainability, cultural inclusion, and the roles and responsibilities of people in design and technologies occupations, were not covered. How might you modify the design briefs to include these? Go back to each of the design briefs (in this book and online) and add your own design specifications and evaluation criteria. Keep in mind some of the critiques of technologies discussed in Chapter 1 as you amend the design briefs.

Figure 2.19 is an example of a design brief that invites you to create your own design brief for survival in the bush. By creating your own design briefs, you will not only practise the skills needed for developing your own activities suitable for the interests and experiences of the children you are teaching, but your design brief will be more in tune with the local materials available to you in your classroom or centre.

Children can also create their own design briefs. An example is shown in Figure 2.20. When you and your children go through the steps of designing a robust and engaging design brief, you are also engaging more consciously in investigating and defining, generating and designing, producing and implementing, evaluating, and collaborating and managing.

You may be wondering how to introduce the concept of design with very young children (Figure 2.21).

> ### Write a design brief relating to survival in the bush
>
> We all need water to survive. Imagine you were on an overnight hike and accidentally lost your water bottle. Discuss with a partner how you might collect water in a bush environment. Use the design brief format in Figure 2.8 to write the criteria for the technological activity of designing and making a device to collect water in the bush (see Figure 2.20).
>
> If possible, give this design brief to someone from a different cultural background and ask for critical feedback. Make your design brief as culturally inclusive as possible.
>
> Test your modified design brief when you next go bushwalking, or set the challenge for children when they are on a school camp. Remember to pack a camera and take photographs of the solutions to the challenge.

Figure 2.19 Generating your own design brief for survival in the bush

Figure 2.20 An example of children's design briefs for collecting water

Figure 2.21 Can we use design briefs in early childhood settings?

Looking inside an early childhood setting: Engaging with the Early Years Learning Framework

In early childhood settings and at Foundation level in school, young children have the opportunity to engage with more adults. Family members are usually encouraged to act as volunteers in the classroom or early childhood centre. The additional adult can work with small groups of children on specific technological design briefs while the teacher is working with other children in the setting. That is, design briefs can be laminated and placed like cards next to materials, such as in the block area or on the construction table, for children to find and invite an adult to work with them. Similarly, design briefs can be given to parents who volunteer in early childhood settings so they can work with small groups of children around a design challenge. Rather than the volunteer family member preparing fruit, for example, a parent helper can use the design briefs for purposeful learning and a guided process to support intentional teaching in technologies.

Video activity 2.3 Design briefs in early childhood settings

Figure 2.22 gives an example of a design brief that can be placed in the block area of an early childhood centre or a classroom. It should be used by adults who are interacting with children in the area.

Design new houses for the three little pigs

Design brief

Design new houses for the three little pigs that are 'wolf proof'.

Evaluating

After reading the story or telling the story of the three little pigs, talk about the design of the three pigs' homes. Talk about:

- What materials were used?
- Which ones were the best for keeping the wolf from entering the little pigs' homes? What materials could the little pigs have used?
- What materials do we have available to us for telling the story?

Investigating

Introduce by saying, 'Let's use the available materials and later the blocks to retell the story of the three little pigs.'

- What materials could we change?
- Try some new materials. Photograph the children before and after trying to blow down each house. Try different ways of building with the materials, for example, different ways to stack the blocks; different ways to join materials together; or different ways to arrange the materials. Photograph the results.
- Talk about why it worked or didn't work.

Generating

Using paper and felt pens, design your new pigs' houses, making sure they are wolf proof. Talk about your designs. Which do you like best, and why?

Producing

Using the materials, follow the design you like best, and make your pigs' homes.

Collaborating and managing

Share your digital photographs and your model of the pig's home you have made with other children and help them to tell the story using your model. You may have to create a new ending for the story!

Figure 2.22 Three little pigs' homes

Download 2.8 Design new houses for the three little pigs

Another way to use this design brief is for the educator to read or tell the story of the three little pigs using large sheets of paper on the easel. This story lends itself well to helping very young children (aged 3 to 6 years) to think about a plan-view orientation when drawing. The capacity to conceptualise a plan view is foundational to technologies education. Mostly, young children draw from a front view orientation, as shown in Figure 2.23. However, after being involved in a unit of technology education, one child was able to draw from a plan view, as shown in Figure 2.24.

Figure 2.23 A common orientation to drawing a house – Heidi's (6 years) design

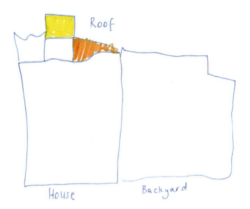

Figure 2.24 Callum's (6 years) design – drawn after learning about a plan view

The following text explains how this transformation from a front-view to plan-view orientation was achieved. The teacher of a multi-age group of children (3- to 6-year-olds) set out to explicitly support her children with this reorientation by using the story of the three little pigs.

After telling the story to the children using blocks (brick house), straw, sticks (found in the garden), puppets of the wolf and plastic animals for the three pigs, she invited the children to look down into the pigs' homes from a 'bird's-eye view'. The teacher took a bird puppet and flew over the pigs' homes, which did not have roofs. This is what she said to the children:

Teacher: This house is special because I can see right down inside it.

Andrea: Cause you didn't have a roof on that house!

Teacher: It hasn't got a roof. I didn't put a roof on for a special reason. I wanted you to have a look inside the house. I am now going to pretend that I am a bird flying over the pigs' homes. If a bird flew over this house and had a look down, I wonder what it might see?

All the children eagerly look down into one of the pig's homes.

Teacher: Andrew, would you like to take the bird puppet and fly over? What can you see?

Andrew: Everything.

Teacher: Eloise, would you like to fly over now?

Eloise immediately stands and takes the puppet and zooms up and down across the top of the largest pig's home.

Teacher: What can you see?

Eloise: Some beds.

Teacher: Can you draw what you see?

Eloise smiles and takes the felt pen, then draws a bed on the large sheet of paper that has been placed on the easel. The teacher invites another child to draw what she sees. After several children have drawn their impressions, the teacher discusses all the things shown in the drawing. She then turns the sheet over and begins to draw.

Teacher: I am going to draw a bird's-eye view of our pig's house and I want you to watch me to see if I do it right.

The children eagerly move forward and follow every stroke of the teacher's pen. Some turn and look closely into the pig's house.

Teacher: It is a bit like a big rectangle.

Eloise: Yes. That is right!

Teacher: And there is a door at the front. We might just put the door like this [makes a line to indicate door space].

The teacher then turns back to the block building of the pig's home and says:

Teacher: I am just going to have a look down inside the building, like a bird, and see what rooms I can see. I can see one, two, three bedrooms and a big, long kitchen. I am going to see whether I can draw that on my paper. Can you help me to count the bedrooms as I draw? Children count, '1, 2, 3'.

Teacher: I wonder if you would like to draw your house plans like that?

Alyssa: I can do that!!

After group time, the children were given the props the teacher had used for the storytelling, A4 sheets of blank paper and felt pens. During the children's play, they retold and role-played the story. They also drew their pigs' homes. The children spent a great deal of time creating models of different kinds of houses for their three pigs, discussing what might be in each of the rooms. Through using blocks as resources for technologies education, the teacher was easily able to support the children to look and think from a plan view, as can be seen in Figure 2.25. These ideas are taken up further in Chapter 4.

The next case study examines technologies learning engineered by Bob, a community volunteer and teacher, as he works with a multi-age group of children in their first year of school through to their third year – that is, 5- to 8-year-olds.

Figure 2.25 Using blocks to help children become oriented to a plan view

Figure 2.26 Processes and production skills learned through making paper planes

Looking inside a classroom: Investigating, making, evaluating and designing paper planes

The processes and production skills of creating designed solutions were introduced to children through the simple activity of making and designing paper planes (Figure 2.26). Bob set up a problem for the children to consider during a storytelling session with puppets of a 'dolly' clothes peg going on holidays to a remote island. The dolly clothes peg needed to be transported out quickly because it had experienced a bad fall on the island while rock climbing. The doctor was called in and dolly had to be taken to a hospital on the mainland.

Design brief: The children were introduced to a decorated 'dolly' clothes peg and told a story about the dolly's adventures on a remote island.

The story had a problem: 'The dolly clothes peg needs to be transported by air to the hospital'.

Investigating and producing: The children designed different planes, tested them, then displayed their designs (and results), explaining how their models worked; they also discussed future modifications. They set about critiquing their designs, as some of the planes they made were not able to fly long distances. Modifications therefore needed to be made and potential solutions tested (Figures 2.27 and 2.28).

Figure 2.27 Making modifications to the design of the plane – will it fly further?

Some of the children reflected on how comfortable the flight would be for the dolly. How could they make their planes fly more smoothly? Other children started to ask questions about the importance of having a flying doctor service available to the local citizens on the remote island. This is in keeping with the goals of the Australian Curriculum: Technologies.

> This sub-strand involves students analysing, exploring and investigating information, needs and opportunities. As creators and citizens they will critically reflect on the intention, purpose and operation of technologies and designed solutions. Analysing encourages students to examine values, and question and review processes and systems. Students reflect on how decisions they make may have implications for individuals, society and the local and global environment, now and in the future. They explore and investigate technologies, systems, products, services and environments as they consider needs and opportunities. They progressively develop effective investigation strategies and consider the contribution of technologies to their lives and make judgements about them. Students develop design criteria in response to needs and opportunities and may respond to or develop design briefs. (ACARA, 2023)

Figure 2.28 Adding weights to the design of the plane – will it fly better?

The children discussed the responsibility of the whole community to support those living in remote regions. They asked, 'How much does it cost to run a plane?' They went online and found out that many groups support the process of fundraising in order to help the Royal Flying Doctor Service. Through these investigations and discussions, the teacher actively supported the children to learn in Technologies.

The experience of making a range of air transport devices, including paper planes, generated a series of design questions by the children:

- How do parachutes work?
- Why do parachutes have holes?
- Does air stop or help aeroplanes fly?
- Why are aeroplane wings shaped the way they are?
- How do the propellers on a helicopter work?
- Why don't helicopters have wings?
- How do birds fly?

This has resonance with the example of Hedy Lamarr (Chapter 1), who spent hours looking at the form and shape of birds and fish to inspire a new design for planes, with the purpose of travelling faster. In today's context, this would also now focus on energy efficiencies for a more sustainable approach.

The children's experiences progressively developed their investigation strategies. The children also began to consider the contribution of technologies to their lives and they were able to make judgements about them based on their investigations. The children started to explore flight in society, and to understand how rules and regulations are formed to protect the pilots and passengers when in the air. Some of the children designed and made an airport, created their own air traffic control rules, then role-played what they had created and the consequences. This is in line with the Australian Curriculum: Technologies, where it is suggested that children should learn how decisions they make may have implications for the individual, society and the local and global environment, now and in the future (ACARA, 2023).

For older children, exploring the flight recorder system and examining the flight paths of planes around the world – particularly in the context of goods being flown from one country to another – is important to understand the footprint of particular food, demand and supply, and also the ethics associated with local production of food not being supported (Engstrom, 2018; Svensson and von Otter, 2018).

Many questions arose for the younger children who were making flight transport systems to help dolly – for example, 'Why do propellers work on a helicopter?' and 'Why don't helicopters have wings?'

Activities that help with answering these questions and those raised above, and that build understandings of design, follow.

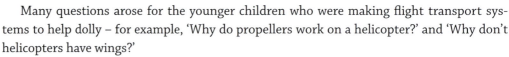

Download 2.9 Whirlybird pattern

Using the whirlybird pattern in Figure 2.29, explain what happens when you experiment with weight and flaps. (You should be able to make the whirlybird spin faster and more accurately.) Questions to ask include: Does air stop or help birds fly? How do feathers help birds fly? Why can't we fly? How do insects and animals fly? Questions give context to technological activities, and in the process of answering these, children prepare reports (see Figure 2.30).

Collaborating and managing: Using an observation booklet, children were encouraged to observe birds at home and at school. How do birds move their wings? Where are their feet during take-off and in relation to the wind?

The children wondered whether these features of birds could be used in the design of their planes. The children worked together to effectively create designed solutions. What Bob noticed was that the children developed the ability to communicate and share ideas throughout the process, negotiate roles and responsibilities and make compromises to work effectively as a team (ACARA, 2023). Assigning roles to group members supported this process.

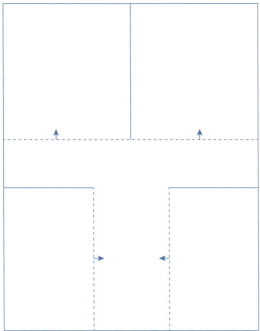

Figure 2.29 Whirlybird pattern

The activities that follow were tried out by the children in order to gain a better understanding of flight in the context of design.

- *Activity 1:* Using two large thick pieces of cardboard tucked under your armpits, run or rollerblade. As you run or rollerblade, flap your 'wings' to feel the air pressure and wind resistance on your wings.
- *Activity 2:* Hold a narrow strip of paper in front of your mouth and blow over it. What happens? (The children discovered that the paper rose because they had blown air away from the top and there was then greater pressure below.)
- *Activity 3:* If you would like to see how the feathers stay together, use a magnifying glass to examine them – what do you notice?

Generating and producing: The activities about how birds fly helped to generate a series of new paper plane designs. To support this process, the students also inquired about how paper planes fly. This is in keeping with Australian Curriculum: Technologies:

Figure 2.30 Michael's thinking report on flight

> This sub-strand involves students in developing and communicating design ideas for a range of audiences. Students generate and iterate ideas, make choices, weigh up options, consider alternatives and document various design ideas and possibilities. They use critical and creative thinking strategies to generate, evaluate and document ideas to meet needs or opportunities that have been identified by an individual, a group or a wider community. Generating creative and innovative ideas involves thinking differently; it entails proposing new approaches to existing solutions and identifying new design opportunities considering preferred futures. Generating and developing ideas involves identifying various competing factors that may influence and dictate the focus of the idea. Students evaluate, justify and synthesise what they learn and discover. They use graphical representation techniques when they sketch, draw, model, simulate and design ideas that focus on well-considered designed solutions. (ACARA, 2023)

The children used a range of techniques, such as drawing, sketching and model-making. Graphical representation was important, as can be seen in Figures 2.31–2.33.

The problem: What happens if:
- you add weight to the nose with a paper clip
- you put flaps on the wings
- the nose is blunt
- you curve the wings?

> Air rises when it is warm. When a bird is in the sky, it can use air currents called thermals. When thermals are very strong, they can lift some birds up into the air. The birds won't even have to flap their wings. Large birds such as eagles and vultures use these thermals to help them.
> **Research:** Strong pectoral muscles help birds fly; the curved shape of wings helps flight.

Figure 2.31 Writing the air report

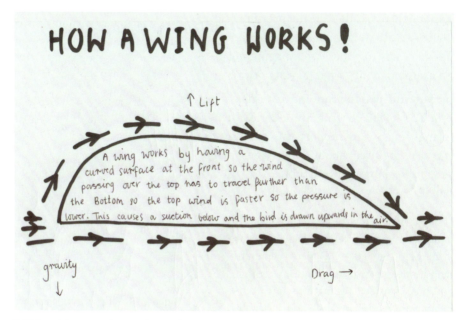

Figure 2.32 Angela's report: how a wing works

SPOTLIGHT 2.2

An iterative, rather than linear approach to design

There is growing evidence that using writing in design and technologies helps children to conceptualise their design ideas more clearly, which supports them in becoming more speculative and creative in their engagement with technologies (von Mengersen and Wilkinson, 2020). In contrast, report writing – particularly for young children – can be supplemented with video, PowerPoint snapshots, digital images and the like, in order to allow children to document their thinking without the constraints of having to write all of their ideas – the younger the child is, the more challenging it is to just physically write (Ordaz, Klapwijk and van Dijk, 2018). This is particularly important as the project progresses and further design challenges are introduced. For instance, the children in the project on flight initially used a design brief that Bob had prepared, as well as being introduced to a series of planes and testing them out (see Figure 2.33). Later, the experience of following a design brief generated new design questions for the children, showing the iterative, rather than linear, approach to design – investigating, making and evaluating – noted by Karina (introduced at the beginning of this chapter) (see Högsdal and Grundmeier, 2021).

Figure 2.33 The simple design worked the best in light wind.

Producing and implementing: Designing and testing a range of paper planes worked well because the children could immediately see the relations between the design (Figure 2.34) and the success (or otherwise) of their planes (Figure 2.35). Testing was quick and purposeful. The children were able to appropriately select materials, becoming more accurate with decision-making over an extended set of flight tests. The children also showed each other what worked and what did not work. This generated a lot of discussion among the children. Because so much testing was taking place in the classroom, the children also had

Design brief

Paper plane throwing competition – design a paper plane that can:

- achieve the longest flight
- make the fastest flight
- be the highest flyer
- be the best stunt plane.

Figure 2.34 Design brief for a paper plane competition

Figure 2.35 Testing design ideas: what happens if you add a paper weight to the nose of the plane?

to think carefully about safe work practices, so the test space was directed away from the children and teacher. This is consistent with the Australian Curriculum: Technologies:

> This sub-strand involves students learning and applying a variety of skills and techniques to make designed solutions to meet specific purposes and user needs. Students apply knowledge about components and materials and their characteristics and properties to ensure their suitability for use. They learn about the importance of adopting safe work practices. They develop accurate production skills to achieve quality designed solutions. Students develop the capacity to select and use appropriate tools, equipment, processes, materials, systems and components; and use work practices that respect the need for sustainability. The use of modelling and prototyping to accurately develop simple and complex simulated or physical models supports the production of successful designed solutions. (ACARA, 2023)

Evaluating: The process of making and testing the paper planes was a productive context in which children could evaluate their design solutions and models. It was important for the children that the individual and group evaluations occurred naturally as they worked. The children discussed:

- the quality and effectiveness of their plane designs, and those of other children
- effective ways to test and judge their designed solutions
- a systems view of their planes (e.g. wind design, front of plane shape, weights – all had to be considered together).

This is consistent with the Australian Curriculum: Technologies:

> Evaluating occurs throughout a design process. It involves students reviewing design ideas, processes and solutions; and seeking feedback and making judgements throughout a design process and about the quality and effectiveness of their and others' designed solutions. Students identify design criteria for needs or opportunities in the investigating and defining stage and then use these criteria to consider the implications and consequences of actions and decision-making throughout the process. They determine effective ways to test, judge and improve their ideas, concepts and designed solutions. They reflect on processes and transfer their learning to other design needs or opportunities. (ACARA, 2023)

The experience with the paper planes sparked a broader interest in flight (as discussed above), and also in making other types of things that used air. Bob seized on this interest and introduced kite-making to the children. He also invited the Year 6 children to help with kite-making. He prepared a design brief for the older children. They worked together with the younger children to investigate, generate, produce and evaluate their kites. The older children also produced their own design briefs, as shown in Figure 2.36.

Design a kite that can fly in light wind

Design brief

Design a kite that can fly in light wind.

Collaborating and managing

Design and test your kite with the 5- to 8-year-olds, explaining your rationale at each step of investigating, generating, producing and evaluating.

Investigating

Fly the different kites provided. They are all made from different materials. They use different construction techniques. What do you notice under different wind conditions?

Generating

Generate a range of design ideas for your kite.

Producing

Explore the possible ways to join the materials together so the kite remains light.

Evaluating

What were the best materials to use? What construction technique worked best? Which design worked well in light winds? What do you now know about materials, design and production processes for kite-making? As a Year 6 group, prepare a brief report as a poster suitable for others to use.

Download 2.10 Design a kite that can fly in light wind

Figure 2.36 Year 6 design brief for making kites with 5- to 8-year-olds

The evaluations of the kite designs are documented in Figure 2.37 (see also Figures 2.29 and 2.34).

Collaborating and managing: brings forward how children collaborate and manage their projects. For instance:

> This sub-strand involves students learning to work cooperatively and to manage time and other resources to effectively create designed solutions. Progressively, students develop the ability to communicate and share ideas throughout the process, negotiate roles and responsibilities and make compromises to work effectively as a team. Students work individually and in groups to plan, organise and monitor timelines, activities and the use of resources. They progress from planning steps in a project through to more complex project management activities that consider various factors such as time, cost, risk assessment and management and quality control. Collaborating and managing occur throughout a design process. (ACARA, 2023)

Reporting results and comparing designs were featured in the kite project. Examples are shown in Figures 2.37 and 2.38.

The parts of a kite

All kites have the same basic structure. The frame, spine and spars frame the main body of the kite. They are covered by the sail. The kite is controlled by the bridles and the main flying line. Many kites also have a tail and a keel, to help stabilise them.

How does a kite fly?

Like an aeroplane, a kite is heavier than air. In order for it to get off the ground, an upward force has to be produced by the wind. The wing is lifted upwards because the air travelling over the top of its curved surface has to go faster than the air passing underneath. Faster-moving air creates less pressure, which means there is more pressure underneath the wing; this helps to force the kite upwards.

Launching a kite

Before you launch your kite, make sure that its balance is correct. Let out a little line and throw the kite into the air. If it hangs down on one side slightly, correct that side immediately. Balance the kite by pressing a small piece of Blu Tack on the other side. Adjust the bridle according to the speed of the wind. An elastic bridle is useful in strong wind as it allows the kite to fly flatter. Finally, check all the knots for tightness.

Figure 2.37 Year 6 report on kites

K1

Kite 1 had an oval head with a 30 metre-long tail; it was made of plastic; the first time it flew approx. 35 metres; the second time it flew about 30 metres and it would have flown better with wings.

K2

Kite 2 was made of plastic; it had a 1 metre-long tail; it flew 25 metres the first time and about 30 metres the second time; it would have flown better if it had floppy wings.

K3

Kite 3 only went 5 metres and 1 metre; it was made of paper and had a 3 metre-long tail made of crepe paper, which was too heavy for its light body.

K4

Kite 4 had a 10 centimetre-long tail. It was made out of material and went 30 metres then approximately 25 metres; this one didn't have any plastic.

K5

Kite 5 was made of a garbage bag; it flew 40 metres high and stayed up the whole time; it didn't have a tail, which probably helped as it was a light build.

Figure 2.38 Year 6 children compare their kite designs

For children to be successful in realising the design briefs, it is critical that they have skills in design – something that, in the primary and early years, draws heavily upon children's drawing skills, and that research suggests needs active teacher support.

SPOTLIGHT 2.3

Progression in design skills of young children

Important research by Milne (2018) investigated children's design drawing skills across the primary years of schooling. From a whole-school perspective, she examined how children represented their design solutions on the technological activity of bridge design and building. Specifically, she gathered design drawings of 5- to 6-year-old, 7- to 9-year-old and 10- to 12-year-old children, and found that within a school year, and over school years, that experience matters in the process of creating design solutions. Creativity in design should take into account children's experiences and developing competencies in design. In the younger children (5–6 years), this included in relation to the structure and shape of bridges – beam bridge, cantilever bridge and suspension bridge:

- being conversant with materials – metal or steel, wood and concrete
- descriptive terms – deck, piers, foundations, cables abutment
- social issues – safety of pedestrians.

Older children (7–9 years) introduced other concepts into their work, such as realistic, view-specific, two-dimensional drawings of bridge design. Specifically, they included in their drawings:

- contours, line drawings shading to show two dimensions
- angled 3D lines
- view orientation – exploded, cross-sectional and plan view.

Finally, the senior students (10–12 years) were able to meet all of the drawing skills to realise their design solutions for bridge building, as described above. In addition, they were able to produce:

- contour drawings
- more detail
- increased annotation to describe how the materials were joined and the construction design
- increased rendering and shading for light and shadow for 3D representation.

Milne (2018) found that children's drawing skills were collectively influenced by their exposure to techniques that supported them with documenting their design ideas. Milne also found that it was important for children to know the purpose and function of using drawing in design. In addition, the teacher creating a nurturing and risk-free environment supports being creative with ideas and encourages children to explore their thinking through drawing. Finally, rich experiences of bridges support children's ability to generate design ideas through drawing.

Video activity 2.4
Thinking about design

Summary

This chapter has looked closely at one of the central characteristics that makes technologies education unique and different from other curriculum areas: design. The key aspect for the youngest children is learning how to conceptualise a plan view so that they can engage in the process of design. Not all children have experiences of designing, or even thinking about a design view. It was noted in this chapter that it is important to introduce this orientation to young children.

The pedagogical feature of design briefs was also specifically examined in this chapter, which looked at how to create a quality design brief and how design briefs can be used in both schooling contexts and early childhood settings. Examples of design briefs were shown for both preschool and school-aged children. It was shown that engaging in the processes and production skills of creating designed solutions requires investigating, generating, producing, evaluating, and collaborating and managing. Two case studies were presented to illustrate the processes and production skills of creating designed solutions.

The next chapter looks at the overarching idea of creating preferred futures.

Acknowledgements

Special thanks to Judith Gomes for providing the infant photo in this chapter and to Bob Greaves for his work on technologies education captured through the case study of making, evaluating and designing paper planes. Thanks to Laburnum Primary School for curriculum development photos. Finally, thanks to Yuwen Ma for support with updating the references for this chapter.

Designing and creating preferred futures

CHAPTER 3

Introduction

Chapter 2 explored the strand of generating designs through two case studies. This chapter and the next continue to show the curriculum in action through a series of case studies. This chapter specifically explores preferred futures as one of the key features of the Australian Curriculum: Technologies (ACARA, 2023).

Creating solutions for preferred futures is the outermost ring of the Australian Curriculum: Technologies, as shown in Figure 3.1, and it is an important overarching idea through which the content can be expressed.

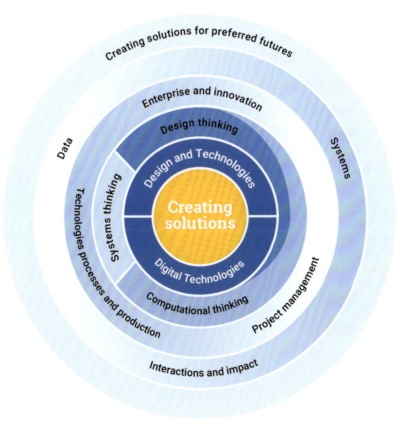

Figure 3.1 Overview of Technologies core concepts
Source: ACARA (2023).

Preferred futures: Identifying compelling visions of the future and making considered design decisions, taking into account diversity, ethics, and economic, environmental and social sustainability factors (ACARA, 2023).

Creating solutions for **preferred futures** is developed through the core concepts of:

- systems
- data
- interactions and impact
- systems thinking
- computational thinking
- design thinking
- technologies processes and production skills
- project-management skills
- enterprise skills and innovation.

This chapter is oriented to exploring the creation of solutions for preferred futures, with subsequent chapters discussing and showing case examples of the above core concepts in action in classrooms and centres.

PEDAGOGICAL REFLECTION 3.1

What does preferred futures mean?

What do you think the concept of creating preferred futures means? Record your ideas below:

Idea 1:_____

Idea 2:_____

Idea 3:_____

Web activity 3.1
Futuristic design

As part of examining the concept of creating preferred futures as it is detailed in the Australian Curriculum: Technologies, this chapter first looks at what children mean by the concept of 'future'. It is important to begin with knowing children's values, attitudes and beliefs before proceeding to prepare teaching programs for them (Figure 3.2).

Figure 3.2 Creating preferred futures
Source: Monash University PlayLab and Laburnum Primary School.

Children conceptualising futures

In her research, Mackey (2014) shows how very young children can and do have agency in their lives when teachers create the right conditions to tap into their thinking about their preferred futures. For instance, she writes:

> We also observed an example of democracy in action where children were given an opportunity to vote. At the kindergarten entrance, the teacher had placed a poster illustrating different playground swing designs that were being considered for the playground. Under each picture she created a space for each child to make a pen mark to indicate the style of swing they preferred. (Mackey, 2014, p. 189)

This example illustrates the simple ways in which educators can begin to teach the concept of preferred futures. We do, however, need to know more about what children think about their future.

What technological experiences do children have at home during their school years and prior to beginning school, and how might these experiences influence their technological thinking about the future? Baker, Le Courtois and Eberhart (2021) and Ma et al. (2022) suggest that children should be positioned as experts and given a voice in the decisions and actions that will influence their lives. In Figure 3.3, Daniel thinks about his current environment and what it may look like in the future.

Figure 3.3 Daniel's thinking about now and the future

PEDAGOGICAL REFLECTION 3.2

Do children think about the future?

This pedagogical reflection considers the range of technological experiences that children might have. Record your responses to the following questions:

1. Why do you think it is important to find out what children know and can do before planning for technology education?
2. The sociological research suggests that some families focus on the 'present situation' and are less likely to discuss 'the future'. How will this influence children's thinking about 'planning' and 'designing preferred futures'?

Video activity 3.1
Futures thinking embedded in design briefs

Do children in the early childhood years also think about their preferred future? It is well recognised that very young children think mostly about the 'here and now', so discussing the concept of preferred futures must begin in early childhood in the context of planning, thus leading to the idea of future planning and thinking, as well as being able to design for the future. For example, when 4-year-old children were asked about their technological experiences at home that featured planning, children had many ideas to share:

Teacher: There are special things that you do with Mummy and Daddy, such as going shopping. How do you go about planning what you will buy?

Sarah: I tell Mummy what I want to buy. We write a shopping list. We have to plan what we are going to buy.

Teacher: What other things do you plan?

Monica: Going on holidays – they [parents] ring up on the phone and we talk about how we are going to get there and see if we need a car. Then we ring up the person. We also need to think about clothes.

Teacher: Any other things you plan for?

Sarah: Dinner – they [parents] choose in their head and then they get an idea and then they use a cookbook to get the recipe.

Tui: We say what we want for dinner. We have a meeting and discuss – only us, Tui and Alex – and then we tell Mum we want spaghetti.

In the following quotations, a group of 5-year-old children explain what they understand about the concept of planning – something that is significant for creating preferred futures.

I can plan. I can plan with my train track. I have got a book about planning about a cat. (Daniel)

My dad is a worker. Sometimes he does a bit of planning. He talks to the people on the phone and plans, and the people help him. (Grace)

When you are planning, you might plan to go to someone's house. (Matthew)

When you plan something, you can then build it. (Alyse)

These children have not referred to writing things down. One might expect that there would be some form of written or graphical planning occurring in families, such as writing a menu or shopping list, or sketching out images. When we examine research into futures thinking for very young children, we notice that although three types of planning are possible – oral, two-dimensional and three-dimensional – it is oral planning that dominates. The least likely form of planning in which young children would participate at home or observe family members undertaking is three-dimensional planning, or model-making. It is possible that some modelling may occur in craft-oriented families; however, it is likely that only the adult will engage in this activity, not the child.

If young children's experiences prior to school involve mostly oral planning, with minimal two-dimensional planning and very little or no three-dimensional experience, it is not surprising that children do not intuitively engage in two-dimensional or three-dimensional planning/design work in school (Milne, 2018). Most of their planning experiences are oral, so they are more likely to use this mode for planning and designing.

A great deal of experience with two-dimensional (written/drawing) and three-dimensional models for planning and designing would be needed by children if they were to engage in anything other than oral planning when in preschool, childcare or school. Milne (2013, p. 351) notes:

> Many primary teachers lack knowledge of and skill in the schemata of communicating design ideas: how to teach and progress students in creating 2-dimesional and 3-dimenational drawn plans, the elements of modelling, creating mock-ups and building prototypes.

Yet this is important, as was discussed in Chapter 2, where research showed how children use drawing to support their design ideas (Hatzigianni et al., 2021; Milne, 2018; Stammes et al., 2021).

PEDAGOGICAL REFLECTION 3.3

What is the range of technological experiences that children have?

Record your responses to the following questions:

- How will children's home experiences influence how they make sense of the technological learning provided in classrooms and centres?
- What does it mean when children come from homes that use a range of high technologies (such as texting, social media apps, tablet devices, gaming consoles, and robotic and electronic toys) and homes that do not have any or only a few? Does it matter?
- How can you find out what children know and can do before they begin school, preschool or child care? How can you continue to connect with their home experiences throughout their schooling?
- What cultural experiences do children have that are likely to facilitate engagement in technology education?

Children's views of the future

The research demonstrates that children have many technological experiences prior to and during their school years (Milne and Edwards, 2013). Children do have strongly held views about their environment and the place of technology in their world. As discussed in Chapter 1, technology is not just artefacts in the children's environment (such as Nintendo Wii, Twitter, Facebook, robotic toys, smartphones, tablets or DVDs), but also the processes of how these and other technologies are invented, designed, made and used. Children are oriented to these processes early in their lives, as shown by the following comments:

> Daddy and I build cubbies together. (Sam)
>
> I collect firewood and help daddy prune the apricot tree. I help him make dinner. (Cynthia)
>
> We make books and we made a bird feeder. (Hannah)
>
> We make castles together. (Feiyan)
>
> I make cakes and things – muffins, pikelets and pancakes. (Shukla)
>
> We make cakes and do the washing. Outside we plant flowers and go for walks. (Jui)

As children grow older and have more life experiences, what do they think about their environments? Do their thoughts change, and do they become increasingly negative? Figure 3.3 shows the response given by Daniel, aged 11, when he was asked about what he thought his environment would look like when he was a grandparent. Like many primary-aged children, Daniel presented a technological view, drawing a picture of a crowded technological environment. Young children include more images of nature in their projected future. For example, when asked about her future, one child responded by writing how new types of flowers could be invented, such as a giant rose, how to bring a kangaroo back to life, and also how to bring extinct animals back to life. When making comments like this, children are projecting into the future. Young children's drawings have generally been found to be positive and cheerful (Fleer, 2002).

Children also make statements about technologically oriented solutions to environmental problems (Svensson and von Otter, 2018). For example, children comment on the world becoming more and more technological. When asked about their future, they often draw images or make statements that reflect pollution. Children also anticipate that life in the future will be very different. They focus on the consequences of these changes by suggesting how they can solve the problem by wearing protective clothing, masks, goggles and the like; this is consequences thinking – using technology to solve problems (Borg and Gericke, 2021; Svensson and von Otter, 2018). These suggestions relate to the need for protection against ultraviolet rays, and sealing out pollution through especially engineered cars or houses. What young children imagine is always positive. Creative inventions about the future also feature in the drawing and writing of young children, as shown in Figure 3.4.

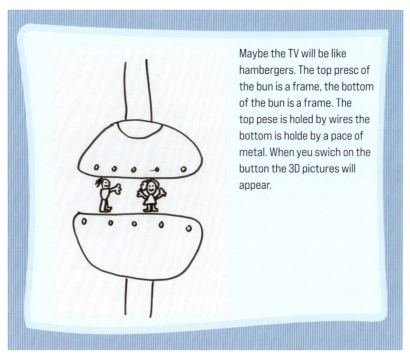

Figure 3.4 Ben's thinking about the future

Preferred futures – Ben's thinking about the future

ACTIVITY 3.1

Reflect on Ben's thinking about the future and consider the following:
1. How might his views have been formed?
2. How might you work with his ideas?
3. How can you engage him in preferred futures thinking?

An analysis of these children's drawings about the future shows that it is older primary school children who include more technological images. Drawings and diary entries can also tell us a lot about children's perceived capacity to *act for the environment* – that is, not just to accept a particular future, but to plan for a preferred future; this is systems thinking (Svensson and von Otter, 2018). Two examples follow that show the concerns children have, but also how they think about their reactive response to solving the problems:

> I think in the future they might clone animals that recently become extinct or endangered that they can get the DNA from and they'll have national parks to keep them in. (12 years)

> Well if heaps of people work together probably but you can't really change it on your own unless you like to do a whole lot of stuff and never get any sleep and you just do nothing. (12 years)

In her research, Mackey (2014) demonstrates how teachers can support children to act collectively. She found that when teachers planned with children how to change the future, a greater sense of child agency to make a difference emerged. As a result, teachers need to:

- ensure that children are given opportunities to create their own vision by planning and changing their environments
- respect that children have opinions and need to be given the possibility to express their views, such as 'What's your favourite space? Where do you like to play? What parts don't you like? Why don't you like them? What can we do to fix it?' (Mackey, 2014, p. 185)
- overcome past barriers by, for instance, challenging policies and risk and safety policies, pushing against government regulations.

Web activity 3.2 Near Future Laboratory

Acting for the environment – what should you do?

Children who are asked about what they can do in the context of looking after the environment or positively changing their environment often include the following statements:

Primary:

- Not wasting so much stuff. My Mum does gardening. Mum normally hangs out the clothes. You don't really need to use the heater so much … Insulation and socks to keep your feet warm. (10 years)
- We are trying to have shorter showers. (10 years)
- You could make more fish farms to breed more fish. You could make fish adapt to chemicals in the water. (12 years)

Early childhood:

- Wash the floors. (5 years)
- You should look after the nature and you should keep all the places tidy and you should keep the house tidy and put your clothes away and clean the roads. (7 years)
- I think we should be looking after penguins that get [hit] with oil tanks that hurt them. (6 years)
- Pollution makes the air. They put rubbish in the air and sea, because people might start reading and then understand. My Mum does that. Because the cars. My Mum told me that you can that people are polluting and when they're polluting it's killing all the coral and starfish. (5 years)
- People will stop littering and make more rules … better rules. (7 years)
- Cut down our factories which make smoke. I'd make differ types of cars and I'd make solar powered things, make more things solar power. (7 years)

Small but significant changes mean that children feel they can contribute to the future that they feel is important. The idea of preferred futures is challenging if children have little experience of thinking about the future (as shown above), or limited opportunities to participate in forward planning (see Milne, 2018). That is why introducing children to design thinking through the concept of a design brief (Chapter 2) is important for a successful technologies teaching program that is geared to creating preferred futures (von Mengersen and Wilkinson, 2020). The Australian Curriculum: Technologies provides insight into the content needed for the preparation of teaching programs that will support the development of this overarching core concept of creating preferred futures:

> Creating solutions for preferred futures is the overarching core concept. It involves identifying compelling visions of the future and making considered design decisions

taking into account diversity, ethics, and economic, environmental and social sustainability factors. (ACARA, 2023)

Planning orally, planning through design and creating the conditions for child agency so children feel they can make a difference to their future are all included in the concept of preferred futures. How might you find out what your children already know about futures thinking? What pedagogical approach could you adopt?

Drawing about the future

The Australian Curriculum: Technologies includes content that will support planning for creating preferred futures. Table 3.1 lists some of this content. Examine this content in relation to the samples of children's thinking about the future (Figures 3.2–3.4) or in relation to your own research (Activity 3.2). This is seen in the content detailed under Technologies and Society content descriptions, as shown in Table 3.1, and also in Table 3.2. Some of these ideas were considered in Chapter 1, and we will return to them in Chapter 4, which looks at the role of technologists.

Table 3.1 Technologies and Society content descriptions

Foundation	Years 1 and 2	Years 3 and 4	Years 5 and 6
explore how familiar products, services and environments are designed by people (AC9TDEFK01)	identify how familiar products, services and environments are designed and produced by people to meet personal or local community needs and sustainability (AC9TDE2K01)	examine design and technologies occupations and factors including sustainability that impact on the design of products, services and environments to meet community needs (AC9TDE4K01)	explain how people in design and technologies occupations consider competing factors including sustainability in the design of products, services and environments (AC9TDE6K01)

Source: ACARA (2023).

Table 3.2 Examples of elaborations for content descriptions for Technologies and Society

Foundation	Years 1 and 2	Years 3 and 4	Years 5 and 6
Asking questions about the design of products from the local store, for example why certain packaging materials might have been selected, and how people design the text and images on the packaging to attract people's attention (ACARA, 2023)	Exploring how people come up with new ideas or modify existing designs, for example preventing water waste when caring for plants (ACARA, 2023)	Exploring how Australian designers consider sustainability when designing products, services or environments, for example designing products for 100% recycled materials, designing services that use minimal energy, or designing landscapes that require minimal water (ACARA, 2023)	Describing the impact and sustainability implications of designed products, services or environments on local, regional and global communities, for example the emergence of small businesses that are recycling materials, such as plastic tags and bottle tops into prosthetics (ACARA, 2023)

ACTIVITY 3.2

How can we find out children's thinking about their future?

Ask a group of children (it could be a small group or a whole class) to draw a picture of what they think the environment will look like in the future.

If the children are very young, you can reference the time period by saying, 'Imagine you are a grandmother/grandfather. When you look all around you, what do you see? Can you draw what it might look like in the future?' If the children are older, you can invite them to write a diary of one day in their life a hundred years from now. Examples are provided below.

Analyse the drawings: What do you notice? Are your results similar to those presented in this chapter? What is the same? What is different? What might the reasons be for the similarities and/or differences?

ACTIVITY 3.3

Children's views of the future

1. Consider what a teaching program that draws upon the concept of preferred futures might look like.
2. Design a unit of work that exemplifies futures thinking.

So how might a teaching program look that draws upon the concept of preferred futures? Three case examples follow, two from a school context (Year 6 and Years 1 and 2) and the other from an early childhood setting (3- to 5-year-olds).

Looking inside a classroom: Year 6 children planning for the design and creation of preferred futures

Year 6 children were invited by their teacher, Tim, to plan interview questions that focused on preferred futures, which they could then ask the other children in the school (Figure 3.5). Tim was interested to find out:

- the sources of the children's ideas – for example, TV, school, family
- their perceived capacity to make changes to their predicted outcome
- what understandings they had and needed to have in order to care for the environment
- the questions they had about the future
- the things they and their family were currently doing or would like to do in caring for the environment.

To achieve this, Tim thought the children should design their own interview questions, as this would provide an insight into the children's thinking, and their questions would also reflect what they were most interested in.

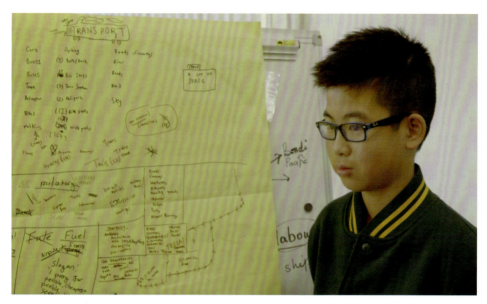

Figure 3.5 Designing the cities of the future
Source: Monash University PlayLab and Laburnum Primary School.

The children came up with the following questions to ask other children in the school:
- What will happen in the future?
- What will the world look like?
- Will we still be here?
- Will the temperature rise?
- Will Antarctica's water level rise?
- Will the countries be the same shape?
- What are the changes we can make to improve the environment?
- Are you thinking of now and not of the future?
- Do you think we can make things in factories without producing carbon dioxide?
- Can we save our planet?

The children also planned questions for the community about design quality. In order to narrow down their questions (they decided the responses to the questions for children were too broad), the children decided to plan interviews that focused on an energy audit of their home and community environment. These are the questions they developed:
- Do you use hot water a lot?
- Do you use a lot of electricity?
- Do you use a bike or a car to get to work?
- Do you have a skylight?
- Do you use gas to keep yourself warm, or do you use a fire?
- What kind of things do you recycle?
- Do you know anything about the greenhouse effect?
- Do you have some ideas about helping to reduce the greenhouse effect?
- If you built a new house, would you make it solar powered?

Tim reflected on the range of questions the children asked in the context of the Australian Curriculum: Technologies:

> When I think about the content in the Technologies curriculum on preferred futures, I recognise that having children ask questions of others is getting them to think about how solutions are created now and will be used in the future. From this, it becomes important to consider how to help children to analyse the possible benefits and risks of creating solutions – ones the adults mentioned or those they thought of themselves. The questions they asked of the adults in their community gave them the opportunity to engage with critical and creative thinking in a meaningful way. It also allowed them to begin to have conversations about how to weigh up possible short- and long-term impact of the solutions. These are all in keeping with the concept of preferred futures in the Australian Curriculum: Technologies.

Looking inside a classroom: Year 1 and 2 children planning for the design and creation of preferred futures

Bob and Renelle use the fairy tale of 'Jack and the Beanstalk' to create a unit of technologies education where the children plan for Jack's future. The teachers read the story to the children as a group and also in small groups. The children discuss with Bob and Renelle how they could 'recreate the story' with wooden puppets. The children make their puppets, both individually and as a group (Figures 3.6 and 3.7), following a model. The children skilfully use hammers to assemble the pieces. For such young children, accurately and safely using a hammer initially presents a few challenges. Figure 3.8 shows a design brief for a puppet play.

The teachers and the children decide that they must create a sustainable garden because the Golden Goose won't lay eggs forever (Figure 3.9). The children discuss how Jack must plan for his future.

Melissa: Jack is not allowed to really steal. So he has to make his own food.

Sylvia: He can grow lots of beans. Not magic beans, but real beans.

Teacher: What do you think he might need?

Melissa: Some beans.

Andrew: Sunshine.

Sarah: We can put beans in a cup and some dirt and grow them.

Teacher: Shall we plan for growing an indoor garden of beans?

Children: Yes!!!! (chorus of replies from the children)

Figure 3.6 Making the puppets for 'Jack and the Beanstalk'

Figure 3.7 'Jack and the Beanstalk' – children make their puppets (Mother, Jack and the Giant)

Design brief for a puppet play

Using the wooden puppets you have made, design your puppet play. Write a play about how Jack plans for his future.

Investigating

Look at a lot of books on 'Jack and the Beanstalk'.

Generating

Using your puppets, role-play the fairy tale of 'Jack and the Beanstalk'.

Producing

Draw pictures of your fairy tale from beginning to end. Make it a picture strip. Role-play a new ending to the story where Jack plans for his future, then draw the new ending and add it to your picture strip.

Evaluating

Perform your new play to another class. Using clapping, ask the children to clap lots if they liked your play.

Download 3.1 Design brief for a puppet play

Figure 3.8 Design brief for a puppet play

Figure 3.9 Planning for an indoor garden for growing beans

The children discuss with the teacher how they can design their stage set.

Teacher: What do we need to do?

Andrew: I have an idea. We could use a table and some chairs to make our theatre.

Teacher: I will make a list of what we need (teacher takes a pen and clipboard and begins to document what the children say).

Melissa: We need a BIG BIG HUGE beanstalk because the giant is really, really big.

Teacher: So what might we need to make this?

Melissa: We need some cardboard …

Andrew: … and scissors and glue

Teacher: What else might we need?

Sylvia: I want to make a production – can I film it?

Teacher: So we might need a …

Sylvia: … camera.

Teacher: I will put that on my list.

The children and teacher continue to document all the things they will need to produce the stage set (Figure 3.10). Later they draw a storyboard of the scenes in the play (Figure 3.11). They draw upon the books and their puppets to help them get the sequence right. Then the children discuss how they have to change the ending to the story so that Jack can plan for his own future without stealing. Sylvia makes a video documentary of the entire process (Figure 3.12).

Figure 3.10 Making the props for the stage set

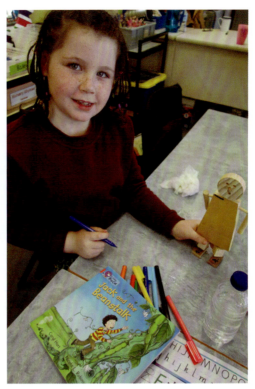

Figure 3.11 Thinking about the story sequence and getting ready to storyboard the fairy tale with a new ending – where Jack does not steal and plans for his future

Figure 3.12 Sylvia making her video documentary of the whole process

Looking inside an early childhood setting: Planning for the future is about young children learning to plan

ACTIVITY 3.4

How do early childhood children engage with futures thinking?

Design a unit of work that supports young children to plan. Refer to the case examples in the rest of the chapter for ideas.

In order to support young children with planning and designing for the future, Wendy, a child-care centre educator, set up a problem that involved the children in planning and designing. She began by telling the children the following story:

> Last night I went out into the garden and you know what I heard? I heard a very sad noise. It sounded like sobbing. I crept out. It was very dark. I went behind a bush and there I saw a little creature. It didn't look like any kind of animal I knew. It was a creature. So I decided to take it inside. I put it into this basket [showing children a cane picnic basket with a lid] and carefully carried it inside and near to the fire so it would be nice and warm. But it was still crying. I tried to give it water. But it didn't want it. I tried to give it food. But it didn't want that either. I asked the creature what was the matter? The creature told me it was very lonely. I said I know some children at Bell Towers Child Care Centre who might be able to help make another creature to be its friend. It is very shy and it probably won't like to come out of the basket. So shall we make a surprise – make a lot of other creatures to be friends with this little creature?

The story set up an engaging context, as the children were really very interested to make a friend for the lonely creature. In order to set up a futures orientation for the children, Wendy set up the following condition:

> We will make friends using our box of construction material. Now tell me what you need. I will make a list. I am going to do some shopping later. If you tell me what you need then I will buy it and bring it in tomorrow to use. The creature is now sleeping. So we will put the creature somewhere where it is quiet now, while you make plans for what you would like to make, and you tell me what you need for the shopping list.

Tony: I am going to make a mummy creature to look after it.

Daniel: I need some sticky tape, some wool and some scissors.

Grace: I need some boxes and some material.

Wendy recorded on her shopping list all the things the children needed to make their design. She noted the oral discussions, but she also took special notice when children drew their designs and discussed what they needed, as shown when Grace talks about her design:

I'll make a crocodile for the little creature. Mine won't talk back. Some jaws and a paddle pop stick. Scissors to make teeth go up and down. I make a crocodile. I put some paddle pop sticks. That's the teeth, the tail. I've finished.

Figure 3.13 shows Grace's design and Figure 3.14 shows what she created.

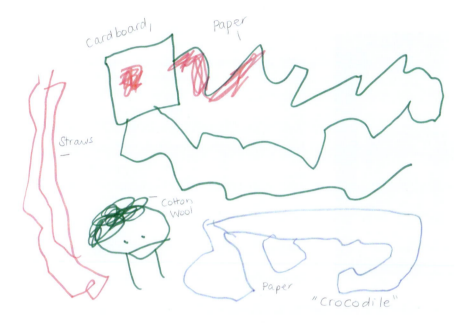

Figure 3.13 Grace (5 years) has designed a friend for the lonely creature

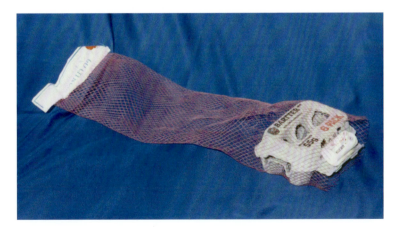

Figure 3.14 Grace (5 years) has made a model of her friend for the lonely creature

Wendy and Grace discussed the design and the final product, evaluating what had been made. Below is their conversation:

Teacher: You were telling me you had a lot of trouble sticking the mouth on. What happened?

Grace: I needed sticky tape. I did use masking tape. So if I was to stick a mouth on, I'd try sticky tape. Masking tape didn't work. Glue didn't.

Teacher: Next time if you made a crocodile what would you use?

Grace: Sticky tape.

Wendy brought along the materials the day after telling the story. She and the children consulted the designs and her list, as she distributed the resources the children had requested. Figure 3.15 shows Alyse's design of some shoes for the lonely creature and Figure 3.16 evaluates what she made after leading questions were asked.

Figure 3.15 Alyse's (5 years) model

Figure 3.16 Alyse (5 years) evaluates her model in relation to the design

After the children had made a friend for the lonely creature, Wendy invited them to think about where the creature could live, suggesting that they could design a house and perhaps some things for the creature to play with. She followed the same process as before, asking the children to tell her what they needed:

Teacher: Andrew, I'd like to know what kind of things you need for tomorrow because Gayle and I have to get some things organised for the creature and the house that you're going to build. What kinds of things do you need?

Andrew: Bricks.

Teacher: How many bricks?

Andrew: Five bricks. Nails.

Teacher: Some nails and … ?

Andrew: A hammer.

Teacher: What else do you think you will need?

Andrew: Some straw.

Teacher: Oh goodness, what are you going to need straw for?

Andrew: For my creature. And I need a chimney.

Teacher: How are you going to make your chimney?

Andrew: With paper … [continues].

An example of a playground design that Daniel created is shown in Figure 3.17. Added to the design shown in Figure 3.17 are the evaluative comments made by Alyse and documented by Wendy.

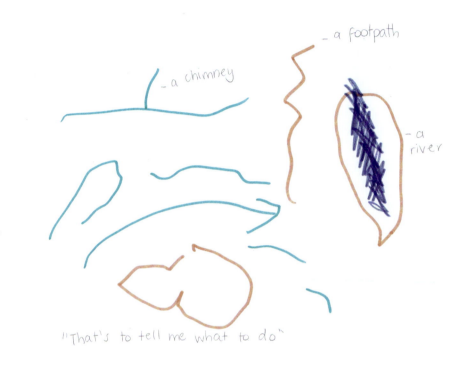

Figure 3.17 Daniel's (3 years) design and model of a playground for the lonely creature

Wendy's unit of work reflects Outcome 4 in the Early Years Learning Framework (EYLF), where, 'Educators promote this learning for all children when they, for example: provide resources for very young children to explore the properties of materials through manipulating, rotating, collecting, transporting and positioning.'

All the examples of the children's designs and discussions with Wendy also show 'explore 2D and 3D forms of expression to develop understandings of different artforms and elements' and 'engage in meaningful conversations about natural and processed materials' (AGDE, 2022, p. 56).

In the design process, Wendy:

- provides resources that encourage children to represent their thinking
- provides sensory and exploratory experiences with a wide variety of open-ended natural and processed materials
- selects and introduces appropriate tools, technologies and media, and provides the skills, knowledge and techniques to enhance children's learning (AGDE, 2022, p. 56).

SPOTLIGHT 3.1

Pedagogy of critiquing: Introducing sustainability and democratic politics as the norm in the design process ethics.

A pedagogy of critiquing

Keirl (2020) introduces the concept of a **pedagogy of critiquing**. This means introducing in the design process ethics, sustainability and democratic politics as the norm. He asks us to think about what kind of technological and design literacy we would want to promote to serve a rich and informed democracy. He invites us to consider whether all students should develop critical 'designerly' behaviours and dispositions, such as:

- values-weighing
- judgement-making
- imagination
- managing discomfort
- meaning-making
- advocacy and defence of design and production decisions
- scepticism about the status quo
- empathy towards other people and other species
- futures thinking
- consciousness-raising
- understanding holism
- question-asking as ordinary
- critical thinking.

This means the teacher is no longer a *transmitter* of knowledge, but rather supports *transformative* and *transactional* engagement and thinking.

Summary

One of the concepts unique to the technologies curriculum is creating preferred futures. This chapter has explored how to support young children in planning in order to think from a futures perspective. It has also examined how older children think about their future, and how teachers can create the conditions for supporting the development of a futures orientation for both younger and older children. Specifically, the chapter has examined the concept of planning, which is critical for the development of early childhood children's ability to think about a preferred future.

Acknowledgements

Many thanks to Bob and Renelle for their work on technologies education captured through the case study of 'Jack and the Beanstalk' and to Wendy, who designed the story and unit of work on the lonely creature. Special acknowledgement is made of all the children who wrote diaries and drew pictures on their thinking about the future. Thanks to Laburnum Primary School for curriculum development photos. Finally, thanks to Yuwen Ma for support with updating the references for this chapter.

Creativity in design

CHAPTER 4

Introduction

The previous chapters examined the idea of a design brief and creating preferred futures. Design thinking that is supportive of the Design and Technologies subject was explored, and through a series of case studies children from birth to 12 years were shown engaging in design thinking to generate and produce solutions to problems they were interested in solving.

This chapter expands on design thinking by examining imagination and creativity in order to support children to ask good design questions (Figure 4.1). It introduces the work of internationally known designer Mary Featherston to show the importance of good design. Through following her work, the chapter will build upon the key ideas introduced in Chapter 1 on the nature and contexts of technology, where the people behind some well-known technologies were discussed.

> Dear Rowan,
> I invite you to come into my room at 1:00 to dskus the cok pen [chook pen]
> Freya

Figure 4.1 Can this be design thinking? Setting up a meeting through a simple note from sister to brother is about communicating about design

The chapter concludes by showing the curriculum in action through a series of case studies that explore the key features of the Australian Curriculum: Technologies.

Design and technologies: Imagination and creativity in design

Read the following questions:

- Why is liquorice twisted?
- Why does my chair have a curved back?
- Why does our chair at home not have armrests?
- Why is there netting over the roast pork?

These technological questions were generated by a young child. She genuinely wanted to know why her constructed environment looked the way it did. Why is liquorice twisted? We take liquorice for granted and never question its design – like many other things in our environment; however, children notice and want to know why things look the way they do (Figure 4.2).

Figure 4.2 What questions arise in digital technologies?
Source: Monash University PlayLab and Laburnum Primary School.

Digital technologies: Imagining and creating digital environments

Families also ask questions about their digital environments, such as:

- What devices of ours can connect to the internet, and how will we keep an eye on their use?
- Do we understand the capabilities of all electronic devices in our home?
- What kinds of activities and online interactions do your children like to engage in?
- What times of day or occasions will we designate as free of high-tech devices?
- What are our house rules for using high-tech devices and internet connectivity?
- What about e-safety? (Steinberg, 2021)

Link 4.1 20 questions for you and your kids

If you were approached by a parent, how might you respond to these questions?

PEDAGOGICAL REFLECTION 4.1

Asking design questions

Have you ever questioned the way your environment is organised or constructed? Did you ever think about why chairs were designed as they are or why the internet of things emerged?

Write down any questions or thoughts you may have had about your designed environment.

Often, little thought is given to the context in which design questions emerge. What environments, including digital environments, need to be created so that children will ask technological design questions? What is possible within the boundaries of the classroom and early childhood centre walls? The design questions drive technological activity. A good design question facilitates quality technological learning, and therefore is an important aspect of the teaching and learning process. The cultural community in which a child lives creates the conditions and the resources for working in design technologies (Kaui et al., 2018).

Educators want children to ask technological questions – questions that can be used to build relevant and interesting technological teaching programs. Children are capable of asking purposeful and insightful questions (see also Chapter 6 on the work of Highfield in relation to computational thinking and robotics). For example, the following questions were asked by a group of preschool children after they had explored a series of robotic toys brought in to the early childhood setting:

- Do they have switches?
- Do they have buttons?
- Do they like to eat oil?
- Do they move on wheels?
- Do they have a motor?
- Do they talk?
- What jobs do they do?
- Do they have beds?
- What time do they go to bed?
- Do they have feelings?

The level of questioning ability of these children is evident when thought is given to the question, 'Do they have feelings?' Vicky, their teacher, supported the children's learning by providing experiences, such as the robotic toys, to actively explore basic programming principles. The children investigated their robots based on the questions they asked. In their investigations, they wrote lists (programs) of what their robots could do, and later what they wanted them to be able to do, such as designing dancing steps. Children asked some very insightful questions, such as 'Why can't my robot remember the steps I put in it?' and 'How do you scroll my list program?' (See Chapters 5 and 6 on digital technology for further insights.)

If young children are capable of asking sophisticated questions such as these, what might be possible with 10- and 11-year-olds? There are many types of questions that children experience (as shown in Table 4.1), but can children be taught to ask questions of their created and designed environment when in a school or preschool context?

Questioning the created environment

If you look around the environment in which you live, it will become immediately apparent that a great deal of it is constructed by humans. We are all born into particular environments and cultural practices. For children, these things are all new and they have many questions to ask; however, adults tend to no longer see or question their environment because it has

Download 4.1 Question types to support technologies education

Table 4.1 Question types to support technologies education

Question type	Example	Purpose
Recall or factual questions	What is this? Can you tell us about … ? How long is it? What do you know about … ?	To identify ideas, recall facts previously presented.
Description-type questions	What did it look like? What happened?	To describe events or objects as rigorously as possible. To restate known ideas in different ways.
Comparative or interpretive questions	What is different about these? How are they similar to each other?	To compare ideas or things and to use these ideas for problem-solving.
Historical questions	How has it changed from before? How is it different now?	To conceptualise a sequence of events over time and to notice patterns.
Prediction questions	What will happen next? What might be the next step? Has anything changed?	In drawing upon known ideas or observations to predict possible outcomes.
Speculative or creative questions	How might we think about this differently? What might be a new way of doing that? What ideas can we bring together for a new way of thinking or working?	To develop new ideas, plans, ways of thinking and investigating.
Research questions	How might we find out the answer to that question? What evidence might we have to collect? What do we have to do to find out the answer? How can we be sure about our conclusions?	To investigate and find out new things. To verify through some data collection process a claim or hypothesis. To document systematically in order to identify understandings about something.
Values clarification questions	Which is the best way to do something? What new understandings have we gained from our research to inform our thinking about something?	Clarification of attitudes and values about specific ideas, events, objects and social actions.
Relevant questions (application)	How can we use this idea in other situations? How can we implement these new ways of doing/thinking?	To use ideas and information gained to solve new and existing problems.
Investigative questions for everyday life activity	What new way of thinking and working do we need to move forward in this everyday situation?	To design investigations for solving problems that matter in everyday life.

become so familiar to them. It is often only when people travel that they begin to think about the differences they see.

Within your lifetime and in your own community, the designs that are created actually come from within the existing culture and environment. Most new designs are only marginally different from those design solutions already in the environment. Radical changes in design are actually incremental.

The designed environment that people take for granted, including their digital environment, influences how they live. Road systems or town planning conceptualised over a century ago influence how people interact today. Many designs outlive the designer and a design continues on in the community. How something is designed has implications for how people work, live and act. For example, examination of an aerial view of Sydney (use Google Map street views) reveals how town planning in central Sydney has evolved since European settlement. The road system meanders all over the place. In contrast, an aerial map of Canberra – a city that was designed before people lived there – shows it is very different. The road system is well planned and has catered for future population growth. Consequently, a design 'always goes on designing – unless destroyed' (Fry, 1994, p. 25). Designs take on a life of their own. People work with good or bad design solutions, but do they question the design solutions with which they live?

Most design solutions are based on some criteria, and it can be useful to question the thinking that supports particular design solutions – for example:

- What is the design solution concealing?
- What limits are imposed?
- What are people now able to do that they could not do before?
- What are the implications of the design and resultant action, now and in the future?

Children do question their environment, and educators need to build upon this curiosity because children see things adults no longer see – things that adults may take for granted. Questioning the thinking that underpins design solutions is a more sophisticated form of thinking and can also be introduced to children.

PEDAGOGICAL REFLECTION 4.2

Encouraging children to ask quality design questions

How can you encourage young children to ask quality design questions? What can you set up in a classroom or centre that will act as a catalyst for asking design questions? What will you do or say? Record your ideas.

To answer these questions, the next section considers a framework that supports children to ask quality design questions.

A framework for stimulating quality design questions

In order to question the designed environment, we need to 'make it strange'. Generally speaking, the school context does not easily support children in asking quality questions of their designed environment because it is separated out from the children's everyday lives. Table 4.2 presents a framework for stimulating quality design questions about one's environment.

Table 4.2 Questioning the designed physical and digital environments

Design questions	Description
What is the life of the design?	Are we living in an environment that was designed last century, such as the road system, railways, etc.?
How does the design influence how we interact?	If we live in Sydney (evolving town planning), as opposed to Canberra (planned from the outset), what does it mean in relation to how we live or interact with each other?
Whose interests are being served?	Are issues of equity compromised in the design solution? What does it mean in terms of power, equity and inclusiveness?
Does the design address cultural sensitivity?	Does the design solution take into account differing world-views?
Is the design sustainable?	Are the availability and use of scarce resources considered in the design solution?
Does the digital solution include ethical considerations?	What perspectives might be designed into the device and the app? For instance, is the digital device or app designed based on explicit assumptions of equity, access, fairness and inclusion? Or what does it 'do' in terms of 'social benefit'?
How safe are the digital environment and digitally enhanced home spaces?	Are there privacy issues associated with questions asked by providers – for example, 'This service wants to turn on your camera' or 'This service needs to access your location'? What about cyber security? Are your data and identity safe? How might young children inadvertently give out private information when using apps online?

How else could it look?

How would this framework translate into classroom practice or how could it be used in an early childhood setting? Perhaps an ecodesign approach would provide the foundation for unleashing children's questions. A key feature of quality design questions and technological activity is that children engage in meaningful experiences – those that have a relationship with the real world – both inside and outside of the school or early childhood setting. It has been suggested by Middleton (2005) that a 'problem zone' needs to be set up in classrooms so children can question all elements of design and technology processes. He argues that, in this zone, children can even ask whether 'the problem presented is worth solving'. Middleton defines this questioning of designs as a 'satisficing zone':

> the term 'satisficing zone' is used … to acknowledge that the act of designing does not result in a correct solution, but rather, one that is the best that can be achieved with the limits of imagination, materials and processes that are available at a particular time. The determination that a solution satisfies requirements is thus a value judgement. (Middleton, 2005, p. 68)

The concept of a satisficing zone puts values in design to the fore. Values can include:

- economic values
- safety values
- environmental values
- cultural values.

Middleton argues that, with this kind of thinking being promoted in design, children won't simply consider creating the biggest, the fastest or even the cheapest gizmos. Harfield (2012) adds to the discussion on satisficing zones by presenting the idea of wicked problems. He introduces:

- problem-finding
- problem-setting
- co-extensive nature of problem and solution
- foreknowledge in the design process
- the 'unknown yet known nature' of true design solutions
- absence of neutrality in the designer
- designer-driven solutions criteria.

Harfield (2012, p. 133) suggests that 'designer-driven solution criteria are central not only to problem-solving, but to the role of the designer as formalizing agent in terms of designer-driven problem establishment', where 'design skills, both learned and taught, are inevitably augmented – or constrained – by notions of position, assumption, desire and expectation'. Once again, values dominate Harfield's idea of wicked problems and their design solutions.

Further below is a case study that is suitable for children in 'Preschool, Foundation to Year 2', and that draws upon ecodesign principles where design problems and design solutions are intertwined. As you read the case study, think about the nature of Harfield's (2012) wicked problem, where he problematises the idea of the neutrality of the designer, and ask yourself:

- What is the distinguishing property of their design that is of overriding importance?
- On what basis?
- How is it to be explicated and supported?
- What does it 'do' in terms of 'social benefit'? (Harfield, 2012, p. 137)

Would the same questions be asked by 11-year-olds? For instance, with design thinking, ACARA (2023) suggests that it helps people to empathise and understand needs, opportunities and problems; generate, iterate and represent innovative, user-centred ideas; and analyse and evaluate those ideas. Can we ask if the digital platform or resource has been designed in relation to a 'social benefit'?

Disruptive technologies (Petrina, 2019) and critical thinking (Brecka, Valentová and Lancaric, 2022) have become important dimensions of design and technologies education (Kafai, Fields and Searle, 2014), but also digital technologies. Nussbaum et al. (2021) argue that critical thinking is fundamental to twenty-first century learning. Critical thinking involves a child's ability to be able to examine, analyse, interpret and evaluate designs and artefacts. Importantly, it also foregrounds asking questions and engaging in conversations and debates about the risks and benefits of technologically designed solutions.

Disruptive technologies, such as autonomous cars, electric cars, drones, the Internet of Things, wrist chips, and the use of robotics in elderly care and education, were topics given to students of technologies education by Axell and Bjorklund (2018). They found that robotic use in elderly care was popular with girls, but that overall the most popular technology was autonomous cars. In critically examining and researching their chosen disruptive technology, students had difficulty with evaluating and problematising the information they researched. Axell and Bjorklund (2018) note that the students did not change their original position, despite undertaking a great deal of research and engaging in critical discussion about their chosen technologies.

PEDAGOGICAL REFLECTION 4.3

Ecodesign teaching

Reflect on the ideas of Middleton (2005) and Harfield (2012) in the context of Table 4.2. How could you use the framework presented in the table to teach values-based design principles? What might be the 'satisficing zone'? How might you conceptualise the wicked problems? Map out a lesson plan for what you might do. A case example follows.

SPOTLIGHT 4.1

Futures orientation in careers

Kaui et al. (2018) argue that a futures orientation is not just for children; rather, what they learn feeds into the new ways of working in their future careers. As shown in Table 4.3, critical thinking appeared midway in the list of the top skills needed in 2015, yet was high on the list in 2020. Similarly, creativity featured highly in 2020, but was at the bottom of the skill set in 2015.

Table 4.3 Top skills needed

What were the top job skills in 2015?	What were the top job skills needed for 2020?
Solving complex problems	Solving complex problems
Coordination	**Critical thinking**
The management of people	**Imagination and creativity**
Critical thinking	The management of people
Negotiation	Coordination
Quality control	Emotional intelligence

Table 4.3 (cont.)

What were the top job skills in 2015?	What were the top job skills needed for 2020?
Service orientation	Decision-making
Active listening	Negotiation
Imagination and creativity	Cognitive flexibility

Source: Kaui et al. (2018, p. 208), citing Gray (2016).

Case study: Practices and content suitable for preschool and Foundation to Year 2

Vicky, a preschool teacher, decided to investigate the 'by-products' of Christmas. She was inspired by Outcome 5 in the EYLF (Table 4.4) and the Designing and Making strand in the Australian Curriculum: Technologies, as summarised briefly in Table 4.5.

Table 4.4 EYLF Outcome 5: Children are effective communicators

Children use digital technologies and media to access information, investigate ideas and represent their thinking	
This is evident when children, for example:	**Educators promote this learning for all children when they, for example:**
• Identify technologies and their use in everyday life • incorporate real or imaginary technologies as features of their play • use digital technologies to access images and information, explore diverse perspectives and make sense of their world • develop simple skills to operate digital devices, such as turning on and taking a photo with a tablet • use digital technologies and media for creative expression (e.g. designing, drawing, composing) • engage with technologies and media for fun and social connection • identify basic icons and keys (e.g. delete button) and use them to support their navigation (e.g. click, swipe, home, scroll) and understand these terms • adopt collaborative approaches in their learning about and with digital technologies	• acknowledge technologies are a feature of children's lives, so will be a feature of their imaginative and investigative play • provide children with access to a range of technologies • integrate technologies across the curriculum and into children's multimodal play experiences and projects • teach skills and techniques and encourage children to use technologies to explore new information and represent their ideas • encourage collaborative learning about and through technologies between children, and children and educators • provide opportunities for children to have access to different forms of communication technologies • research topics and search for information with children • teach children critical reflection skills and encourage them to evaluate the quality and trustworthiness of information sources • have opportunities to develop their own knowledge and understanding of appropriate digital technology use and safety with children and families • assist children to have a basic understanding that the internet is a network that people use to connect and source information

Source: AGDE (2022, p. 63).

Vicky focused her attention on the excessive drain on people's resources during the Christmas season – wrapping paper, Christmas decorations and Christmas cards. She began her unit by telling a story about three animals that wished to celebrate Christmas. The

Table 4.5 Australian Curriculum: Technologies Designing and Making strand

Creating designed solutions by:	Foundation
generate, communicate and evaluate design ideas, and use materials, equipment and steps to safely make a solution for a purpose (AC9TDEFP01)	• identifying a purpose for designing and making a solution, for example the sand keeps blowing out of the sandpit, the birds keep flying into the waste bin and taking food scraps or people with disability need to know where they can park at school • exploring ideas by drawing or modelling and choosing the most suitable idea, for example drawing or modelling designs for bee hotels to attract native bees to the school garden and choosing one to make, and changing perspectives from front view to plan view • evaluating what they have made using personal preferences, for example using a smiley face Likert scale • exploring how available materials can be used or re-used in construction play, for example using blocks and rain gutters or cardboard to make a ramp to roll a ball or toy car down • practising a range of technical skills safely using equipment, for example joining techniques when making a product from materials, such as a greenhouse to keep a seedling warm or a trellis for holding up tomato plants • assembling components of systems and checking they function as planned, for example making and testing a bowling, stacking or obstacle game with discarded food containers or packaging

Source: ACARA (2023).

animals wrapped their gifts in different types of materials. She then drew the children's attention to some ecodesign principles:

- Would you put the wrapping paper in the bin?
- What else could the animals have done with the wrapping paper?

Vicky asked the children to consider the following:

- Have these materials been used before?
- Can we use them again?
- Can these materials be used in a different way?
- Could other materials have been used?
- What materials could be used again for wrapping presents?

The children progressed to using recycled materials to create their own decorations, cards and wrapping paper. The children also used a digital tablet to design and create their own Christmas cards on recycled paper. As a result of this experience, they asked questions about the 'nature of recycling': 'What things can or cannot be easily recycled?' and 'Why do people design things which waste so many resources or can't be recycled?'

With the children, Vicky prepared a list of their questions about other materials in their environment. The children called these their *ecodesign questions*. They are shown as a framework in Table 4.6. This framework outlines how quality questions were asked by the children about materials, the design of the product and the process, and the system itself.

Critical frameworks are also relevant for children engaged in digital technologies. For Year 6 children, the key ideas to be considered are:

- Design algorithms involving multiple alternatives (branching) and iteration (AC9TDI6P02)

- Design a user interface for a digital system (AC9TDI6P03)
- Generate, modify, communicate and evaluate designs (AC9TDI6P04).

What might be the questions to ask? See Table 4.6 for ideas.

Table 4.6 A framework for stimulating quality design questions by children

Materials	Examples
What happens to the material afterwards?	Does it go down the drain hole?
Where does the material come from?	Rainforests?
Can you recycle it?	Does it have a recycle symbol?
Do we need to use so much?	Is there a lot of packaging that is not necessary?
Does the material grow again?	Is it made of cotton (which grows) or is it a manufactured substance?
How long does it take to make the material?	Paper: Is it made from wood, which takes a lot of time to grow and to process, or is it made from hemp, which is easily grown and processed?
Are natural resources used?	Is sunlight important/used?
Who benefits from the use (or over-use) of particular resources?	What policies are in place to protect rainforest timber harvesting – for example, importing restrictions, logging restrictions, council rules with building permits?

Design system	Examples
Is there a recycling system?	Has the council set up easy-to-access recycling?
Do they have a recycling policy?	Is a policy on display? Have they thought about writing one?
Are the recycling bins easy to get to?	Where are the bins in the school?
Are useful products made from the recycled materials?	Paper
Do they have a policy of buying recycled materials?	Tin cans or bottles
What are the social factors that have allowed particular systems to evolve?	Demand for attractive items, where over-packaging results

Information systems	Examples
How do we tell others about the recycling?	Designing information for presentation on computer, tape, video, diorama, noticeboard, maps, poster and letter
How do we present information on the different ways of recycling?	Fridge magnet, poster, brochure, bookmark
Where can we access information about how to care for the environment or deal with violations (actual or proposed) to the environment?	Websites, council newsletters, signs and newspaper articles

Download 4.2
A framework for stimulating quality design questions by children

You could also jump into the ACARA (2023) website and look at the cross-curriculum priorities. Consider questions associated with the three cross-curriculum priorities:

- Aboriginal and Torres Strait Islander Histories and Cultures
- Asia and Australia's Engagement with Asia
- Sustainability.

It is suggested that the Sustainability cross-curriculum priority is futures-oriented and encourages students to reflect on how they interpret and engage with the world. It is designed to raise student awareness about informed action to create a more environmentally and socially just world (ACARA, 2023). You will notice that there are four sets of organising ideas:

- *Systems*: The interdependence of Earth's systems (geosphere, biosphere, hydrosphere and atmosphere) that support all life on Earth, and social and economic systems.
- *World views*: The role of world-views (sets of attitudes, values and beliefs) that shape individual and community ideas about how the world works and our role in the world.
- *Design*: The role of innovation and creativity in sustainably designed solutions, including products, environments and services, that aim to reduce present and future impacts or to restore the health or diversity of environmental, social and economic systems.
- *Futures*: Ways of thinking and acting that seek to empower young people to design action that will lead to an equitable, sustainable and inclusive future. (ACARA, 2023)

Conceptualising technologies education from a sustainable perspective has become increasingly important (Johansson, 2021). In this context, we also see the concept of creativity emerging (Henriksen et al., 2021). Key aspects of the literature on design in technologies have broadened our understandings to include the concept of *imagination and creativity*. It is argued that to effectively design means to act and think imaginatively and creatively. This next section looks at a well-known designer in Australia and discusses how she thinks and works to illustrate the importance of quality design questions. This is followed by a theoretical discussion of Vygotsky's (2004) conception of imagination and creativity.

How do designers in the community work?

Web activity 4.1 Designers in the community: Mary Featherston

The design work of Mary Featherston has for many years focused on simplicity and functionality so that the manufacturing process elegantly brings to the general population well-designed everyday products. In partnership with Grant Featherston, Mary had a set of well thought-out design principles that were based on the idea of the minimal use of materials, the concept of modularity and a focus on 'production techniques to create well-designed, affordable pieces'. Mary captured this central idea when she said, 'We shared the belief that the role of design was to enrich people's everyday lives' (Featherston, 2014, p. 144; see also Figure 4.3).

Design following these principles meant that Mary and Grant worked together with manufacturers, so design solutions took into account the best available materials and production processes while achieving the overall goal of producing high-quality, affordable items to support everyday living. This holistic view of design necessitated a great deal of research, visits to many production companies and 'animated exchanges' with 'adventurous engineers and chemists' who 'were intrigued' by the design project Mary and Grant had conceptualised.

Mary (Featherston, 2014, pp. 144–5) writes about the challenges faced by designers when designing and producing a chair 'moulded to shape' the human body:

Figure 4.3 Mary Featherston's belief is that everyone deserves to be enriched by quality design.
Source: Mary Featherston.

> We had to convince their American parent company, the global automotive parts manufacturer Uniroyal, which was based in South Australia. Grant initially won their interest with a series of evocative, luscious-coloured crayon sketches that illustrated the furniture potential of their technology. We suggested that there was a market for affordable, modular lounge units for informal living/rumpus rooms, 'where people spend most of their time'. But the item that really captured their imagination and a contract was the prototype of the Obo chair. The idea for this radical chair sprang fully formed from Grant's head one day as he was experimenting with forms to exploit the plasticity of the moulded urethane. He formed a prototype from sheet foam, cut and glued to simulate the hollow sphere, which he partially filled with polystyrene pellets, before setting off for Adelaide with a chair over his shoulder in a large drawstring bag. It looked rather like a bundle of laundry.

In her account of the development of Australian furniture, Whitehouse (2014, p. 147) states:

> Featherston's 'House of Tomorrow' furniture won almost universal approval, and the demand for the Relaxation range and private commissions enabled him to establish a small factory in Collingwood, where he set about educating himself in the art and practicalities of furniture manufacture. The archives indicate a period of intense experimentation with materials and forms as Featherston studied the mechanics of things – upholstery, componentisation, structure and detailing – while developing his design toolbox – sketching, technical drawings, promotional graphics and photography – all the time reading about art, aesthetics and design.

Whitehouse (2014, p. 150) writes that Grant and Mary formed a team in 1965 and set about designing the world-famous 'Talking Chair'. They 'continued pushing boundaries and produced some of the most aesthetically and technically sophisticated furniture of the 1970s: the Poli lounge suite, 1971, the Numero IV lounge, 1971–74, the Numero VI lounge, 1973–74, and the Obo chair, 1974, the last significant chair developed by the Featherstons'. The designs in the context of Mary's archives can be found at: www.featherston.com.au.

Figure 4.4 Mary Featherston designed quality learning environments with children.
Source: Mary Featherston.

Mary continued her work through researching and designing learning environments for children from early childhood settings through to secondary schools. Her design principles were now focused on the experience of the child in the learning contexts that she designed. Whitehouse (2014) describes the design issue that Mary concentrated upon as 'overcoming the lack of research into the perspective of children within the educational setting'. Mary designed the Children's Museum in Melbourne and, according to Whitehouse (2014, p. 152), broke the traditional museum 'conventions by designing exhibitions according to children's needs and curiosity that actively encouraged children and families to physically touch and explore displays'. Her design principles set new standards by building the child's perspective into learning spaces, but also introducing alternative pedagogical practices (see Figure 4.4).

Examples of Mary Featherston's designs for learning environments include Wooranna Park Primary School, Alphington Primary School and Dandenong High School. In discussing her work at Wooranna Park Primary School, Mary outlines the 'Inside-Out' design project:

Web activity 4.2 The Featherston Archive

> The intention of the 'Inside-Out' Project was to refurbish an area within a Victorian government-funded school to support and reflect contemporary understandings about children and learning. The design process was to include all the participants (students, staff, parents) and to seek design solutions that might have broader applicability.

The process of working together with children and the broader community began with older children (Figure 4.5). Mary wrote:

> During the first term all students and staff in the 5/6 Unit were involved in the design process, from analysis of needs, to assessment of existing space and resources and finally development of design solutions. At the initial meeting, with all school staff, research into children's perceptions of their physical environment was discussed.
>
> This discussion led to a decision to ask all the students 'What is it like to be a student at WPPS? [the school]' The children's responses, in words and drawings, indicated their strong priorities – play and friendships, followed by anything involving activity and comments about the importance of learning and working hard. Students were then invited to name the qualities that were important to them in the environment: friendship, happiness, resilience, respect. To the same question staff nominated: comfort, spaciousness, welcoming, purposeful, interactive, stimulating … This raises another design challenge: what is an appropriate ambience for a school learning environment: domestic, corporate, workshop, community centre, children's museum?

From this research, the design began to crystallise. A series of photographs and the evaluative comments from staff and children can be found in the report. This site has an example of the full project, with the final designs of the new learning spaces for the children.

Mary's design philosophy centres on three important dimensions:

1. conceptualising and designing new learning spaces (i.e. the buildings) based on the needs of all those who work and learn in them
2. designing the furniture so that it supports the children's learning and the teachers' innovative pedagogies
3. designing how the materials and resources are displayed, accessed, stored and used so that quality experiences are had by all.

What might be learned from Mary Featherston's design work? How could her design principles be applied to children's design work in schools and preschools? This challenge is returned to in the case studies later in this chapter. One key feature that stands out is Mary's creativity during the design process and the design studio in which she works. Mary brings together the perspective of the children – their needs in their learning spaces, but always in the context of the pedagogical practices of the teachers.

Figure 4.5 Mary Featherston listens to the children as they share their research into what makes a quality learning experience.
Source: Mary Featherston.

Design contexts

SPOTLIGHT 4.2

Stables (2020) argues that it is not possible to know everything in relation to a design challenge. Children engage in and learn repertoires of skills, such as imaging, modelling, reflecting, investigating and prototyping.

Context

Stables (2020) argues that the context of designing for successful solutions to everyday problems may be quite new for children. For example, Stables suggests that in setting a design brief that is about helping a child with cerebral palsy, a child may have a range of designing skills, but may not have experiences of being with children who have a disability, such as cerebral palsy.

Signature pedagogies: Gaining wisdom-in-action

SPOTLIGHT 4.3

This is an everyday situation that requires thoughtful consideration by the child. It is both the context and the 'designerly' way of thinking – how architects or engineers might tackle solving a problem through design – as we see with Mary in the case example. Emerging from this are specific ways of 'thinking', 'performing' and acting with integrity in that particular profession. Wells and van de Velde (2020) suggest that, when thought about in the context of education, these habits of the mind (lawyer), habits of the heart (clergy) and habits of the hand (surgeon) become *signature pedagogies*.

What will be the pedagogy of the studios that feature engineers (Chapter 8), food technologists and e-textiles (Chapter 7), and architects (this chapter)?

SPOTLIGHT 4.4

Design studios

When these habits of mind are examined in specific studios, then the spaces and workplaces suggest particular ways of working and 'designerly' thinking. Stables (2020) argues that the *studio* becomes an important space for learning, and it has its very own signature pedagogy. She believes it removes the teacher from the centre of learning, and provides a more student-centred approach. The concept of a studio also foregrounds dialogue, peer engagement and peer learning, and creates a community of practice and design culture. Taken together, Stables (2020) suggests that the studio, with its *project* and *design brief*, create a signature pedagogy, which she believes is project based and gives opportunities for experiential learning. She argues that this kind of project-based learning has open-ended outcomes, where the outcomes are unknown at the outset by teacher or student. Learners have autonomy, but she warns that this might also be unsettling for both the learner and the teacher.

Stable argues that the following questions need to be asked in the studio:

- What is the role of the teacher?
- What will be the nature of the activity in the studio?
- How will time be organised?
- What will be the levels of abstraction (potentially characterised through imagination and creativity)?
- What will the role of the learner be in the studio?

These questions and their responses are accompanied by a set of considerations, such as:

- Will the teacher facilitate or will there be direct teaching in the studio?
- Will the activities be authentic or contrived?
- Will the children be tied to a timetable or will they have possibilities to go beyond classroom time constraints? How will this be organised?
- Will the children manage their own learning and activity or will they be directed more by the teacher in the studio?

Stables (2020) argues that the pedagogy of the studio could be as diverse or as expansive. This is in keeping with what is to follow:

- pedagogies of speculation (see Chapter 1)
- pedagogies of imaging and modelling (this chapter)
- pedagogies of materiality (see Chapter 7)
- pedagogies of need-to-know (see Chapter 5)
- pedagogies of critiquing (see Chapter 3)
- pedagogies of collaboration (see Ordaz, Klapwijk and van Dijk, 2018).

Children don't just bring their prior experiences to the studio in relation to the design challenge; they also create and imagine solutions not previously experienced or considered. The studio acts as a site for designerly thinking (imagining) and action (creating), and as Stables (2020) suggests, can draw upon a particular signature pedagogy of a particular profession – such as Mary working with children in the case example discussed above.

What follows is a discussion of creativity and imagination, and how this is foundational for design and technology education.

Creativity and imagination

The technology and design education literature suggests that a certain level of creativity is needed for children to engage in design and technologies activities. Creativity and imagination are important elements of technologies education. A psychological perspective on these terms is needed to fully embrace creativity in design and technologies (Fleer, 2017). Vygotsky (2004, p. 88) states that, 'The development of a creative individual, one who strives for the future, is enabled by creative imagination embodied in the present.'

What is imagination?

When a cultural-historical view of imagination is drawn upon, it is possible to move from the traditional belief in an internal, subconscious and biological process of imagination to seeing imagination as a conscious and social act, in which the role of teaching is very important. Vygotsky (2004, p. 13) argues that 'imagination is not just an idle mental amusement, not merely an activity without consequences in reality, but rather a function essential to life'. Imagination becomes the means for broadening a person's experience. Vygotsky (2004, p. 17) suggests that humans imagine what they cannot see, conceptualise what they hear from others and think about what they have not yet experienced – that is, a person is not limited to the narrow circle and narrow boundaries of their own experience, but with the help of their imagination can venture far beyond these boundaries, assimilating someone else's historical or social experience.

Creative imagination embodied in the present

According to Vygotsky (2004, p. 25), 'Every act of imagination has a very long history'. The creation of new ideas and inventions requires a particular form of imagination that is culturally and socially located. Vygotsky (2004, p. 30) argues that everything that is created is really an accumulation of designs and creations from the past. For example, a newly designed washing machine represents the creativity and imagination (not to mention field-testing and production process trials) of previous designers of washing machines.

Imaginative creations arise when the material and psychological conditions that are necessary for their formation are available. The need for greater food production, for instance, emerges as communities grow in size, and through this change in societal circumstances, new technologies – such as tools for cultivating the soil – are invented. Access to materials, such as wood, stone or metal, determines the nature of particular technological inventions. Cultural and social histories build, and inventions are generated incrementally. A contemporary example can be seen in the culturally specific invention of the clothesline. The expansive Hills Hoist washing line (a rotating clothesline that looks like the metal frame of a large outdoor umbrella – see Figure 4.6) in Australia, where horizontal space is plentiful, is very different from the creation of a pole washing line projected out of windows from high-rise buildings (like a mast angled at 45 degrees to the building – see Figure 4.7) in Singapore, where vertical space is utilised.

Figure 4.6 The Hills Hoist clothesline is a common everyday technology in Australia.

Figure 4.7 In this small village, washing hangs on lines between houses – a different environment with a different need, and therefore a different design solution.
Source: © Getty Images/Walter Zerla.

Collective designing

In a cultural-historical reading of creativity and imagination, it is important to acknowledge both the collective and the individual constructions of creativity. In collective creativity, all individual acts of creativity are clustered together as a product of a generic created humanity. Many of today's artefacts, systems and processes were originally created by unknown inventors. When individuals design in classrooms, they do not act independently of what exists or of each other. They work within the context of a historical and collective created humanity.

Creativity for sustainability

Web activity 4.3
Creativity

When thinking about design and creativity in school classrooms and early childhood centres, educators need to look not only to the past to understand the context of creativity, but also to the future. For example, Vygotsky (2004) maintains that when something completely new is imagined and created, it becomes a real and tangible artefact or process. It exists in our world and we can act and think differently because it has been invented. This marks the future orientation of design.

Creativity and design in practice

When we think about design from a cultural-historical perspective, our attention is drawn to the historical, futuristic and collective reading of this technological process. Soomro, Casakin and Georgiev (2021) argue that creativity is the most valuable component of design activities. Creativity includes:

- being different
- thinking divergently
- making new connections
- challenging barriers to existing knowledge
- being comfortable with developing ideas/solutions not yet approved within society.

Supportive environments for fostering creativity in schools and centres

In reviewing the literature, Casakin and Georgiev (2021) note that creative thinking requires a supportive environment. An emotionally safe setting is needed so children are not afraid to take risks or explore new ideas. Warm-up activities help to increase creativity. Howard-Jones (2002) cites the example of a *brain train*, where an imaginary train stops at different moments in the child's mind or problem area, and every two minutes children are invited to stop at each station to think up new ideas. Howard-Jones (2002) terms this the 'emotional space for design and technology education'.

Casakin and Georgiev (2021) also draw attention to the importance of the physical space for design and technology education. Here they include time and space. Spaces that are inviting and challenging, and that display children's work or portfolios, are said to give inspiration to children and increase creativity. Wang, Peck and Chern (2010, p. 91) have shown that the time of the day when children are invited to be creative matters:

> As design educators who considers [sic] creativity the most valuable component in design activities, difference should be recognized and appreciated as a gift, not a burden [where] a learning environment respects creators' 'timing' differences.

Lewis (2009) suggests that competition can also be helpful for stimulating creativity. He cites the following examples of successful international competitions:

- teams creating fuel-efficient cars that build, test and demonstrate the power of the designs under a series of different conditions
- designing and building robots to perform under specific conditions
- evaluating bridge designs through building bridge kits and testing them.

Creative process

Many researchers have drawn upon foundational work by Wallas (1929) for increasing creativity in design and technology education. They discuss the elements of preparation, incubation, inspiration and verification:

- *Preparation:* Children concentrate on analysing the problem itself.
- *Incubation:* This is a period of time when the child may not be thinking consciously about the problem.
- *Inspiration*: This is a period of time when knowledge or ideas, often only remotely connected to the original problem, illuminate a solution.
- *Verification*: This refers to the process of insightful and critical evaluation, analysis or extension of the idea.

PEDAGOGICAL REFLECTION 4.4

Analysing practices for opportunities to build creativity

On your next field placement, look around the classroom or early childhood centre and examine the learning climate and the resources available. Analyse this context.

The following are some key questions that may be helpful for your analysis:

- What are the creative prospects of technology education?
- What pedagogic strategies seem likely to stimulate the inventive urges of children?
- What kinds of emotional conditions are created in the classroom/centre for supporting creativity?
- What kinds of physical spaces (including time) are available for children to engage in creative design?

Some have suggested that although many curriculum documents around the globe – and particularly in the United Kingdom – call for the introduction of creativity, in reality most programs foster formulaic rather than creative responses from children, most focus on the individual rather than the team and most programs are safe and known rather than offering innovation. For instance, Kimbell (2006, p. 162) notes that programs that support creativity:

- *have* ideas
- *grow* their ideas
- *prove* their ideas (emphasis in original).

Creativity can also be found in the range of experiences that teachers organise through their early childhood programs. In the following section, we discuss how play is a foundational pedagogy for supporting 'designerly' thinking in young children, in both the early childhood and primary contexts – and many would argue that this is also foundational for older children and even adults.

Play as foundational to design thinking

One of the defining features of Vygotsky's (2004) conception of imagination and creativity introduced in the previous section is his concept of play (Vygotsky, 1966). In play, children change the meaning of objects, giving them a new sense. For example, a child who finds a stick on the ground and no longer views the stick as something that has fallen from a tree can create an imaginary situation where the stick represents a wand and the child becomes Harry Potter. The child may turn the stick into a hobby-horse and become a rider, galloping away over the imagined mountains to bring in the cattle.

When children change the meaning of objects and actions to give them a new meaning, they are projecting into the imaginary situation. They are imagining not what is in front of them, but other realities. Play provides a strong conceptual basis for design and technologies because it gives children a basis upon which to design something that does not exist, or to bring together things that do exist but to conceptualise them in new ways – just as designers do in real life. The Early Years Learning Framework (AGDE, 2022) has play as its cornerstone. This means that when teachers support children in their play, they are supporting children's present and future design thinking. A case example of an early childhood setting follows to illustrate how design thinking can be introduced to toddlers.

Looking inside an early childhood centre: Toddler play as creative design

It is difficult to imagine how infants and toddlers might engage in a process of design. However, Alita, a teacher of a group of toddlers, set about using the LEGO DUPLO® pieces that were in her centre as the basis for building a design process into her teaching program.

Alita sang the song 'Old MacDonald Had a Farm' as she turned the pages of a book, punctuating each page with the noise made by the particular animal. The children were aged between 18 months and 2 years, and they were seated on the floor next to Alita. Lucy, Ashleigh, Yuan and Alita sat snuggled up, singing and making the sounds of the animals appropriate to each page of the book.

Alita then introduced DUPLO® blocks and animals to the toddlers. She sang the song again, introducing each animal as she sang. She gave one animal to each of the children who were seated with her and participating in the singing of 'Old MacDonald Had a Farm'.

Alita then said to the toddlers, 'We are now going to make our farm and draw it'. This was the design brief she had planned and thought most relevant to the toddlers.

The toddlers, with some suggestions from Alita, decided to make a farm for all the animals. They decided to call it 'Lucy's Farm'. Alita wrote the words on a piece of cardboard and put it next to the gate and fencing the toddlers had erected. She asked the toddlers to make an enclosure for each of their animals on Lucy's Farm.

Alita: Lucy, you have the horse. Do you think you can make a stable for it? Yuan, you have a pig. You could make a pigsty. Ashleigh, we can make a hen house together.

The toddlers looked at the book in relation to their animal, while Alita supported them to think about all the different parts they could see, such as the roof, floor, walls, doors and windows (as appropriate) and features inside the enclosure they were designing with the DUPLO® blocks. The toddlers then went about making their enclosure on the farm with support from Alita.

After this, Alita invited the individual children to draw the models of the farm they had created using the DUPLO® blocks. An example of Lucy's design (with labels written by the teachers) is shown in Figure 4.8.

Alita was very thoughtful about how she individually supported the toddlers with their design and building of a farm. An example of Alita interacting with Ashleigh follows:

Figure 4.8 Toddler play as the conceptual basis for design thinking

Ashleigh, we can build the hen house for the chickens. Can you put one brick next to this one? [Ashleigh smiles and moves the bricks closer to the chicken.] There, let's see if we can put another one on the other side. We need to put one more brick on this side. There. [Ashleigh continues to add bricks to create a wall] We have a wall on each side now. Can we make it higher? [Ashleigh smiles and nods] Fantastic, you are putting a brick on top. Another one, and another one … and another one. [Ashleigh smiles and motions to her high wall] You now have a high wall on each side. Shall we put the roof on? [Ashleigh nods] What shall we use? [Ashleigh puts out more blocks] Oh, that is a good idea. The long piece – is it the right size? Let's try. Does it cover the hen house? [Alita and Ashleigh smile at each other] Yes it does! Let's find the chickens. Oh you have one, two, three, four, five chickens altogether, in your hen house. Let's sing together. [Ashleigh sings along with Alita] Ashleigh has a hen house EIEIO. And in that hen house she had five chickens, EIEIO. With a cluck, cluck here, and a cluck, cluck there, here a cluck, there a cluck, everywhere a cluck, cluck, Ashleigh had a hen house EIEIO.

Ashleigh drew a picture of her hen house (Figure 4.9). Alita put all the toddlers' designs onto a pin-up board, and as she did this she said, 'With our drawings we can remember what our farm looks like. We can make it again by looking at our drawing.' Lucy jumps up and smiles, holding her drawing.

Alita: Here we have Lucy's drawing of her stable. We can put Lucy's design of her hen house here next to Yuan's drawing. Yuan, where should we put your pig sty?

Yuan lifts up his drawing into the air and laughs, then makes pig sounds.

Alita: Ashleigh has put her picture over there. Is this big picture of the farm the same as what we have made here on the carpet?

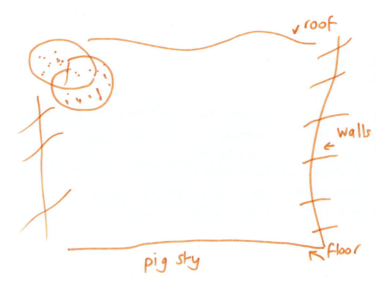

Figure 4.9 Ashleigh's design for her hen house

This example illustrates how a song centred around a set of plastic blocks and animals that are already available in an early childhood setting can be transformed into a design activity. The toddlers in this example stayed with the activity because the teacher engaged them in a known song with familiar objects, but introduced them to a new challenge of drawing and displaying what they had made with the LEGO materials. In the example that follows, we see the same principles of playfully engaging with design being foregrounded by the teacher, but with much older children.

Can toddlers design?

ACTIVITY 4.1

Having read about Alita's classroom, consider the following questions:
1. What was the key pedagogical approach used by the teacher?
2. List three challenges and ways you could overcome these.

Looking inside a classroom: Primary children's play as creative design – architect's studio

Vanessa, Tim and Alison work together in an expansive learning community of 75 children. The children were in Years 3 and 4, and they came back from the school holidays to find their learning space set up as an architect's studio. The idea was to give them time for pretend play as architects. On entering the space, the teachers gave the children clipboards and pens with the following task:

> You have just entered an architect's studio. You will see Mary and Jules at work. You are to observe what they do, how they work together, what design challenge they are working on, and to prepare a set of questions that you will use to interview them. You should also be part of what they do, by pretending to be architects yourself.

The children wandered around the studio. They observed and they role-played. In the space, they found:
- a range of architectural plans – front view, cross-sections, plan view
- service models – made from a range of materials, scaled and with plans
- computer with sophisticated programs for drawing up designs.

They played with the equipment, then they prepared their questions. The children asked:
- What do architects do?
- What do you do to build a house?
- How do you plan for this?
- How do buildings get water and electricity?
- How do you design so that the building is energy efficient?
- What are the different materials from which buildings are made, and how do you know if they are sustainably harvested?

Then Mary asked the children, 'What do you know about architects and their work?'

Angela: We are building new rooms on our house. There is a real mess now. My mum is always looking at plans and talking to the builders.

Mary: My job is to talk to builders too, just like your mum. The plans your mother is looking at are something I prepare on my computer. What other things do you know about architects?

To answer these questions, Mary invited the children to participate in the development of a genuine plan and model. The children were apprenticed to Mary, and they set to work researching, exploring the different tools and materials to create service models and using the software to design. Small groups took it in turns to join her at their meetings with her client. They analysed the design brief that Mary had developed jointly with her client.

In small groups, the children took the client's brief and began to prepare sets of concept designs. They prepared questions to ask the client. Mary supported the children as they worked in their groups.

Using icy pole sticks the children made simple models of their floor plans. The children explored 3D and 2D forms. In groups, the children drew cross-sections of their constructed models. They also used Unifix® Cubes to build a 3D model. The children drew plan views and side views of their Unifix® models. The children also explored size and scale. They were shown a two-bedroom house plan drawn to a scale of 1:100. In the gymnasium, the children laid down ropes to match the home plan. They used graph paper and experimented with scale.

Challenges in realising imagined designs on paper

The children began to draw plans of a basic front view. Drawing from a plan view was something new, and the children needed support in thinking about how to do this. The size of the plans also presented a challenge. Figure 4.10 shows Tejh's design. Tejh's idea of proportion and conceptualising the space on the paper within which the children were working was also difficult. A number of children became frustrated, making comments such as, 'I can't do it right' and 'Look what I've done. Everything is too small, it is all squished up.'

The children imagined what they wanted, but did not have the technical skills to know how to draw it – for example, one child said, 'I want to put a hall in, like in my house, but I can't do it. I don't know how to draw a hallway ... Look, all the rooms are pushed together and that's not what I have imagined I want' (Figure 4.10). Learning about cross-sections was important to help children realise their imagined designs on paper – for instance, 'My house has more than one storey, but if I draw it like it is in real life then everything will be on top of each other and no one will understand it.'

Many of the children initially had difficulties. It was really very challenging for them to 'just design' something without the support of knowing how to draw from a range of perspectives, or how to draw cross-sections. This is an important dimension of producing quality designs and of empowering children with the skills they need to be successful in their design work. For instance, these model-making challenges were heard:

Figure 4.10 Tejh's design – how do you put in a hall?

- 'I couldn't make the model with paper and glue because it was too hard.'
- 'The paper was too light and wouldn't really stand up, like I could make one side but then I wouldn't be able to put anything heavy on it or it would just fall over. I tried folding the paper in all different directions but nothing really worked. Also, the glue took too long to dry and it made the paper go soggy. I should have used the other glue. There's no way that an architect would make a very strong model with paper and glue. I didn't think that – *cardboard and this glue might work better*!!'

One group of children had shown interest in sustainability. They researched and identified local materials and craftspeople who could work on the project with Mary. They prepared an evaluation poster that they initially presented to all the children, and then used later with each of the small groups that were designing plans and making models, to support a sustainable edge to their work.

Mary also brought together a finance group of children who worked with her to research the cost of materials. They prepared a spreadsheet of the associated costs of building the various designs that were being prepared by the small groups. This 'accountants group' prepared a financial statement and presented it to the respective groups.

The designs, models, environmental impact statement and financial report for each of the groups were then presented to the client.

The children learned that annotated drawing can help with:

- identifying the different parts of a design
- easily seeing what materials need to be used in the designed object
- stepping someone through the processes to be followed
- showing an intended sequence of movements or actions.

The children as a group discussed their experiences and prepared a class book, *What Do Architects Do?* They also prepared a concept map of what they knew at the end of the unit:

- Architects build little models to show the builders what the materials are, and what the front, back and side would look like.
- There are architects all over the world.
- Architects have lots of rulers and pens and stuff like that.
- Architects draw plans to show builders and people who own the house how the house would look like inside.
- An architect is someone who designs buildings.
- Without an architect, houses and buildings will not be very stable.

This case example has also shown that children need a lot of experience in drawing from a range of angles (front, plan, side and cross-section). These skills support them in being able to express their design ideas on paper.

This case study of an architect's studio demonstrates the challenges children have with drawing something they see as 3D into a 2D format (Figure 4.11). Learning drawing techniques helps children with their design work. A range of examples follow. These techniques should be embedded in the teaching program, so doing these activities is meaningful and has a sense of purpose.

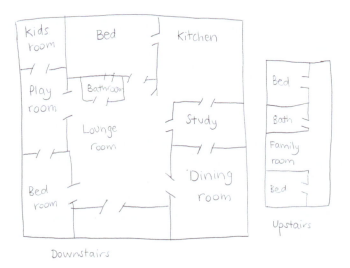

Figure 4.11 How do you show a two-storey building?

Idea 1

Drawing objects from direct observation is critical for supporting very young children. This can be supported by asking children to:

- make something, then draw it from the top and from the side, not just from the front

- cut out their different drawings and put them together on one A3 sheet, as their architectural plan or design
- take a photograph of their actual model and attach it to the A3 plan.

When children talk to an architect about the design process, they discover how designs keep changing – from concept sketch, to working with the client, to draft and then to final design (Figure 4.12). This process can be documented by making a design plan.

Figure 4.12 Making a design plan – concertina fold

Idea 2

Another way to support children with learning how to prepare quality designs is through preparing exploded plans. The teacher can invite children to:

- pull apart an object, such as a torch
- lay out the pieces on an A3 sheet of paper
- arrange the pieces ready for drawing, thinking about which small part might need to be drawn bigger than the others (i.e. exploded plan) so it is easier to see
- draw each item, leaving enough room for the exploded drawing of the small parts.

Summary

This chapter has specifically concentrated on one of the main subject areas found in the Australian Curriculum: Technologies – Design and Technologies. It follows on from the discussion on preferred futures (Chapter 3) and expands understanding of design thinking and imagination and creativity to support creating design solutions.

The chapter also analysed how play can be foundational for design thinking for toddlers and preschoolers. Through a case example of primary-aged children role-playing being architects, it demonstrated how play is foundational for developing design thinking in this age group too. The chapter specifically noted how design thinking is a key concept in the subject Design Technologies.

Part 2 of the book discusses the contexts of the Australian Curriculum: Technologies and more attention is given to the subject Digital Technologies.

Acknowledgements

Special acknowledgement is made of the teachers who have supported the curriculum work that was published in M. Fleer and J. Sukroo, *I Can Make My Robot Dance* (Curriculum Corporation, 1995), and who are once again represented in this chapter – Alita, Vicky and Vanessa. Thank you also for the photos provided by Mary Featherston. Thanks to Laburnum Primary School for the curriculum development photo. Finally, thanks to Yuwen Ma for support with updating the references for this chapter.

PART 2

The curriculum in action

This part of the book will examine valued forms of knowledge that are sanctioned through the national curriculum development processes.

Both the Early Years Learning Framework and the Australian Curriculum: Technologies have brought new ways of teaching and learning into centres and classrooms. For updates on the EYLF, please reload the web content. Part 2 will showcase examples of the curriculum in practice.

In Chapter 3 we examined the creation of solutions for preferred futures. The overarching core concept was shown as identifying compelling visions of the future and making considered design decisions, taking into account diversity, ethics and economic, environmental and social sustainability factors.

Sitting under this overarching core concept are the following core concepts:

- *Systems:* Comprise the structure, properties, behaviour and interactivity of people and components (inputs, processes and outputs) within and between natural, managed, constructed and digital environments (ACARA, 2023).
- *Data:* Can be acquired, interpreted and represented to help inform decision-making and can be manipulated, stored and communicated by digital systems (ACARA, 2023).
- *Interactions and impact:* Need to be considered when creating solutions; this involves examining the relationships between components of technologies systems, sustainability and the effects of design decisions on users (ACARA, 2023).
- *Systems thinking:* Helps people to think holistically about the interactions and interconnections that shape the behaviour of systems (ACARA, 2023).
- *Computational thinking:* Computational thinking helps people to organise data logically by breaking down problems into parts; defining abstract concepts; and designing and using algorithms, patterns and models (ACARA, 2023).

- *Design thinking:* Helps people to empathise and understand needs, opportunities and problems; generate, iterate and represent innovative, user-centred ideas; and analyse and evaluate those ideas (ACARA, 2023).
- *Technological processes and production skills:* Help people to safely create solutions for a range of purposes and involve investigating and defining, generating and designing, producing and implementing, evaluating, and collaborating and managing. (ACARA, 2023)
- *Project-management skills:* Help people to successfully and efficiently plan, manage and complete projects to meet identified design criteria. (ACARA, 2023)
- *Enterprise and management skills:* Help people to identify opportunities to take action and create change; follow through on initiatives; and generate new ideas, processes and solutions (ACARA, 2023).

You are invited to consider these concepts as you read Part 2. These core concepts are taught in the specific technologies contexts of:

- Food and fibre production
- Food specialisations
- Engineering principles and systems
- Materials and technologies specialisations.

These contexts are presented as chapters in Part 2. To bring the digital concepts further forward, Part 2 also includes two chapters with case studies of teachers and children engaged in core concepts of data and computational thinking. For systems thinking it is suggested to look in detail at the Australian Curriculum, Assessment and Reporting Authority (ACARA) website for content descriptions and also resources showcased in previous versions of the curriculum.

As you read the chapters in Part 2, also think about the following questions:

- What are the unique dimensions of the technologies curriculum in action (in both the classroom and early childhood setting)?
- What is the content that is foundational for designing and implementing a technologies curriculum (Grobler & Ankiewicz, 2021; Mosely, Harris and Grushka, 2021)?
- What are the big ideas in technologies education that link to other curriculum areas (Yliverronen, Kangas & Rönkkö, 2021)?
- How does the content of the technologies curriculum become personalised knowledge for children?
- How can the same curriculum outcomes be taught differently so they build upon what children bring to the classroom or early childhood setting?
- What might be some political issues associated with introducing a technologies curriculum in the community (Owen, Davies and Iles, 2021)?

CHAPTER 5

The curriculum in action: Digital technologies in everyday life, the community and the classroom/centre

Introduction

In the first part of this book, the unique nature of technologies education was examined, with a focus on design thinking. Design thinking is central to learning in both subjects in the Australian Curriculum: Technologies – Design and Technologies and Digital Technologies. This chapter looks more closely at Digital Technologies.

The Australian Curriculum, Assessment and Reporting Authority (ACARA, 2023) suggests that digital systems support new ways of collaborating and communicating, and require new skills such as computational and systems thinking. These technologies are an essential problem-solving toolset in our knowledge-based society. The Australian Curriculum: Technologies recognises the need for different types of thinking. Although design thinking was featured in Part 1, this chapter takes a deep dive into the place of digital technology in children's lives to set the foundation for examining computational thinking in Chapter 6.

This chapter begins with a general discussion of digital technologies, followed by an introduction to ethics and myths associated with digital technologies (which in Chapter 6 are shown embedded in case examples), and concludes with reflections on the case examples from early childhood (see Figure 5.1) to the primary years (see Figure 5.2), where digital technologies in action are showcased in the classroom/centre.

Link 5.1 Digital Child blog

Digital technologies in everyday life

Concerns have been expressed in the media about the nature and use of digital technologies, with reports in the literature on successive waves of moral panic within communities (Laidlaw, O'Mara and Wong, 2021). Pedagogical Reflection 5.1 asks you to consider your position on the use of digital technologies by and for children.

It is suggested that digital technologies have become central to the lives of children and young people, and that 'many people are now regulated by smartphones, tablets, Wi-Fi and other requirements of being "always on"' (Selwyn, 2014, p. 155). How this is talked about has changed over time too (Arnott and Yelland, 2020; Yelland, 2021; Yelland and Waghorn, 2020). The COVID-19 pandemic has not only increased our reliance on the digital environment to

121

Figure 5.1 Representations of digital systems by 4-year-olds

Figure 5.2 Eleven-year-olds engaged in digital technology in children's lives
Source: Monash University PlayLab and Redeemer Lutheran College.

> **PEDAGOGICAL REFLECTION 5.1**
>
> **The digital age**
>
> What is your position on:
>
> - the use of digital technologies in the community
> - the place of digital technologies in the home
> - the amount of screen time children should have
> - how we should use digital technologies in the classroom or early childhood centre?
>
> Document your thoughts. There will be an opportunity to review these questions at the end of the chapter.

support everyday lives, such as online ordering of groceries, takeaway food purchases, use of QR codes for a broad range of purposes to minimise contact and to track and trace (see also Vargo et al., 2021); as Selwyn and Jandrić (2020, p. 989) point out:

> We've seen teachers in Australia (and I'm sure this has been the case in North America and Europe) suddenly have to run two or three different strands of remote schooling provision for their classes – catering for the 5G households, the dial-up households, and those with little or no connectivity at all ('home-schooling six children with just one phone' as a BBC News report (2020) put it).

Digital technologies do pervade the lives of people in the community, including children. Digital technologies encompass a vast range of experiences, such as blogging, flogging (i.e. online bartering, trading), building home pages, instant messaging and text messaging, and Google Maps and Google Earth for navigation. The list goes on. There is a suggested gap for those who did not grow up 'connected', such as the elderly and those who are living in low socio-economic status contexts.

Although the technologies themselves continue to change, this long-standing tension with the 'digital' in education has generated a sizeable body of academic literature around the technical dimensions, the pedagogical affordances and the psychological aspects of technology and education. When thinking about working with young children, what might this education tension mean? Do we also bring AI-interfaced robotic toys into this conversation (Kewalramani, Kidman and Palaiologou, 2021)?

Web activity 5.1 AI and education – podcast

Ethics and digital technologies

Research tends to support the view that digital technologies and their applications to everyday life are broad and that the education system (both early childhood and primary) must embrace these, but with this comes a particular 'duty of care' from the teacher. For instance, Mannheimer Zydney and Hooper (2015) raise the issue of ethics in the documentation and use of images of others – now possible through the range of digital tools available to children. They argue that in the context of designing apps, a number of ethical questions present themselves, which are also useful to think about in relation to the nature of digital documentation in classrooms and early childhood centres more generally. They ask (adapted from Mannheimer Zydney and Hooper (2015, p. 42):

- What are the goals of recording and how many images are necessary to meet this goal?
- Who needs to provide permission?
- Who needs to see the image collected?
- What level of consent is needed?
- What level of confidentiality is wanted?
- What level of protection is needed for storing the data?
- Who controls how an image gets recorded, edited and uploaded?
- How long is it necessary to archive an image and when (if at all) will the image be deleted?

PEDAGOGICAL REFLECTION 5.2

The ethics of using digital devices

Examine the questions raised by Mannheimer Zydney and Hooper (2015). Are these questions that you have considered when making digital observations of children or when inviting children to visually document others? What about e-safety and cyber-bullying? What policies are in place in centres and schools or developed by departments of education to address concerns?

There are now many kinds of computer clubhouses and maker spaces with digitally enabled devices, community oriented digital experiences, such as immersive technologies, and the everydayness of the digital world, such as designing digital projects where animation software, video editing software, photo editing programs, game design platforms, and other design programs, now form the basis of many children's lives. These computer clubhouses create contexts that involve not just developing imaginative online images and programs, but also the digital documentation of others, raising potential ethical issues about the use of other people's images. In order to effectively deal with these ethical issues, Mannheimer Zydney and Hooper (2015) have designed a useful protocol that children (as well as teachers and researchers) can use when visually documenting for digital production. The protocol includes:

- digitally documenting in neutral settings and with neutral clothing – for example, no school uniforms or sports team t-shirts that can give away identifying information
- avoiding accidently recording non-participants in the background
- being careful not to accidentally record copyright material, such as music playing, in the background if planning to distribute widely
- familiarising all participants with the digital recording process in order to support a more mature visual documentation – for example, not acting for the camera or digital capture
- reminding children to avoid revealing personal information during the digital documenting process (Mannheimer Zydney and Hooper, 2015, p. 45).

The digital age brings with it many questions that educators must consider. Broader issues of ethics include piracy, plagiarism, cyber-bullying and behaving ethically online. What other ethical issues might arise in digital contexts? Go back to the comments you made for Pedagogical Reflection 5.1 and consider what you wrote down. Compare it with the aims described in the Australian Curriculum: Technologies:

- Use design thinking to design, create, manage and evaluate sustainable and innovative digital solutions to meet and redefine current and future needs.
- Use computational thinking (abstraction; data collection, representation and interpretation; specification; algorithms; and implementation) to create digital solutions.
- Confidently use digital systems to automate the transformation of data into information efficiently and effectively, and to creatively communicate ideas in a range of settings.
- Apply protocols and legal practices that support the ethical collection and generation of data through automated and non-automated processes and participate in safe and respectful communications and collaboration with audiences.
- Apply systems thinking to monitor, analyse, predict and shape the interactions within and between information systems and the impact of these systems on individuals, societies, economies and environments (ACARA, 2023).

PEDAGOGICAL REFLECTION 5.3

Digital childhood

In pairs, discuss the following questions, note your views, then read the text below:

- Childhood and digital technology don't mix.
- Young children are 'digital natives'.
- Technology hinders social interactions.
- Technology dominates children's lives.
- If it is interactive, it must be educational.
- Children need to get tech savvy for their future lives.

Do you hear families making these comments? Do you think crises, such as the pandemic, mobilise new thinking as children and adults increase their screen time, use a broader range of devices, apps and media, and discuss challenges of data security? What is your position? Document your thoughts.

Although it is well understood in education that digital technologies are a key component of the Australian Curriculum, and most families have become proficient in the use of QR codes, internet banking and more, the place of technologies continues to be debated in the community – most notably in the context of learning from home, where sharing of digital devices and screen time has emerged as an issue across the school years. Some of the arguments made reflect myths put forward more than a decade ago by Plowman and McPake (2013). The myths formed the basis of Pedagogical Reflection 5.3. Consider the content in the context of your own position. You will return to these questions and content in Chapter 6, where computational thinking and coding are discussed.

Digital childhood: Debating the myths

The digital world moves fast – often well beyond the pace of research. Here are some of the most common myths and the ways in which they have been contested.

Myth #1: Childhood and technology don't mix

The first myth is that childhood and technology don't mix, yet most families have access to simple technologies – for example, smart TVs with interactive interface; engagement in play practices such as interactive dolls and pets; extensive use of the internet. Technologies continue to change, and so will children's engagement with digital devices. A range of apps are now available for the iPad that have turned this device into a multifunctional piece of equipment that is bringing to young children a broader range of tools for many things that only adults had access to just a few years ago. For instance, apps and touchscreen interfaces allow for:

- screen images and sound to be streamed from an iPad to a computer system
- apps to edit or create binders on cloud sites
- the ability to create professional-looking e-books that feature photographs, narratives (voice and text) and animation (e.g. Book Creator from Red Jumper Studio; My Story – Storybook Maker for Kids)
- conversion of spoken words into text (e.g. Dragon Dictation)
- playing virtual musical sounds (e.g. free apps – Guitar Free, PianoAngelFree, iCanDrum)
- creating content in e-book format and reading literature in e-book format
- viewing space (e.g. SkyView), weather (e.g. The Weather Channel app), satellite view of the planet (e.g. Living Earth app)
- expanding scientific understandings (World Book® – This Day in History app; Science360) (Siegle, 2013).
- AI by creating a sustainable city for their robot and 'his' family to live happily. Children play with the AI robot-fostered inquiry literacies – namely creative inquiry, emotional inquiry and collaborative inquiry (Kewalramani et al., 2021).

Myth #2: Young children are 'digital natives'

The term 'digital natives' was first introduced by Marc Prensky (Koutropoulos, 2011), and there are now other terms for children and young people who have only ever known digital technologies, such as 'net-generation'. However, Sorrentino (2018) suggests that:

> A growing body of recent studies have questioned the validity of the digital native metaphor showing that Prensky's assumptions lack empirical evidence and that they are supported mostly by anecdotes and appeals to common sense beliefs.

Historically morphed into conversations about digital immigrants and intergenerational learners using digital technologies, Garvis (2018, p. 183) introduces the idea of digital narratives to capture the 'dynamic places in which children's inner lives and their external worlds meet each other'. To understand this fuzzy zone, Garvis (2018, p. 188) argues that it is important to ask:

- Who initiates the digital narrative?
- What is the narrating situation like?

- Who are present, and how do they participate in narrating?
- How do children express themselves in the digital narrative?

The concept of the digital narrative moves the debate forward and provides teachers with a different way to think about children who are growing up in a digital world.

Myth #3: Technology hinders social interactions

The myth that technology hinders social interactions is often presented as a problem with the introduction of digital devices. Research by Boland et al. (2022) and Busch (2018) shows many examples of how communications within families are actually opened up, as all members – including children – engage in long-distance communications with other family members, such as Skyping and Zooming with grandparents, as shown in Figure 5.3.

Children learn valuable internet search skills during interactions at home and in preschool with adults (Davidson et al., 2018), and digital devices help support social interactions for children with disabilities (Fleer, 2018). Indeed, children prefer to use digital devices with others, and this creates more opportunities for social interactions (Konca & Tantekin Erden, 2021). There is now a great deal of research that refutes the isolationist perspective; rather, families have learned to manage the rules of engagement, as an international study of digital use in family homes has shown (Chaudron et al., 2018). For example, in another study of parents and children engaged in digital devices at home (Khoo, Merry and Nguyen, 2015, p. 36), families commented:

Figure 5.3 In Australia, Judith supports Alfie to Skype with his grandfather in Bangladesh.
Source: Judith Gomes.

> We are told to assist our kids while brushing their teeth until they are seven but we let them play computer games at four and that's not very sensible, of course they need heaps of guidance …

> We have the same rules at home as at the centre …

It can be concluded that digital learning in schools and preschools, as well as at home, is valued by families and contributes to children's social engagement.

Myth #4: Technology dominates children's lives

The increasing use of digital technologies does not necessarily equate with digital domination over children's lives. The research found that families were aware of the dangers of screen time but reported that this was not an issue for them. Interestingly, very little research is available on what constitutes the amount of screen time that optimises children's development. Walker, Danby and Hatzigianni's (2018) longitudinal study of Australian children demonstrates that digital play of up to 240 minutes per week is associated with better scores in literacy and mathematics thinking. Interestingly, lower levels of play (120 minutes) did not show achievement gains. Their research also found that higher levels of play (421 minutes) were shown to raise problems with cognitive development, self-regulation, academic performance and emotional development of children aged from 8 to 10 years.

Myth #5: If it is interactive, it must be educational

The myth that if it is interactive, it must be educational can also be disputed because devices may initially be engaging, but many apps have been designed so that they simply reproduce boring drill and practice activities where learning is not meaningful. 'Interactive' can refer to the process of clicking, scrolling and pressing only. The latter is particularly evident in studies that have followed children in early childhood settings across school (Kalamatianou and Hatzigianni, 2018) and home (Chaudron et al., 2018), where children have access to a variety of digital devices and apps (Davidson et al., 2018; Roos and Olin-Scheller, 2018). Even if parents do not always feel confident about selecting appropriate apps for their children (Kervin, Verenikina and Rivera, 2018), children still have richer experiences through the digital technologies; however, this depends on how families created these conditions for their children (Highfield, Paciga and Donohue, 2018; Scriven, Edwards-Groves and Davidson, 2018). It has been found that much of the interaction around the software is dependent upon the design (Nikiforidou, 2018) – for example, whether it allows children to play collectively and whether it supports social pretend play, where children are able to have higher levels of agency. The apps open up learning opportunities, rather than restricting what might be possible, as nuanced further by Hvid Stenalt (2021, pp. 60–1) who identified five areas of child agency in digital contexts:

1. *Agentic possibility:* What power do students have to achieve the intended outcomes in the particular context of action and interaction?
2. *Digital representation:* How can students manage and adapt their self- representation in the digital context of learning?
3. *Data uses:* How are student data circulated or recirculated?
4. *Digital sociality:* How is sociality constructed, and how can students manage sociality?
5. *Digital temporalities:* How are student actions constructed in terms of time?

Video activity 5.1
Technology-driven world

Myth #6: Children need to get tech savvy for their future lives

There is a great deal of information available in the community that can be digitally sourced, which supports the view that children are growing up in a digital age. For example:

> What are the skills students will need in the 21st century? The 21st century dawned as the beginning of the Digital Age – a time of unprecedented growth in technology and its subsequent information explosion. Never before have the tools for information access and management made such an impact on the way we live, work, shop and play. New technologies and tools multiply daily and the new technologies of today are outdated almost as soon as they reach the market. (Beers, 2022)

As a future teacher, you may be wondering how you might debunk the myths held by peers or families and work together to enrich the digital experience of children. Rather than investing in a conceptual challenge about the nature of digital technologies, screen time and more, you would invest that energy into setting up a maker space inside or outside the classroom.

SPOTLIGHT 5.1

Maker Movement

Digital and traditional technologies can be brought together in the Maker Movement or Maker Education. This is a group of children and adults who come together outside of school time to make things. According to van Dijk, Savelsbergh and van der Meij (2020), a typical example of a Maker Movement or Maker Education activity or design involves hacking a toy.

Hacking a toy

1. Bring a toy from home and make it move/blink or do other cool things with it.
2. Make a light object with LEDs.
3. Build an automaton in which a rotation is converted to another movement.
4. Build a marble track that takes exactly 60 seconds to complete.
5. Make something you really want to make.
6. Build an object that clearly shows a physics principle.
7. Build an object that shows how the liver works.
8. Build a musical instrument. You have to play a song on it that the teacher is able to recognise.

Hacking your school

1. Build something that improves your or the teacher's school life.
3. Build a box with something locked inside that takes considerable effort to open (no force!).
4. Make a game about your school.
5. Build a mousetrap car: a car that goes as far as possible only driven by the potential energy of a mouse trap.

The pedagogy that dominates these after-school activities is: think, make and improve. For instance, in the *make* part, children and adults will 'Play, Build, Tinker, Create, Program, Experiment, Construct, Deconstruct, Test Strategies/materials, Observe Others, Borrow and Share Code, Document Process, Look for Vulnerabilities, Ask Questions, Repair' (van Dijk, Savelsbergh and van der Meij, 2020).

In Australia, the use of digital devices is actively supported through their inclusion in the curriculum from Foundation level onwards (ACARA, 2023), and even from birth to 5 years (AGDE, 2022). The concepts, contexts and processes are complex. The next section walks you through some core concepts and teaching ideas about digital technologies. Chapter 6 provides further insights and case studies of teaching practices.

Video activity 5.2 How might you use SMART Boards in early childhood settings and primary schools?

Understanding the Australian Curriculum – Digital Technologies

Digital Technologies has been conceptualised in the Australian Curriculum as including two sub-strands in the strand of Knowledge and Understanding (also see Chapter 1). One sub-strand focuses on Digital Systems and the other on Data Representation. The other strand of Processes and Production Skills includes many sub-strands: Acquiring, Managing and Analysing Data; Investigating and Defining; Generating and Designing; Producing and Implementing; Evaluating; Collaborating and Managing; and Privacy and Security.

Table 5.1 provides details of the two strands in Digital Technologies. It is suggested by ACARA (2023) that when teachers bring these strands together in their programs, children have opportunities that develop their knowledge, understanding and skills, and can thereby safely and ethically use the capacity of information systems (people, data, processes, digital systems and their interactions) to systematically transform data into solutions that respond to the needs of individuals, society, the economy and the environment.

Table 5.1 The two strands in the subject Digital Technologies

Knowledge and Understanding strand	Processes and Production Skills strand
Digital Systems This sub-strand focuses on the components of digital systems: hardware, software and networks. In the early years, students learn about a range of hardware and software and progress to an understanding of how data is transmitted between components within a system, and how the hardware and software interact to form networks. **Data Representation** This sub-strand looks at how data is represented and structured symbolically for use by digital systems. Different types of data are studied from Foundation to Year 8 including text, numeric, images (still and moving) and sound, with relational data being introduced in Years 9 and 10.	**Acquiring, Managing and Analysing Data** Students explore the properties of data, how it is acquired and interpreted using a range of digital systems and peripherals, and analyse data when creating information. Students use computational thinking elements such as pattern recognition, abstraction and evaluation. They progress from exploring data acquisition strategies and looking for patterns to validating the data and data integrity. **Investigating and Defining** Students create solutions and define problems clearly by identifying appropriate data and requirements. When designing, students consider how users will interact with the solutions, and check and validate their designs to increase the likelihood of creating working solutions. Defining and communicating a problem precisely and clearly is an important part of specification. **Generating and Designing** Students develop computational thinking by creating algorithms which clearly define steps which may lead to creating a digital solution. Students progressively move from following algorithms in their daily activities to designing algorithms and validating them against test cases. They make choices, weigh up options and consider alternatives. Students use critical and creative thinking and systems thinking strategies to generate, evaluate and document ideas to meet needs or opportunities that have been identified by an individual, a group or a wider community. Generating creative and innovative ideas involves thinking differently; it entails proposing new approaches to existing problems and identifying new design opportunities considering preferred futures. It also involves identifying errors that may occur within an algorithm and how control structures can improve the flow through a program. **Producing and Implementing** Students apply their algorithms as a program through systems to make products or content which have been designed to meet specific user needs. They apply knowledge about components and how digital systems use and display data to ensure the success of their program. Students develop accurate production skills to achieve quality digital solutions. They develop the capacity to select and use appropriate systems, components, tools and equipment; and use techniques and materials that respect the need for sustainability. They use modelling and prototyping to accurately develop simple and complex physical models that support the production of successful digital solutions. **Evaluating** Students evaluate and make judgements throughout the design process and about the quality and effectiveness of their digital solution. They identify design criteria and develop user stories to support success of the digital solution. In the early years, the teacher may guide the development of these criteria and user stories. Progressively, students develop criteria which become increasingly more comprehensive. Students consider the implications and consequences of actions and decision-making. They determine effective ways to test and judge their digital solutions. They reflect on processes and transfer their learning to other solutions and opportunities.

Table 5.1 (cont.)

Knowledge and Understanding strand	Processes and Production Skills strand
	Collaborating and Managing Students learn to work collaboratively and to manage time and other resources to effectively create digital solutions. Progressively, students develop the ability to communicate ideas and information and share ideas throughout the process, negotiate roles and responsibilities and independently and collaboratively manage agile projects to create interactive solutions. Students share information online by creating websites and interacting safely using appropriate information system protocols and agreed behaviours. They are progressively guided by trusted adults to account for risks when working individually and collaboratively. **Privacy and Security** Students develop appropriate techniques for managing data which is personal, and effectively implementing security protocols. In the early years, this begins with knowledge that data can be personal, collated and connected and progressively moves to students developing skills in managing the collection of their own or another user's data. Students investigate how online applications and networked systems curate their data and explore strategies to manage their digital footprint. Students learn the importance of effective security protocols. They effectively access school or personal accounts and progress from using simple usernames and passwords in the early years to using unique passphrases and multi-factor authentication which considers cyber security threats.

Source: ACARA (2023).

This overview is important because it frames the content to be taught. To better understand this overview, we now turn our attention to examples of some of these sub-strands from the Digital Technologies curriculum subject.

Looking inside a classroom: A snapshot of teaching programs

Table 5.2 presents snapshots of how the knowledge and understandings (Column 1) are operationalised in the classroom or centre (Column 2).

Table 5.2 Teaching ideas for the Knowledge and Understanding strand

Knowledge and Understanding strand	Teaching ideas
Data Representation This sub-strand looks at how data is represented and structured symbolically for use by digital systems. Different types of data are studied from Foundation to Year 8 including text, numeric, images (still and moving) and sound, with relational data being introduced in Years 9 and 10. (ACARA, 2023)	**Years 5 and 6 example** The students are preparing for the end of year school play on the story of *Charlotte's Web* and decide to have a light and sound performance instead. To achieve this, they: • Study a range of sound effects found as free source material • Explore ways to bring light together with their music – searching for a suitable open access app • Prepare their scripts as digital text, but also include symbols to illustrate light and sound effects at appropriate points • Rehearse, time, evaluate, adjust and reproduce iteratively

Table 5.2 (cont.)

Knowledge and Understanding strand	Teaching ideas
	• Record digital version (just in case a family member cannot make it to the performance)_ • Prepare the video as YouTube • Set up electronic newsletter, with schedule release of the YouTube link – set to private access and use password protocols to send out e-newsletter **Foundation to Year 2 example** The children have been reading the story *Where the Wild Things Are*, and are preparing a stopmotion animation to share with their families. To achieve this they: • Prepare a diorama as a backdrop for the story so as to frame the scene for photographing • Prepare the characters for photographing by drawing and cutting out the images • Script the narrative, rehearse and record • Use functions on the stopmotion, so the children add music • Edit their movie by including credit and text for scene changes in the story • Put their video on YouTube and share the link with their families

Table 5.3 presents examples of teaching practices for students for the Processes and Production Skills strand in Foundation to Year 2 and Years 5 and 6.

Table 5.3 Teaching ideas for the Processes and Production Skills strand

Processes and Production Skills	Teaching ideas
Privacy and Security Students develop appropriate techniques for managing data that are personal, and effectively implementing security protocols. In the early years, this begins with knowledge that data can be personal, collated and connected and progressively moves to students developing skills in managing the collection of their own or another user's data. Students investigate how online applications and networked systems curate their data and explore strategies to manage their digital footprint. Students learn the importance of effective security protocols. They effectively access school or personal accounts and progress from using simple usernames and passwords in the early years to using unique passphrases and multi-factor authentication which considers cyber security threats. (ACARA, 2023)	**Years 5 and 6 examples** The students have identified a problem in their classroom. They do not know how to keep their personal devices safe when not in use or when they are out in the playground. They solve this problem by: • Undertaking a general security audit of the school – who can enter/exit the carpark, the front office, and other access points • Examining/interviewing leadership on the policies on devices, internet access, etc. and existing safety protocols. • Using Google Earth, they explore the school surroundings for tracks and other obstructions or access points • Going onto council websites and retrieving data on who lives in the community, statistics available on safety, and what Council has put in place to keep people and property safe • Researching generally about cyber safety, and noting how to use passwords and simple user names to protect the content of their device. • Preparing their plan, implementing and evaluating whether it works – why or why not; adjusting and putting new protocols and procedures into place

Table 5.3 (cont.)

Processes and Production Skills	Teaching ideas
	Foundation to Year 2 examples The children have re-created the story of 'Goldilocks and the Three Bears' in their classroom. The design challenge is to set up a security system so that Goldilocks cannot come to their house uninvited. To achieve this, the children: • Do a security walk of the school – what systems are in place – locks, cameras, passwords? • Undertake a security audit of the digital devices in the school – passwords and protocols for using the internet. • Research how to set up a security system by studying content on YouTube. • Plan their security system – who will be the guards, what might be the password and how do we remember it but also change it? • Prepare a map of the area to be secured using Google Earth.

If you were to prepare teaching content for students in Years 3 and 4 or from birth to 5 years, what would that look like? Add your ideas to Table 5.4.

Table 5.4 Your teaching ideas

Knowledge and Understanding strand	Teaching ideas
Privacy and Security Students develop appropriate techniques for managing data which is personal, and effectively implementing security protocols. In the early years, this begins with knowledge that data can be personal, collated and connected and progressively moves to students developing skills in managing the collection of their own or another user's data. Students investigate how online applications and networked systems curate their data and explore strategies to manage their digital footprint.	**My teaching ideas for children in the birth to 5 years sector:**
Students learn the importance of effective security protocols. They effectively access school or personal accounts and progress from using simple usernames and passwords in the early years to using unique passphrases and multi-factor authentication which considers cyber security threats. (ACARA, 2023)	**My teaching ideas for students in Years 3 and 4:**

Download 5.1 Your teaching ideas

We now turn our attention to two case studies to illustrate how teachers bring core concepts of digital technologies into their program so that what children learn is personally meaningful to them.

Looking inside a classroom: Years 3 and 4

Julie is the teacher of a group of Year 3 children. In drawing upon the Australian Curriculum: Technologies, she introduces computational thinking through exploring a range of digital technologies by designing a school-based radio station, where she uses the achievement standards from the Australian Curriculum: Technologies (ACARA, 2023): 'By the end of Year 4 students create simple digital solutions and use provided design criteria to check if solutions meet user needs ...'

According to the Australian Curriculum: Technologies (ACARA, 2023), the achievement standards assist teachers to monitor student learning and to make judgements about student progress and achievement. Teachers may also use the achievement standards at the end of a period of teaching to make on-balance judgements about the quality of learning demonstrated by students and to report that information to parents.

Julie considers what is expected, then records the following in her program:

- How does a radio work? Use inquiry-based approach to investigate.
- Establish prior knowledge. (Children to draw a picture of where the announcements come from and how they reach our room.)
- List any questions the children may have.
- Suggestions of how to investigate them.
- Investigate questions. (Gather information from books, experiments, experts, internet, etc.).
- Support the development of computational thinking.

Julie begins her program by focusing on planning for Book Week. She sets a design brief for the children (Figure 5.4).

Book Week

Produce a radio broadcast (using the intercom system) for the children in the school.

Radio investigations

Listen to the radio. Time it so that the children hear a few different segments (music, news and talk). Record what you find out.

Your understandings

Draw a picture of what you understand about radios and radio stations. Think about the person and where they might be. Think about what kinds of computer systems there might be.

Figure 5.4 Design brief for Book Week

Julie suggests to the children that they should prepare a program that features Book Week in some way. They consider both the broadcasting program and the project of Book Week.

Radio announcements

Investigate what information needs to be given – language style, scriptwriting and verbal skills when presenting.

For Book Week, the children consider how they might set up a book display and how they could use what they learn about producing a radio announcement/radio station to support their promotion of Book Week.

Book display

- Factual.
- Fiction.
- Poetry.
- Play/drama.
- Ask children what sort of books.
- Read a section (pre-marked and same for all) to child.
- Ask again what sort of writing/book this is.
- Ask about the purpose of the writing/book.
- Ascertain when we use this sort of book.

Julie takes the children on an excursion to a radio station. Before they leave, the children draw a picture of what they think happens at a radio station. The children visit the radio station and document their visit on an iPad and by drawing pictures (they have clipboards) about what they learned at the radio station.

The children documented what they learned about the technologies in the radio station. They found out how computers are used at a radio station (see also Figure 5.5):

- Computers are used to survey people about what they like to listen to.
- Computers help by getting the music.

Figure 5.5 How are computers used at the radio station?

- Computers link to other radio stations.
- They control the volume of voices.
- They can send messages between the technician and the other people.
- They show what is planned next and make it happen.

When the children return to school, they generate a series of questions about which they are curious and discuss how they could answer these questions.

Questions we have:

- How does the radio get the sounds?

What do we think?

- By the radio waves.
- A little magnet picks up the sounds.
- It just goes into the radio.

What we could do:

- Open up a radio from the tinkering table and look inside.
- Look in books.
- Make a crystal radio.

To support the children's curiosity, Julie sets up a tinkering table with a large number of different types of radios to investigate (Figure 5.6). This is what she documents in her program:

Tinkering table:

- Pull apart – microphones, telephones, radios, speakers, switches, circuits.
- Compare different machines – can you find similar parts?
- Encourage children to find connections between different pieces.

The children prepare a group poster on their activities:

What we found out
Radio stations have radio waves and the antennas put up the waves and the wires take them to the speakers and the speakers make it louder.

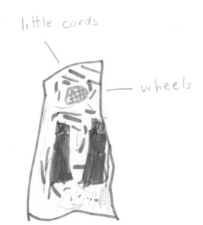

Figure 5.6 What is inside a radio?

As part of the children's investigations, they decide they now know enough to design their own radio station to broadcast news about Book Week.

To prepare for the radio program, it is important to have something interesting to share with the audience. Because it was Book Week when Julie did this unit of technology, she encouraged the children to also ask about their favourite books. A survey about Book Week is a good way to share something interesting that could be broadcast.

Julie works with the children to gather the data needed to prepare a successful radio broadcast. The children want to know 'What is the best way to advertise Book Week?'

What we did to answer this question:

- We surveyed people about what they like to hear.

- We listened to different kinds of programs – jazz, pop music, classical, stories being read, news, weather reports, interviews.
- We interviewed the children in the school (see Figures 5.7 and 5.8).

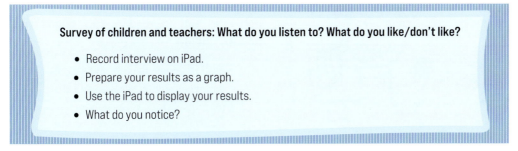

Download 5.2 Survey of children and teachers: What do you listen to? What do you like/don't like?

Figure 5.7 Gathering and analysing data about what children like to listen to on the radio

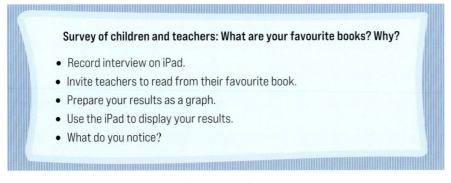

Download 5.3 Survey of children and teachers: What are your favourite books? Why?

Figure 5.8 Gathering and analysing data about favourite books

This research helped the children to prepare something interesting that they could broadcast.

As part of using the topic of preparing a program to broadcast, Julie also wanted the children to learn about digital systems. She was keen for the children to have an opportunity to think about all the components of the digital system with which they were working as part of creating their own radio station and preparing something to broadcast. Figure 5.9 shows one child's design for a radio station.

Through Julie's teaching program on designing and broadcasting a radio program during Book Week, the children had the opportunity to better understand not just how to represent data but, as with the Foundation year unit designing a system of care (see below), they were also learning about systems – in this case, digital systems.

Digital systems

Investigating all the digital devices that made up the radio station, then using the school PA system, the children were able to recreate a digital system of their own. Here they learned about the broader idea of digital systems through exploring data, people and processes. They

Figure 5.9 Michelle's design for a radio station

also focused on the components of digital systems, such as the hardware and software (computer architecture and the operating system) and the networks and the use of the school internet (wireless, mobile and wired networks and protocols). This aligns with ACARA (2023):

> *Digital systems*: explore and describe a range of digital systems and their peripherals for a variety of purposes (AC9TDI4K01) & explore transmitting different types of data between digital systems (AC9TDI4K02)

Interactions and impacts

The children not only created their own data through surveying the other children in the school, but learned about how to safely and ethically store their results, how to analyse data and how to use their analysis for making informed decisions about broadcasting during Book Week. The children also discussed the concept of copyright, and what they could or could not broadcast during Book Week. This aligns well with data representation, evaluating, and aspects of privacy and security (ACARA, 2023):

> *Data representation*: recognise different types of data and explore how the same data can be represented differently depending on the purpose (AC9TDI4K03)
>
> *Evaluating*: discuss how existing and student solutions satisfy the design criteria and user stories (AC9TDI4P05)
>
> *Privacy and security*: identify what personal data is stored and shared in their online accounts and discuss any associated risks (AC9TDI4P09)

Computational thinking

Computational thinking is discussed in full in Chapter 6. However, as we can see in this case study of Julie preparing for Book Week, the children also wrote their own radio broadcast, giving step-by-step instructions to all those involved in the successful broadcast. For instance, the children prepared a song list based on what children like to listen to, organised a system for how the songs would be played on the PA system (including dealing with copyright) and decided when and how all the announcements would be made. Writing and following the steps in their radio program was the key to the successful broadcast during Book Week. The children used flow charts to help them organise what they needed to do.

Systems thinking

Taken together, this unit, with all of the complexity of designing and running a radio station, has contributed to holistically supporting children's systems thinking in digital contexts.

Looking inside a classroom: Foundation level

In the Foundation year, it is possible for children to have many opportunities to create a range of digital solutions through guided play and integrated learning. We see this through examples of using robotic toys at home (Kewalramani, Palaiologou et al., 2021; Palaiologou, Kewalramani and Dardanou, 2021) or through using personal devices to play (Arnott and Yelland, 2020). The case example that follows shows how Mandy, a teacher in the Foundation year, introduced her children to a range of robotic toys. One of the toys introduced to the children was a Furby. This particular toy, although not programmable, did provide children with many opportunities to explore the relations between the Furbies as they interacted, and to consider the patterns of sounds noted by the children. The children were able to give instructions to the other robotic toys that they brought in from home. In the example that follows, the practices and investigations with the Furbies are presented as an example featuring digital toys. This unit, as shown in this case study, shows how Julie connected with the Achievement Standard:

> By the end of Foundation students identify familiar products, services and environment and develop familiarity with digital systems, using them for a purpose. They create, communicate and choose design ideas. Students follow steps and use materials and equipment to safely make a designed solution for a school-selected context. They show how to represent data using objects, pictures and symbols and identify examples of data that is owned by them. (ACARA, 2023)

Digital toys

The example of a Furby is introduced, but any digital toy that is available and of interest to the children could be used (see Ling et al., 2022 for a range of Internet of Things devices).

Design brief: Adopting a Furby family and friends

Our class has been asked to adopt a Furby family and their digital friends. Figure 5.10 shows the letter that arrived with the Furby.

After exploring the Furby – what it could do in the context of the other Furbies – the children documented what they had found out. They wrote a class book on Furbies. As part of their investigations, the children, with support from their teacher, Mandy, decided that the Furby could have overnight stays with children. To do this, they needed to set up a system of care for the Furby. The children explored what this might mean (Figure 5.11).

> **Volunteers and Furby carers**
>
> Dear Friend,
>
> Thank you for volunteering to take me home with you. I am looking forward to meeting your family. I will be bringing my backpack with me, and my bus pass in case I have to catch a bus home with you. Please treat me like one of your family and let me join in with you. I like watching TV, and I shall try to be quiet! I would love you to write in my diary, just a short note about what I did at your house. Please write your name in my address book too.
>
> Please bring me back to school the next school day. I don't want to miss out on my school work!
>
> Thank you for volunteering to care for me. You are very kind. I hope we have lots of fun!
>
> Love from your Furby friend and family.

Figure 5.10 Letter from Furby

> **What we already know**
>
> **We care for:** Each other, plants, environment, pets, sick people, animals, babies, environment.
> **We are cared for by:** Parents, grandparents, relatives, babysitters, cottage care, teachers, friends, volunteers.
> **A caring environment:** Kind, warm, safe, clean, healthy, carers.
> **What the Furby needs:** Volunteers, sleepover brag book, overnight bag.

Figure 5.11 Creating a system of care

The children documented what might go into a backpack for the Furby to take with it. This is what they came up with.

List to go into overnight bag:

- Soap
- Face washer
- Toothbrush
- Brush
- Book
- Folder
- Toy
- Paper and pen
- Postcard.

The children decided it was important to put a note with the Furby and its backpack, so the families that looked after it would know a little about what the Furby liked and needed (see the pro forma for the personal details in Figure 5.12).

Furby personal note

Name: _____
Food: _____
Diet: _____
Sleep: _____
Book (reading): _____
Shop: _____
Medical details: _____
Birthday: _____
Story writing: _____
Base – chair, beanbag, TV: _____
Toys: _____

Download 5.4 Furby personal note

Figure 5.12 Personal details of Furby

An overview of Mandy's program is shown in Table 5.5. It includes details of the focus questions that she introduced to the children, the discussion points to cover with the children and the specific activities she planned. This overview program shows the integration of technologies with other key areas of learning, such as literacy. Below this are the learning outcomes for digital technologies, linked specifically to the detail of Mandy's program.

Download 5.5 Overview of teaching program

Table 5.5 Overview of Mandy's teaching program

Week	Focus questions	Points for discussion	Activities
1	Who cares for you? What does it mean? What makes a caring environment? What would you take with you to stay overnight?	We are cared for by parents, grandparents, relatives, babysitters, cottage care, teachers, friends and volunteers.	Refer to our needs for a sleepover and compare your needs with those of the Furby. Introduce the Furby's backpack. Lucky dip: take one item at a time, discuss the item's use and say whether it should be included to take home. Place it in the Furby's backpack.
2	What kind of room or home do you think Furby would like? Why? What different uses could your room have? What makes a room special? What is your favourite room? What does 'design' mean? Could you design a room for Furby? How would you make this room?	Names of different rooms in a home. An individual name, perhaps? Purposes of different rooms. Design and 'look' of a type of room.	Design a room in your big book. Try to recreate your room with boxes, fabric, paper, etc. Use a Furby to see how it likes the new room. Appraise – change/add/take away from your room.

Table 5.5 (cont.)

Week	Focus questions	Points for discussion	Activities
	What materials could you use? Will you add extra things – e.g. for comfort, play, interest?	Materials used outside and inside a room or home. Finishing touches and special items in a room.	Test drive your room at home or at school with Furby.
3	In what kind of restaurant would the Furby like to eat? In what shops would the Furby like to spend money? Would the Furby enjoy using a library? What would the Furby need for a day at the beach? What does a hospital need to look after sick Furbies?	Discuss what worked well and if anything was missing for future Furby visits.	Brainstorm the items needed for the venues for the Furby. Collect and check off items needed. Arrange classroom to accommodate the different venues. Form teams and visit each venue created in rotation.

Mandy's program, with its design brief of adopting a Furby, provided a meaningful context for the children to develop their thinking. Through guided play with the Furbies, the children documented how the Furbies moved about and what sounds they made when interacting with the children or other Furbies (data). Through this, they noticed patterns (analysis) that they could use to purposefully prepare an appropriate system of care (forerunner for systems thinking). These hidden dimensions of the Furbies were important characteristics that the children experienced during their play, but that they visualised and abstracted when discussing the system of care needed for the successful adoption and home visit of the Furby in their care.

The children not only designed, but also produced, a system of care that was made concrete through the backpack and home visits with the children over time. This example shows the development of key concepts for the Foundation level, as was evident when the children worked out a system of care for the Furby. The children also produced a Furby book, which documented the data they had gathered about the Furby.

Through the experiences at the Foundational year, as shown in the example of adopting a Furby, we can see how children develop familiarity with representing data.

PEDAGOGICAL REFLECTION 5.4

Same materials, different year levels

The design briefs that follow illustrate how the same materials used in the example of Mandy's project on Furbies can be used for children in Years 5 and 6.

- *Design brief 3 (Year 5/6): Auditing Santa Claus.* You are to audit the work of Santa Claus. It has been reported that he has been delivering politically incorrect toys to children. Your role is to examine the Furby, Tekno Robotic Puppy, Meow Chi Interactive Robotic Cat and Diva Starz toys. When children play with these toys, what are they learning ... about culture, gender, technology? Prepare a report.

- *Design brief 2: Furby investigations.* You have just landed on a Furby planet. Your mission is to learn the language of the Furby, record its habits in your explorer book, and write up a report to take back to Earth (after many hours observing, drawing and discussing with your friends).
- *Design brief 3: Furby visits the preschool/childcare centre.* The children find Furby in the middle of their mat storytelling area. There is a note. It reads: 'I am new to your preschool/childcare centre. I am lonely because I have no friends. I do not know about your routines. Can you help me settle in and make friends? Love from Furby.'

What do you notice about the examples? Can you think of other teaching ideas that could be used at the beginning and end of primary school? What about over the five years for which children attend child care? How can you use the same ideas to plan for learning so it builds children's conceptual knowledge and thinking in the subject area of Digital Technologies?

Summary

This chapter considered the place of digital technologies in children's lives. It was also shown how an exploration of digital technologies by young children in classrooms/centres can lead to thinking in new ways. It also looked at how teachers can use children's robotic toys from home as a motivation for digital learning. For younger children, this meant experimenting with very simple, step-by-step procedures to explore digital toys, to represent their ideas as data and experience systems thinking in a digital context. In Chapter 6, we take this further with older children, who design digital solutions as simple visual programs involving branching, iteration (repetition) and user input.

Acknowledgements

Thank you to Judith Gomes for providing the infant photo in this chapter. Special thanks go to Mandy (Foundation teacher), Julie (Year 3) and Charina Pumpa (Redeemer Lutheran College) for their work on technologies education, captured through the case studies presented in this chapter.

CHAPTER 6

The curriculum in action: Digital technologies – computational thinking

Introduction

In Chapter 5, Digital Technologies as a subject area was discussed. This chapter continues the exploration of concepts and teaching practices for Digital Technologies by going more explicitly into computational thinking.

This chapter begins with a general discussion of computational thinking and concludes with case examples of digital technologies in action in the classroom/centre. Through studying computational thinking in action, it is hoped that you will come to understand this concept and develop a range of ways in which you can teach it meaningfully to children in the early years and from the Foundation to Year 6 levels (Figure 6.1).

Figure 6.1 The embodiment of computational thinking as children guide the Wild Robot across the school wilderness using hexadecimal code
Source: Monash University PlayLab and Redeemer Lutheran College.

What is computational thinking?

In your reading of the Australian Curriculum: Technologies, you would have noted that in Digital Technologies one of the aims is for children to use computational thinking (abstraction; data collection, representation and interpretation; specification; algorithms; and implementation) to create digital solutions. You would also have noted that the two strands in Digital Technologies are conceptualised as 'an iterative process including computational thinking, where students evaluate, collaborate and manage throughout the process' (ACARA, 2023). But what is computational thinking?

Computational thinking involves a set of concepts and thought processes that help a person to formulate a problem and find a solution. What makes it computational is that it is usually thought to involve digital processing in some way. Computational thinking has also been termed 'programming', but there are many who suggest that programming – or coding, as it has increasingly become known – is the process and computational thinking is the concept (Lavigne, Lewis-Presser and Rosenfeld, 2020). In looking at this area in the literature, you will notice that the term is constantly being developed as more teachers and children engage in computational thinking in the classroom, and as more apps are developed to make coding more accessible to younger children (Relkin, de Ruiter and Bers, 2020).

There is now an increasing level of interest in computational thinking worldwide. Should coding be part of the school curriculum for all age groups? What is your view? When should computational thinking begin? Some have suggested that computational thinking is a new form of literacy (Kyza et al., 2022) to add to the suite of twenty-first century thinking skills (Wong and Cheung, 2020), suggesting that it is now essential for everyone. But how did this all begin?

Video activity 6.1 What is computational thinking?

SPOTLIGHT 6.1

Historical accounts of computational thinking

Jeannette Wing (2008), credited as the pioneer of computational thinking by many (Kyza et al., 2022), has given new directions for digital technologies by introducing this concept. Her work is discussed extensively in this section. While some suggest that computational thinking was alluded to by Seymour Papert (1980) in his famous book *Mind Storms* (see Relkin, de Ruiter and Bers, 2020), many have stated that it was Wing who brought this forward as a concept. Wing (2008, p. 3717) states, 'Computational thinking is taking an approach to solving problems, designing systems and understanding human behaviour that draws on concepts fundamental to computing'. Computational thinking is a type of analytical thinking that can also be found in scientific thinking, mathematics thinking and engineering thinking (Ehsan, Rehmat and Cardella, 2021). Specifically, it mirrors the way people and children might approach designing and evaluating the real-world systems they see in everyday life.

Wing (2008) suggests that the essence of computational thinking is abstraction. This term is also mentioned by the Australian Curriculum: Technologies (ACARA, 2023) as part of the definition of computational thinking. Although coding is thought of as an abstract activity, it should always be connected to the real world in some way – that is, the problem must be about everyday life. For instance, a robot is not coded simply to move; rather, a problem is set up – such as asking how a robot might move around a playground or the wild terrain (Figure 6.1). In working with students in Year 5, Kopcha, Ocak and Qian (2021) note that computational thinking is actively supported when it is an embodied interaction.

Computational thinking is the essence of digital technologies. To build it into our teaching, we need to think through the essence of the concept. The first key idea involves helping children to work with rich abstractions, and to know how to define the right problem as part of one of these abstractions. Wing (2008) suggests that the abstractions in computational thinking always involve layers, such as defining an abstraction, exploring the many layers of the abstraction, then developing an understanding of the relations between the multiple layers. The layering has also been noted by Mannila et al. (2014) in their review of computational thinking across a broad range of countries, where they found a distinct need to switch conversations from coding to the idea of problem-solving. The complexities of computational thinking need to be captured by stating what is meant – for example, computational thinking involves:

- conceptualising problems in a way that allows digital devices to act as a tool to help solve the problem
- organising data so it can be analysed with the aid of digital devices
- finding ways to automate solutions so that they are a series of ordered steps (algorithmic thinking)
- being able to identify a series of possible solutions, and being able to analyse these for efficiency of steps and combinations of resources
- being able to apply the problem-solving processes to a range of problems, thus generalising and transferring processes to other contexts and problems.

The second key idea in conceptualising computational thinking is considering the relations between abstraction and automation. This means seeing computing as the automation of abstractions, or problem-formulation and solution-finding. Within this framework, Wing (2008) argues that, although a computer can automate abstraction, so too can the human mind. Computational thinking therefore does not need a machine; however, the human mind combined with a machine can bring together a higher level of processing power. For instance, computational thinking can support everyday activities in society through automating processes, such as:

- statistical analysis – identifying patterns and anomalies in large volumes of data
- processing of large data sets – for example, magnetic resonance imaging scans, credit cards and credit card machines, maps of the solar system, and even shopping, where ordering and receipting are connected
- scientific work – for example, the sequencing of the human genome
- business models – for example, following online purchasing and then selecting advertisements appropriate for the history of the shopper
- health – for example, searching for donors for n-way kidney exchange.

Computational thinking involves data mining of large data sets to discover new trends, patterns and links. Further, it is seen in computer simulations that draw upon powerful mathematical models for:

- aerospace science – simulation of an aircraft or space mission
- geosciences – simulating the Earth, from the inner core to the Sun's surface
- humanities and the arts – digital libraries.

> The power of computational thinking lies in taking all the above ideas and projecting these into the future for:
>
> - modelling systems, including time scales and use of three-dimensional space
> - modelling interactions, including the identification of conditions that predict tipping points and other behaviours
> - adding to the models more parameters and conditions
> - playing models back and forth in time
> - validating models against evidence or practice (Wing, 2008).
>
> As societies continue to deploy more digital tools and gather more data, there is a greater need for computational thinking. For instance, communities already use and collect data across a range of sensors for:
>
> - routine monitoring and surveillance systems
> - social media and the prevalence of digital images captured through mobile phones
> - digitised global weather systems
> - simulation models of systems (Wing, 2008).
>
> This would suggest that computational thinking is relevant to everyone. Wing (2008) brought into our world a concept to name some powerful existing and future practices.

There is evidence to show that schools already engage learners in a broad range of computational thinking. For instance, a study was done by Mannila et al. (2014) to find out what parts of computational thinking are already integrated into teachers' practice – that is, what part of their everyday classroom activities is related to computational thinking. The researchers surveyed secondary teachers in Finland, Italy, Lithuania, the Netherlands and Sweden, and found three clusters of activities where teachers already taught their students to engage with computational thinking. Cluster 1 involved collecting, analysing and representing data. Cluster 2 included simulations, automation and parallelisation. Cluster 3 was problem composition, algorithms and abstraction. Teachers used interactive whiteboards, iPads, web resources, including social media production tools such as Office suites and graphics software, graphical programming environments such as Scratch, programming languages, simulation software (NetLogo) and robotics (LEGO MINDSTORMS).

There are also studies that show how computational thinking, supported through ScratchJr, looks conceptually different with 6- to 9-year-olds compared with 10- to 12-year-olds (Kyza et al., 2022). Through being introduced to the problem of designing a digital story to present to their families about environmental waste management actions, children used block-based programming tools for their digital solution. They found that 'children's collaborative performance with coding aligned with children's age, as children's projects increased in sophistication' (p. 250) from the 6- to 9-years group to the 10- to 12-year-olds. While this was to be expected, they suggest that their research shows children's coding practices and their computational thinking are a progression, something that has not previously been identified through research. They found that younger children needed more support with abstraction and problem decomposition.

SPOTLIGHT 6.2

Technology and design in New Zealand

Fox-Turnbull (2018) explains that in 2016 in New Zealand, the education sector introduced digital technology into the Technology curriculum. Over 10 years, digital technology has developed an important role in education, but there is a shift from learning how to *do* technology to knowing how to *use* it in new ways. The IT industry wants more graduates with a broader set of expertise. For instance, Fox-Turnbull (2018) explains that in the area of computational thinking, parents are frightened by the view that their child might be learning computer science but support their children learning computational thinking.

The first rationale for implementing digital technologies from 5 years of age in New Zealand is that this is when they can easily learn computational language, and develop the dispositions needed to be oriented to digital technologies – this view is similar to ideas about learning an additional language. The second rationale is that digital technologies are a part of being in the twenty-first century. Digital citizenship and the need to be digitally literate are seen as important. Technology and design education, and digital technology, are about designing and development (not just using). Digital technology is well placed in a design and technology curriculum because learning is culturally situated and learning outcomes are centred on human interactions.

One question that is discussed is whether digital technologies should be a part of the technologies curriculum or separate.

SPOTLIGHT 6.3

ScratchJr, Fiona Morrison (junior school teacher)

ScratchJr (Figure 6.2) is a fantastic tool for younger students to begin building the knowledge, language and key understandings of basic block coding. It is one of our favourite coding tools in the Year 1 classroom as students are highly engaged, motivated and keen to develop their coding skills through this application. As a teacher, it is easy to navigate and simple to teach the key blocks that students would need to use to begin creating code. Our students enjoy the creative opportunities this app offers, not only in the variety of blocks available to create code with, but the vast array of characters and backgrounds to use (not to mention the option of adding your own details!).

One of our students' favourite activities on ScratchJr is navigating a character through a maze, which is created by uploading a maze background image using the camera feature. This lesson allows students to engage in creative problem-solving, critical thinking and collaboration as they work together to decide which blocks to use in their code, and how many of each block is required. For an added piece of fun, students can upload their face as the character – squeals of delight always ensue as students see themselves moving and jumping through the maze!

Another activity that is well suited to the ScratchJr app is the literacy outcomes of retelling a story. Students can retell the full story or their favourite scene (depending on their skill level), including details such as character, setting, complication, resolution and moral (depending on the year level).

Figure 6.2 ScratchJr in action

We find that this is another way whereby students can demonstrate their understanding of a text while removing some of the barriers of 'traditional' learning that may be problematic for some of our students, such as those with learning disabilities or undeveloped literacy skills. I have yet to meet a student who was not able to fully participate in or engage with ScratchJr after teaching and initial support from a teacher – further evidence of the wonder of this app!

Source: Fiona Morrison.

What are the core concepts that make up computational thinking?

As more research is being undertaken, greater insights are emerging into what constitutes the concept of computational thinking. While ACARA (2023) defines the concept as including abstraction; data collection, representation and interpretation; specification; algorithms; and implementation, many studies show a nuancing of these, as shown in the following examples.

Example 1: Bers (2019) and Bati (2021) show that computational thinking has a stepped logic:

- representing a problem
- systematic generation and implementation of solutions
- examining multiple solutions
- systematically approaching problems – complexity is represented from 'de-bugging' to 'trouble shooting' with a set of problem criteria

- a productive attitude to 'errors' or lines of inquiry that lead to understanding why 'that did not work'
- a disposition to approaching open-ended and difficult problems
- building general skills that are applicable beyond robotics and computational thinking.

Algorithm: A step-by-step series in instruction.

Abstraction: Generalising and transferring the problem-solving process to similar problems.

Automation: Using digital and simulation tools to mechanise the problem's solution.

Problem decomposition: Breaking down a complex problem into smaller parts, reducing complexity.

Synchronisation: Synchronising events between sprites, for example: Use of only 1 Wait 'Control' block in combination with any of the 'Looks', 'Motion' and 'Sound' blocks.

Parallelism: Making things happen at the same time.

Example 2: There exist computational practices, computational perspectives and computational concepts. The last of these include syntactic, semantic and schematic knowledge commonly used in programming, such as variables, loops (repeat, do … while), conditionals (e.g. if … then … else), operators (e.g. arithmetic and comparison). It is suggested by Wong and Cheung (2020) that this can be mapped as critical thinking and problem-solving.

Example 3: Seven powerful ideas of computational thinking have been described: algorithms, modularity, control structures, representation, hardware/software, design process and debugging (Relkin, de Ruiter and Bers, 2020).

Example 4: Barak (2019, p. 8) states that in computational thinking, students engage with three concepts:

1 **algorithm**
2 **abstraction**
3 **automation**.

Example 5: In their research with ScratchJr, Kyza et al. (2022) put forward the following seven computational thinking concepts: abstraction and problem decomposition; logical thinking; synchronisation; parallelism; algorithmic notions of flow control; user interactivity; and data representation.

These examples show how computational thinking has been given a range of meanings in the literature. But how do these dimensions of the concept of computational thinking play out in the classroom and in how children learn over time? In drawing on Kyza et al. (2022), we provide a broad overview with definitions in Table 6.1. Progression of computational thinking is shown. Table 6.1 could act as a pro forma for preparing a rubric for other kinds of programmable tangibles.

Table 6.1 Computational thinking progression when using ScratchJr

Computational thinking concepts	Definition	Level 1	Level 2	Level 3
Abstraction and problem decomposition	Breaking down a complex problem into smaller parts, reducing complexity	One script or sprite or none	More than one script and sprite in project pages	More than one script and sprite in all project pages
Synchronisation	Synchronising events between sprites	Absence	Use of only one Wait 'Control' block in combination with any of the 'Looks', 'Motion' and 'Sound' blocks	Use of Wait 'Control' block in combination with any of the 'Looks', 'Motion' and 'Sound' blocks on one or more sprites on same page
Parallelism	Making things happen at the same time	No script or only one script on green flag	Two or more scripts on green flag, but not all of them running correctly	Two or more scripts on green flag, and all of them running correctly

Table 6.1 (cont.)

Computational thinking concepts	Definition	Level 1	Level 2	Level 3
Algorithmic notions of flow control	Blocks are arranged in sequences	No sequence of blocks	Sequence of blocks	Repeats of sequences (use of the 'Repeat' block, the 'Repeat forever' and the 'End' block)
User interactivity	The user clicks on a sprite and triggers an action	There is no interactive capability	Start on green flag	Includes 'Trigger' block: start on tab
Data representation	Modifiers of sprite properties	No sprite properties have been modified	Use of the 'Shrink' and 'Grow' blocks within a script with the default value (2)	Use of the 'Shrink' and 'Grow' blocks within a script within a sequence of blocks using customised values (not the default value)

Source: Adapted from Kyza et al. (2022, p. 233).

An interesting aspect of Kyza et al.'s (2022) research is that they identified from the literature that ScratchJr was more suitable across the primary years than Scratch. Through their synthesis of the literature, they identified that there are still many questions about the nature of computational thinking, such as 'How to assess it?'

PEDAGOGICAL REFLECTION 6.1

Computational thinking in the curriculum search

The Australian Curriculum: Technologies (ACARA, 2023) provides definitions of some of these concepts that underpin computational thinking. Jump onto the website and complete Table 6.2. Add what you find. Consider the year level you would be teaching and put in some ideas of what the content might look like in practice.

Table 6.2 Computational thinking as presented in the Australian Curriculum: Technologies

Computational thinking concepts:	Definition:	Practice example for chosen year level:
Abstraction		
Data collection		
Representation and interpretation		
Specification		
Algorithms		
Implementation		

Digital design practices: Such things as being incremental and iterative, testing and debugging – for instance, using sequences, loops and events.

Kyza et al. (2022) discuss how there are frameworks that go beyond computational thinking concepts, such as sequences, loops and events, and bring forward **digital design practices**, such as being incremental and iterative, testing and debugging. This nuancing of computational thinking is also evident in the research of Wong and Cheung (2020) who, alongside computational concepts, include *computational practices* and *computational perspectives*, as shown in Table 6.3.

Table 6.3 Conceptual framework for computational thinking

Concepts	Definition	Practice examples of concepts in action	Twenty-first century skills
Computational concepts	Syntactic, semantic and schematic knowledge commonly used when coding	Variable loops – repeat, do ... while; conditionals – if ... then ... else	Critical thinking Problem solving
Computational practices	Strategic knowledge to solve coding problem during the process of thinking and practices	Being incremental and iterative, testing and debugging, reusing and remixing and abstracting and modularising	Creativity Critical thinking Problem solving
Computational perspectives	Understanding of personal, social and technological relationships around them in connection to coding	Expressing and questioning the technological world through computation – create their own digital stories with Scratch	Creativity Critical thinking

Source: Adapted from Wong and Cheung (2020, p. 440).

Consistent with the *computational perspectives* shown in Table 6.3 is how Kyza et al. (2022) show that research is still emerging on perspectives of computational thinking and how what we know about this area also changes over time.

PEDAGOGICAL REFLECTION 6.2

What does computational thinking look like in practice across the school years?

1. How has 'computational thinking' been shown in practice on the ACARA (2023) website or in the EYLF? Record your ideas below:

    - _____
    - _____
    - _____

2. Can you find examples of both content descriptors and indicators of computational thinking for the following bands:

    a. Foundation
    b. Years 1 and 2
    c. Years 3 and 4
    d. Years 5 and 6?

3   What might be an example of computational thinking observed in:

    a   a preschool
    b   a classroom
    c   everyday life at home
    d   everyday life in the community?

    How are they the same? What might be different? Record your analysis.

4   You will be able to return to your suggestions at different points throughout the remainder of this chapter.

When should children begin learning computational thinking?

Following on from the foundational writings of Wing (2008), who theorised that under the right conditions children as young 5 years of age could engage in computational thinking, we have seen an emergence of studies into early childhood children's digital engagement with computational thinking, primarily through visual-based coding (Lavigne, Lewis-Presser and Rosenfeld, 2020; Relkin, de Ruiter and Bers, 2020) and robotics (Yang, Ng and Gao, 2022). Those arguments that express concerns can be summarised as follows:

1   Young children are just starting to learn to read and work with mathematical symbols, and computational thinking presents an additional conceptual area or literacy.
2   The fine-motor skills of young children are still developing, and therefore typing is difficult.
3   Young children are still developing their critical thinking skills.
4   Computational thinking deals with rules, logic and syntax – all of which do not yet sit within young children's experiences or conceptual framework, such as if–then conditions.

The long-standing research that has been done presents a positive view about children's capacity to code, such as those studies that have examined the coding of robotics:

- Children as young as 4 years of age can and do build simple robots, engaging in foundational levels of coding (Monteiro, Miranda-Pinto and Osório, 2021) and computational thinking (Yang, Ng and Gao, 2022).
- Children in the early years of primary school who work with robots are also able to engage in coding (Shively, 2014).
- Through coding robots, children learn powerful ideas that support their thinking in areas such as engineering and computer coding, while building computational thinking skills (Chou & Shih, 2021).
- Robotics play supports children to learn about and from technologies in meaningful ways that are engaging and that motivate them (Bers, 2008).
- Robots act as objects to think with, and create contexts for meaningful problem-solving (Bers et al., 2014).

Figure 6.3 Florence uses the Star Tracker App, which maps and tracks the constellations in real time.
Source: Kelly-Ann Allen.

More recently, research has shown how some of the original concerns about coding not being supportive of children's development can be addressed. For instance, studies into block-based coding are emerging as programmable devices and tangibles show features that support younger children's engagement in coding and the development of computational thinking, such as drag-and-drop of visual objects called 'blocks' and modular editing interface, that are more intuitive. These features contrast with text heavy coding approaches of the past, and they show how visual-based tools work on touch devices and have interactive interfaces which are more physically accessible for children. Some have shown how visual-based environments, such as ScratchJr, not only sustain engagement but provide instant outputs so that children become creators of games, animations and a variety of interactive stories. But there are also many programmable tangibles now available that are easy for very young children to use (Figure 6.3). These bring into play higher levels of physicality and interactivity between what children code and what the tangibles can do.

Link 6.1 Visual coding apps suitable for children

PEDAGOGICAL REFLECTION 6.3

Planning for the introduction of computational thinking

Some key questions need to be considered when examining the concept of computational thinking:

1. What might be the most effective way of organising computational concepts so children's learning develops over time?
2. How should I integrate the concept of computational thinking into my teaching?
    - The tangibles and programmable device should not get in the way of children's learning of concepts.
    - Children should not just learn to use a programmable device rather than learning computational thinking.
    - Similarly, it is important that children do not think that because they can use the programmable device, they have learned computational thinking.

How might we, as teachers, work with children in order to engage them in coding and to support computational thinking? The following section has three case studies. The first is an example of a Conceptual PlayWorld to support coding and computational thinking of 11-year-old students. This is followed by an example of a Y chart approach for introducing robotics into the classroom for 11-year-olds. We then turn our attention to the practices introduced by early childhood teachers to set up for computational thinking for toddlers and preschoolers.

Looking inside a classroom: Year 6 computational thinking Conceptual PlayWorld

Charina is a Science, Technology, Engineering and Mathematics (STEM) specialist who drew on the pedagogical model of a Conceptual PlayWorld (Fleer, 2022a, 2022b) to teach computational thinking to her Year 6 students. She began by looking at the band level descriptions (Table 6.4), followed by checking in with the achievement standard relevant for her cohort (Table 6.5). This gave her the curriculum content needed to plan a Computational Thinking Conceptual PlayWorld.

Table 6.4 Band level descriptions for Years 5 and 6

Process and Production skills	Definitions
Investigating and defining: define problems with given or co-developed design criteria and by creating user stories	**Design criteria** Criteria used to determine if the proposed solution meets the requirements. They are drawn from the solutions requirements, user stories, if appropriate, and constraints. **User stories** Short, simple descriptions of key software features that end users want from a digital solution. They often describe why the user wants particular features, and are part of the iterative design process.
Generating and designing: design algorithms involving multiple alternatives (branching) and iteration	**Algorithms** Precise description of the steps and decisions needed to solve a problem. Algorithms often involve iterative (repetitive) processes and can be represented, e.g. as flowcharts and pseudocode. **Multiple alternatives** (branching) Algorithmic expressions that involve making multiple yes or no decisions based on defined conditions and the data provided. **Iteration** Repetition of a set of steps or instructions in an algorithm or program, e.g. a loop in a flowchart, a repeat block of FOR, WHILE statements.

Source: ACARA (2023).

Table 6.5 Year 6 achievement standard for the subject Digital Technologies

Strand	Description
Knowledge and Understanding (Year 6)	By the end of Year 6 students develop and modify digital solutions, and define problems and evaluate solutions using user stories and design criteria. They process data and show how digital systems represent data. Students design algorithms involving complex branching and iteration and implement them as visual programs including variables. They securely access and use multiple digital systems and describe their components and how they interact to process and transmit data. Students select and use appropriate digital tools effectively to plan, create, locate and share content, and to collaborate, applying agreed conventions and behaviours. They identify their digital footprint and recognise its permanence.

Source: ACARA (2023).

Selecting a dramatic story

Charina chose the story of *The Wild Robot* by Peter Brown (2018). In line with Wing (2008), who argues that computational thinking needs to be set within a frame of a meaningful purpose, Charina planned her Conceptual PlayWorld by reading parts of this story to set the scene of Roz the Robot being washed up on a deserted island in a crate. In the story, the robot is presented as not having feelings, but as having machine learning capability, which means it knows it is on its own and needs to get along with all the other animals living on the deserted island – it needs their help to repair and sustain itself. The story is dramatic (Figure 6.4). It poses many contradictions and emotional responses for children – being a robot yet appearing human like (empathy), needing help (from the children in role as characters in the story) and needing to machine learn (but what and how?).

Figure 6.4 Beginning the Conceptual PlayWorld – Charina reads a chapter from *The Wild Robot* by Peter Brown.
Source: Monash University PlayLab and Redeemer Lutheran College.

Designing the imaginary space

As a STEM specialist, Charina wanted to provide a holistic approach to the students' learning through motivating them with an emotionally charged problem, in a learning context that was both familiar and unfamiliar – a natural area of bushland with a dam that became the island the children explored as part of the drama of being with Ros the Robot (see Figure 6.1). In her planning notes, Charina wrote:

> Utilising the natural scrub areas of our school for inspiration in design. Utilising the natural area of our school dam … uneven ground … 'hazards' all around … natural elements … wild … remote …

On this imaginary island, the children initially jump into the story and relive the narrative as presented in the book. The environment is rocky, has different inclines, has dangers (keeping the robot out of the water) and has overhead tree obstacles in which to become entangled.

There is no obvious point of reference for Roz because she was washed up on a deserted island and didn't know where she had been stranded.

Planning entering and exiting the Conceptual PlayWorld

In the story, Roz is washed up on the deserted island in a crate. Charina uses the idea of the crate as the portal into and out of the imaginary Conceptual PlayWorld of the island. The children know they are on Roz's island when they go through the crate and know that when they leave the island through the crate (Figure 6.5), they are back in the STEM classroom as regular students. In Charina's planning notes, she states:

> Entering the dam through a wooden crate 'door' in the same way that the robot arrives on the island in a wooden crate …
> Possible placement of one of our robotic devices in the natural area …

Figure 6.5 Computational thinking in action – setting up motivating conditions for coding
Source: Monash University PlayLab and Redeemer Lutheran College.

Planning the problem to arise in the Conceptual PlayWorld

The children build empathy with the hero of the story – Roz – and are keen to help her in her new environment. The problem that arises is simple, as shown in Charina's planning notes:

> Roz (the robot) needs to learn to survive on this remote, wild island, so must adapt to her surroundings …

But this simple problem demands a great deal of computational thinking from the children. They need to break down the problem into smaller steps because Roz's survival on the island means navigating around the difficult terrain. This is in keeping with the computational thinking concept where '[p]recise description of the steps and decisions needed to solve a problem' is demanded (ACARA, 2023).

After establishing empathy, visiting the island to find Roz and role-playing the storyline, Charina amplifies the problem by leaving a message from Roz to the children in the STEM lab. The message is written in hexadecimal code. Around the STEM classroom are resources to support the children to decode the message. Roz leaves a long message explaining her situation and her urgent need of help. The children set to work to decode the message in order to learn of her plight: her vision sensors have malfunctioned and the children need to provide a conceptually coded map of the terrain so she can navigate safely around the island. This amplified problem introduces algorithms to the children so they can move beyond simple steps and begin to introduce 'if … else' statements and iterative processes for efficient navigational code for Roz.

SPOTLIGHT 6.4

What is hexadecimal code?

Hexadecimal code is used by coders in digital systems to reduce the long list of numbers or strings of binary code. It is more manageable than using long number lists. You may see this numbering system referred to as a byte, or a multiple of the byte (16 bits, 24, 32, 64, etc.). Using hexadecimal numbers just makes these large binary numbers easier to write.

The numbering system with which we are all familiar is base 10. Hexadecimal uses base 16.

Link 6.2 Hexadecimal numeral system

To support the children to build the flowcharts and pseudocode, Charina introduces Google Earth to the children so they can locate the dam and other features, and use this to support their emerging skills in writing code for Roz's navigational system. Links with machine learning and how AI are used in some cars provide real-world contexts for the children to consider or reference as they undertake their research.

Importantly, the children need to test out their emerging code. This means visiting the island through the crate and undertaking the debugging process as both an embodied action together with Roz (Figures 6.1, 6.4–6.6) and as code presented by the children to discuss with each other as a group (Figure 6.7).

Figure 6.6 The debugging process is embodied
Source: Monash University PlayLab and Redeemer Lutheran College.

Figure 6.7 Code is presented and discussed
Source: Monash University PlayLab and Redeemer Lutheran College.

Precise descriptions of the steps and decisions are needed to solve the problem. Algorithms often involve iterative (repetitive) processes and can be represented, for example, as flowcharts and pseudocode (Figure 6.7).

To position the children as coders and as occupying other professional roles in computer science, Charina makes up relevant lanyards that the students use to support their role in the imaginary situation (Figure 6.8). As professional coders, the students go onto the island to visit Roz, to assess the situation, and then to return to the STEM classroom to prepare the code for the navigational map.

Figure 6.8 The coders land on the island, crawl through and out of the crate, and begin their reconnaissance mission – building a profile of the terrain ready to take back to the STEM lab for coding
Source: Monash University PlayLab and Redeemer Lutheran College.

The lanyards support the learning of the students in two important ways. First, they position them as coders undertaking an important role in the support of Roz, and second, they build a sense of identity that computational thinking is meaningful and leads to a purposeful profession that they could consider later in life. That is, computational thinking is more than coding. Set within the drama of Roz needing help, with a personally meaningful problem to solve, computational thinking as a concept brings together social and ethical issues (see Chapter 5), and moves beyond a conception of computer science being about just an isolated task of coding.

We now turn our attention to a different example of computational thinking in action with the same age group, but using a different model of teaching.

Looking inside a classroom: Years 5 and 6

Jackie and her Year 5 and 6 children embark upon a unit of work that features an exploration of robots. Specifically, Jackie wishes to consider ethical issues alongside supporting her children with coding and designing algorithms. In studying the Australian Curriculum: Technologies (Tables 6.4 and 6.5), Jackie notes that she can explore coding by using apps such as Alice, GameMaker, Kodu, LEGO MINDSTORMS, MIT App Inventor and Scratch (Build Your Own Blocks and Snap). She notes that visual programming languages or environments are where the program is represented and created visually rather than presented as text. Because the children have not done any computational thinking activities in her classroom before, she is interested in exploring how they code and how they make judgements as they observe a robot moving around the classroom.

Link 6.3 Visual programming software suitable for children

Jackie looked into the Australian Curriculum: Technologies (ACARA, 2023) as shown to see what the achievement standard is expecting of her children by the end of Year 6. She also looked closely at the band level descriptions and identified what was relevant for planning and supporting her children's computational thinking, as shown in Table 6.5.

Jackie began her program by finding out what children thought about and knew about robots (Figures 6.9 and 6.10). The children created Y charts about their understandings (Figure 6.10). The children also explored the old robots they had, as well as the robotic toys they had brought to school to share with their friends.

In Jackie's classroom, the children were experimenting with different ways of representing an instruction about their robots. In particular, the children wrote programs that allowed for a choice. For instance, Emily extended her program by including the following commands when programming her robotic toy to move down a road she had pre-prepared (Figure 6.11).

Emily continued to experiment and worked out that, rather than continually typing the commands into her robot, she could include a repeat function so the robot could keep making the same movements. She used this repeat function to make her robot dance (Figure 6.12).

> **My experiences:** When I was a toddler, I was given a remote-control car that I did not like and I pulled, unscrewed and basically tinkered it to bits. And I have had a microwave cook my dinner.
>
> **What I know:** I know that robots can be programmed to do things for humans.
>
> **What I would like to know:** I would like to know whether humans will ever create a robot that can think for itself.
>
> **A robot is:** A robot is a machine that can be programmed to do things for humans. Some examples are:
> - a remote-control car
> - a microwave
> - a television
> - a computer
> - a valiant roamer.

Figure 6.9 What Mere knows about robots

Emily's robotic program is much more efficient and effective than Brett's program for making his robotic toy dance (see Figure 6.13).

Jackie noted that the children had gained a lot of experiences with the robotic toys, which supports the content descriptions found in the Australian Curriculum: Technologies. In particular, the children prepared a range of designs for their robotic toys, supporting some of the content descriptions shown in the curriculum. In order to further the children's computational thinking, Jackie prepared a 6 x 6 square grid on the asphalt outside that was lettered and numbered. She used chalk to mark up the squares and included a few obstacles in the grid. She gave the children a set of whiteboard markers and a set of clear laminated cards and the design brief shown in Figure 6.14.

The intersection of the groups on the grid created a range of humorous obstacles for the children as they tried to avoid each other. They noted that the 'if ... then' command worked well for effective navigating. Having cards with the capacity to change the program steps – that is, wipe off the cards and begin again – allowed for a lot of experimentation and discussion.

ROBOTS

My experiences
When I was a toddler I was given a remote-control car that I did not like and I pulled, unscrewed and basically tinkered it to bits. And I have had a microwave cook my dinner.

What I know
I know that robots can be programmed to do things for humans.

What I would like to know
I would like to know whether humans will ever create a robot that can think for itself.

A robot is a machine that can be programmed to do things for humans. Some examples are:
- a remote-control car
- a microwave
- a television
- a computer
- a valiant roamer.

Figure 6.10 Y chart about what Mere knows, and would like to know about robots

Turn on Robot (on)
Press R 90 (for turning right 90 degrees)
Press F and 10 (for forward 10 steps)
IF robot meets a block THEN Press B and 10 (to go backwards) ... Press L 90 ... Press F and 10
IF robot does not meet a block THEN Press L 90 (for turning left 90 degrees)
Press F and 10 (for forward 10 steps)
Press GO

Figure 6.11 Emily's program for her robot using IF and THEN statements

Turn on Robot (on)
Press R 90 (for turning right 90 degrees)
Press L 90 (for turning left 90 degrees)
Press F 10 (for forward 10 steps)
Press R 90 (for turning right 90 degrees)
Press L 90 (for turning left 90 degrees)
Press B 10 (to move her robot backwards 10 steps)
REPEAT 5 TIMES
Turn off Robot (off)
Press GO

Figure 6.12 Emily's program for making her robot dance using a REPEAT function

1	Switch on			**9**	Press	↱	1-8-0
2	Press	▲	1	**10**	Press	▲	1
3	Press	↰	9-0	**11**	Press	↰	9-0
4	Press	▲	2	**12**	Press	▲	2
5	Press	↱	9-0	**13**	Press	↱	9-0
6	Press	▲	1	**14**	Press	▲	1-1
7	Press	↱	9-0	**15**	Press		GO
8	Press	▲	2				

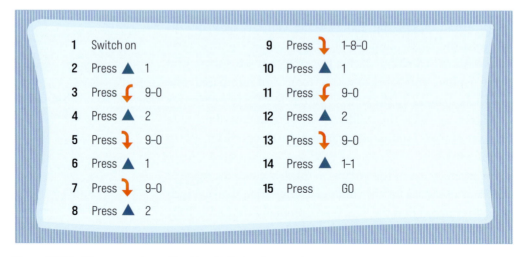

Figure 6.13 Brett's program for making his robotic toy do a rap dance

Programming games

Form a group of three – a card writer (programmer), Freddo frog searcher and caller (processing unit that tells the searcher what to do).

Using the cards, prepare a list of commands (one command per card) that will allow your Freddo frog searcher to navigate through the square grid to the end, where a Freddo frog is waiting for the winner.

The biggest challenge will be avoiding the other children who are also engaged in the same challenge. Only one child is allowed on a square at a time.

The first person through the maze wins the Freddo frog and shares the winnings with their group.

The card writer prepares the cards with input from the group. The caller reads out to the Freddo frog searcher what is on the cards. The Freddo frog searcher follows the actions on the cards.

Think about the most efficient way to go through the grid. Only have one instruction per card. Hint: you could include 'repeat' and 'if then' commands.

Download 6.1
Programming games

Figure 6.14 Design brief for the Freddo frog challenge

The great debate: Ethics and digital technologies

As the children explored the robotic toys and discussed robots, a range of highly motivated questions emerged around the concept 'What if robots had feelings?' To support the children's thinking, Jackie engineered a debate between the children (Figure 6.15).

Debate: What if robots had feelings?

Pros
Robots are mechanical device they had been made for people they make things and clean thing they help us do thing and that's all. I don't think robots have feelings if they did they would do what we say. They would get angry and turn and greet us. They would make cars. Won't do their work. If they had feelings they would cry and blow up pice would be ever were that's why I don't think robots have feelings.

Cons
I think robots do have feelings. If they didn't why would they do want we tell them to because they love us or if they don't they don't get payed theyre be whating for a long time they mite cry I haven't seen one. But I haven't seen a robot be for. So that's barly why. That why I think robot have feeling.

Figure 6.15 If robots had feelings

In preparation for the debate, teams were set up and research was done in order to put forward the pros and cons of this question. The children then voted. The children also debated whether robots could replace teachers (Figures 6.16 and 6.17).

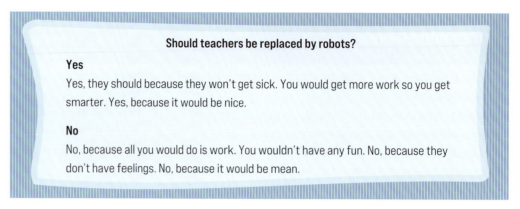

Figure 6.16 Should teachers be replaced by robots?

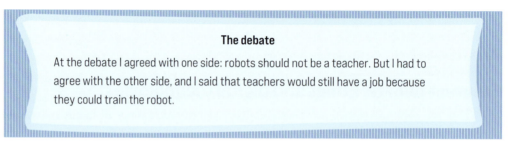

Figure 6.17 The debate – what Laura thought

When taken together, it is possible to see that Jackie introduced the children to a project that drew on personal (do robots have feelings), ethical (should robots replace teachers) and prior understandings (Y chart) to locate developing competencies in computational thinking of the children. She created a challenge (Freddo frog) to motivate the children to code the robot with a specific purpose, and this supported them to work out different ways to represent their thinking, enact their digital solutions, debug and successfully undertake their challenge. The children demonstrated that they were working towards the achievement standards through Jackie's project on robotics (Table 6.1).

PEDAGOGICAL REFLECTION 6.4

How different pedagogical models work

Consider the different pedagogical models used in the two examples – Charina used a Conceptual PlayWorld and Jackie used a Y chart.

- What did each of these approaches enable for the teaching?
- What were the different outcomes you noted?

Looking inside an early childhood centre: Preschoolers

Highfield (2010a) argues that robotic toys – or 'techno-toys' – offer many possibilities for learning in classrooms. There are a range of ways to classify these 'techno-toys':

- screen-based toys
- moveable toys
- responsive toys.

Following her own research, Highfield (2010b) suggests that there are three ways to think about how to embed robotic toys into classrooms:

1. *structured tasks*, such as when a teacher leads how the robots will be used in activities (e.g. the teacher models movements of the robot and children try to work out the steps)
2. *exploratory activities*, such as when children use their prior understandings to interact with the toys (e.g. an open challenge – Can you race your robots to the end of the Olympic circuit?)
3. *extended tasks*, which is where the experiences are initiated by the children and expanded on in relation to prior learning (e.g. children use their knowledge of how robots move to program a treasure hunt on a floor map or on a screen).

In the case example that follows, Vicki has introduced into her preschool different robotic toys that the children have brought in from home.

Exploratory activities: At group time, Vicki placed all the toys in the middle of the circle, then invited the children to talk about their experiences of robotic toys. Vicki documented the children's ideas (Figure 6.18).

> What do you know about robots?
> - Robots don't sleep.
> - Robots keep working, they don't need to stop for food.
> - Robots don't get bored.

Vicki invited the children to explore how robots move. As part of their explorations, Vicki invited them to talk about any questions they had.

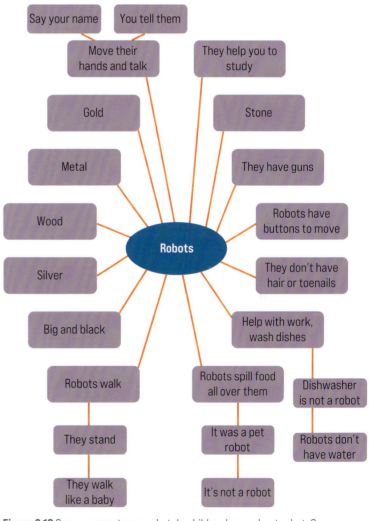

Figure 6.18 Group concept map: what do children know about robots?

What do we want to know about robots?

- Do they like to eat oil?
- How do they move?
- Can they talk?
- Do they have feelings?
- What time do robots go to bed?

The questions acted as a framework for the children's investigations, setting the foundations for computational thinking to emerge. To support this, Vicki set up block mazes during free choice time in the preschool and, together with interested children, worked out how to move the robots through the mazes. The children later designed their own mazes and challenges by inviting other children to join them and test out the codes they had created and additional problems that emerged, such as:

- My bird robot (robot with feathers added) cannot find her mother. Can you help her – as per *Are You my Mother?* by P.D. Eastman (1960)?
- Can you make a map of the farmyard for my chicken robot to follow, so she gets home in time for dinner – as per *Rosie's Walk* by Pat Hutchins (1967)?

SPOTLIGHT 6.5 — Children collaborating while coding robots

Recent research by Kuperman, Aladjem and Mioduser (2018) investigated two different scenarios for children collaborating when coding robots (Kinderbot) to move around a block maze in a preschool.

Scenario 1

In groups of three, preschool children designed their maze, then designed and built their robot. Using a desktop computer, one child entered the commands while the other children stood over the robot and called back to the child programmer. For instance, one child followed the robot and called back to the child at the computer the commands using technical language, such as, 'Forward two steps'.

The children appeared to go through three modes of activity as they programmed the robot.

- Mode 1: immediate execution command-by-command
- Mode 2: immediate execution of a sequence of commands
- Mode 3: planning and programming a script.

Debugging

Due to the child programmer being spatially at a distance from the robot, the strategy used was to correct the robot through writing another sequence of programming steps and then to test it out. Kuperman, Aladjem and Mioduser (2018) term this coding approach 'replacement'.

Scenario 2

As with Scenario 1, the preschool children were placed into groups of three. They designed their maze, then designed and built their robot. The children used an iPad to control their robot. One child held the iPad and stood over the robot, entering the commands, while the other two children made encouraging calls to the coders from the side, such as, 'Yes, it is going well. The robot is moving' as the children squealed with delight.

Debugging

With the mobile device, the child coder appeared to go through the same three phases identified by Kuperman, Aladjem and Mioduser (2018); however, due to the in situ nature of the debugging, it seemed that the child coder immediately corrected the program with small tweaks. This they termed 'counterbalancing'.

Kuperman, Aladjem and Mioduser (2018) found that the children who used the desktop computer rather than the mobile device (iPad) used more technical language when coding the robot and acted more collaboratively when coding (calling out instructions to each other). They termed this the 'desktop program-first-then-run' approach. With the mobile device, however, this approach disappeared and the coding was 'in situ'. The actions of the coder encompassed both the spatial environment and the robot's behaviour as if in unity. This suggests that the coding becomes 'almost wearable' (p. 81) – that is, the child who is doing the coding embodies the actions of the robot as they enter the commands and then observe and adjust the results. The other children in the group encourage and look on, rather than actively participating in collaborative coding.

In the next section, one of the most challenging dimensions of introducing digital technologies into early childhood education will be examined: the development of computational thinking for toddlers. As you read the last case example, think back to Charina's Conceptual PlayWorld, Jackie's Y chart, and Vicki's robotics maze play, and consider the progression of computational thinking over time (see Table 6.1).

Looking inside an early childhood centre: Toddlers

Computational thinking for the early childhood period – with its focus on problem-solving, where infants, toddlers and preschools create solutions using digital technologies – can be realised in the areas of toys, digital and printed photo sorting, and action card games, as detailed below.

Toddler toys

- Infants and toddlers, together with their educators, explore a range of push and pull toys, some of which have battery powered features for programming musical tunes.
- Key questions can be posed during exploration with each toy, such as:
  – What can this toy do (especially for infants – winding, pushing, pulling, squeezing, sucking, blowing and so on to make the toys move/interact)?
  – Can we put all the toys together that do the same things?
  – Can we draw a picture of what we want the toy to do, then try to make it do it? Can we draw some signs?
  – Let's draw a road with chalk on the carpet/cement path. Can we make our toys go along the road we have drawn?

- What are the steps we have to remember to make it go down our road?
- Can we pretend to be this toy and move the same way? Let's try to get X [child] to move like this toy. What might we tell them to do? Can we make some pictures to show this? Let's try to find others who can do this by showing them our cards.

Digital and printed photo sorting

- Infants and toddlers can take digital photographs of the things that are important in their everyday world and document them in digital frames for others to view, assemble them in printable form on display boards or laminate photos onto cards for sorting, discussing and sharing with others.
- Key questions can be posed when looking at the photographs, so they can be organised according to criteria, or the problem set up by the educator; these might include:
  - Can we find all the photos of you?
  - How might we show what we did today – what you did first, then second, etc.?
  - Let's find all the photos of our group and put them together on the wall.
  - Let's find a quicker way to sort the photos so we have them ready at the end of the day to show the families. We could work together with Toddler A finding all the … and Toddler B finding the …

Action card games

- The educator takes photographs of the infants and toddlers in the centre engaged in different everyday actions (e.g. sleeping, jumping, singing, crawling) and creates laminated cards showing one action per child on each card. These cards are then used by the toddlers and preschoolers to create a sequence of actions (e.g. a set of five actions), which the children can design in the order they want, including duplicates (two cards that are the same). Preschoolers could draw pictures to add to their sequence of steps. The children then invite other children to follow their action cards – onlookers check whether they get it right.
- The action cards could also be used as a transition from group time to outside time, where the educator shows a series of cards, and small groups follow the steps as they jump, crawl and hop out the door.
- Action cards could be used in the outdoor area too, but with the added complexity of suggesting 'directions' for the hopping, jumping and so on through adding arrow cards, a stop sign, a give-way sign and so on. The educator or the child can initiate and design the sequence.

When playing with the toys, action cards and photographs, these infants and toddlers are organising the toys, cards or photographs (data) logically, breaking down problems into parts, interpreting patterns and models, and designing and implementing their cards (or algorithms). This is computational thinking for infants and toddlers, but with guided support by the educator.

As suggested in the Early Years Learning Framework (AGDE, 2022, p. 15), educators 'know children engage with popular culture, media and digital technologies so they build partnerships with families and others to keep children safe and families aware of e-safety information'. Educators also support 'the integration of popular culture, media and digital technologies which add to children's multimodal play (AGDE, 2022, p. 22).

Technologies are the diverse range of products that make up the designed world of infants, toddlers and preschoolers. These products extend beyond artefacts designed and developed by people to include processes, systems, services and environments. Toys, cards and photographs are some examples. Can you think of other resources by which infants and toddlers are surrounded that you could use for supporting computational thinking?

The Early Years Learning Framework (AGDE, 2022) invites educators to plan to support children to become confident and involved learners through Outcome 4. The document suggests that this is evident when children:

- explore their environment through asking questions, experimenting, investigating and using digital technologies
- use a range of strategies and digital tools to organise and represent mathematical and scientific thinking
- use a range of media to express their ideas through the arts, e.g. clay, drawing, paint, digital technologies. (AGDE, 2022, p. 53)

Educators promote digital learning of all children when they, for example, model the use of digital technologies and media to assist children to investigate and document their findings (AGDE, 2022, p. 54) but also in Outcome 1 (Children develop knowledgeable confident self-identities, and a positive sense of self-worth). This is evident when children 'share with others how they have learned to use digital technologies' (AGDE, 2022, p. 34) as shown in Figure 6.19, where two children draw and explain, 'We press L. That is for Laura you know.'

Table 6.6 provides an overview of what digital learning looks like for children from birth to 5 years (Column 1) and how educators and teachers support their learning (Column 2).

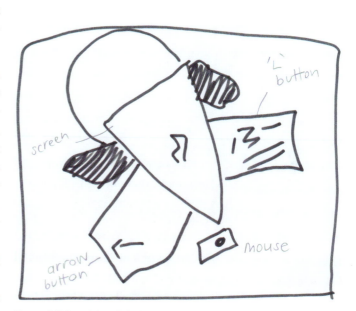

Figure 6.19 Imagining digital solutions

Table 6.6 Children resource their own learning through connecting with people, place, technologies and natural and processed materials

This is evident when children, for example:	Educators promote this learning for all children when they, for example:
• identify technologies and their use in everyday life • incorporate real or imaginary technologies as features of their play • use digital technologies to access images and information, explore diverse perspectives and make sense of their world • develop simple skills to operate digital devices, such as turning on and taking a photo with a tablet	• acknowledge technologies are a feature of children's lives and, as such, will be a feature of their imaginative and investigative play • provide children with access to a range of technologies • integrate technologies across the curriculum and into children's multimodal play experiences and projects • teach skills and techniques and encourage children to use technologies to explore new information and represent their ideas

Table 6.6 (cont.)

This is evident when children, for example:	Educators promote this learning for all children when they, for example:
• use digital technologies and media for creative expression (e.g. designing, drawing, composing) • engage with technologies and media for fun and social connection • identify basic icons and keys (e.g. delete button) and use them to support their navigation (e.g. click, swipe, home, scroll) and understand these terms • adopt collaborative approaches in their learning about and with digital technologies	• encourage collaborative learning about and through technologies between children, and children and educators • provide opportunities for children to have access to different forms of communication technologies • research topics and search for information with children • teach children critical reflection skills and encourage them to evaluate the quality and trustworthiness of information sources • have opportunities to develop their own knowledge and understanding of appropriate digital technology use and safety with children and families • assist children to have a basic understanding that the internet is a network that people use to connect and source information

Source: AGDE (2022, p. 63).

Have you noticed these outcomes and indicators of learning in early learning settings? How might these be realised for infants and toddlers? In your view, what might be an indicator of computational thinking in Table 6.6? Could you re-write or add an indicator that shows both what computational thinking in action (Column 1) and what an educator or teacher would do to promote this learning (Column 2)? When you look at what is written in the Australian Curriculum (ACARA, 2023) for computational thinking, what might be evidence of early progression of learning of computational thinking for children in the preschool years (see Pedagogical Reflection 6.5)?

PEDAGOGICAL REFLECTION 6.5

How does computational thinking progress?

After reading the case examples, return to the comments you made in Pedagogical Reflection 6.2. Now consider:

- What core concepts were evident in the case examples?
- How did the teachers create the motivating conditions for children's development of computational thinking? What was unique to:
    - **a** toddlers
    - **b** preschoolers
    - **c** Year 5 and 6 students?

Record your analysis.

Summary

This chapter has considered computational thinking across the birth to 12 years age span. This chapter and the previous one have brought together some key aspects of digital technologies. Go back to Pedagogical Reflection 5.1 and consider whether your position has changed with regard to:

- the use of digital technologies in the community
- the place of digital technologies in the home
- the amount of screen time children should have
- how teachers should use digital technologies in the classroom or early childhood centre.

This chapter has shown how an exploration of digital technologies by young children can lead to thinking in new ways. It looked at how children can program robots and robotic toys. For younger children, this meant experimenting with very simple, step-by-step procedures to explore programmable devices (Foundation to Year 2 – ACARA, 2023) and for older children it meant implementing digital solutions as simple visual programs involving branching, iteration (repetition) and user input (Years 5 and 6 – ACARA, 2023).

The chapter revealed that issues of ethics are important questions for older children too, as shown when the Years 5 and 6 children debated what might happen if robots had feelings or if robots replaced teachers. Examples illustrate the depth of children's thinking when examining digital technologies.

The next sets of chapters will examine core concepts taught in the specific technologies contexts of:

- Engineering principles and systems – Materials and technologies specialisations
- Food and fibre production – Food specialisations.

Acknowledgements

Special thanks go to Vicki (preschoolers), Kay (toddlers), Jackie (Year 5/6) and Charina Pumpa from Redeemer Lutheran Primary School for their work on technologies education, captured through the case studies presented in this chapter, to Bas Gerald for photos of the Wild Robot unit and to Dr Rebecca Lewis for supporting the Wild Robot curriculum project.

CHAPTER 7

Technologies contexts: Food and fibre production and food specialisations

Introduction

Chapters 5 and 6 examined the subject Digital Technologies in detail. In this chapter and those that follow, the contexts of Technologies will be studied: food and fibre production and food specialisations (this chapter); and engineering principles, and systems and materials and technologies specialisations (Chapters 8 and 9). This chapter will look specifically at food and fibre production and food specialisations (Figures 7.1–7.3). In the process of studying fibre production, the fashion industry will be explored.

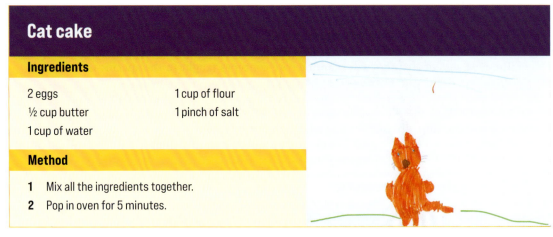

Figure 7.1 Designing recipes – the cat cake

Figure 7.2 Lani is inspired to become a fashion designer.
Source: Trisha Gleeson and Lani.

Figure 7.3 Fashion design
Source: Trisha Gleeson and Lani.

Approaches to technologies education

A defining feature of technologies is the range of contexts that exist for learning. Included in these are food and fibre production and food specialisations. As discussed in the Australian Curriculum: Technologies, the technologies context focuses on the process of producing food and fibre as natural materials for the design and development of a range of products, which brings with it many opportunities for exploring concepts (ACARA, 2023). But what does this really mean for teaching in classrooms and early childhood settings? The scope and sequence detailed for food and fibre production and food specialisations helps with establishing the potential content to be covered in the particular year levels (Table 7.1).

Table 7.1 Technologies context: Food and fibre production; Food specialisations scope and sequence

Context	Foundation	Years 1 and Year 2	Years 3 and 4	Years 5 and 6
Food and fibre production	No explicit content description	Explore how plants and animals are grown for food, clothing and shelter (AC9TDE2K03)	Describe the ways of producing food and fibre (AC9TDE4K03)	Explain how and why food and fibre are produced in managed environments (AC9TDE6K03)
Food specialisations	No explicit content description	Explore how food can be selected and prepared for healthy eating (AC9TDE2K04)	Describe the ways food can be selected and prepared for healthy eating (AC9TDE4K04)	Explain how the characteristics of foods influence selection and preparation for healthy eating (AC9TDE6K04)

Source: ACARA (2023).

PEDAGOGICAL REFLECTION 7.1

Teaching about fibre and food

How might you teach young children about fibre or food from a technologies perspective? What might be some of the challenges you would face in designing and teaching a unit or a design-based project on food or fibre? List your ideas and potential solutions below:

Challenge 1:_____
Solution 1:_____
Challenge 2:_____
Solution 2:_____
Challenge 3:_____
Solution 3:_____

ACTIVITY 7.1

Planning for fibre technologies in support of food specialisations and food and fibre production

Design a unit or design-based project for one of the year levels in Table 7.1. The following are some topics you could use:

- Design a model of a pig farm.
- Design a new 'Free-Range Pork' brand.
- Design and make a solar oven.
- Design and produce a scale model of a fence that will keep sheep and cattle in a paddock.

- Design and make a water filter.
- Design and make a long-handled dip net for picking up fish out of the water after having been caught.
- Design a model to simulate the process of moving water from a source to an irrigation channel.
- Design a tree-planting program for the school grounds.
- Design a forest plantation for a farmer.
- Design and make a nesting box.
- Design and make paper.
- Design some environmentally friendly packaging.
- Design a marketing campaign for dairy products.
- Design a new process to do an everyday task that relates to food and fibre production.
(Primary Industries Education Foundation Australia, 2015, p. 22)

Consider the following:

1. What concepts would you want to introduce?
2. What pedagogical approach might you adopt?
3. How might you evaluate the unit of work? That is, what kind of tool might you use?
4. How would you know if you were successful? That is, what kind of evidence would you gather using that tool and how would you know it was assessing what you were interested in finding out?
5. If you chose to design a unit for Years 5 and 6:
   - How might you explore *sustainability and fashion* as part of this unit of work?
   - How could ethics and fashion be considered? Revisit previous chapters.
   - Would marketing be an important component?

Web activity 7.1
Investigating technologies for food and fibre production

The sections that follow explore the pedagogical approaches available to teach food and fibre production and food specialisations by looking at case examples of practices in classrooms and early childhood centres. Specifically, we will examine practices in the context of the literature on what constitutes effective practices for technologies education. Before introducing the case studies, the research on concepts in fibre production, as noted in the literature for the fashion industry, will be examined.

Approaches to technological contexts: Background information on fibre and fashion

When thinking about fibre, a number of key areas need to be considered as background reading for teaching, including:

- pattern-making and sewing
- sustainability and fashion
- ethics and fashion
- fashion and marketing
- YarnCAD.

Although there are many other areas that could be covered, this chapter will explore only these, to gain some knowledge of the concepts that underpin fibre (Figure 7.4).

Pattern-making and sewing

Pattern-making is the craft of preparing a design of a garment in 2D form and creating a pattern that is laid onto fabric and used to guide the cut of the fabric. Pattern-making is an important design skill that can be taught. In schools, this might be done when children design and make clothes for dolls, or when early childhood centre children make paper clothing for their paper dolls.

In the world of fashion and fibre, Ashdown (2013) argues that the skills needed for learning about pattern-making include:

- understanding the contours of the body (adding darts and seams)
- capturing shape (truing, notches and seam allowances)
- fitting the body or dress form (ease, line, grain, balance and set)
- maintaining the garment silhouette while choosing different style lines (shifting darts and seams)
- fitting active body parts (creating sleeve and pants patterns)
- adding fullness (gathers, flair, pleats and cowls)
- creating shape within the fabric panels (eased seams and tailoring techniques)
- interactions between fabric and form (bias cut and fabric properties).

Figure 7.4 Technologies context of food and fibre production – the fashion industry, the catwalk and the design of costumes create motivating conditions for learning about sustainability and fashion.
Source: Beau and Emma.

These are complex ideas. Which do you think might be relevant for young children to learn? Pattern-making is just one key dimension of studying fibre. Joining fabric through sewing is another key skill and concept for working with fibre. Like other forms of technology, sewing involves processes. For instance, the sewing or construction process involves:

- joining fabric (various seaming techniques)
- finishing the edges from which the garment falls (facings and interfacings)
- creating edges that fall from the garment (hems)
- fastening the garment (zippers, buttons and buttonholes, hooks and eyes, and snaps)
- care and durability issues (finishing seams and creating linings) (Ashdown, 2013, pp. 115–16).

What processes or construction skills are needed for young children making dolls, puppets, hats, party accessories and other artistic creations that might support their play or social development? In Chapter 2, a number of design briefs were shown that required children to be able to work with fibre. Although some of the skills detailed above may not be taught to primary-aged children, some of them are relevant when children are designing and making dolls' clothes and in other design briefs that use fibre. For instance, a good fit means thoughtful designing, where patterns include darts and contours. A fuller fit means designs that include pleats and gathers. What aspects of pattern-making and sewing do you believe are important for young children to learn during the process of studying technologies?

Sustainability and fashion

A focus on sustainability through design in fashion and the manufacturing industry more generally has recently emerged as an area of importance (Mukendi et al., 2020). For instance, zero-waste design practices in fashion are a sustainable way of manufacturing products. Zero waste means designers and pattern-makers cut fabric so less is wasted. Children who use templates on colourful card, fabric or paper can also consider the idea of zero waste. This is not something that children will necessarily consider. Often, they take a template – such as a star when making Christmas decorations – and place it in the middle of a large sheet of card. They then cut into the card, discarding most of the material. Children can be introduced to sustainable ways of working when designing and making their creations. By placing the templates or patterns carefully (or designing them to suit the paper sizes and shapes), waste is minimised and children learn important skills for supporting sustainability. In Chapter 2, a values-based approach was discussed, where students brought in objects they were happy to discard and used these as their source materials for designing and making costumes.

Even in the fashion industry, it has been shown that designers and creators do not always work together to develop a sustainable approach to their work. Carrico and Kim (2014) argue that by bringing together the designers and the pattern-maker, a more holistic approach to creating garments is fostered during both the design and manufacturing phases. They suggest that zero-waste design practices are not yet commonly used in the fashion industry.

The fashion industry does employ different methods for minimising waste, such as using software to plan the placement of pattern pieces for cutting (which is much like solving a jigsaw puzzle on the computer) or cutting multiple sizes and styles together, providing increased chances for pattern pieces to interlock efficiently. Those methods, however, do not completely eliminate the waste of fabric that ends up on the cutting-room floor – the scraps can be recycled (denim insulation) or repurposed (appliqués, pillow stuffing), designing garments that produce no waste in cutting (Carrico and Kim, 2014, p. 58).

How might the concept of zero waste be fostered in classrooms? Children working on their technology projects in groups have the opportunity to discuss collectively the idea of zero waste, and to build this idea into their design solutions. Zero waste is a useful concept for children when studying fibre in technologies education. Children could be introduced to zero waste by noting how this concept is already used across cultures. For example, when considering traditional practices in many countries, it is possible to note that a range of different cultural practices already exist that use zero waste design practices – for example:

- the Indian sari – a length of cloth is draped and wrapped around the body without being cut or stitched
- the Japanese kimono – made of cut and sewn pieces of fabric.

These patterns for clothing leave little waste. Western fashion, with its tailored look, draws on contours and darts to present tight-fitting garments. This Western design approach to fitted clothing reveals a real need to develop manufacturing practices that employ zero-waste design principles. What other cultural practices across countries that do or do not support zero waste might go beyond fibre and production technologies?

Employing zero-waste design practices in fashion means that both aesthetics and function are conceptualised simultaneously. The design approaches to zero waste for sustainable ways of manufacturing are:

- tessellation (one shape that repeats by fitting perfectly together)
- jigsaw and embedded jigsaw (where the pattern is made to fit within a length of fabric)
- multiple cloth approach (two or more patterns are designed to be cut from the same fabric length)
- patterns in combination from the same cloth
- minimal cut (the garment is designed through draping with limited fabric cuts).

Children already explore tessellations in school. Applying these mathematical ideas to fashion projects for designing and producing dolls' clothes, for example, gives meaning and a useful context for learning about the concept of tessellation. Children explore a jigsaw approach when cutting paper and card (not just fabric), which gives them new ways of reducing waste during craft work and other activities at home in their everyday lives.

Considering pattern-making and zero-waste principles in the primary years adds complexity to children's design capabilities and deepens their technological understandings. Go back to the design briefs from previous chapters and see how the concept of zero waste might improve the technological practices of children. How might you add this concept into those design briefs so that children work with the criterion of zero waste?

Paper dolls

Paper dolls and the range of clothes and accessories that can be created for them give children opportunities to explore a range of fashion possibilities, promoting the principle of multiplicative thinking. For instance, children can explore concretely the possibilities for different 'outfits'. They should list all the possibilities and count the number of outcomes for the range of clothing and accessories. Ura, Stein-Barana and Munhoz (2011, p. 33) suggest that:

> This material allows students to construct knowledge about the multiplicative principle in an active way. If, for instance, the student separates three blouses and four shorts, the event A would be the three blouses ($m = 3$) and event B the four shorts ($n = 4$). Therefore, the number of possible combinations of shirt and shorts is as follows: $m \times n = 3 \times 4 = 12$

When children design their own patterns for making the clothing for their paper dolls, they can explore a range of ways of laying out the pattern on the coloured paper. Similarly, felt board dolls can be made and put onto boards. Children can use a range of different cloths to make clothing and accessories, and even street or farm scenes, and place these on the felt boards. It is possible to introduce the zero-waste principle during the cutting out of the fabric or coloured paper. Children can also explore the 'stickability' of the fabrics to the felt board. When groups of children are laying out their patterns on the cloth, the idea of tessellating shapes can be applied, as the children can discuss how they might change their designs so that they can fit better onto the cloth and reduce waste.

Issues of sustainability and ethics can also be discussed. Finding out the names of fabrics (investigating their own clothing) and searching online to see whether the materials are natural or synthetic, identifying where they are made, and analysing the production processes all contribute to a deeper understanding of fibre production.

Through examining a range of natural fibres to see how they were originally used in societies (and returning to use of these in recent years), children have the opportunity to see how fibre production has changed and continues to change in communities. Children can also explore the source of the natural materials – paper (forestry), wool (history of merino wool), hemp (alternative and sustainable product for paper and fabric) and so on. Sustainability is therefore clearly more than considering zero waste. Thinking about the type of materials used, their suitability and their ecological footprint provides a holistic context for sustainability. Ashdown (2013, p. 119) argues that 'the current shift to local, more meaningful and sustainable clothing forms will initiate a change in our industry'. Key ideas and questions about sustainability were introduced in Chapter 3, where the concept of preferred futures was discussed. Return to that chapter to see what other sustainability concepts might improve the study of fibres for primary-aged children. The next section turns from sustainability to ethics in the study of fibres – clearly a context of technologies that is not values-neutral.

Figure 7.5 shows a design brief and teaching rationale for making paper dolls.

Design your own paper doll

1. Trace around the doll.
2. Make a pattern for the doll's top.
3. Make a pattern for the pants.
4. Place both patterns together on your chosen 'fabric' (coloured paper).
5. Can you move the patterns around so that you do not waste too much fabric? Keep changing and moving the patterns.

Figure 7.5 Design brief for making paper dolls

Ethics and fashion

A growing community concern is the exploitation of children in poor developing countries for the sewing of garments and the development of accessories (such as embroidering of scarves). This is just one example of the ethical issues facing countries that import cheaply produced clothing. Orzada and Cobb (2011) have sought to institute projects that examine ethics in the fashion industry. They address ethics through a problem-based learning format, where students are challenged to design and produce garments, drawing on ethical principles in collaboration with the Fair Labor Association. They suggest (p. 173) that ethical design includes:

- a choice of materials that benefit the environment
- a choice of suppliers with verifiable fair labour practices
- responsible interactions and exchanges between the buyers/designers and suppliers.

What constitutes ethical fashion and how might this be addressed with young children? Orzada and Cobb (2011) argue that ethical fashion goes beyond simply incorporating organic cotton into a clothing line; rather, they suggest that, 'Ethical fashion represents an approach to the design, sourcing and manufacture of clothing which maximises benefits to people and communities while minimising the impact on the environment' (Ethical Fashion Forum, 2018). What has made it confusing is that the terms 'ethical fashion', 'socially responsible apparel business' and 'sustainable fashion' have been used frequently, but essentially mean the same thing. What might be some other ethical issues to consider when exploring fibre and fashion with young children? Chapter 10 will show how children as young as 6 years of age can, with the right support, discuss the ethics of purchasing bags that were made by children in a poor majority country.

The next section examines another aspect of fibre and production technologies: yarn. This product is a 'hidden' material that is simply taken for granted. This content is relevant for you as a teacher, rather than content designed to be taught to young children.

YarnCAD

CAD is the acronym for computer assisted design. Cassidy, Grishanov and Hsieh (2008) have shown how a CAD interface can be used to help learning about fashion and textiles, specifically in the area of yarn design and production. In their research, students were asked to design their own yarn and then to try to simulate a given real yarn through the use of YarnCAD. YarnCAD is designed to close the gap between the textile designer and the technologist as they jointly produce new yarn. Cassidy, Grishanov and Hsieh (2008, p. 13) state that the 'designer expresses his [or her] ideas about new yarn in a form of visual image whereas the technologist thinks in terms of technical specification of yarns and fabrics'. Areas for joint focus for technologists and textile designers in yarn are:

- diameter
- hairiness
- twist
- density.

Thinking about the design of the yarn is an important part of fibre and production technologies. Yarn can also be thought about from an environmental perspective. For instance, in New Zealand, a new yarn made from possum fur was designed specifically to help the environment. Possums are viewed as a real pest in New Zealand because of their destruction of the environment. They are out of their natural habitat and have grown in size and number:

> Introduced to New Zealand in 1837 from Australia and with no natural predators, the possum is New Zealand's biggest ecological threat. Possums occupy 95% of New Zealand, with an estimated population of 60 million. They are legally classified as pests. (Merinomink™, 2018).

Through clever technology, a new yarn that uses possum fur was developed, with the following characteristics noted by one of the manufacturers:

> Brushtail Possum fibre has a hollow structure, this means the fibre has an extremely high warmth to weight ratio. Air is trapped both within the fibre and in the fabric. When blended with high crimp, fine Merino, it creates a luxuriously soft, lightweight

and very warm garment. The fibre has no scales so resists pilling and has outstanding durability and excellent performance characteristics. (Merinomink™, 2018)

The result is a yarn known as Merinomink™ (possum fur, merino wool and silk). Designers and technologies can be found in many areas of the fibre and production technologies in the fashion industry. For young children, exploring different kinds of yarn that are used for specific purposes, such as selecting gold yarn for making cards and gifts, is relevant. However, studying yarn in itself may not be something specifically planned for and done in primary schools.

The next section looks at a topic that is of interest to children in the latter years of primary school: fashion and marketing.

Fashion and marketing

Foster and Yaoyuneyong (2014) have brought together marketing and fashion merchandising in order to give students the opportunity to engage with real-world businesses through introducing *client-based projects* where the students work with real companies and discuss real projects. In these contexts, students develop insights into client needs and become familiar with new concepts, such as 'competitors'. Foster and Yaoyuneyong (2014, p. 154) argue that, through bringing together marketing with fashion, a context is created that supports thinking and acting in new ways where professional collaborations and 'problem-solving skills, including effective teamwork, critical thinking/reasoning, innovative thinking/creativity, and information gathering and analysis' are featured. In reviewing the literature, they found that when *client-based projects* were introduced to students:

- learners took more ownership of their learning
- learners developed workplace skills
- learners' motivation increased
- realism was introduced into the classroom
- concepts came to life in the classroom.

The literature suggests that client-based projects give students the 'ability to translate customer needs into product characteristics' (Drechsler, Natter and Leeflang, 2013, p. 298). Some ideas about customer or client needs were introduced in Chapter 4, and further detail is given in Chapter 9, where project management is considered.

---

e-textiles

SPOTLIGHT 7.1

There is growing support for innovation in design in fabrics through the introduction of e-textiles (Litts et al., 2017; von Mengersen and Wilkinson, 2020; Wu, Mechael and Carmichael, 2021). For instance, von Mengersen and Wilkinson (2020) draw attention to a new textiles economy – redesigning fashion's future.

The Ellen MacArthur Foundation (2017), an organisation dedicated to promoting an economy dedicated to 'restorative and regenerative design', proposes that:

> Fashion is a vibrant industry that employs hundreds of millions, generates significant revenues, and touches almost everyone, everywhere. Since the 20th century, clothing has

> increasingly been considered as disposable, and the industry has become highly globalised, with garments often designed in one country, manufactured in another and sold worldwide at an ever-increasing pace. This trend has been further accentuated over the past 15 years by rising demand from a growing middle class across the globe with higher disposable income, and the emergence of the 'fast fashion' phenomenon, leading to a doubling in production over the same period.
>
> Van Dijk, Savelsbergh and van der Meij (2020), drawing on the literature, discuss e-textiles as stitched electronic circuitry in textiles and note that children learn circuitry and coding and teachers better understand children's abilities within the context of design. In addition, von Mengersen and Wilkinson (2020) draw attention to the Future Fabrics Virtual Expo in which e-textiles are featured.
>
> The Sustainable Angle (2018) argues that:
>
>> The Future Fabrics Virtual Expo is now a more advanced online research and sourcing platform, with increased search capability, and opportunity for direct contact with mills. The fabrics are searchable by categories from fibre type and price, to certification and provenance, and educational background information alongside each fabric makes it a valuable tool for both designers and buyers new to the area of sustainable textiles and materials, as well as those with established sustainable sourcing strategies.
>
> The introduction of e-textiles is considered by Kafai, Fields and Searle (2014) as a form of disruptive technology because it works actively against commonly assumed practices and ways of conceptualising design.

The Australian Curriculum: Technologies (ACARA, 2023) brings forward in the subject of Design and Technologies a content description related to food and fibre production:

> *Content description:* Explain how and why food and fibre are produced in managed environments
>
> *Related elaborations:* Sequencing the process of converting on-farm fibre products into a product suitable for retail sale, for example creating a digital flowchart to record the fibre-to-garment life cycle (fibre, yarn, fabric, garment).

What might learning about fibre production mean for younger children? What might the progression in learning for this context area look like in classrooms across the primary and early childhood years? How could you introduce this content so it is personally meaningful to children? The next section presents case examples of children learning about fibre production. These are pedagogical examples of how fibre can be studied by young children, presented as a series of case studies of fibre for Year 6 children, then for Years 3 and 4 children, followed by infants in the early childhood period. If you return to the design briefs in Chapter 2, you will find classroom examples of clothing design and exhibition (catwalk) for children in Years 5 and 6. We take those ideas one step further in this chapter. Together, these give examples of how fibres can be studied in primary and early childhood classrooms.

Critical materials: Pedagogy of the material world

In line with Keirl's (2020) pedagogy of critiquing, and as suggested by von Mengersen and Wilkinson (2020, p. 3), there is also a critiquing pedagogy of the material world because designers and manufacturers must make material choices. They ask the following moral question:

> What is an 'appropriate relationship' with materials in design education? Each time a person or a child selects a particular material, they engage with another person's culture, their environment, and ecology. There is a life cycle in using materials, from sourcing, to application, usage through to disposal or repurposing.

A life-cycle analysis of materials can be undertaken by children in a very active way. Teachers can use a pedagogy of:

- design-for-sustainability (DFS)
- design-for-environment (DFE).

According to von Mengersen and Wilkinson (2020), these pedagogies can be realised through design topics such as:

- climate injustice
- world food and water shortages
- finite materials economy.

These topics lend themselves to 'a clear circular-economy', which is an 'alternative to a "take, make, waste" linear-economy approach' (von Mengersen and Wilkinson, 2020, p. 4). In addition, there are movements such as:

- design-for-recycling (DFR)
- design-for-disassembly (DFD)
- extended-producer responsibility (EPR)
- design-for-repair, whereby material choices are integral.

This is particularly important in the context of the fashion and textiles industry, where the fast-fashion phenomenon has emerged in recent years. It has become acceptable to order an item of clothing online and to wear it for just one day. There is the need for a counter-scenario of post-growth fashion that sees the repurposing of clothing, but also a critical look at which cloth or materials need excessive care – for example, in cleaning – hence polluting the environment.

Von Mengersen and Wilkinson (2020, p. 14) argue for a

> pedagogy for understanding the material world in which design development (including material testing) and quality prototype construction relies upon a combination of material (including sustainability), technical (construction processes) and social (ethical) knowledge dimensions.

Web activity 7.2
Critiquing pedagogy for materials technologies

Go back to Chapter 4 and consider what this pedagogy might look like. Do any of the tables of questions (Tables 4.1, 4.2 and 4.6) inspire you to think about this critiquing pedagogy that von Mengersen and Wilkinson (2020) and Keirl (2020) have introduced?

Von Mengersen and Wilkinson (2020, p. 5) state that

> a pedagogy for understanding the material world considers the conscious material choices by both educators and students to be a pivotal factor in sustainable design

systems and proposes how Design and Technology educators might collaborate with their students to develop more appropriate relationships with the material world around them informed by principles of ecological sustainability and social justice.

We now turn to case examples.

SPOTLIGHT 7.2

Fashion hub

Figure 7.6 Florence immersed in the digital experience – secret message projected into the classroom
Source: Kelly-Ann Allen.

Helena has transformed her classroom into a design hub for fashion using the long corridor leading to her classroom as a catwalk. It is the beginning of Term 3 and she has been actively engaged in children's conversations about fashion for some time. As the children arrive in the classroom, they are not greeted by the usual classroom layout, but rather have entered the world of fashion. Before they enter, they put on 'critical lenses' and are given a lanyard with a professional role stamped on the front: Designer, Model, Seamstress, Fabrics Engineer, e-Textiles Computer Engineer, Social Media Guru, Communications Consultant, Project Manager, Finance Officer and so on. As they enter, they observe an immersive experience (Figure 7.6) (an interactive board could be used) with images of models walking the catwalk, with all the glitter, pomp and music that might be expected. Drawn to the screen, the children sit and listen as Ameillia and Jacque tell their story of being a fashion designer (Ameillia) and model (Jacque). The story sets the scene for the problem that emerges:

> We are stuck in the fashion industry. We have sent you this secret video message because we need your help. We see many problems with how fibres are produced in managed environments. But now we have to go before we are caught – here is the link to get you started. We will try to send you more secret messages, but hope in the meantime you can research the problem and design a solution. Your new fashion friends.

Link 7.1 Wearable technology

Looking inside a classroom: The fashion industry under the microscope for Year 6 students

Towards the beginning of the chapter (Figure 7.4) we saw Beau wearing a jumper designed by his mum, Emma, which dynamically sets off the yellow dress and pink-topped beanie.

How do families and teachers support their children to have agency in the design of their outfits? Not all children grow up in homes where they can learn to be imaginative, creative and agentic designers of their own fashion as we saw for Beau in Figure 7.4. The Australian Curriculum: Technologies explains that children need to learn 'how fibre is produced in managed environments' (ACARA, 2023). As part of this management, we can introduce values and social needs surrounding fashion. In the case example that follows, we go deeper into the Wardrobe Wonder design brief (Figure 2.13) and superhero catwalk (Figure 2.14) introduced in Chapter 2 and exemplified in practice by Florence in Figure 7.6. Rather than the context of preservice teachers, in this chapter we look at a design-based project that draws on a Conceptual PlayWorld pedagogy (Fleer, 2022a, 2022b) in the context of 10- and 11-year-old children.

Looking inside a classroom: Fibre production in Year 3 – knitting

Many classrooms organise experiences for children that are related to the context of fibres. For instance, Figure 7.7 shows an image of Rowan's knitted bunny and his evaluation. Rowan is in Year 3. He wanted to knit a finger puppet bunny. He needed to find a pattern for creating the right-sized bunny, with instructions he could follow, to select appropriate yarn and needles, and to design the facial features of his bunny (Figure 7.8).

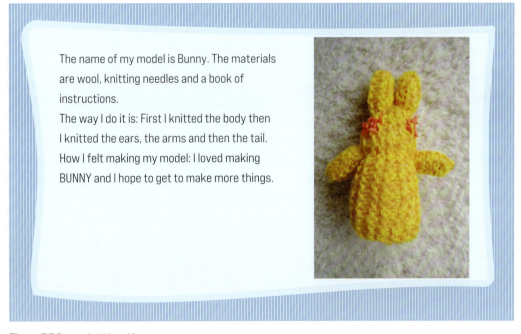

Figure 7.7 Rowan's knitted bunny

> ## Make your own finger puppets
>
> 1. Choose a material with which you would like to work.
> 2. Draw around your finger (or hand) to make a 'pattern'.
> 3. Make a paper pattern for your puppet.
> 4. Use the paper pattern to help you cut out the fabric ready to sew or glue.
> 5. Add your accessories – selecting from cotton, wool, silk and synthetic materials.

Download 7.1 Make your own finger puppets

Figure 7.8 Design brief for making finger puppets

Figure 7.9 French knitting – what might children be interested in creating?

Although Rowan could knit his bunny evenly and successfully produce something he really loved, it is important to select activities that young children can manage with their fingers. Knitting is of great interest to many children, but it is not suitable for all children if they have difficulties coordinating the needles and wool. Another approach suitable for very young children is French knitting. While there are French knitting kits, it is also possible for children to design their own, as shown in Figure 7.9.

As children gain more experience in making finger puppets, the level of design and production can be increased so that children can:

- weave their own fabric by making or using a basic loom
- weave together many different types of yarn to create interesting fabrics (e.g. like Merinomink™)
- sew together different pieces of fabric
- add buttons, and sew basic embroidery threads following their own designs
- design and make accessories using a range of materials and yarn.

In this example, knitting is shown as an activity with some design elements. The project is about producing something, and it was through inviting children to make their own finger puppets that the project became more design based. The experience of making something enabled the children to explore fibres.

Looking inside an early childhood setting: Fibre production in early childhood

An important question to consider is what infants and toddlers are interested in investigating and designing. Fabrics surround young children and form an important part of life and living. How might you find out what children know and can do in relation to fibres? What understandings do the infants and toddlers bring into the early childhood setting?

For infants and toddlers investigating fibre, the focus is on the feel of the different textures, experiencing their characteristics, as shown in Figure 7.10, where a newborn infant feels the fibres in her mother's clothing, and in Figure 7.11, where Catalina experiences the softness and pliability of the fabrics she is stroking.

Preschool children and toddlers can also investigate the fibres in their everyday lives. For instance, inviting children to document their experiences through drawing (preschoolers) or using digital devices (toddlers), gives the educator a real sense of what children know, can do and are interested in regarding fibre. Storyboarding is one such example of how to engage with children's interests (see Figure 7.12). Storyboarding at the level shown in the figure is a foundational step in learning about design processes.

Figure 7.10 Infants also study fibres: Amelia experiences the fibres in her mother's clothing.

Approaches to technological contexts: Background information on food specialisations

Food technology has a long history in the secondary area in Australia, through the Home Economics Institute of Australia (HEIA). The next section looks at food as a specialisation in the Australian Curriculum: Technologies, and considers the central concepts of this technologies context. Taking the same conceptualisation of learning area achievement standard, subject

Figure 7.11 Catalina experiences the softness and pliability of the fabrics she is stroking.

Draw a picture of what you did over the weekend

Getting up

Draw yourself dressed and ready for the weekend.

Breakfast

Draw a picture of the materials you used before and during breakfast (e.g. flannel, tea towel, cotton buds).

Playtime and other things you did

Can you draw what you did before lunch?

Lunchtime

Draw a picture of the materials you used.

Afternoon

Prepare a list of all the materials you used.

Dinner

Draw a picture of the materials you used.

Bedtime

Draw yourself getting ready for bed.

Evaluation

What fibres and fabrics did you use over the weekend? What fabrics were used for washing, drying, clothing, toys?

Figure 7.12 Storyboarding everyday life

Chocolate cake

Ingredients
1 cup of floulwr
1 cup of chocolate
2 eggs
3 cups of warttr
Then pop it in the oven 6 minits.

Figure 7.13 Alex has researched and selected the best recipe for a more sustainable option for cooking a chocolate cake, or it could have been designed for healthy eating – no sugar?

achievement standard and content description for fibre from this chapter, we can use the same elaboration but in the context of food specialisation.

Through a content description lens (ACARA 2023), it is possible to see how to focus on food and engage children in design thinking in the design and technologies context in the areas of food and fibre production and food specialisations. An example is shown of Alex (Figure 7.13), who has researched a range of recipes. With this knowledge, he has designed his own recipe for a chocolate cake that has no sugar. Questions about the source of the chocolate – cacao bean – and the different percentages within the chocolate bars selected at the supermarket could be planned. Additionally, learning whether the cacao bean had been sourced as a sustainable product and about the relative carbon footprint of importing products could support students to begin thinking about how and why foods are produced in managed environments.

Researching recipes in relation to healthy eating brings into focus the content description 'Explain how the characteristics of foods influence selection and preparation for healthy eating' (ACARA, 2023). In designing a recipe without sugar, and in considering the percentage of sugar and cacao in the cup of chocolate, Alex is making informed decisions about healthy eating in terms of the characteristics of the food he is making.

Concerns for healthy eating have emerged over time in relation to food safety (Kansou et al., 2022) and it is in this context that new directions for studying food technologies can be found. For instance, an area that has been around for some time, but that recently has gained more attention, is nanotechnology. Relevant for thinking about packaging and storage of food, with implications for concerns about plastic particles, broadens and stretches what could be considered as food production and associated technologies. Bryksa and Yada (2012, p. 188) state:

> Nanotechnology is the application of scientific knowledge to manipulate and control matter in the nanoscale range to make use of size- and structure-dependent properties and phenomena that are distinct from those at smaller or larger scales.

Nanotechnology in food technologies allows for a detailed study of 'Environmental sources, plant and animal production, release from packaging materials, and food processing aids or equipment surface coatings', which are 'all potential sources of unintentional nanomaterial contamination in foods' (Bryksa and Yada, 2012, p. 188). However, the ability to engage in the analysis of nanomaterials in food is still emerging.

What is becoming more evident is that food technologies are essentially multidisciplinary, covering knowledge in food science, food engineering and food management (Owen, 2020). Food engineering focuses on nutrition, health and security; however, food engineering also covers packaging and logistics, where international rules and guidelines surrounding water, energy, wastes and cost are considered, providing a global scale to food technologies.

The context of food technologies is broad and provides many opportunities for designing diverse activities for children (Slatter and France, 2018). For instance, programs in food technologies should consider:

- diversity and quantity of products
- safety, security along the chain (cold chain, storage, packaging)
- continuous process improvement, with progress in equipment, measurements, renovation of products, trying to get better understanding by research, modelling (Trystram et al., 2011)
- new product development to improve quality/security, to attract consumers
- costs of goods, which must be optimised
- sustainability regarding all considerations of environment, limitations of impacts, selection of raw materials (choice of process, recycling, cleaning).

These considerations are beyond what might be done in an early childhood setting or primary classroom. A more child-centred and effective teaching of food technologies should include:

- a clear statement of the design decisions that children should be making
- a description taken from curriculum that informs children's design decision-making
- details of the activity on a session-by-session basis, where each activity builds towards the final goal
- design specification against evaluation of a product
- the use of digital information
- the integration of food technologies with other subjects.

Slatter and France (2018) argue that there is a real need for food literacy. For instance, they give the example of the death cap, a toxic mushroom that killed three people in Canberra in 2012 because of the confusion between edible field mushrooms and death cap mushrooms. They ask:

- What are the attributes of a food-literate person?
- What components are deemed essential for a food literacy education program?
- What are the important concepts to be planned for in a food literacy program?
- How essential are these concepts for the development of food literacy?

They recommend that a literacy model includes four key characteristics:

- food
- social dimensions
- biological
- environmental.

They also suggest that the program of twenty-first century technological food literacy be based on nutrition science and a philosophy of food technology. A number of suggested components of technological food literacy are shown in Table 7.2 (Slatter and France, 2018, p. 456).

Consider the content of Table 7.2 in relation to key twenty-first century technological food literacy skills, dispositions and knowledge. How does this compare with what is promoted in the Australian Curriculum: Technologies (ACARA, 2023)?

Table 7.2 A conception of twenty-first century technological food literacy

Type	Theme and sub-theme	Component of food literacy	Examples (extracts from Slatter and France, 2018)
Disposition	Authentic	Food preparation from scratch	'I think teaching people basic cooking skills and how to use raw ingredients and make food that tastes good is important' (p. 456)
Knowledge	Culture	Knowledge of the cultural dimension and significance of food	'food is not just about eating. It's used for all sorts of other things in society' (p. 457)
Knowledge	Food systems	Knowledge of the systems that underpin food	'the systems that underpin food production, distribution, advertising, gardening and marketing' (p. 457)

Table 7.2 (cont.)

Type	Theme and sub-theme	Component of food literacy	Examples (extracts from Slatter and France, 2018)
Knowledge	Nutrition	Knowledge of health-giving properties of food	'how to create good health' (p. 457)
Skills	Critical thinking	Critical thinking and decision-making about food	'Learning to question too, I think is very important, that they can look critically at the way in which food is advertised, the way in which it's marketed, and what's in it, like in the millions spent on advertising fast food.' (p.457)
Skills	Hygiene	Food hygiene	'how to handle food … food-borne illness and contamination can generate illness' (p. 457)
Skills	Shopping	Menu planning and food purchasing decisions	'They need to know how to plan ahead and to do it within a budget.' (p. 457)
Skills	Tasting	Sensory experience of food	'Developing a palate and actually tasting a wide variety of foods is an essential.' (p. 457)
Skills	Cooking	Application of cookery skills	'All cooking skills are absolutely essential, far more important than an ability to play the violin, do karate, or swim four stroke.' (p. 458)
Skills	Learning	Use of literacy and numeracy skills	The ability to follow a recipe.

The next section presents a series of case studies of food specialisations in action, beginning with Years 5 and 6, followed by Years 3 and 4, and concluding with a case example of Foundation to Year 2.

SPOTLIGHT 7.3

What is food education?

Rutland (2018) undertook a survey to identify the key issues associated with food technologies. She found:

- obesity is a national issue in society
- food sustainability and global security
- scientific understanding
- links between food technology and science
- the impact of a modern food technology curriculum.

In her critique of technologies education, Rutland (2018) asks, 'What is food education? What is it that we want children to learn? What does design mean in this context? What are the design decisions that are made?' She suggests that food technology has featured a number of challenges. For instance, she asks what product development would look like in practice. What might be the concept of making, and what are the 'design decisions' that children make or should make? She argues that food technology is more than simply developing a food product or following a recipe. Further, she asks what 'modelling' might look like in food technologies. Key issues to consider according to Rutland (2018, pp. 462–3) are:

- changing lifestyles and the increased consumption of ready-made meals and highly processed foods, as well as the increased availability of supermarkets
- the need for pupils to understand the scientific concepts related to food and their application in a practical, visual context
- linking practical food-based activities to an understanding of nutrition and making healthy choices, knowledge of the sources of food and the functionality of ingredients
- knowledge and understanding of new technologies and processes, and their application and benefits, which would help the public to make 'informed choices'.

National and international food availability and sustainability are key issues, and will become even more important in the future.

In foregrounding a pedagogy of critiquing for food technology (Keirl, 2020), how might you introduce children to the topic of food politics? One example is the introduction of sugar in processed food to make it taste better without consideration of the net effect on a community's health – obesity in children, an increase in tooth decay and the health concerns for type 2 diabetes. This creates a new curriculum need for knowledge about a balanced diet, nutrition and wise shopping habits. However, Rutland (2018, p. 463) suggests that, 'Currently, it was not clear what will happen in schools if they focus on "learning to cook" rather than wider issues of food technology'.

Overall, design and making in food technology are different from other areas of technology because children need to make conceptual, marketing, constructional, technical and aesthetic decisions as they work with food. They are not just following a recipe (Rutland, 2018).

Video activity 7.1 Food specialisations

Figure 7.14 A Year 5 student holistically explores designing in the specialisation of food and fibre technologies
Source: Kelly-Ann Allen.

Wand-making (sticks, ribbon), dress-up party and a silent disco workshop are all preparation for attending the school café (Figure 7.14). These bring different contexts of food and fibre.

Looking inside a classroom: Food specialisations – starting with children's everyday experiences with food

Children have many experiences of buying and eating food; however, they may not have examined their food explicitly, critiqued where their food comes from or considered important ideas associated with food technology, such as organic food, sustainable food and companion planting. Some of the techniques for designing with food that are available for exploration, and that may be relevant to the community in which you are teaching, could include:

- kebabs
- soup
- stews
- sandwiches

- pizza
- bread-making
- rice-based meals
- party snacks
- cakes
- biscuits
- jams
- stir-fries
- curries
- roasts
- barbecues
- deep frying
- confectionery
- smoking
- dry curing
- boiling
- dehydrating
- poaching
- blanching.

A design brief can frame the exploration of what children already know and do in relation to the preparation or purchase of food. A series of examples follow in Figures 7.15–7.17.

Thinking about food in new ways means connecting with children's prior understandings and introducing them to new ways of preparing, planning and exploring food. This gives children new ways of thinking about their everyday life that impact their health, sustainability through food selection, and agency and knowledge when designing their own recipes.

A nutritional audit

You have been invited to undertake a nutritional audit of a favourite takeaway food.

1. In a group of four, select a favourite takeaway food.
2. Gather promotional material on the takeaway. What does the information say it contains?
3. Buy the product (with support from your teacher).
4. Investigate the contents. List the food in the takeaway. Weigh each type of food product.
5. Search the internet for the nutritional value of each food.
6. With support from your teacher, calculate the nutritional value of your takeaway.
7. Then examine the advertisement for your takeaway:
   - What does it say?
   - What message is given?
   - How persuasive is it?
   - How is food presented (if at all)?
   - Does the advertisement just show 'lifestyle', and does this relate to the food?
8. Compare the results of your analysis of the advertisement with the results of your nutritional audit. What do you notice?
9. Compare your nutritional and advertising results with those of others in your class (their audit of their favourite takeaway).
10. What can you conclude?

Download 7.2
A nutritional audit

Figure 7.15 Design brief for a nutritional audit of a favourite takeaway food

> ## Studying the school canteen
>
> In groups of five, you are to undertake an inspection of your school canteen. You have been issued with latex gloves, a clipboard and a camera. You are to examine:
>
> - safety
> - finances
> - nutritional value
> - cultural appropriateness of the food
> - service
> - work flow
> - recycling
> - where the basic ingredients come from: school garden, imported, etc.
>
> You also need to take photos and interview staff.
> 1. What can you conclude about your canteen?
> 2. How might you redesign your canteen to deal with the problems you have identified, or how might you advocate for the approach already taken by the canteen?

Download 7.3 Studying the school canteen

Figure 7.16 School canteen inspection

Figure 7.17 From school canteen inspection to Florence designing her own healthy pizza options
Source: Kelly-Ann Allen.

Looking inside a classroom: Years 5 and 6 designing and setting up their own café

Lara is seeking to bring into the children's world a new way of organising lunchtime at her school. She sets up a design brief (Figure 7.18) of a school café.

To support the children's research, they visit a local restaurant. Armed with questions, digital devices to capture what they see and hear, and notebooks, they begin their research. The results of their excursion are documented collectively and discussed. The children examine their results from visiting the local restaurant and identify some important features needed for designing their own café, as shown in Figure 7.19. Their list gives them a framework. They vote on which area they wish to design and produce, and teams are formed. In

Café or restaurant investigation

1 Visit a local café or restaurant and investigate by asking the following questions:
   - What do the staff do?
   - How is food stored?
   - What is in the cool room? Write down the food types.
   - What is on the menu? Photograph the menu for the day.
2 Draw a floor plan of the spaces in the restaurant. Investigate this further by:
   - taking photographs of all the food-preparation spaces
   - video-recording what the waiter does.
3 Interview the chef about how the kitchen is managed.
4 Design your own restaurant.
5 Set up a plan for managing a restaurant in your school.
6 Role-play your plan. Prepare badges for each of the roles that you have identified from your research.

Download 7.4
Café or restaurant investigation

Figure 7.18 Designing and setting up a café

What we found:
- There are flowers on the table.
- The menu is on a blackboard – for specials.
- Tablecloths are made of thick paper.
- Napkins are all sorts of designs.
- The shapes of the tables are different at the front of the café – round – and inside they are square.
- There is a waiter, manager, chef, dish stacker, kitchen hand, barista.

Figure 7.19 The children's research

their groups, they undertake further web-based searches, phone retailers for material costs, scout the school for equipment and furniture, and prepare an e-newsletter with calls for things still needed for setting up their café. The management team works out a project plan for implementation, and a supply chain from paddock-to-plate is prepared. The finance team works out the budgets associated with menu choices, and the social media team begins preparations on launching the café.

Closer to the time of officially opening their café, the children invite a chef from their local restaurant to visit their school (see Figure 7.20). Alison reflects on the visit:

> Today we had a chef come and visit our school. She showed us all her tools and her special book of recipes. She wore a special hat. She showed us many ingredients. We also smelt a lot of spices and herbs. A lot of food has spices in it. We learned that this makes them hot!

Figure 7.20 Chef's visit

> We had a chance to explore all the things she brought in for us to see. I wore the chef's hat and apron – it was a bit big. Later we role-played being chefs in our café.

Looking inside a classroom: Food specialisations – a snapshot of Year 3 and 4 children

Beginning with what children know about food and building upon their understandings, ensure that children experience meaningful learning activities. How might this project have evolved? How were the children motivated to want to talk about all they know about food production, preparation and tools?

In preparing the birthday charts of the children in her Year 3 classroom, Kelly-Ann notices that in the first week of the school year, three children have birthdays. She decides that a birthday party will be the best motivation for beginning a food technology unit.

As she does calendar work with the children on the first day of school, she plots out the week and draws attention to Friday – this will be a special day for Alicja, Henry and Charlotte. She introduces the children to the design problem: How do we prepare for this special day? What should we do on this day? As expected, the children all suggest a class birthday party.

Preparations begin and teams are formed. The children break down the design challenge into specific areas:

- What food to prepare and eat at the party – design the menu?
- Where to have the party – environment to plan and decorate?
- What to do at the party – games to design?
- How to organise the day – project manage the party plan and clean up?

The major criterion she asks the students to consider is how the party plan can be healthy so no family complains and everyone can eat the food prepared.

Each morning there is a planning meeting to see how things are going in each team – collective reporting supports collective problem-solving, as the children help each other, and Kelly-Ann adds key information/sources/suggests supporting their technologies studies. For example, she suggests to the children in the group preparing the menu that they run a digitally organised survey of what each member of the class likes to eat.

On Day 3, Kelly-Ann reads out a newspaper article on her phone at their morning meeting. It says:

> Breaking news – People from all over the world are asking about the footprint of their food. How can food production, food security and food sustainability be better understood? What can you do to help?

Kelly-Ann invites a discussion on the party plan that each group is preparing, and the children decide to prepare a mind map poster (Figure 7.21) of what they know about food so they can consider the footprint of their party plan. The children research and revise their original party plan, particularly the group working on the menu. The newspaper article creates the motivating conditions for thinking more about what they know and what they can do in a way that is personally meaningful – preparing for a birthday party and wanting to help with reducing their carbon footprint.

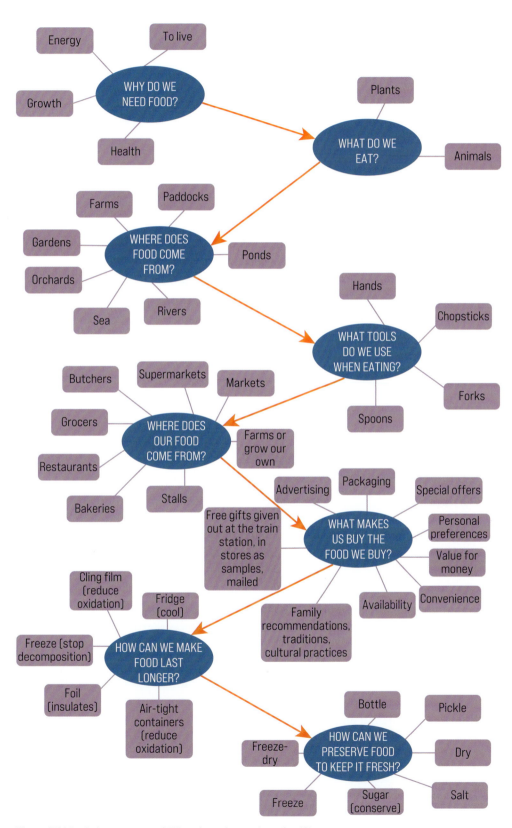

Figure 7.21 A mind map poster of 'What do we know about food?'

Each of the groups brings its work to a close on the Thursday, and first thing on Friday morning the children celebrate at their party and discuss their successful party plan and what they would do differently for the next one. This project illustrates how children can explain how the characteristics of foods influence selection and preparation for healthy eating.

The next example looks at the youngest children engaged in food specialisation and considers more closely the pedagogy needed to support learning in food technology.

Looking inside a classroom: Food specialisations – a snapshot of Foundation to Year 2 children

Younger children have many experiences with cooking; however, food technologies are more than simply preparing and eating food. The unique aspect of food technologies is that children can design their own recipes. To be able to design recipes means that children need experiences of analysing recipes before they can create their own. But how do we set up this experience for Foundation children or children in Years 1 and 2?

Andrea plans a Conceptual PlayWorld for supporting children to 'explore how food can be selected and prepared for healthy eating' (ACARA, 2023). (See previous chapters for other working examples of a Conceptual PlayWorld or jump on to the website at: www.monash.edu/conceptual-playworld.)

Overview

1. *Selecting the story:* Andrea plans her Conceptual PlayWorld using the story of *Little Chef* by Matt Stine and Elisabeth Weinberg (2018). (www.youtube.com/watch?v=rY3MMdHrOHE) It is a story about Grandmother coming over for dinner. Lizzy, the main character, asks her mum: 'What shall I cook?' Lizzy decides to cook her favourite meal, smashed sweet potato. In the story, Lizzy makes a list of the ingredients. They go shopping to the farmers market to find the best produce. Lizzy prepares her dish, and wants to add the secret ingredient, but she doesn't know what it is, because secret ingredients are not written in the recipe. Lizzy must find her own secret ingredient. The story concludes with Grandma enjoying the smashed sweet potato and asking about the secret ingredient. The final page asks, 'What should I cook tomorrow?'

2. *Designing the space for the Conceptual PlayWorld:* Andrea uses the art room in the school as her kitchen. She puts a sign on the door, 'Lizzy's secret recipe: Do not enter'. Inside the art room, she moves tables and chairs together to form groups, and on a higher table she places cooking facilities, such as a microwave and an electric frying pan. There are cooking books on display, magazines with recipes, and a range of cooking tools, pots, pans and bowls.

3. *Entering and exiting routine:* To enter the Conceptual PlayWorld of 'Lizzy's secret recipe: Do not enter', the children put on chefs' hats. To exit, they remove their hats and hang them on hooks ready for the next visit.

4. *Planning the problem to be solved:* The story sets up the problem that the children discuss: What is your favourite recipe? Can you prepare and cook your favourite recipe to share? What might be your secret ingredient to introduce into your recipe?

After reading the story to the children, the children go into character as chefs, and enter 'Lizzy's kitchen'. They role-play the story and discuss the secret ingredient in the recipes they love. The next time the children enter 'Lizzy's kitchen', they research their chosen recipe – using the books, digital devices and magazines.

In Figure 7.22, Alice shares what she has learned about recipes as a result of reading many different ones. In Figure 7.23, Zac shares his recipe for making damper – he interviewed members of the local community to learn about the traditional approaches to making damper that they knew or used. In Figure 7.24, Lia lists the steps for making scrambled eggs. Lia made eggs at home with her father and then made them at school. She wrote down the steps after she had made her scrambled eggs. Each of the approaches (Alice, Zac and Lia) suggests a way to engage with food technologies at the Foundation to Year 2 level.

> I learnt new ideas from the chefs cooking. We had some piaclets.

Figure 7.22 Alice learned about new recipes

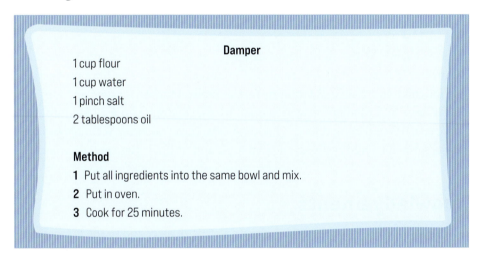

Figure 7.23 Zac's recipe for making damper

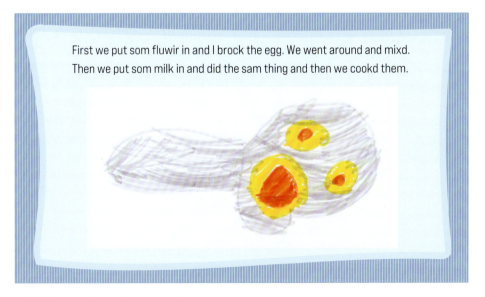

Figure 7.24 The steps for making scrambled eggs

On subsequent days, the children prepare their own recipes and share their designs with the whole class. The children select three of their favourites that everyone can enjoy and, like Lizzy, prepare lists and visit the supermarket/farmers market and return to later cook up all their recipes. They taste test and discuss the secret ingredient in each of the three chosen recipes. They evaluate and adjust their recipes as needed, but mostly the children loved the food because they had made it.

In this section of the chapter, examples from classrooms and early childhood settings were presented to illustrate how food specialisation can be introduced to children from birth to 12 years. Although food is common across the year levels, the levels of complexity were shown incrementally. The key to successfully designing and implementing these examples was finding out what the children know, working with their interests and beginning with something motivating.

Summary

This chapter examined the technologies contexts of food and fibre production and food specialisations. It looked at case examples of food technologies and fibre production technologies for children from Foundation to Year 6. It also touched on food and fibre technologies for infants and toddlers as experiential, where children gain insights into the range and characteristics of fibre and food. Chapter 8 examines two other Technologies contexts: engineering principles and systems; and materials and technologies specialisations.

Acknowledgements

Special thanks to families for the infant photos in this chapter and to the teachers who implemented the technologies program and the children who participated, and whose work has been captured through the case study presented. Special thanks to my colleague Associate Professor Kelly-Ann Allen for the photos of Florence and to Emma for her photo of Beau. Finally, thanks to Yuejiu Wang for support with updating the references for this chapter.

Technologies contexts: Engineering principles and systems, and materials and technologies specialisations

CHAPTER 8

Introduction

Chapter 7 examined food specialisations. This chapter continues to examine the contexts of technologies by looking at engineering principles and systems, and materials and technologies specialisations. Engineering as a context for the study of technologies is an area for primary and early childhood teachers to consider when planning for children's learning. This area opens up new possibilities, particularly for girls (Figure 8.1). As a profession in Australia, engineering is male dominated. Engineers Australia (2022, p. 17) found that:

Figure 8.1 Engineering technologies for girls – Florence designs and engineers a forest cubby, paying special attention to structure, material load and force.
Source: Kelly-Ann Allen.

201

The low rate of female entry into engineering degrees stems from a simple fact: most girls do not even consider engineering as an option. Only 7% of women who pursued other fields say they seriously considered studying engineering. A further 16% say they considered it only briefly or in passing. This means that about 3 in 4 never considered engineering at all.

Teachers have a real opportunity to make a difference, not just through supporting the learning of engineering principles but also through engaging and motivating young girls with regard to the delights of studying important engineering concepts.

Engineering covers a broad classification of professions, and this term brings forward many specialisations. In this chapter we will look at engineering principles and concepts from the Australian Curriculum: Technologies. This chapter and Chapter 9 on project management will provide foundational knowledge and pedagogical examples of engineering in practice. This chapter will also look at early childhood engineering, because internationally this area has gained real momentum.

There are many types of engineers

The focus on engineering principles and systems, and materials and technologies specialisations provides a foundation for engineering education. But what is engineering? Most people think of hi-vis vests and hard hats. Engineering is both intellectual and practical, and sits in a social context. Engineers begin with social needs, find solutions and predict how they will work. These needs become projects – both small and large – where engineers coordinate people and professions, safely deliver solutions and predict and work within/manage budgets.

Engineers have huge responsibilities and need a broad range of skills because they:

- work closely with clients to understand their needs
- need to understand the materials required
- create systems and technical specifications
- liaise with other professionals who have specialist knowledge needed for realising the engineered solution
- consider social, environmental and economic conditions in which the engineering solution is being designed.

There are many kinds of engineers. Often people think about the most obvious or stereotypical engineer, such as a mechanical or civil engineer. Other engineering professions are:

- *Electrical engineering*: a field characterised by electrical energy – how it is produced and used.
- *Aerospace engineering*: a field characterised by design, construction and the operation of aircraft, aerospace vehicles and the system of differing aircraft – jets, planes, helicopters, gliders, missiles and spacecraft.
- *Chemical engineering*: this field covers the design and management of technologies and large-scale conversion of raw materials for commercialisation or general utility.

- *Environmental engineering:* an area of engineering focused on environmental protection through assessment of impact on the waterways, soils, air quality and noise.
- *Mining engineering:* a field oriented to the investigation and extraction of mineral deposits, ore bodies, non-metallic ores and fuels.

As societies develop, more specialist expertise is needed, so new types of engineers are needed. This list will continue to grow and change. Yet Engineers Australia (2022, p. 5) found in its Women in Engineering survey that the main reason why 'women who didn't study engineering was lack of familiarity of engineering, there is little awareness of what engineering involves'. This statement is often heard, and is coupled with a view of half the population missing out on important career possibilities. Generally, the community does not know much about what is involved in engineering professions, and there is still a need to bring more women into the profession. As suggested by Engineers Australia (2022, p. 5), some of the factors preventing women entering the profession include:

- a lack of positive perceptions of the engineering profession – seen as male dominated and challenging, and not impactful or fulfilling
- poor Science, Technology, Engineering, and Mathematics (STEM) engagement throughout schooling – many girls don't feel supported to do well in STEM
- students feeling less supported to do well in their studies, compared with other degrees, despite a generally positive experience studying engineering at university.

In fact, the report by Engineers Australia (2022, p. 5) found that most female engineers feel valued at work and are passionate about their work; however there are significant issues for women with workplace culture and unequal opportunities.

Once again, teachers can make a big difference to some of these key reasons, and this chapter goes some way towards addressing STEM engagement by showcasing how teachers can create motivating conditions for all children, but especially for girls in engineering.

PEDAGOGICAL REFLECTION 8.1

Engineering as a specialist profession

There are several key thinking skills that characterise an engineer (Dowling et al., 2022):

- *Systems thinking:* engineers consider all of the elements of a problem. Problem identification, problem boundary, and components that make up the problem, are considered in relation to each other.
- *Design thinking:* engineers engage in conceptual design and detailed design. The former involves the identification of a suitable solution to the problem. The latter is where the conceptual design is detailed in relation to the components ready for implementation.

Dowling et al. (2022) summarise the engineering method used by professional engineers as involving five processes:

1. *Research:* gather together data and knowledge to clearly define the problem and specify criteria.
2. *Generate:* a range of possible solutions to the problem.

3. *Evaluate:* the solutions in relation to the specified criteria.
4. *Monitor and review:* considering impact and outcomes.
5. *Communicate* the engineered solution to the client.

Thinking point: How does the specialist profession of engineering relate to what children need to know in schools and early childhood settings? As you read through this chapter, consider the profession and what is discussed in Australian Curriculum: Technologies (ACARA, 2023) and the Early Years Learning Framework (AGDE, 2022). Do these documents mirror what an engineer does and how they think? What might be the special focus for girls that you would consider key, given the findings of the Women in Engineering report (Engineers Australia, 2022)? Record your thoughts. We will return to this question at the end of the chapter.

My ideas: _____

Knowledge and approaches to learning in engineering contexts

How should engineering education be taught? The Australian Curriculum: Technologies (ACARA, 2023) gives some direction for supporting teachers. An overview of the scope and sequence of the two technologies contexts detailed under the engineering principles and systems, and materials and technologies specialisations is provided in Table 8.1. This scope and sequence help with establishing what might be the content to be covered at the particular year level for each of the contexts. However, it is also possible to see how these are related to each other and how the concepts build over time across the different year levels.

Table 8.1 Technologies context: engineering principles and systems, and materials and technologies specialisations scope and sequence

Technologies context	Foundation	Years 1 and 2	Years 3 and 4	Years 5 and 6
Engineering principles and systems, and materials and technologies specialisations	No explicit content descriptions	Explore how technologies including materials affect movement in products (AC9TDE2K02)	Describe how forces and the properties of materials affect function in a product or system (AC9TDE4K02)	
Engineering principles and systems				Explain how electrical energy can be transformed into movement, sound or light in a product or system (AC9TDE6K02)
Materials and technologies specialisations	No explicit content descriptions			Explain how characteristics and properties of materials, systems, components, tools and equipment affect their use when producing designed solutions (AC9TDE6K05)

Source: ACARA (2023).

As Table 8.1 shows, engineering principles and systems, and materials and technologies become more differentiated for students in Years 5 and 6, while they are much more integrated for Years 1–4. The engineering context is not given for the Foundation year – even though there is an increasing emphasis in the research internationally on the prominence of engineering education for 3- to 8-year-olds (Tunnicliffe, 2022).

What might be some of the pedagogical practices relevant to teaching engineering principles and engineering concepts? What might be specific engineering knowledge? Is this knowledge different from science, literacy or mathematics?

PEDAGOGICAL REFLECTION 8.2

Teaching about the engineering principles and systems, and materials and technologies specialisations

1. How might you teach engineering principles and systems, and materials and technologies from a technologies perspective to young children (Figure 8.2)?
2. What might be some of the challenges you face in designing and teaching a project-based unit on engineering principles and systems, and materials and technologies?
3. How might you draw upon some of the existing resources available to you in the classroom (e.g. see Figure 8.2) and work with these to explore engineering principles, especially when it comes to engaging girls? List your ideas and potential solutions below:

Challenge 1:_____
Solution 1:_____
Challenge 2:_____
Solution 2:_____
Challenge 3:_____
Solution 3:_____

We will return to your challenges and suggested solutions at the end of this chapter.

Figure 8.2 Exploring forces and materials in everyday life supports children's experiential learning of engineering principles.

It is suggested by Yu, Fan and Lin (2018) that there are four dimensions of engineering knowledge:

- nature of engineering
- theoretical engineering knowledge
- knowledge through engineering
- engineering design and problem-solving processes.

They state (p. 404) that exploring the nature of *engineering knowledge* is about studying the 'meaning of engineering, and its relationship with various disciplines, the society, and the environment'. This would involve having an understanding of what engineering is (definition of this discipline area or profession) and how engineering relates to other disciplines (e.g. as STEM and Science, Technology, Engineering, Arts and Mathematics (STEAM)) and a relational understanding of engineering and society. The *theoretical dimensions of engineering knowledge*, such as mechanics and electronics, bring forward specialised forms of knowledge of the engineering (see earlier on the different engineering professions). *Knowledge through engineering* is understood as problem-solving and the maintenance of common engineering products, material processing methods and procedures, and the operation and use of common tools and equipment (e.g. the five steps of the engineering method discussed above). *Engineering design and problem-solving processes* include a focus on creativity and problem-solving to meet practical needs. The core content features the ability to complete technical drawings, creative thinking processes, engineering problem-solving, design thinking and product design and development. Pedagogical practices for developing this form of knowledge were discussed in Chapter 4.

Teachers' pedagogical content knowledge (see Chapter 1) specific to engineering can be conceptualised as follows (Yu, Fan and Lin, 2018, p. 404):

Engineering-focused pedagogical content knowledge

1. Teaching strategies for engineering design thinking
2. Teaching strategies for project-based learning
3. Teaching strategies for technological problem-solving skills
4. Teaching strategies for creative thinking
5. Teaching strategies for interdisciplinary integration

Knowledge of learners

1. Students' physical and mental development and corresponding characteristics
2. Prior knowledge and abilities of students at different learning stages
3. Students' personality traits and cultural backgrounds
4. Misconceptions of conceptual knowledge
5. Misconceptions of procedural knowledge

Knowledge of educational contexts

1. Designing the classroom for technology teaching
2. Managing the classroom for technology teaching
3. Industrial safety and hygiene
4. School characteristics and local culture

Collectively, expansive sets of knowledge forms are featured in studies of engineering.

> ### Engineering design principles
>
> SPOTLIGHT **8.1**
>
> It is suggested by Yu, Fan and Lin (2018) that engineering concepts should be embedded meaningfully in the everyday classroom. By infusing engineering design principles into the day-to-day activities of children, both concept-driven (e.g. studying engineering principles inherent in bridge design) and activity-oriented (e.g. making bridges and learning the engineering principles by doing) approaches are brought together. In their study of teachers in Taiwan, the authors found that:
>
>> Teachers are uncertain about the breadth and depth of the content range of engineering-focused curricula; (2) teachers are concerned about the transformation process from the traditional technology education to an engineering-focused curricula; and (3) teachers are worried about their own professional knowledge and ability. (Yu, Fan and Lin, 2018, p. 409)

Part 1 of this book discussed design making technologies different from other curricula. Design through engineering becomes an important aspect of learning about engineering principles. Knowledge of engineering principles, systems and design thinking (both concept-driven and activity-oriented approaches) is brought together in engineering education contexts. Consequently, the contexts of engineering, with its focus on both engineering principles and systems, and materials and technologies specialisations, are presented in this chapter through project-based learning and design-based thinking units. We also introduce an Engineering Conceptual PlayWorld (Fleer, 2022a, 2022b). The activity-oriented, project-based approaches are well supported in the community (van Dijk, Savelsbergh and van der Meij, 2020) and many primary schools interested in the study of engineering principles are using these methods to introduce engineering principles and systems, and materials and technologies specialisations. Mills and Treagust (2003, p. 4) state that:

> Design is one of the fundamental processes and activities in engineering (and basically all other engineering activities relate to it e.g. implementation or construction of designs or processes and maintenance of facilities or products).

Accordingly, the next section considers engineering design holistically, followed by engineering principles and systems, and finally materials and technologies specialisations.

Web activity 8.1
Engineering principles and systems

Engineering design principles

This next section explores possible approaches to teaching engineering principles and concepts to children with a focus on design-based learning or, as it is known in the engineering profession, design thinking and the five-step engineering method (see Pedagogical Reflection 8.1).

As a profession, engineering has also had its own pedagogy and ways of working. Engineering habits of mind have been suggested as signature pedagogies for engineering education. For instance, Hanson and Lucas (2020) examined how engineers work, and suggested that a particular signature pedagogies was needed. By studying how engineers work, they found the following habits of mind:

- *creative problem-solving*, which involves generating ideas and working in teams
- *improving*, which includes experimenting and evaluating
- *problem-finding*, where engineers check, clarify and investigate
- *adapting*, which involves critical thinking and deliberate practising, even when faced with challenges
- *visualising*, which includes thinking out loud and model-making
- *systems thinking*, which involves looking for links, working across boundaries and pattern-making.

With these habits of mind, Hanson and Lucas (2020) consider the pedagogy needed for promoting these ways of working and thinking. They were engineering design processes, tinkering approaches (playful experimentation) and authentic engagement with engineers. In introducing a critiquing pedagogy, Keirl (2020) also invites other kinds of thinking that can be applied to thinking like an engineer, such as questions of ethics, values and the footprint of the engineering solution. Similarly, von Mengersen and Wilkinson (2020) encourage asking questions about the materials, which also speaks to broader societal values and ethics associated with food production, food waste and, as discussed in Chapter 7, the ethics of processes associated with the production and delivery of the fast clothing industry. Von Mengersen and Wilkinson (2020) and Keirl (2020) suggest that other kinds of habits of mind need to emerge.

A *five-step engineering design process* has also been suggested by DiFrancesca, Lee and McIntyre (2014) when working with students:

1. *Ask:* children define the problem and begin to identify the constraints.
2. *Imagine:* children brainstorm ideas and work out which might be the best one to work with.
3. *Plan:* children draw their ideas, create diagrams and collect the materials they need.
4. *Create:* children follow their design and plan of action to realise their product/idea, and then test it to see if it works as planned.
5. *Improve:* children discuss what they might do differently to improve their product or idea.

They then repeat steps 1 to 5.

The five-step approach provides some insight into what is unique about learning engineering principles from a design perspective. DiFrancesca, Lee and McIntyre (2014) state that engineering learning needs to be considered holistically, and therefore in the context of technologies as presented in the Australian Curriculum: Technologies. This means that design processes need to be employed by students when investigating specific content, such as force, electrical energy, and sound or light production to support systems thinking.

Wolfinbarger et al. (2021) show that engineers must be technically competent. They have responsibilities that include interfacing between social and physical environments, and understanding the needs of their clients in the context of society. It can therefore be argued that children who are learning engineering principles should also have experiences of thinking about the interface between the social and physical environments in which they live, and that they need to gain insights into how to work with clients in the context of their community. Examples of the development of both these skills were given in Chapter 4, where the role of architects was examined.

Problem-based learning has been used in engineering to support the development of technical competence for engineering and to support a team-based approach. According to Mills and Treagust (2003, p. 4), problem-based learning has been used as the main pedagogical practice of educators in many fields such as medicine, and has also been deployed to teach engineering principles. They suggest that the 'strategy for teaching design as has been practiced in engineering programs for many years' and that it 'has many similarities with the problem-based learning strategy'.

Problem-based learning has generally focused on identifying and solving genuine problems – usually those relevant to students' everyday lives. This might be seen when children find a problem with their play equipment in the playground – something is not working as it should (e.g. the see-saw or a rocking rider). Problem-based learning projects are usually open and connected to real-life problems that students are keen to solve. Key questions that can be asked to support children in thinking creatively might be:

- Why has this problem arisen?
- What is causing the problem?
- How does this situation arise?
- When does it happen?
- Where does it happen?
- Who makes this happen?

How do we systematically bring experiential learning into project-based learning? In problem-based projects, the content for learning is always the group rather than the individual. Problem-based learning projects support group collaboration in searching for solutions. Problem-based learning also supports a focus on learning for a specific need (i.e. to solve a problem for a client or self), rather than the explicit teaching of engineering principles (which could be decontextualised and provide limited motivation for the learner).

Related to problem-based learning is *project-based learning*. Mills and Treagust (2003) discuss how in project-based learning in engineering, 'the project' is the unit of work. In the context of tertiary engineering education, Havenga and Swart (2022) have also shown the value of project-based learning for setting up real-world problems for students. The differences between project-based and problem-based learning are shown in Table 8.2 (summarised from Mills and Treagust, 2003) and they are relevant for primary classrooms – but what about early childhood education settings?

Problem-based learning has also been characterised through seven steps (Buck Institute for Education, n.d.):

1. *A challenging problem or question:* The project is framed by a meaningful problem to be solved or a question to answer, at the appropriate level of challenge.
2. *Sustained inquiry:* Students engage in a rigorous, extended process of posing questions, finding resources and applying information.

Table 8.2 Differences between project-based learning and problem-based learning in engineering education

Project-based learning	Problem-based learning
Project tasks are closer to the professional reality of engineers. They take longer to complete.	Usually shorter in duration.
Project work is directed to the *application* of knowledge.	More directed to the *acquisition* of knowledge
Project work is usually accompanied by subject courses or discipline knowledge, such as mathematics.	Not based on doing courses or oriented to other discipline areas.
Project management (time, resources, role differentiation) is very important.	Not required.
Self-direction is important for project completion.	Less need for self-direction.

Source: Adapted from Mills and Treagust (2003).

3 *Authenticity:* The project involves real-world context, tasks and tools, quality standards, or impact, or the project speaks to personal concerns, interests and issues in the students' lives.
4 *Student voice and choice:* Students make some decisions about the project, including how they work and what they create, and express their own ideas in their own voice.
5 *Reflection:* Students and teachers reflect on the learning, the effectiveness of their inquiry and project activities, the quality of student work and obstacles that arise and strategies for overcoming them.
6 *Critique and revision:* Students give, receive and apply feedback to improve their process and products.
7 *Public product:* Students make their project work public by sharing it with and explaining or presenting it to people beyond the classroom.

A related strategy to problem-based learning is introducing levels of critique by children, such as when considering the most appropriate technologies or design solutions for a particular problem, as we might see with environmentally friendly engineered packaging or products:

- Is it inexpensive?
- Does it use materials that are sourced locally or are recycled?
- Is it robust and easy to maintain?
- Does it include information on their safe use?

These ideas were considered in Chapter 1 in relation to appropriate technologies. However, more specific to the area of engineering are strategies for supporting the practice of sustainable engineering (von Mengersen and Wilkinson, 2020). For example. sustainable engineering could focus on asking questions about:

- maintaining ecological integrity
- applying precautions

- consulting stakeholders
- promoting equity
- conserving resources
- limiting emissions
- practising industrial ecology.

Web activity 8.2
Materials and technologies specialisations

We know from research into the use of social media that there are other ways to conceptualise approaches to teaching engineering. For instance, Khosronejad, Reimann and Markauskaite (2021) state that engineering is designed to be a collaborative profession, with teams working together. Yet, often learning about engineering principles occurs in an information silo. It is suggested that using social media as a tool for communication greatly enhances understandings of tacit knowledge – that is, engineering principles that are experienced but not considered consciously. While this concern is directed at the profession, the argument is equally valid in early childhood and primary education, where children experience engineering technologies (e.g. when playing in the playground) without ever really noticing or understanding them, or working as a team to explore them.

Social media can also offer motivating conditions for learning (Willbold, 2019) and teachers can use social media to support each other in learning more about engineering principles. Table 8.3 presents an adapted summary of digital tools suitable for teachers in supporting each other to learn engineering principles.

Table 8.3 Using social media to support teachers in your school in the learning of engineering principles

Type	Function	Tools	Example	Type of knowledge
Communicating	Share ideas, innovations and information found Build a relationship with others (or a following)	Social networking	YouTube, Twitter, Snapchat, Facebook, WhatsApp, Instagram	Socialisation
Collaborative documentation	Teachers discuss specific projects – such as pedagogical practices	Wikis, virtual communities of practice, websites of practical ideas and resources	Wikipedia, Wordpress	Information exchange and problem-solving
Engineering concepts	Present data on practices that have been tried out and that work	Blogs, YouTube videos	Google Docs, YouTube	Sharing of working examples
Generative	Develop new programs for teaching engineering concepts	Virtual learning community	Amazon, Flickr, YouTube	Sharing examples of new practices and approaches
Interactive	Exchange information, ideas, resources, materials	Social bookmarking, virtual communities of practice	Facebook, WhatsApp, Twitter	Seeking feedback or asking for information or giving feedback and sharing information

Source: Adapted from Murphy and Salomone (2013, p. 32).

ACTIVITY 8.1

Engineering is designed to be a collaborative process

Social media can offer motivating conditions for learning (Table 8.3). How might you use social media to support the learning of engineering principles? You could consider (with family approval) drawing on some social media to encourage children to communicate with each other on projects after school hours, or with children in other schools working on similar engineering projects.

Following on from Table 8.3, teachers could use digital tools to motivate children in the learning of engineering principles (Table 8.4).

Table 8.4 Using digital tools to motivate children in the learning of engineering principles

Type	Function	Tools	Example	Type of knowledge
Communicating	Share ideas, innovations and information found Build a relationship with others (or a following)	Robots and children's programmable toys	In teams code a robot to navigate the classroom or set up a robotic challenge among teams. One child pretends to be the robot and the others prepare codes.	Socialisation
Collaborative documentation	Teachers introduce specific projects – such as writing code for a class/group picnic (list of instructions to plan)	ScratchJr Google Earth	Children design the invitations, menu and how to get to the picnic.	Information exchange and problem-solving
Engineering concepts	Present data on practices that have been tried out and that work	YouTube videos – content for children only, preselected and loaded on school intranet	Children plan their project in groups using Google Docs.	Sharing of working examples of engineering projects
Generative	Develop new movie to showcase engineering concepts	Stopmotion project	Children present their projects through slowmotion, such as building different kinds of bridges and structures.	Sharing examples of engineering projects as stopmotion
Interactive	Exchange information, ideas, resources, materials	Interactive whiteboard, Google Earth, school intranet	Children engage in civil engineering project using interactive whiteboard and Google Earth for town planning project.	Seeking feedback or asking for information or giving feedback and sharing information

In engineering, Dowling, Carew and Hadgraft (2015) argue that community consultations are another important aspect of how engineers work when solving problems with integrity. In drawing upon the Code of Ethics of Engineers Australia (2010), which discusses that engineers must respect the inherent dignity of the individual, act on the basis of a well-informed conscience and operate in the interests of the community, Dowling, Carew and Hadgraft (2015) suggest the following key questions for community consultations:

- Who should the team invite to attend the local community meeting?
- How do we begin the discussion so that there is a productive and positive process of debate and discussion?
- How do we ensure that everyone has the opportunity to express their views?
- How do we guide the community members towards a constructive decision?

Engaging with the community can also go beyond the borders of the country, which is now increasingly possible for primary-aged children to do through Skype and other forms of social media. This could occur in considering community-engaged, sustainable technical solutions more globally, and particularly in the context of poor, under-developed countries and their needs, in order to promote the social and human components of engineering solutions (Gilbert et al., 2014).

How community engagement might translate into primary education programs is not well understood because teaching engineering principles in the context of client-based and community-oriented projects has a very short history in primary education. Mostly, engineering principles are taught through science programs, rather than as a dedicated area of study. Two examples to illustrate engineering principles in practice follow:

- *Engineering for Foundation to Year 6:* Children were given a brief to work with two kinds of model boats (one in water and one using springs). The students finished both a science problem (examining and explaining the effects of various mechanical factors on spring length) and a conceptually related engineering problem (increasing the speed of model boats being pulled through a canal system).
- *Engineering for 5-year-olds:* Young children were given engineering challenges that were related to distributing water – for example, designing and building a system to deliver equal amounts of water to two 'apartments', one higher than the other. In this example, the effects on flow rate of differences in reservoir elevation and pipe diameter were considered by the children (Cunningham and Carlsen, 2014, p. 203).

Careful thought must be given to ensuring that the conceptual content of engineering is not lost in the process of teaching integrated units of work in schools (integrity of the conceptual learning). Engineering design projects can support the learning of a broad range of concepts from other curriculum areas (integration of discipline concepts for transfer and/or to be a personally meaningful experience).

The next section presents a case example of an engineering context of designing a city by Year 6 students and their teachers. This example brings together the content discussed so far and presents a holistic picture of the technologies contexts of engineering. This is followed by case examples of engineering principles and systems, and case examples of materials and technologies specialisations. The examples are structured in this way to show, through the first example of designing a city, how knowledges and concepts in engineering are considered through the lens of design and project-based learning (see also Chapter 9 on project management). Then the specific concepts of materials and systems that are embedded in this holistic approach are both drawn out. These concepts are also shown through further examples of looking inside a classroom for system and for materials, respectively. Where possible, the latter two will feature from preschool to Year 6 – sometimes as design briefs and sometimes as worked examples from children.

Looking inside a classroom: Designing a city for Year 6

The staff in the school planned a Conceptual PlayWorld with integrated STEM for their Year 6 students. While their central focus was on mathematical concepts, they used the framework of a Conceptual PlayWorld to create motivating STEM conditions – where the children wanted to learn concepts in order to solve the problem that was the focus of their attention: how to design a city.

Characteristic 1: Selecting a book/story

To kickstart the program, the teachers chose to read the story of *Imagine a City* by Elise Hurst (2016). The story is about going through a make-believe city, captured magically through illustrations on each page of the book, including flying machines. As a simple illustrated book, the teachers decided to launch from the illustrations of the book by listening to a WebEx message from a Billionaire, Mr Chazman (one of the teachers' fathers), who sent a message to them asking for their help:

> I have heard you have the finest minds at your school. I want to be a mayor of a city. But the problem is I don't have a city yet. Please design me a city. My assistant (Year 6 teacher) will work with you. You can pitch your designs to me. I look forward to hearing about your ideas.

Characteristic 2: Planning the imaginary space

The teachers set up a board room for all the Year 6 students to attend (Figure 8.3). The board room was where the messages were given, the pitches were received and the decisions were made about the designs to go forward to the Billionaire.

Figure 8.3 Children meet in the board room
Source: Monash University PlayLab and Laburnum Primary School.

Coupled with the board room were the companies that worked on the design pitch. Each of the students' classrooms was turned into companies. This is where the groups worked on their pitch – researching, preparing and presenting (see Figures 8.4 and 8.5).

Figure 8.4 Children back in their companies (classrooms)
Source: Monash University PlayLab and Laburnum Primary School.

Figure 8.5 Children in groups preparing to research and engineer solutions
Source: Monash University PlayLab and Laburnum Primary School.

Characteristic 3: Entry and exit into the Conceptual PlayWorld

Entry and exit were through setting up a schedule of meetings to take place in the board room, and the exit routine was the assistant to the Billionaire making the announcement, 'Now go back to your companies'.

Characteristic 4: Problem to be solved

The story and the WebEx message set up the problem for the students. However, the teachers spent time studying what content they wished to introduce within the environment of the Conceptual PlayWorld. Some of the engineering concepts that the experience supported related to the technologies context of materials and technologies specialisations (ACARA, 2023), where children needed to explain to each other (as they prepared their pitch), and in the board room, their pitch to the Billionaire: 'How electrical energy can be transformed into movement, sound or light in a product or system' (ACARA, 2023) (Figure 8.6).

Figure 8.6 Mind mapping energy systems for their city
Source: Monash University PlayLab and Laburnum Primary School.

In Figures 8.7 and 8.8 we can also see how the children 'describe the materials and systems used in public places and facilities that benefit the way people live, for example a community' as they plot the transport system.

Finally, 'how characteristics and properties of materials, systems, components, tools and equipment affect their use when producing designed solutions (AC9TDE6K03)' (ACARA, 2023) was considered, as the students examined what social media to use for communications (technologies) (Figure 8.9) and what kinds of materials were needed for construction of the buildings, when visiting Mr Con Crete (teacher in hi-vis vest as a contractor) to get specifications and quotes.

Figure 8.7 Explaining their system of transport
Source: Monash University PlayLab and Laburnum Primary School.

Figure 8.8 Children's pitch for their engineered solution of a transport system for their city
Source: Monash University PlayLab and Laburnum Primary School.

Figure 8.9 Working on their pitch: a system of people movement and communications in their designed city
Source: Monash University PlayLab and Laburnum Primary School.

Video activity 8.1
Conceptual PlayWorld:
Design a city

While much more learning was achieved, it is possible to see in this one example how the Conceptual PlayWorld brought with it integrated learning, at the same time as setting up the need for the engineering design process (design a city) and the study of systems, as well as considering material choices when designing solutions. Different groups in their companies researched different things and this was in keeping with responsive teaching and differentiated learning. Board room discussions provided a cohesive overview of the collective learning experience of all the children from all the companies.

Looking inside a classroom: Engineering principles and systems when looking at human movement for Foundation and Years 1 to 4

As discussed at the beginning of the chapter, understanding force is fundamental to engineering principles and systems. The Australian Curriculum: Technologies (ACARA, 2023) suggests that children should be invited to explore how technologies use forces to create movement in products. The concept of force is also detailed in the Australian Curriculum: Science (ACARA, 2015a).

Force is often experienced viscerally by children, so may not be thought about consciously. Force can be also experienced through human movement, and this is often a good place to start at the Foundation to Year 1 level as part of exploring how technologies use force to create movement in products. Examples of children's thinking are shown in Figure 8.10 as a group concept map. Force can also be discussed through exploring a range of verbs, as shown in Table 8.5.

Figure 8.10 A mind map about 'How do our feet move?'

Table 8.5 Doing words: clues about the forces experienced in our everyday lives

Bending	Circling	Twinkling	Twisting	Skipping
Cycling	Punching	Walking	Swinging	Pointing
Marching	Jumping	Running	Pumping	Rolling
Stepping	Turning	Singing	Waving	Squatting

Making the forces acting in their everyday lives explicit to very young children enables them to begin thinking consciously about this concept; they are thus able to use this concept when investigating the engineering principles at work in a product. As shown in Figure 8.11, mind maps help support children to think more deliberately about the concept of force.

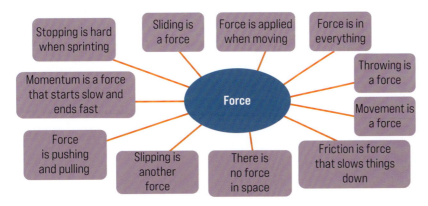

Figure 8.11 Children's mind map about force

The concept of force can help children to understand how the technology of a windmill harnesses the force of water or wind to create movement, as shown in Figure 8.12.

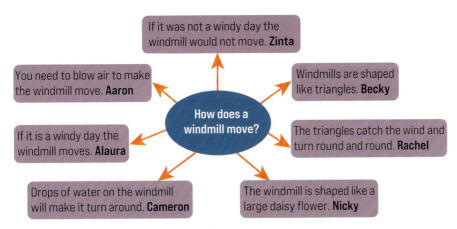

Figure 8.12 Engineering: how does a windmill move?

The concept of force is foundational for learning the principles of engineering, as shown in Table 8.6, where an explanation of the content of the Australian Curriculum: Technologies is presented. Notice the qualitative change from 'Explore' to 'Describe' and to 'Explain' in the content descriptions across the year levels.

Table 8.6 Content descriptions for the Technologies context: engineering principles and systems, and materials and technologies specialisations

Foundation	Years 1 and 2	Years 3 and 4	Years 5 and 6
No explicit content description	Explore how technologies including materials affect movement in products	Describe how forces and the properties of materials affect function in a product or system	Explain how electrical energy can be transformed into movement, sound or light in a product or system

Source: ACARA (2023).

Turning a study of force into a project on windmills requires a different kind of pedagogy and an engineering design process:

1. *Ask:* transforming the school playground into an adventure park can be supported by a windmill to move water from one level of the play space to another (children define the problem and begin to identify the constraints).
2. *Imagine:* children brainstorm their designs and work out how to build a windmill to support their designs (this should involve researching a range of windmills to gain insights into the relevant mechanisms and design principles needed to be used for the design and eventual product).
3. *Plan:* children draw their designs, creating diagrams, making a model of their windmill and playground, and collecting the materials they need to build the actual windmill and playground.
4. *Create:* children follow their design and make their windmill in the context of an adventure playground, then test it to see whether it works as planned.
5. *Improve:* children discuss what they might do differently to improve their windmill.

Download 8.1 Different kinds of pedagogy and an engineering design process

They then repeat steps 1 to 5. Specifically, they include a consultative phase in their project by inviting peers (their clients) to try out (test) the playground.

This example of the engineering design process in action shows how a project is more engaging and expansive than a simple study of the way the human body moves. The motivation for doing a project on designing a windmill with a purpose gives an engaging engineering context. These human dimensions of the project versus the content alone add a context for a client-based approach to engineering and the community consultative dimensions of being an engineer, as well as drawing upon engineering principles for understanding the forces inherent in existing and newly designed windmills for moving water through the different levels of the playground.

We move from the content associated primarily with engineering principles and systems to a focus on the materials and technologies specialisations in the next section.

Looking inside a classroom: Learning about materials and technologies specialisations through bridge-building for Years 1 to 4

Civil engineers are described by Dowling et al. (2022, p. 14) as being 'concerned with the undertaking of civil works that contribute to how people live their everyday lives, mainly focusing on the physical infrastructure of the urban community', such as bridges. With regard to bridge-building, it is important to know the engineering principles behind what works and what does not work. As in the previous section, the central engineering concept of bridge-building is force.

In the example of the bridge-building project that follows, the teacher documents in her program her intended strategies for supporting the learning of materials and technologies specialisations through engineering:

1. Gain a base to begin their own investigations.
2. Investigate how paper strips can be made stronger.
3. Devise a simple test to determine the strongest structure they design.
4. Measure the strength of a variety of paper structures.
5. Infer why some paper structures are stronger than others.
6. Construct simple bridges of varying materials and measure the mass they can support.
7. Modify the bridges so they can support a greater mass than the simple bridges.

The teacher began her program by consulting the content descriptions for the year level of the children (Table 8.7) and noted how the complexity of learning about materials developed conceptually for children from Years 1 to 6. She noted that the change from explore, describe and explain became more explicit in Years 5 and 6. In Years 1 and 2, the focus is on how materials affect products. In Years 3 to 4, it is about how the properties of materials affect function. Finally, the orientation is on the characteristics and properties of materials and how they affect their use when producing designed solutions.

Table 8.7 Content descriptions for the Technologies context: materials and technologies specialisations

Foundation	Years 1 and 2	Years 3 and 4	Years 5 and 6
No explicit content description	Explore how technologies including materials affect movement in products	Describe how forces and the properties of materials affect function in a product or system	Explain how characteristics and properties of materials, systems, components, tools and equipment affect their use when producing designed solutions

Source: ACARA (2023).

The teacher said:

> In our project we documented on cards all the questions the children had about bridges. In small groups they sorted the cards and came up with the questions they wanted to investigate. The children chose how they would like to work – individually, in pairs or in small groups. By generating a problem-based project, I hoped to create motivating conditions for children to explore materials.

Questions the children came up with:
- Who invented the first bridges?
- Why were bridges invented?
- What were the first bridges made from?
- Where were the first bridges built?
- How do they build bridges that open and close?
- How do they test the strength of bridges?
- How do they make sure the bridges meet exactly when they are built from the two sides of a river or bay – like the Sydney Harbour Bridge?
- What is the strongest type of bridge?
- How do they secure pylons in the sea or riverbed?
- What is the strongest type of material to build a bridge from?
- How many types of bridges are there?
- Why doesn't the water wear away the pylons?
- What is the longest bridge in the world?

Questions that were investigated:
- Who invented bridges?
- Why were bridges invented?
- What is the strongest type of bridge?
- How do they test bridges?
- How do bridges open and close to allow boats to go under?

The children worked in small groups initially, but as the investigations proceeded they started to work across groups, helping each other. There was a real sense of wanting to know the answers to the questions – *their* questions. The teacher gave the children an investigation booklet to document their ongoing thinking, as shown in Figure 8.13.

Download 8.2 Our investigations book on bridges

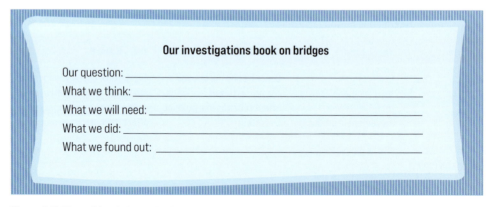

Figure 8.13 The children's investigation booklet

Examples of the children's work from Year 3 from their booklet are shown in Figures 8.14–8.17.

Our question: What is the strongest type of bridge?

What we think: I thought I would make a sourt of long bridge but it turned out as a schock because I didn't think it would b so strong.

What we did: I made a beem bridge and I ment to make a contiuos bridge And it turned out to be quite a good bridge. And I used foam with the pots and fences and the houses were you pay.

What we found out: I made a model bridge and it will hold 9 kg and we ran out of waights. So we got some from the TV room and thats all.

Our beam bridge was the strongest.

Figure 8.14 Ang's group – our investigation book on bridges

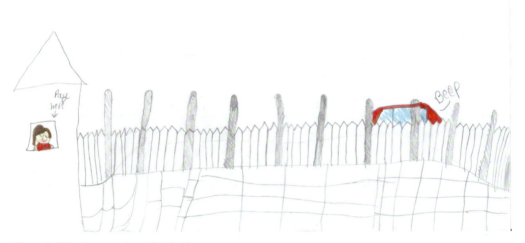

Figure 8.15 Ang's group draw their bridge

Our question: How bridges open and close to let boats go under.

What we think: I thought I could build a bridge that could open and close. But it didn't turn out the way I thought it would.

What we did: I got to bits of bulsor wood and put them on either side and then put a pice of cardboard across.

What we found out: I found out that I could build a bridge and me and my partne tryid hard to make it. But I thought I made it very good.

Figure 8.16 Alex's group – our investigation book on bridges

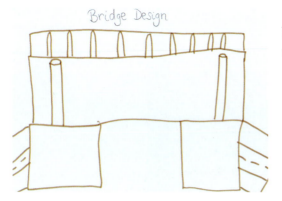

Figure 8.17 Alex's group draw their bridge

The teacher prepared an evaluation of the unit of work on bridges to reflect what worked in the context of the learning about materials and technologies specialisations:

> When we started this unit of work, the children found it very difficult to write about their ideas on bridges. However, once the children began to make models it was easier for them to draw and write about their ideas.
>
> The exploratory activities were designed to support the children to think about some of the key principles to do with engineering. It also gave them practical experience of designing, testing and evaluating their bridges. The children were most enthusiastic about building the bridges. This led to real interest in how particular bridge designs worked. The children cheered when they worked out which design was the strongest.
>
> The children had many questions about bridges. The challenge was narrowing down the questions so that a real sense of a bridge-building community could emerge. To do this, I wrote all the questions up on cards and displayed these so they could consider the questions they were most interested in. This allowed the children to form groups – children selected a card and then those children with the same card worked together. It was important for the children to form their own groups, because they could then work on problems they were really interested to solve. The result was six questions and 10 groups.
>
> The investigation booklet was given to each group. This helped them to organise their thoughts as well as their materials. Doing it this way meant a lot of discussion took place in each group.
>
> Interestingly, almost all of the children began building their models immediately. Only one group did their design before they began making their model. In addition, the group that researched the question about who invented the first bridge was drawn into the other groups' model-making, completely forgetting about their own investigation.
>
> One of the challenges was to keep each group focused on their question. I achieved this by bringing the children back as a whole group at the end of each session, and by asking each group to give a progress report.
>
> What emerged was a level of competition between the groups, which supported the children testing out their bridges in their small groups in order to build the strongest and most stable bridges possible.
>
> At the end of the unit, the children were invited to prepare a report to share with the whole class. This gave the possibility to evaluate their thinking, but also for the children to self-evaluate, and to evaluate each other – a collective form of assessment resulted. I found that through listening and watching, the children had learnt much more about design, testing and the construction of bridges than I had thought possible. The children really engaged with the concept of force and came to understand the key engineering principles needed for building bridges (at their level, of course).

In this problem-based project, engineering principles were drawn upon to build and test model bridges. Through the activities of the children, and their continual reflections through documenting their learning in their investigation booklets and providing ongoing reports, key concepts were examined more consciously, rather than simply tacitly experienced. The booklets and the progress reports were key pedagogical features of this project.

PEDAGOGICAL REFLECTION 8.3

Projects or models?

Creating models, rather than making actual bridges, is achievable in a classroom. But what might be the limitation of simply model-making?

What might be the benefits of children designing and making a model bridge? What might be the limitations of designing and making a bridge in the school playground? Record your ideas. You will return to these later in the chapter.

SPOTLIGHT 8.2

Progression in design thinking about materials

A study of the design drawing skills of children in early, middle and senior years of primary school was undertaken by Milne (2018). She was interested in knowing how students' drawing skills progressed across primary school and how their representations of materials changed. A unit of engineering was developed for each age group.

Project on bridges

Year 6 children made a bridge that was strong, while Year 4 children were asked to design a bridge that would hold a specific weight.

Year 6

The children experienced presentations from a designer and a structural engineer. They learned about materials and the structural properties of the town bridges. The children designed bridges and made models of bridges.

Year 4

The children learned about the function of a bridge through storytelling about bridges. The children designed bridges and made models of bridges.

Milne (2018) gathered children's drawings of bridges prior to the unit of work, and again towards the end of the unit. Milne encouraged the older children to experiment with different orientations and design perspectives of bridges prior to drawing the final design for their bridge.

Milne (2018, p. 504) found that when children had experiences of the form and function of materials through exploring materials and designing bridges:

1   There was a 'predictable progression of students' drawing skills across the class levels, with the junior students creating "after" drawings, which showed enhanced detail of the features

> and function of a bridge, and the middle and senior school students beginning to construct drawings that also communicated information'.
> 2 The purpose of drawing and the skill development noted in the research were directly related to the context of bridges. Through a meaningful context of studying bridges, children showed progression in drawing and design capabilities.

Video activity 8.2
Analysis of engineering concepts

The next section looks at how materials can be explored in early childhood settings with an engineering design orientation.

Looking inside an early childhood setting: Materials and technologies specialisations using blocks

Figure 8.18 Kim is using the blocks to build a very high tower – engineering and materials exploration: 'I am playing with blocks in the block corner. I am playing with my brothers. I like playing with brothers and Carris (sister) and Bianca (cousin).'

There are many resources within early childhood settings that can support the development of engineering education, such as those shown in Figure 8.18 where children use the block corner in completely new ways.

With some small changes to how the resources are introduced to children, these everyday activities in early childhood settings can become important sites for engaging in engineering practices and an exploration of materials. Following are a series of design briefs or pedagogical ideas for supporting engineering practices in the preschool learning centres (block area, box construction area, construction area, home corner, etc.) with materials already available, as outlined in Figures 8.19–8.28.

Adding resources to change the children's block play

Include the following items in the block corner:
- strips of different types of floor covering (carpet, tile, cord, wood)
- various fabrics in a range of different colours and shapes
- plastic people
- dolls' furniture
- mirrors, rugs, a dog kennel.

Figure 8.19 Adding resources to the block area

Combining learning areas to create new ways of working

Add box construction material to the block area so children can make the things they need for their block play, such as beds. For example, the following materials are easy to use and can be played with instantly:
- pipe cleaners
- bottle tops
- coloured and floral paper
- lids
- scraps of wood
- toothpicks and play dough
- Blu-Tack
- masking tape
- an array of boxes and cylinders.

Figure 8.20 Combining learning areas

Designing constructions

Invite the children to draw pictures of their blocks, LEGO and other constructions. Invite them to draw from a range of angles, to give them experience with drawing from a plan view, front view and even a cross-section (with you showing them how this might be done) for particular building types. To encourage this:
- provide boards and pens
- display children's drawings of their plans in the block area
- laminate children's drawings, inviting others to try to reconstruct them using their plans and a photo of the construction.

Figure 8.21 Including design in all the construction areas

Changing the focus of the block area

Use the block area to set up a theatre. The blocks are excellent props and stage effects.

Figure 8.22 Creating imaginary spaces in order to change the focus of the play and construction work

'Goldilocks and the Three Bears'

The blocks can be transformed into bear-sized furniture – chairs, tables for porridge, and beds. On each retelling of the story, encourage the children to suggest a new ending. This will allow the children to use the blocks as a story prop for a variety of endings.

Figure 8.23 Design briefs that draw upon fairy tales

Build a boat for *Mr Gumpy's Outing*

Build a boat using the blocks from the block corner to re-enact the story of *Mr Gumpy's Outing* (Burningham, 1970). The children can plan this by discussing how many of them can fit into the boat. The seating arrangement can also be planned – perhaps having name tags for the seat. Drawing a floor plan is also helpful. Boat-building could be expanded by searching the internet for a range of boat styles, finding the plans for this, and printing them off for adoption or adaption.

Mr Gumpy's Outing can then be acted out within the boat. *Who Sank the Boat?* (Allen, 1982) is another story that could be acted out in the boat.

Figure 8.24 Design briefs that draw upon popular books

Create an imaginary situation from the story of *Where the Wild Things Are*

After reading *Where the Wild Things Are* (Sendak, 2001), return to the phrase 'He sailed off through night and day and in and out of weeks and almost over a year to where the wild things are'. Organise a small group of children to design a shelter that will keep Max safe. This structure could be used to re-enact the story, with the children making masks to represent a particular 'wild thing'. Remind the inventors (children) to plan for 'their terrible roars, their terrible teeth, their terrible eyes, their terrible claws'.

Figure 8.25 Design briefs that draw upon popular books

Create a farmyard, following the map in *Rosie's Walk*

Recreate the story of *Rosie's Walk* (Hutchins, 1967) with the children in the block area. On the first page before the story begins, there is a full map of the whole farmyard. Use this double page as the map or floor plan for recreating the farmyard. Plastic animals, dry grass and other box construction materials may add to the authenticity of the recreation once the farmyard is complete. Retell the story using plastic animals or organise the children to design costumes so they can be the farmyard animals.

Figure 8.26 Design briefs that utilise picture books

Song: 'The Wheels on the Bus'

Using the block area, build a bus that will seat all the children. This structure could also be transformed into a train. Encourage the children to collect tickets and to plan their journey.

Figure 8.27 Design briefs that use well-known children's songs

Song: 'London Bridge is Falling Down'

Build a bridge for the song 'London Bridge is Falling Down'. Encourage the children to test out their design by placing successive weights upon the bridge. The children could start with dolls and puppets as they overcome their engineering problems. The teacher could also have children walk across the bridge – leading to another potential song or storytelling, such as the Three Billy Goats Gruff crossing the bridge.

Download 8.3 Design briefs supporting engineering practices

Figure 8.28 Design briefs that use well-known singing games

The diversity of materials will change the nature of the play that occurs in the block corner. In each of the design briefs, it is important to include some element of design before, during or after the children's play. Children can also be encouraged to create play plans – that is, to discuss with a teacher what play they would like to do in a particular area or what they might do that day in the early childhood setting. Children should be encouraged to consult with the other children around them, who may have other ideas about how to construct in the learning areas. Books are also a great way to support children (see Figure 8.29) in thinking about key ideas to explore in their play. Finally, the children should be encouraged to evaluate their designs and constructions. The teacher plays a key role in discussing the engineering principles at work as the children are working on their constructions.

Figure 8.29 Books are a great way to begin a unit on engineering.

Teachers should also comment on the stability of the structures, supporting solutions where all the forces are acting to help problem-solve why some structures are stronger than others. Children could also prepare 'engineering reports' on their structures, testing out whether they are 'earthquake safe', for instance. Play provides an important narrative about everyday life, where key engineering principles can be explored. This might be seen during discussions about shopping trolleys in the real world during play (see Figure 8.30) as they push and pull across a range of surfaces.

Web activity 8.3 Engineering concepts

Figure 8.30 Children working with materials in engineering contexts in preschool settings – feeling the push and pull of the shopping trolley

This section has looked at the contexts of technologies and presented a range of ways of teaching engineering principles and systems, and materials and technologies specialisations. Return to Pedagogical Reflections 8.1 and 8.2, and reread your comments. Are you able to imagine how you might introduce engineering contexts to children in meaningful ways? What insights did you gain from reading the literature on the range of pedagogical approaches to teaching engineering that have been presented in this chapter? Return to each of the teaching examples and include a section on teaching for:

- encouraging girls into engineering (How might you privilege this more in your program?)
- creating authentic engineering projects that have a purpose for children (How might children conceptualise a 'client' or 'consult with the community'?)
- creating learning across the curriculum (How might technology support literacy learning, mathematics or science?)
- sustainable engineering (What kinds of questions or design briefs might you create to support children with thinking about sustainable engineering?)
- materials and sustainability (What is the footprint of the materials used for the engineering projects?).

Summary

This chapter has considered the technologies contexts of engineering principles and systems, and materials and technologies specialisations, and how concepts could be taught from early childhood to the end of primary school. One key dimension of technologies specialisations (engineering) is project management. Chapter 9 is devoted totally to this important way of thinking and working, and these key ideas should also be drawn upon when planning for engineering principles and systems, and materials and technologies specialisations.

Acknowledgements

Special thanks to families for the infant photos in this chapter, to the teachers who implemented the technologies program and to the children who participated and whose work has been captured through the case studies presented. Thanks to Laburnum Primary School (especially Kelli Simmons, Student Engagement and Achievement – Numeracy) for curriculum development photos and to Bas Gerald for filming the project presented in the chapter. Finally, thanks to Yuejiu Wang for support with updating the references for this chapter.

The curriculum in action: Project management

CHAPTER 9

Introduction

> Everything is a project, from planning to go on a picnic to designing and building the space shuttle. (Portz, 2014, p. 19)

This chapter introduces the concept of project management through a community project approach. Several examples are provided to show a range of products that have been designed and produced for 'clients' in local communities. The advantages of incorporating a community project approach as part of a balanced technologies curriculum are discussed and the benefits are highlighted. This is in keeping with the definition in the previous version of the Australian Curriculum: Technologies (Version 8.4), which states that a project represents a

Project management skills: Help people to successfully and efficiently plan, manage and complete projects to meet identified design criteria (ACARA, 2023).

> set of activities undertaken by students to address specified content, involving understanding the nature of a problem, situation or need; creating, designing and producing a solution to the project task and documenting the process. Project work has a benefit, purpose and use; a user or audience who can provide feedback on the success of the solution; limitations to work within; and a real-world technologies context influenced by social, ethical and environmental issues. Project management criteria are used to judge a project's success. (ACARA, 2015b)

The most recent version (Version 9 – ACARA, 2023) foregrounds **project management skills**.

The project approach became popular in the United States after being promoted by Dewey and Kilpatrick (Pomelov, 2021), and in children's work in England in the 1920s (Isaac, 1996). Project work was central to the 'integrated day' or 'integrated curriculum' in Britain (Plowden Committee, 1967) and also in the Bank Street curriculum in New York (Zimilies, 1987). This approach supports Design and Technologies, where the content description associated with processes and production skills of collaborating and managing is featured (see Figure 9.1 and Table 9.1). The progression from Foundation to Year 6 is shown. A qualitative change is seen from recognising and planning a sequence of steps (Years 1 and 2) through to developing project plans (Years 5 and 6).

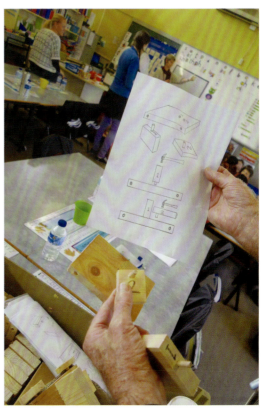

Figure 9.1 Project management in action

231

Table 9.1 Design and Technologies: Content description for processes and production skills – collaborating and managing

Foundation	Years 1 and 2	Years 3 and 4	Years 5 and 6
No explicit content description	Sequence steps for making designed solutions cooperatively (AC9TDE2P04)	Sequence steps to individually and collaboratively make designed solutions (AC9TDE4P05)	Develop project plans that include consideration of resources to individually and collaboratively make designed solutions (AC9TDE6P05)

Video activity 9.1 Project management

Source: ACARA (2023).

The community project approach in technology

A community project approach encourages children to identify needs or problems that are relevant to people in the local community (clients), and to generate products to make the clients' lives easier. These products must work and not just be models. When using a community project approach, the children write the design briefs, carry out interviews with members of the local community, conduct investigations and supply the necessary materials. On a need-to-know basis, they learn to use tools and equipment safely while acknowledging the individuals who assist them. There is ongoing student–client dialogue as the product is being devised, with the design drawings facilitating communication. An important feature of a community project approach is the client's evaluation of the product's durability, appearance and effectiveness.

Many children use recycled materials to minimise costs and for reasons of sustainability. Although community project approaches generally do not require children to identify the science concepts underpinning the products, the children's science understandings are often revealed in their narratives (Xu, Williams and Gu, 2021). As discussed in the previous chapter, the technological process can be the organising process that integrates other subject areas, such as science, art and environmental education, and gives a context for learning (Jurayeva, 2021).

In a community project approach, the design task is embedded within a framework of helping people in the community. A community project approach incorporates technology in the curriculum in the form of authentic tasks in which children are genuinely engaged (Fox-Turnbull and Snape, 2011). The value of 'authentic' activities must be stressed.

Children using a community project approach design and produce technological products that clients evaluate by determining how effectively the products work to meet their particular needs or solve their problems. What makes this approach authentic is that children have to negotiate the projects with clients in the community. Children keep 'process diaries', in which they record all their original ideas, sketches and designs. Teachers encourage children to use digital cameras, including video cameras, to capture a visual record of their involvement in a technological process. When children make presentations to their peers and show their completed projects, photographs, design sketches and models, it is important to encourage reflection on and evaluation of how well the project worked. Some examples of evaluation criteria are shown in Table 9.2.

Table 9.2 Community project evaluation criteria

Criteria	High	Medium	Low
Design brief outlining authentic task			
Evidence of communication and negotiation with client			
Product responds to the design brief			
Quality of product			
Presentation of product			
Evidence of all phases of the design/technology process			

Download 9.1 Community project evaluation criteria

Web activity 9.1 Project-based engineering

SPOTLIGHT 9.1

A pedagogy of critiquing

Keirl (2020) suggests that narrow views of design and technology focus on teacher-centred instrumental pedagogies, such as doing, making and skilling. He notes a spectrum from total design avoidance to tokenistic closed design briefs ('designing with the corners knocked off'), prescribed but open design briefs and student-determined research-based designing. To deepen the learning experience and the outcome of design and technology, Keirl (2020) suggests that all technology and design projects, including community-based projects, should be critical in their approach – that is, they should demonstrate a higher-order form of analysis and critical awareness. Keirl (2020) argues that in order to really understand critique in design and technology, it is important to study the context and to reflect on what kind of education society is wanting for children. This foregrounds community, which means it is vitally important in a community-based approach to include a focus on the ethical and environmental aspects, and to engage in political interrogation.

This pedagogy of critiquing in community-based projects should centre on all the phases of the project development. Keirl (2020) recommends that this should occur during the *initial conception* or *intention*; during *design*; during *realisation*; during *use*; and with regard to *consequences* – it is through the lens of a pedagogy of critiquing, he suggests, that the future is impacted by how we design and the designs we embrace (Keirl, 2020). A pedagogy of critiquing that is embedded into the community-based project should be considered as you progress through the content of this chapter.

PEDAGOGICAL REFLECTION 9.1

Community project approach

In your view, what might be a suitable community project for primary school children? Explain your reasons. Can you think of a community project that may be possible to do with children in an early childhood centre? Could you do this with infants and toddlers? What digital technologies could support them as they document and manage the project?

Drawing up a contract

Early on in the course of a community project, children need to draw up a contract with the client. This is an agreement between the two parties concerning what is to be made and who is to pay for the materials. Figure 9.2 shows an example of a contract.

> Date: _____
>
> This letter certifies that _____ is conducting a technologies project as part of their learning and that the class teacher has agreed to let them design a product that will be beneficial to assist them in the classroom. After observation in the community, _____ has suggested they design in order to help the community. The teacher has agreed to this and looks forward to having this design as a benefit for all.
>
> It has been agreed by both parties that any prices involved in the making of this product will be split evenly and that the maximum amount to be spent should not exceed $X. Recycled items will also be used when possible. The process of making the product will take around six weeks, during which time the teacher will communicate on a regular basis with _____ as to their progress in completing the product. Any concerns that either party has, throughout the six weeks, will be addressed promptly and appropriately.
>
> Name of student: _____ Date: _____
> Name of teacher: _____ Date: _____

Download 9.2 An example of a contract

Figure 9.2 An example of a contract

The contract is important for making the technological process proceed effectively, as evidenced by the client evaluation shown in Figure 9.3.

> Working with you to design and produce these products has been a smooth and enjoyable process. Both the talking wheel and the traffic light system are working brilliantly in the after-school program. Students are responding particularly well to the traffic light system, as I have noticed a significant change in their behaviour. They are also encouraging each other to do the right thing so that their card doesn't get changed from the green light to the yellow or red light. Thank you again for approaching me with your intentions to assist me in creating these new behaviour-management systems.

Web activity 9.2 Community project evaluation criteria

Figure 9.3 Client evaluation from an after-school care program

Once the school year starts, a community project should be introduced early so children have plenty of time to select a client and identify a need or a problem to be solved.

A balance of activities in the technologies curriculum

A combination of technological challenges and authentic project tasks provides a balanced Technologies curriculum. In the primary school, once the children have participated in several design process tasks (see Chapter 2), a community project approach can be introduced. Katz and Chard (2000, p. 8) suggest that a significant portion of early childhood and primary school practices should involve project work, as it 'stimulates emerging skills and helps children to master them because it provides contexts in which they are applied purposefully'. Since this work was published, less attention has been paid to project work in primary schools, even though projects create authentic learning contexts for children (Wells and van de Velde, 2020). A project is emergent and negotiated, rather than being pre-planned by the teacher, thereby encouraging children to generate creative solutions to problematic situations. Projects tend to be long term in nature, rather than just short-term activities, and they present occasions when some things have to be done over again to meet the client's standards or expectations. Perseverance is fostered and children gain satisfaction from hard work and from overcoming the obstacles encountered during their project work.

Project management

Another important feature of learning about community projects is the concept and skill of project management. It is suggested in the previous version of the Australian Curriculum: Technologies (ACARA, 2015b) that project management should be defined as the 'responsibility for planning, organising, controlling resources, monitoring timelines and activities and completing a project to achieve a goal that meets identified criteria for judging success'. As noted in Chapter 8, project management is already an important part of engineering, where project management includes:

- scheduling (What tasks are required? What time is available?)
- Gantt charts (client need, planning, problem definition, research, selection criteria, alternative solutions, analysis, decisions, evaluation)
- resources (making use of abilities of the team members; variety of members, such as creative thinkers, managers, implementers; contingency plan if someone is sick)
- risk management (identifying impact, potential consequences, calculating risk) (Dowling et al., 2022).

How might you introduce project management to young children, and what content might be learned?

PEDAGOGICAL REFLECTION 9.2

Project management

- Do you think you could teach project management to infants and toddlers? What might project management look like in early childhood settings?
- How might you introduce project management to school-aged children? What content might be learned?
- Document your views. You will return to them later in the chapter.

The previous version of the Australian Curriculum: Technologies suggests that in learning about project management, children should:

> develop skills to manage projects to successful completion through planning, organising and monitoring timelines, activities and the use of resources. This includes considering resources and constraints to develop resource, finance, work and time plans; assessing and managing risks; making decisions; controlling quality; evaluating processes and collaborating and communicating with others at different stages of the process. (ACARA, 2015b)

Project management also stretches children's thinking as they grapple with issues of managing sustainability, as noted in the previous version of the Australian Curriculum: Technologies (ACARA, 2015b): 'Students are taught to plan for sustainable use of resources when managing projects and take into account ethical, health and safety considerations and personal and social beliefs and values.'

The next section includes some working examples of project management in the context of community projects. These examples provide some insights into what project management looks like in practice in schools and early childhood settings.

Looking inside an early childhood setting: Project management

The experiences children have during the early childhood and primary years provide a strong basis for developing specific project-management skills. By the time children enter secondary school, they should be able to work effectively together towards developing the process and production skills of project management, as shown in the content description for collaborating and managing in Year 9:

> develop project plans for intended purposes and audiences to individually and collaboratively manage projects, taking into consideration time, cost, risk, processes and production of designed solutions. (AC9TDE10P05) (ACARA, 2023)

Where does this all begin? In the early childhood years, children work together with adults to realise their designs – for example, an adult can be present at the carpentry table with the child, cooperating to project manage the process of successfully completing a child's creations.

It is also important to create an inviting environment that children are interested in exploring – somewhere they can use real tools so they can effectively engage in carpentry themselves. A wish list or an ideas book can help children to identify projects on which they can work with adults; it will also provide an opportunity and a space where they can document their designs or illustrations of what they have made, to add to the ideas book for others to consider (see Figures 9.4 and 9.5). Authenticity is foregrounded, as is respect for children's ideas about a project, and their ability – together with an adult – to project manage their ideas into creation.

Buddy programs can be organised so that older children can work together with young children in realising projects. For instance, the transcript in Figure 9.6 details an interview undertaken by a group of Year 6 children who visited their local child-care centre and interviewed the teacher, Deanna, about the female tradespeople who had come into the centre,

Figure 9.4 Wish list – creating a table of off-cuts and recycled materials for carpentry

Figure 9.5 Ideas book on the carpentry trolley – projects to consider and a place for children to put their designs and images of their final project

and who worked with the children on real projects. The children used a digital recorder to document the interview, and replayed the interview in order to prepare their report.

Children make links between the activities available in the early childhood setting and the professions where specific skills are needed for the successful completion of something. Finding out about the different tradespeople in the children's community helps them to build a holistic understanding of their community. This is the community with which they will later be collaborating in the identification of meaningful community projects.

Alice:	Could you tell us who visited the child-care centre?
Deanna:	Yes. A chef, a plumber and a cabinetmaker visited the child-care centre.
Erica:	What did they do?
Deanna:	The chef cooked, the cabinetmaker planed some soft wood and the plumber showed us how she joined the pipes together.
Jamie:	Who watched them?
Deanna:	All the children in the childcare centre watched them for half an hour in their groups.
Alice:	Why did they visit the childcare centre?
Deanna:	They visited so that the children could see that girls can be chefs, plumbers or cabinetmakers. They also spoke to each group to let the children know that girls can really choose whatever career they are interested in.
Erica:	What did the children think about it?
Deanna:	The children liked it and thought it was most helpful. Alice learnt new ideas about it, Jamie learnt how to do stuff and Lisa was most interested in the plumbing.

Figure 9.6 Year 6 children conduct an interview

Figures 9.7–9.9 show children's reports on what they learned about their community, the specific roles people in the community had, and the kinds of projects on which they worked.

Figure 9.7 Esme (5 years) writes. 'The carpenter is building a fence.'

Figure 9.8 Lisa (3 years) draws and the teacher scribes what she has learned about her community – the plumber.

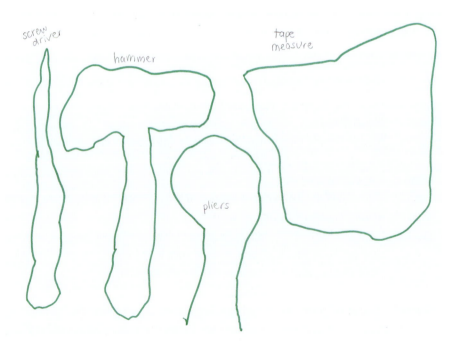

Figure 9.9 Andy (4 years) investigates the cabinetmaker's toolkit by examining each tool and tracing around it on paper.

In the Foundation year, projects can also be fostered through designing and making wooden characters for the storytelling session of 'Jack and the Beanstalk', as shown in Chapter 3. Bringing such a project to fruition requires a great deal of scheduling, preparation, resources and risk management (Dowling, Carew and Hadgraft, 2015). For instance, the project of 'Jack and the Beanstalk' required the following steps, and a number of questions needed to be asked:

- *Scheduling the working with wood project*. What tasks are required? What time is available? What equipment is needed? Do we read the story first and then plan for the making of the wooden characters so they can be used for future storytelling?
- *Preparation of a chart on wood-working project*. Who is the client? Is it the teacher or the children? What does the client need? What is the problem we are solving in this project? Is it how to make a series of wooden dolls? Should there be moving parts? What do we need to find out before we start (our research)? How many characters do we need to make? How will we know whether we have been successful with our project – how will we judge this?
- *Allocating resources*. How do 21 children make the wooden characters – do we organise them as groups or individuals? How best can we use the abilities of the team members? Do we have a variety of team members, such as creative thinkers, managers and implementers? What is our contingency plan if someone is sick?
- *Developing a risk-management plan*. What happens if the wooden characters don't work and we have to cancel the storytelling session? What will we do? What is our back-up plan?

Looking inside a classroom: Project management

The example that follows examines how a community project can be developed and managed. Vanessa and her Year 2 and 3 multi-age group worked together with the teachers and children from the Year 5 and 6 multi-age group on a design brief that arose from a problem they noticed in their community:

> The local newspaper said that oil was found in their waterways. The children draw a map of the problem on the whiteboard [see Figure 9.10]. They created posters and notices to inform the community about the problem [see Figures 9.11 and 9.12]. The children also wanted to create a short documentary on the problem and to show it on the local TV station.

The Year 5 and 6 multi-age group was set the task of helping the younger children to inform the community about caring for their environment. The Year 5 and 6 multi-age group worked with its clients (the Year 2 and

Figure 9.10 Whiteboarding the problem – a child's drawing of their problem

Figure 9.11 Posters were made to inform the community

Figure 9.12 Notices to inform the community about the problem

3 children) to develop a project brief. The children did this through the process of identifying the various perspectives on the problem (see Table 9.3). They:

- researched the technical requirements by visiting the local TV station and the radio station
- learned how to use digital cameras and editing software to support the production
- learned about how to create special effects and the necessary stage props and backdrops
- researched what community (i.e. families from the school) resources were available to help them
- worked with their client to get the right message – slogan, script, credits, etc.
- filmed and produced the media production
- evaluated the success of their production with the Year 2 and 3 children.

Web activity 9.3
Issues-based approach to technologies

The children researched with a critical eye, as is noted in Table 9.3.

Table 9.3 Issues-based approach to technologies – using a critical lens

Perspectives	Technological questions	Project management
Personal perspective	What sorts of TV programs do young children like watching?	
Reorienting to the other's perspective	What sorts of TV programs do other children and their families like watching?	
Historical perspective	How has TV viewing changed over time and why? How might that inform us about what type of program to produce?	
Environmental perspective	What messages are already out there in the community about sustainability, environmental issues and resource use and consumption?	
Producer perspective	What are the social consequences of screening the program being produced? Who gains and who loses?	

Download 9.3 Issues-based approach to technologies – using a critical lens

The teacher asked, 'How can we tell others about how to look after our environment better?' The children suggested the following ideas:

- 'We can create posters of the messages they wish to give.'
- 'We can prepare models and backdrops for the production, where we represent the problem to the community.'
- 'We can examine the drains in their schools to see how water flows through their school.'
- 'We can engage in research to follow the waterways in their community.'

Progression in project management

When setting design briefs to support the creation of mini-enterprises and other community projects where a level of project management is needed, there are many things that children need to think about. These include:

- the needs of the client
- the preferences of the client
- the importance of consumer choice
- product quality
- costs, including for time, people, skills, equipment and materials
- how advertising helps
- control of stock
- supply and demand.

It is important to consider the level of understanding and skills that children already have in project management. Understanding what children already know and can do in relation to client needs and preferences, consumer choice, product quality, costs, advertising, and even

Web activity 9.4
Project-based engineering

supply and demand is the first step in identifying what should be the focus of the program. It is crucial to identify where the child is at and where the teacher wishes to take them.

Progression in project management is shown in Table 9.1 (above).

As you read the examples that follow, consider what kinds of project management skills are being expected and developed. For example, how might you begin the project (see Figure 9.13)? With whom do you need to consult so you can engage the community (see Figure 9.14)? What follows is an example of how a group of young children set up a newspaper and how the project was managed by the children.

> To: Canberra Times
> A group of young children (5–7 years old) at our school are currently involved in creating a school newspaper. We were hoping that you would be able to write or email us with some simple information about how many people are involved in making a newspaper and what their specific roles are – e.g. journalist, reporter, etc. We look forward to hearing from you very soon as we meet again on Wednesday.
> Thank you very much.
> Karen and the children

Figure 9.13 Email to a newspaper to research the process

> Dear Parent,
> Your child is currently involved in creating a school newspaper during our Wednesday afternoon science and technology groups. We have decided that in creating a newspaper it is important to consider the audience, which is you and the children, so we are conducting this simple survey to find out what you would like to see in your newspaper. Simply jot down your ideas about what you think would be appropriate for you and your child to share together in a newspaper. Please send your ideas to school by Wednesday or put them on our blog.
> Karen and the children

Figure 9.14 Letter prepared for families

Project management: Setting up a class newspaper
How might you begin the project?

The class sent an email to a newspaper company to learn more about the process involved in creating a newspaper.

The teacher, Karen, developed a set of badges for the children to wear, which displayed all the roles for preparing and publishing a newspaper:

- Reporter
- Illustrator
- Journalist
- Cartoonist
- Advertising
- Photographer
- Graphic Designer.

Who do you need to consult?

The children in the class surveyed their audience to see what they wanted to read about. The ideas that were returned included:

- book, TV and DVD reviews
- pet tips
- for sale column
- gardening month
- recycling tips
- recipes
- photographs
- poems
- sports page
- environment news
- kids' page
- theatre events.

From there, the children developed their ideas.

Story ideas

News stories

Esme brought her new chicken to school. It is a special breed from Germany called a Hamburg.

Lilly hurt her leg because she forgot to have a seatbelt on. Remember to always wear a seatbelt.

Angela's mice have had more babies.

Hugh's cat Roger hurt his head. He has a big scar.

Marita had to go to hospital because she got a really big bump on her head.

Lost and found

LOST: Different-coloured LEGO – Denise

WANTED: Someone to teach my dog how to be a good dog – Deanna

Obituaries

Tina's dog died. Bye Bye Ginger.

Sam (Sally's fish) died and so did Max (Jenny's fish).

IMPORTANT NOTICE: Emma looked after a baby kookaburra but it died.

Interviews

As discussed previously, in project management children take on different roles. The reporters had some key questions that they used to frame their interviews. For instance, when the children decided to interview visitors to the school, they started their interviews with the following comment, 'We are reporters for the school newspaper', and followed this up by asking:

- Who visited? (Can you tell me your names please?)
- Why did they visit? (Why did you come to our school?)
- What did they do? (What is your role?)
- Who watched them? (Who came to see your performance?)

An example of Sylvia's newspaper plan, which she presented to the class, is shown in Figure 9.15. Other children discussed their role as reporters when they presented back to their class – for example, 'When I was doing the newspaper, I interviewed Alan and Carla.'

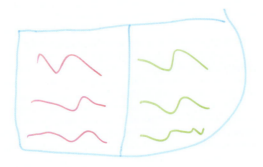

Figure 9.15 Sylvia: I made the newspaper

Project management: Setting up and curating an art gallery

Planning an art show would provide children with an opportunity to have an authentic audience for their artwork, and also to develop skills in design, curating and project management (see Figure 9.16).

Design brief

You are to redesign your classroom into an art gallery so that one piece of artwork from each child is displayed. You should plan an opening night.

Figure 9.16 Design brief for curating an art gallery

The children brainstormed what they needed to do, such as:

- how to display the artworks so they could be seen easily (see Figure 9.17)
- advertising the event so that people would come to see the artworks
- having an opening night
- catering for the opening night
- inviting someone important to open the art gallery
- working out how to display 29 pictures in the classroom
- developing a catalogue for the visitors.

The children followed up after the event with reports and evaluation (see Figures 9.18, 9.19 and 9.20).

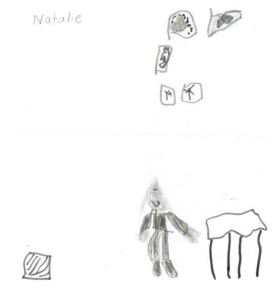

Figure 9.17 Natalie's design of how to display the artworks

Today mum is coming to the art show.

Figure 9.18 Melinda's report

Today we set up an Art Show. Me Gen Dorothy and Danielle set up the Wattle paintings.

Figure 9.19 Nathan's report

> Yesterday we had an Art Show. We made food and coffee for the parents. Before we put the paintings up Karen got some paper and we wrote about all the Art we did. Merideth said Anna liked all my Art the best.

Figure 9.20 Natalie's report

Evaluating

Questions we asked our visitors

- Does the room look nice?
- Does the room feel friendly?
- Can you easily see the artworks?
- Did you like the food?

Questions we used to evaluate the art show

- Was the room attractive?
- Did we start the show on time?
- Did we have lots of visitors?
- Did our advertising work?
- Was the food presented well?
- Could the artwork be seen easily?

We asked the visitors to evaluate our art show on a score of 1 to 3.3, with 3.3 being the best.

What we liked

Our parents came. The wattle pictures. The morning tea. We had fun.

What we could have done better

More art would have been good. A big welcome sign at the door. Some lighting effects.

Teacher reflections

The technological component was invaluable. The children really owned the art show. They created the artworks, designed the art gallery in their classroom, made the gallery appear and continuously appraised various parts of the process. The children also investigated various modes of presenting information.

Project managing mini-enterprises

Below are a range of design briefs that illustrate what the design process for generating a project of a mini-enterprise might entail (see Figures 9.21, 9.22 and 9.23). Each of these mini-enterprises will need children to consult in one way or another. For instance, they could:

- consult the coordinator of environmental education and the school principal
- organise group discussions/meetings with all the Year 6 students
- collect children's ideas together
- draw up proposed plans or designs
- consult the buildings and grounds chairperson – discuss materials and funding
- consult specialist teachers in the school, such as the art teacher, about ideas/suitable techniques
- consult the school board – submit their proposed project to the school council and buildings and grounds committee; they will need to supply a copy of the proposed plan
- organise Year 6 to view the plan – write up proposed questions or criteria for discussion and evaluation of the success of the project.

In addition to giving children a design brief, or children identifying a need in their own community, children can also use planned excursions to practise or develop project-management skills.

Project managing: Setting up a travel agency

- Systems – receipting, accounting, recording holidays, deposits, final bills
- Information – holiday brochures
- Booking accommodation
- Help – visas, itineraries, passport, medical insurance, currency arrangements
- Role-play inquiring, buying and selling tickets to test out system.

Figure 9.21 Project managing a travel agency

Design and planning tasks

- Create the agency logo and corporate message
- Develop a poster or webpage to advertise the travel agency
- Will there be a uniform? Design the uniform
- Phone message – friendly message
- Design the email signature
- Advertisement – for radio, TV, internet
- Use storyboarding, video record advertisement, field test advertisement, document results in spreadsheet
- Role-play advertisements.

Figure 9.22 Design and planning tasks that need to be project managed

Project managing: Setting up a café

Questions to consider

- What type of food will be sold?
- What will be the speciality of the café?
- Where will the café be located?
- Who might eat at the café?
- How do we run a café in such a way that the school routines and activities are not disrupted?
- How do we store unsold food?
- How are staff trained?
- How do we balance the costs against the sales?

Figure 9.23 Project managing a café

PEDAGOGICAL REFLECTION 9.3

Project managing an investigation at the zoo

How would you project manage an experience of investigating the science at a zoo?

Examine the achievement standards for project management in the Australian Curriculum: Technologies (ACARA, 2023). Identify the achievement standards for bands 3 and 4. Using the topic of 'Science at the Zoo', plan how you would help children learn to project manage an investigation so learning takes place in both science and technologies.

Figure 9.24 shows what Sarah knows and would like to know about science at the zoo. Figure 9.25 shows data gathered about the zoo. Use this information as the basis of your teaching plans. Some examples might be:

- designing good enclosures
- deciding what is good or bad for animals
- finding out about the trees needed for particular animals
- special food requirements
- being aware that if the animals are not well, the zookeepers need to give them medicine – how do they know this?

Figure 9.26 shows one child's report on the visit to the zoo.

Return to Pedagogical Reflections 9.2 and 9.3, where you were invited to consider whether young children should be taught how to project-manage, and where you had to consider what this might look like in practice. Now that you have read the case examples from early childhood through to the end of primary school, have your views changed or deepened? What is your opinion about what should be the key concept for children to learn about project management?

CHAPTER 9 PROJECT MANAGEMENT 249

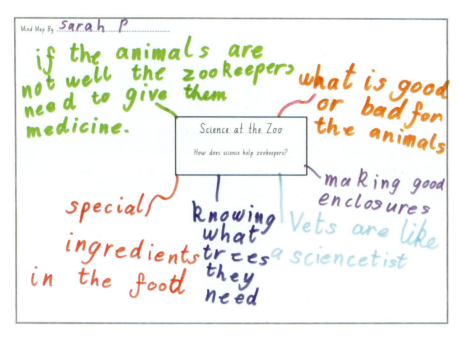

Figure 9.24 What Sarah knows and wants to know about science at the zoo – how can the class project manage these investigations?

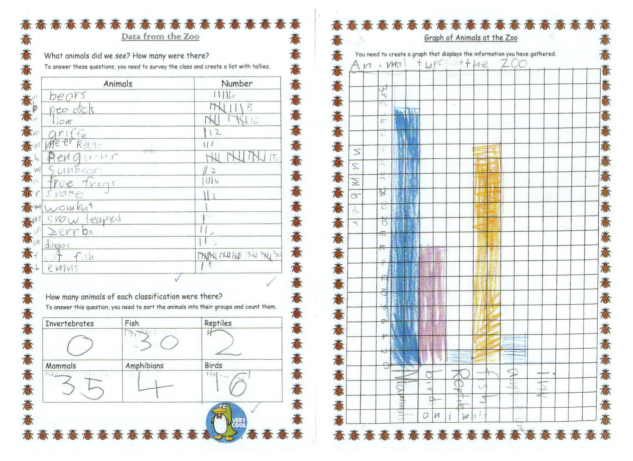

Figure 9.25 Data gathered from the zoo visit

> **Sophie's report**
>
> Science helps animals with food and water. At te shops ou by dog food, cat good and other animal food. Scintists need to know what's poisonous for animals. Dog food has rice, meat, other stuff like healthy food, and some vitamins.
>
> Cat food has fish meat. Vitamins, nutritions, scientist tell us what the wethers going to be like so we know to keep our pet outside or keep our pet inside.
>
> So now I know about pets I would like to know how to care for animals and look after one of my own.

Figure 9.26 Sophie's report

Figure 9.27 What might project management look like for infants? Could it be a system of care or a routine to pack-up toys?

Various approaches to teaching project management were shared across the case examples. Is there a specific pedagogical framework that you feel is best for achieving learning in the key concept you have identified? How do you now feel about teaching project management in early childhood settings and/or primary schools (see also Figure 9.27)? Share your insights with others.

Engaging children holistically

A balanced technologies curriculum that includes community projects can motivate children to learn project-management skills. A project approach relies on the children's own interest in the authentic task and on the appeal of the technological product. A project approach enables children to select the products to be designed and made, and to progress at a pace that suits them. Children can choose the level of difficulty and the degree of challenge required in order to solve problems. Further, projects can be introduced to bring together a range of curriculum areas, thus making learning in the primary school connected and more meaningful to children (see Fox-Turnbull and Snape, 2011). Where possible, children can draw from mathematics, literacy, science and other curriculum areas to generate content that can help them to better engage in the technologies, and to manage their projects more effectively.

Engaging holistically can also mean that children draw their topics and activities from the community. For instance, children can volunteer to assist a client in their community. Volunteerism has many benefits for children, including developing their willingness to help others and learning to communicate with people of different ages. Important social skills such as negotiation, decision-making and compromise are fostered. Therefore, community projects allow children to participate in activities that engage them holistically. Values are foregrounded, as over time children share with their client their creative ideas, technological expertise and endeavour. The requirement that the product must work to the client's satisfaction results in the children persevering to product completion, and thus being rewarded for their involvement in a technological process.

Summary

This chapter has examined project management in the context of technologies, where the concept of a project was discussed. The community project approach introduced at the beginning of the chapter provided insights into how project management can be enacted. In addition, presenting the range of ways in which project management can be enacted in classrooms and early childhood settings has allowed for a better understanding of how the concept of project management can be built over time.

Project management as a new way of working and thinking for young children in primary classrooms and early childhood settings opens up new possibilities for them, and also generates the need for teachers to use different pedagogical strategies. The case examples in this chapter illustrate how teachers can introduce the concept of project management to children through enacting it *together with them*, thus paving the way for children to work more independently of the teacher later on in secondary classrooms. Further insights into the special pedagogical approaches needed for teaching in the area of technologies follow in Part 3, where planning, assessment and evaluation are discussed specifically in relation to the pedagogical approach adopted.

Acknowledgements

Special thanks to the families at the play centre who agreed to be photographed and filmed for this chapter, and the other teachers and children who explored and developed competencies in project management. Acknowledgement is also made of the families at the play centre who agreed to be photographed and filmed undertaking everyday technologies as they played and worked in the centre, and to Bob, Renee and the children, who also allowed filming and photographing as they engaged in rich technological activities. Finally, thanks to Yuejiu Wang for support with updating the references for this chapter.

PART 3

Pedagogical practices for technologies

In this final part, different approaches to technologies education are examined. Both pedagogy and assessment practices are examined, and at the end you are invited to take a position on your own personal approach to teaching technologies to young children.

CHAPTER 10

Planning, assessment and evaluation in technologies

Introduction

In organising technological learning environments for young children, educators need to ask themselves three fundamental questions:

- How can educators find out what young children already know (assessing)?
- How can this process of assessment be a part of the teaching–learning sequence?
- What is the unique nature of assessment of technologies for determining capability, quality and judgement?

Figure 10.1 Assessing about learning, assessing for learning, assessing during learning – what can we find out about children's learning during their exploration of materials when making a simple kite?

This chapter looks specifically at these questions through considering the planning, assessment and evaluation of technological learning. Case studies are presented to illustrate what this means in practice. Each case example will examine a different way of planning, assessing and evaluating in technologies education. This chapter builds upon the planning sections covered in Parts 1 and 2. It begins by examining a range of ways of finding out what children already know in technologies (see Figure 10.1), followed by a spectrum of planning approaches; it concludes with a discussion of assessment in technologies.

Finding out what children know

Determining (or assessing) how much children already know and can do in technologies education sets the stage for designing learning experiences that are meaningful because they build upon children's existing competence.

Examples of subject achievement standards in each band in the primary school in Design and Technologies were shown in Part 1. Examples for subject achievement standards in each band in the primary school in Digital Technologies were shown in Part 2. In both Design and Technologies and Digital Technologies, ACARA (2023) presents level descriptions, achievement standards and content descriptions. What might this all mean for planning, assessment and evaluation?

ACARA (2023) gives guidance on content descriptions:

How content descriptions are used
Content descriptions are not all of 'equal size', so it's not expected that teachers will allocate equal time to each in their planning and teaching. While some content descriptions are so fundamental and critical to a student's development they should be revisited and retaught numerous times during the year, others might only be taught in a few lessons. Teachers, schools and/or jurisdictions will make decisions about the time required to address content descriptions depending on the complexity within each content description and on local context.

ACARA (2023) also gives guidance on achievement standards:

How achievement standards are used
The achievement standards assist teachers to monitor student learning and to make judgements about student progress and achievement. Teachers may also use the achievement standards at the end of a period of teaching, to make on-balance judgements about the quality of learning demonstrated by students and to report that information to parents.

The use of Australian Curriculum achievement standards as a common reference point for reporting to parents supports national consistency in reporting.

Assessment practices should be embedded in the social and cultural life of the classroom or early childhood setting (Tamati et al., 2021). Assessment should not be an adjunct to teaching in technologies. Generally, there is a distinction between two types of assessment approaches: **formative assessment** and **summative assessment**. Formative assessment informs teachers throughout the teaching unit, while summative assessment gives a summary of their outcomes at the end. An integrated system of assessment on the go (e.g. adding to student portfolios – formative) and assessment at the end (presentation of final portfolio – summative) is needed so that older children can reflect on their own learning and take greater control through the outcomes of assessment (Fox-Turnbull, 2015).

By 'unpicking their portfolios', children can examine explicit examples and gain insights into their own learning. For the younger learner, personal reflection would look quite different. For instance, for a 3-year-old child, educators would expect technological capability that is focused on experiential learning, design work based on modelling, and learning about what the materials will do or how they behave.

Only later would early childhood educators expect children to produce plans for their technological work, although they may invite a 3-year-old to draw or photograph their creation, as was seen in Chapter 4 when Alita invited her toddlers to draw pictures of the farm they had made from DUPLO® blocks. For older children, educators might expect *an analysis of designer competence* by looking for evidence of:

- novel and unexpected solutions
- being able to tolerate uncertainty and working with incomplete information
- an ability to apply imagination and constructive forethought to practical problems
- using drawing techniques and other modelling media as a means of problem-solving
- resolving ill-defined problems
- adopting solution-focused strategies
- using non-verbal, graphic/spatial modelling media.

Formative assessment: Teachers assess children's work throughout the teaching period, and not just at the end.

Summative assessment: Children are assessed only at the end of a unit. This feeds into making an overall judgement about the achievement of children in a learning area at the end of that band (e.g. F–2, 3–4 or 5–6) for Technologies.

Embedded assessment practices in technologies education have been specifically examined in the seminal research undertaken by Moreland, Jones and Chambers (2000, p. 3), Jones and Moreland (2001) and Moreland and Cowie (2009), who have noted important findings about how to assess in technologies education.

In the first phase of the research undertaken by Moreland, Jones and Chambers (2000), the researchers noted that during the assessment of children's technological work, teachers found it difficult to make judgements about the conceptual and procedural technological knowledge of the children. Due to the teachers' limited knowledge, or not having clear technological outcomes in mind, they tended to make judgements about children's behaviours, such as praising the children and making summative assessments. For instance, the teachers mostly commented on whether or not the children had completed the technological work. The study also found that the children appeared to not have a clear understanding of what they were being assessed on. For instance, some students thought it was more important to draw cooperatively with their partner than to create a drawing that would show their initial product ideas (Moreland, Jones and Chambers, 2000, p. 8).

During the second phase of this research, teachers were involved in extensive collaborative and in-service work. A change in the assessment practices of the teachers and the way they interacted with the children took place:

Figure 10.2 Assessing about learning, assessing for learning, assessing during learning – making observations of young children's learning during their play

> This resulted in teachers moving from using general concepts about technology to more specific concepts within different technological areas. For the first-time teachers were able to identify the specific technological learning outcomes they wished to assess and thus enhance the formative interactions. (Moreland, Jones and Chambers, 2000, p. 10).

> Teacher–student conversations became consultative rather than praise-based, students were assisted and encouraged to undertake an iterative problem-solving process, teacher modelling and the scaffolding of tasks became critical, and teachers began to focus on assessing the overall dimensions of technology as well as specific learning outcomes. (Moreland, Jones and Chambers, 2000, p. 2)

The teachers in Moreland, Jones and Chambers' (2000) study were looking at their interactional behaviours in the context of assessing learning objectives. Specifically, the researchers and the teachers were not trying to remove the children from their everyday classroom experience in order to assess them, but rather wanting to understand how the learner changed as a result of the technological activity while they were experiencing it (see Figure 10.2 as an example of a key observation about how children use technological resources in their everyday play).

Milne et al. (2002) examined technological assessment within the context of successful classroom planning and formative interactions. Their ideas are summarised in Table 10.1. Their work is useful for examining children's competence in technologies education in detail. Through examining what children know and can do in technologies, educators can better plan for learning in this key curriculum area.

Download 10.1
Assessment in technologies in the classroom

Table 10.1 Assessment in technologies in the classroom

Feature	Characteristic	Framing tasks	Assessment focus
Lesson selection	Known environment Carrying out familiar and real activities	Anchoring activities to everyday meaning to improve outcomes	'Designerly' play – playing, making and exploring ideas
Student drawing	Familiar and real	Drawing what they know or drawing what they see	Drawing representations or drawing accurately
End-point focus	Making clear the purpose of the activity in which children are involved	Discussing how their image works	Possible mismatch between planning and construction to be highlighted/noted
Modelling and planning	3D and 2D	• Playing around with hands-on exploration – 3D prototype or model rather than making • Children to make their 3D plan/design	Building experience for later design work
Information transfer	Recognising similarities of tasks previously completed	Remember when we talked about …	Learners need to 'notice' similarities
Consideration of variables	• Thinking about more than one or two variables • Formative interactions • Considering methods of gathering and analysing their work	Task selection is important: • Challenging • Open-ended • Multiple solutions • Number of unrelated variables	Unidimensional reasoning: • Unfamiliar tasks • Quantitative comparison • Choice between alternatives • Dominant dimensions

Source: Adapted from Milne et al. (2002).

In looking for the concepts that are foregrounded in Table 10.2 during a technologies activity, educators can have an embedded and meaningful formative assessment interaction with a group of children. The fourth column of the table highlights those areas that are to be assessed. Assessment cannot sit independently of the context, the purpose (for the child and the adult) and the overall plan of learning being considered over time. A holistic view of assessment in technologies is needed.

Video activity 10.1
Technological assessment in the classroom

As discussed in Chapters 1 and 2, one of the key dimensions of technologies education that makes it unique is design. Table 10.2 presents an example of a finely graded analysis of design performance and provides insights into what teachers might look for when observing children working technologically.

Most assessment practices tend to focus on the personal knowledge of individuals (Fox-Turnbull, 2015). As discussed briefly in Chapter 1, knowledge is socially produced, and

Table 10.2 Taxonomy

Level	Description
Abstract	Structures knowledge to solve problems, using relational and creative ideas and mature design development concepts.
Relational	Considers a range of design solutions, investigates possibilities, proposes a design solution and gives a rationale for best option for solving challenge. Can link design ideas to technological specifications.
Multi-structural	Provides a range of design solutions. Technological challenge is broadly conceived, and main components are considered and used for generating design solutions. Consistency in judgements and rationale is still developing.
Uni-structural	Design challenge is understood as one focused problem. One or two components feature in the design solution that is generated.
Pre-structural	Design solution does not relate to the technological challenge.

Source: Adapted from Leung (2000, p. 157).

groups of children often work together with their teacher on technological challenges. How is it possible to assess only individual capacity when that capacity is supported through interacting with others?

There is a growing body of literature in technologies education research (e.g. Zhao, Llorente and Gómez, 2021) that is moving away from the idea of the individual child constructing knowledge for themselves (a position influenced by a constructivist theory of teaching and learning) and moving towards more of a sociocultural approach (it tends to be named in this way in North American contexts) or cultural-historical (as named in Russia – see Kravtsova, 2008 from the Vygotsky Institute) view of learning and assessment. In this perspective of learning and assessment, the role of other children and the teacher must also be considered. It can be argued that the technologies lesson/event should not be analysed simply as a 'solo activity' or viewed as individualised, where the focus is centred on the assessment of the individual. Rather, educators should be thinking about assessment of technological activity as a social process, undertaken by 'collectives', where meaning and activity are socially negotiated. Technological knowledge should be viewed as distributed between people, and skills should be thought about as negotiated and mediated through others. A cultural-historical view of assessment in technology education leads to a very different kind of assessment practice.

Rogoff (2003) introduced the idea of using three lenses to make personal, interpersonal and cultural/contextual dimensions of an assessment perspective visible. Using three lenses to make judgements about the same observation of technological activity helps focus attention on:

- the *personal* (how an individual child is experiencing something)
- the *interpersonal* (how they are communicating together about something)
- the *cultural/contextual* (how the tools or artefacts available shape what might be possible) dimensions of working and thinking technologically.

The personal

Most of the literature on assessment across a broad range of curriculum areas provides insights into how to assess individual children. The next section has examples of approaches to assessing individuals, within the context of interpersonal and cultural/contextual dimensions of technologies education.

The interpersonal

In researching assessment practices from a sociocultural perspective, Compton and Harwood (2003, p. 7) found that

> a strong focus on the interaction between the 'mind and hand' demanded a high level of interest in finding out 'why and how pupils chose to do things' rather than focusing on the somewhat easier task of establishing 'what it was they chose to do'.

The assessor asking this kind of question invites a fuller reading of the assessment context. Harrison (2009) suggests that teacher talk in assessment for learning should include statements and questions that concentrate on the group of children as they are discussing and thinking about the technologies. For example, this could involve:

- inviting a group of children to predict:
    - How do you know if your design will work/is safe?
    - How might you check if your design is safe?
    - Which of your design features is key to ensuring this works/is safe?
- inviting a group of children to clarify:
    - What do you mean by that? Say a bit more.
    - Can you give an example?
- probing children's assumptions:
    - What do you think happened?
    - Might another group use it differently?
    - Is that always what happens?
- probing children's reasons:
    - What are your reasons for saying that?
    - Are you saying ... ? Which means ... ?
    - Which part of your design fits with that idea?
- inviting a group of children to consider the implications:
    - What might happen if you did this ... not that ... ?
    - What other reasons might there be for that happening?
    - What might you do to strengthen that feature?
    - How might your design work if it were used with younger/older children in different weather conditions/for several weeks?
- gaining children's viewpoints:
    - How do [child's name]'s ideas differ from those of [child's name]? What is similar and what is different about all these ideas?
    - Would the user look at the design in the same way? (adapted from Harrison, 2009, pp. 455–6)

These formative interactions support teachers in establishing understandings about the nature of children's design thinking and capabilities as they are working. Listening to the conversations that children are having as they try to solve problems, or generate design ideas, or work with materials to test their characteristics is also key to assessing children in technologies education. These insights can support teachers in making better decisions about what to plan for in subsequent lessons or units of work (Fox-Turnbull, 2015). Importantly, these insights help to better support children in technologies education as the teacher is interacting with them.

Cultural/contextual

The third lens is one of the most challenging areas of assessment. This lens invites a critical edge because it examines many aspects of the assessment net that are often neglected. De Vries (2005) argues that many people make normative judgements – for example, 'a computer functions well' or 'the computer does not function well'. De Vries (2005, p. 149) says that, 'In knowledge of technical norms, rules and standards as another type of technological knowledge we also find a normative component. This characteristic has consequences for our assessment of knowledge'. For instance, when children design technological solutions to a technological problem, such as designing a new school system for going to the canteen at playtime, the children refer to people-movement strategies that do not yet exist, but instead have to be imagined. They have to think about what might be fair, and the subtleties associated with making decisions, such as whether the Year 1 children get priority at the canteen.

De Vries (2005, p. 153) states that when children work technologically, they must also consider ethical and other values in their project work. For instance,

> pupils should be aware of the ethical aspects of technology. Sometimes curriculum developers shy away from doing that because they are afraid to indoctrinate pupils. This need, however, not be the case. It is important to help pupils to acquire analytical tools, with which they can recognize when a value dilemma shows up and how to deal with it through proper reasoning. Each individual teacher/school can then decide whether or not to add specific ethical content to that.

Ethical, moral and even aesthetic judgements made by children in their technological work are difficult to assess because these judgements are culturally and socially embedded and contextualised. A norm does not exist. This third lens, which takes into account the cultural/contextual dimensions, is a highly contested area of assessment, and is often not foregrounded when thinking about assessment practices in classrooms and early childhood centres.

Another key dimension for assessment when drawing upon this third lens is the assessment context created for children – that is, have children been asked to engage in a technological activity that is appropriate, meaningful and relevant to children's lives, and therefore engaging for them to work with? Asking this question ensures that the assessment is fair. If a child is not engaged in a technological task, they are less likely to demonstrate their capabilities or understandings because they may be bored, not interested or even offended by what is being asked of them. The latter might be seen when children are asked to do things that feel culturally unsafe or uncomfortable, or that position them in gendered ways, such as expecting boys or girls to engage in specific technological activities with which they have limited experience or that they see as unrelated to their personal lives.

> ### SPOTLIGHT 10.1
>
> ### Learners' experience of assessment – the journey
>
> Kimbell (2020) argues for the importance of determining the learner's experience of assessment. He suggests that in the assessment of a student's technological capability, the teacher should consider the unique nature of technologies, which involve practical task-based actions. These actions are visible, different approaches to working that are explored by the learner, and both the process and result are shared and can be measured against particular assessment criteria.
>
> Kimbell (2020, p. 203) argues that the assessment of Design and Technologies, such as when making a product or designing a system, is also related to our capability to *make explicit* what we know. The learning process is therefore practical or action oriented and visible, so the learner can see the assessor in action during the process of doing technologies education (formative) but also notice the assessment of the final tangible result (summative). Consequently, Kimbell (2020) argues that it becomes 'important to recognise however, that autonomous technological capability does not exist as a state – but rather describes a journey upon which learners are embarked'.
>
> Kimbell (2020) suggests that in a capability curriculum, the learner is on a journey in technologies, where they develop imagination and experience emotional subtlety in their action-oriented work, and in this context assessment must consider:
>
> - the affective aspect – specifically regarding trust, because the assessment is highly visible to the learner
> - assessment in-the-moment
> - agentic assessment by the learner.
>
> #### The affective
> Kimbell (2020, p. 204) raises the point that for a design and technologies teacher to be effective, they need to be a trustworthy supporter of the student, and ensure they feel comfortable to take risks. But the design and technologies teacher must also be a sufficiently critical external presence to offer challenges, make assessment and carry intellectual authority.
>
> #### Assessment in-the-moment
> It is suggested by Kimbell (2020, p. 204) that assessment is always immediate, because it is a 'personal reflection by the designer at the moment of creation'. For example, the learner usually engages in an iterative process of imagining/modelling. Each iteration is based on some kind of assessment by the learner about their design, product or system. Kimbell believes the process of student reflection and iteration is not typically called 'assessment', but nevertheless is an act of assessment on the part of the student. It is also a visible and action-oriented phenomenon that is public, so it forms part of the assessed process of the teacher.

Agentic assessment: Considering the agency of the learner as an assessor of their own work.

> ### Agentic assessment
> Kimbell (2020) argues that considering the agency of the learner as an assessor of their own work is different from formative assessment because the assessment process locates the agency with *learners* rather than with the *teachers*. Specifically, to say that 'capability assessment is driven by learners continually challenging and reviewing their own performance on task is not to say that teachers have no role in it, for clearly learners can elicit informed judgement from any number of sources' (p. 205). This is a form of **agentic assessment** by the learner.

PEDAGOGICAL REFLECTION 10.1

Planning for assessment – thinking about technologies activities/unit of work

Briefly write down an example of a technologies lesson/activity you have seen in a school or early childhood centre and consider the following questions:

- What was the intended learning outcome?
- Who decided what was to be made/evaluated – the teacher or the children?
- What was the role of the teacher?
- What was the role of the children?
- Was it part of an ongoing lesson sequence or a one-off experience?

Compare your analysis with the following case example of 'Bags with Attitude'. Consider whether your example highlights values in technologies. How might you assess values in your example? Record your ideas.

Case study: The cultural/contextual lens in action – 'Bags with Attitude'

A good way to help children learn about values inherent in designed objects is through taking an everyday object, such as a shopping bag, and experiencing it from a range of perspectives. When given experiences with an object from a personal perspective, someone else's viewpoint, or an historical, environmental and producer perspective, children begin to notice how objects are value laden. For example, Bev France brought a group of children together to explore a range of bags. These included:

- an army back-pack
- a school bag
- a blingy evening bag
- a Harrods shopping bag
- a traditional Aboriginal carrying bag, sometimes known as a 'dilly bag'
- a paper bag
- a garbage bag
- a briefcase

- a knitting bag
- a reusable plastic shopping bag
- a nappy bag.

Bev invited the children to form small groups, then to take a bag and role-play being the person holding the bag, imagining what might be inside the particular bag. She knew from her research that children would take a personal perspective, but she wanted them to go deeper into thinking about their designed environment, as shown in Table 10.3.

Table 10.3 A range of perspectives about everyday designed objects, such as bags – draw a picture of someone holding 'this' bag

Perspective	What might be expected	How to develop children's perspectives
A personal perspective	Young children are likely to draw a picture of themselves carrying their special bag.	If children put these up as posters to view, then they see a range of ways in which they can think about an everyday object, such as a shopping bag.
The perspective of the other individuals and groups	Children analyse the different bags and think about who might use them (knitting bag, briefcase, army back-pack, nappy bag).	If children draw the bag and the person, they then go out into the community and research who carries particular bags.
An historical perspective	Children research how their fellow students bring their lunch to school.	Children interview a grandparent or elder in the community about how they brought their lunch to school. Children bring their findings back to the class to share and discuss.
An environmental perspective	The children take the common reusable plastic shopping bag and discuss what happens to it. They document their ideas.	The children research what happens to the reusable plastic shopping bag, creating a flow chart to illustrate the pathway. They also examine canvas or cloth shopping bags.
The producer perspective	The children are presented with a plastic handbag and are asked to think about who made the bag and why.	The children are asked to critically examine the design process (local product/imported – resource footprint), whether it was made in a poor, under-developed country and whether anyone was exploited or the conditions in which they worked – and to think about the marketing surrounding the item – that is, creating a 'need' or 'want' for the product.

Download 10.2 A range of perspectives about everyday designed objects, such as bags

The children then drew their bag, the imagined contents and the person who was holding the bag on an A3-sized card. These drawings became their posters to display.

The children walked around each of the posters and talked about the range of perspectives represented – the way the bag was linked with the people who were holding the bag. Some of the perspectives that were noted were:

- nappy bag – a female dressed casually holding a baby
- briefcase – a male dressed in a suit
- Harrods shopping bag – someone wearing expensive clothes and jewellery
- reusable plastic shopping bag – a European-heritage child holding a toy, and a Chinese child making the toy in China.

In this example of a values-based approach to technologies, assessment included looking for drawings and comments from children throughout the unit of work that featured:

- asking about, researching or commenting on who might benefit from these technologies
- comments on sustainability
- discussing a range of alternative materials to be used that focus on local community
- the environmental footprint of transporting the product
- asking questions about the production of the bags in relation to who benefits – is it the local community?
- commenting on everyday artefacts in their own lives and homes and asking questions about them.

ACTIVITY 10.1

Planning a values-based approach to technologies – 'Bags with Attitude'

Refer to the case example 'Bags with Attitude' for a unit of work that foregrounds values.
Design a unit of work that takes this critical edge and foregrounds values. In your planning, include:

- a personal perspective
- the perspective of others
- an historical perspective
- an environmental perspective
- the producer perspective.

In Chapter 3, the idea of children's future thinking and designing was discussed. This way of conceptualising children's design capabilities and technological knowledge must be matched with an assessment approach that is future focused – that is, it must be situated within a futures orientation. For instance, students do not necessarily progress through what they are not able to do, but must be extending to what they can do to bring in what they cannot yet do. This perspective mirrors the general assessment literature, which in recent times has focused on a future orientation to assessing children's achievements. A cultural-historical perspective of assessment is noted by Kozulin (1998, p. 69):

Vygotsky argued that the task of assessment must identify not only those cognitive processes of the child that are fully developed, but also those that are in a state of being developed at the time of assessment. This development, according to Vygotsky, depends on a cooperative interaction between the child and the adult, who represents the culture and assists the child in acquiring the necessary symbolic tools of learning.

Vygotsky's theoretical work in relation to the zones of proximal and actual development has also been used for theorising assessment practices to draw attention to assessment for the future (Fleer, 2010). Assessment for the future takes account of the expansive work of Kravtsova (2008) on actual, proximal and potential zones of development. Kravtsova's model for the zones of development is shown in Figure 10.3.

In this model, Kravtsova maps Vygotsky's (1997) actual and proximal zones and adds to this the idea of a potential zone of development. By this she means all the experiences that a child has had, which may not yet be understood – for instance, a primary-school child visiting an architect's studio and observing the practices of her mother engaged in drafting plans or spending time in an engineering workshop supporting the activities of the adults by sweeping the floors may not actually understand or take part in the drafting or engineering activities in meaningful and knowledgeable ways; however, these experiences are important because they orient the child to related events later on in school or everyday life, where learning activities can be connected with these earlier experiences. Taking these zones of development and using them to theorise assessment practices in technologies education generates the concepts of proximal assessment and potentive assessment.

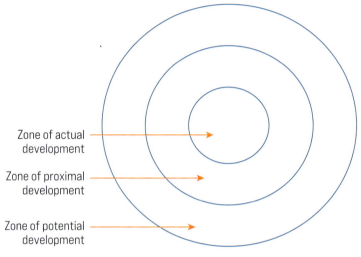

Figure 10.3 Zones of actual, proximal and potential development

Proximal assessment seeks to capture all the dynamic interactions associated with a performance as it is enacted by a child, a group of children or adults interacting with children (or vice versa). Through the wholeness of this performance, the assessor makes judgements about individuals or groups of children in the context of their interactions and in terms of the wholeness of their cooperative task. Within this *dynamic assessment context*, it is possible to document proximal performance, as made visible through the carefully organised interactions between children and staff, and through the children themselves. In these situations, it is not just the wholeness of the performance that is important, but also the support received that allows individuals to engage in the collective task or performance.

Potentive assessment allows teachers to organise learning situations that project children into future learning contexts, where they observe or gain insights into the learning that is still to come. Potentive assessment is a concept that will help teachers in their observation and planning for children's learning.

The assessable moment

Proximal assessment involves not only assessing the children's proximal capacities as enacted through interactions with more highly performing others; it is also about teachers making judgements about when, in everyday practices, assessments should be made about children's actual and proximal zones of development. The timing of these assessments is significant, as teachers must make judgements at times when children can best show their capabilities. This kind of teacher judgement is termed the *assessable moment* and it mirrors the established and well-known idea of the 'teachable moment'.

These concepts are important because they represent a just-in-time moment for furthering learning (teachable moment) and a just-in-time moment for measuring or observing the proximal, actual and potentive development of children (assessable moment). A cultural-historical view of development, as shown in Figure 10.3, provides the theoretical foundation for building assessment practices into the technology teaching programs of all educators working with young children.

Evaluating

Before evaluating a teaching program in technologies, it is important to think about the purpose of the evaluation. Is it to find out how the pedagogy went? Is it to provide data on outcomes of the whole teaching–learning program to the school or state? Is it for self-reflection – how should things be done differently?

Once the purpose has been established, the task of collecting information begins. What tools are needed – for example, survey, interview, student assessment records, workshops, discussion groups, panels or school–community conferences?

When teachers are undertaking an evaluation, it is important to consider:

- real-world programs that relate to the children's everyday world:
    - Does the technologies program being implemented fit into the curriculum in the school or early childhood setting?
    - Have the children been given the opportunity to go outside of the school or early childhood setting and into the real world with all its problems?
    - Is there any industry or service near the school or early childhood setting that could be utilised? Could they offer children rich and worthwhile real-world experiences?
- the effectiveness of the learning and teaching process:
    - Is the teacher aware of the understandings the children are bringing to the particular unit of work before it begins?
    - Are the children central to the learning process?
    - Are the children actively engaged and participating (rather than passively receiving)?
    - Do all the children have an opportunity to contribute, and are the broad interests of the group being taken into account – that is, is inclusivity being considered?
    - Are various strategies being used to determine the understandings of the children, so that different ways of making learning visible are possible?

- Is the technologies program supporting an integrated approach to learning so that learning is meaningful to the children?
- Are learning experiences relevant to the children's lives?
- Are safe practices being adhered to by all?
- Do the children ask questions?
- Are the children being encouraged to plan their own investigations?
- Are the children being encouraged to talk and play with ideas?
- whether learning outcomes documented in the program were achieved and why
- self-evaluation:
  - How did the teacher feel about the technologies teaching approach that was used?
  - Did the topic lend itself to stimulating and challenging technologies questions?
  - Did the management of the children and the resources influence the program outcomes?
  - What did the teacher learn about technologies teaching and children's thinking?

This section has brought together some of the long-standing assessment research undertaken in the area of technologies education. Beginning with the area of assessment is important because it invites us to think about what children know and can do in technologies and, armed with this knowledge, to better plan for learning. The next section looks at a range of ways in which learning can be set up for children. Technologies education has been shown in the previous chapters in both expansive and simple one-off lesson contexts. As such, the examples that follow highlight a range of pedagogical approaches. In each case example, planning and assessment practices are foregrounded.

ACTIVITY 10.2

Evaluating your technologies program

Select one of the case examples of teaching technologies from the textbook, or the values-based unit you designed. Evaluate that program in relation to:

- real-world programs that relate to the children's everyday world
- the effectiveness of the learning and teaching process
- whether or not learning outcomes documented in the program were achieved and why
- self-evaluation.

Reflect upon the following:

- What did you learn from doing this?
- Did you have enough information to undertake the evaluation?
- What information do you need to collect in order to evaluate your program?

SPOTLIGHT 10.2

Assessing quality

Kimbell (2020) has introduced the term 'connoisseurship' to capture the idea of quality in technologies education from the perspective of the student. He says that, as educators, we invite our students to reflect upon their design/products/systems by asking them questions such as:

- What do you like/not like about your X?
- What would you change?

He suggests that this very pedagogical action is like an inquisition, which has the effect of determining quality as something that emerges 'from the work itself and that (for learners) are seen to be indicators of quality'. Discussions about quality in technologies education are important for teachers, who need to write school reports. Kimbell (2020) argues that, rather than attribute a 'numerical grade' for a 'design, product and/or process/system', it is more reliable to make judgements between actual tangible artefacts as a 'comparative judgement' rather than an 'absolute', book-based criterion assessment. He says that we make comparative judgements and these are simpler than absolute ones. He suggests that it is easy to say that *this* shopping bag is heavier than *that* one. But what we find difficult is saying exactly how much heavier it is in terms of kilograms. An absolute judgement about kilograms is difficult, but direct comparison is easy.

In summary, Kimbell (2020) states that the judging process should be seen through the lens of how the learner is grappling with their *emerging connoisseurship* as they join us within our community of practice. This is a very different way of conceptualising quality in technologies education, and reflects the unique way we can frame achievements in the process of assessing outcomes in technologies education.

Setting up the learning environment

Figure 10.4 Alicia has drawn how learning is organised in her preschool – what it means to her at group time. All the children can see each other at group time and this makes her feel happy.

The ways in which learning environments are set up show both the philosophy of the teacher in action and the possibilities for what children can do in a classroom or early childhood centre. Young children are already aware of the special learning spaces that are created in preschools and schools, as shown in Figure 10.4.

Alicia has drawn a picture of how learning is organised for her at preschool. She has focused on group time, which is a key characteristic of setting up learning in preschools and classrooms. What we notice from her picture is that all the children are seated in a type of semi-circle – presumably with a teacher somewhere in the circle. This configuration means that all the children can see and hear each other. When children are clustered together, one behind the other on the mat, it means that the children at the back may not actually be able to hear what another child is saying when responding to the teacher.

Alicia's drawing is a powerful image because it shows an effective pedagogy for technologies education, where children frequently discuss ideas and show designs. If only some of the children can hear each other or see each other's faces, then valuable learning opportunities are lost. The worst-case scenario is captured by Madison (10 years):

Madison: I hate group time on the mat. I can see and hear the teacher. But I can't hear the others [children] – what they say back to Ms X.

Interviewer: How is the group organised?

Madison: Oh, we all sit bunched together. All I can see is the back of other children's heads. I can't hear anything at all!!!

Interviewer: So you cannot see or hear the children in your class?

Madison: Yes, and it is so boring. I can't wait for it to be over. We do it every day!

Setting up for technologies education can also involve changing a part of the classroom, as might be seen when a large technologies project is introduced. Figure 10.5 shows Freya's drawing of how the classroom had been changed to reflect her local community.

This simulation is an example of what teachers do when creating new spaces in their classroom or early childhood centre. In Freya's classroom, her teacher changed the whole space so that when the children entered they had a supermarket, a garage, a nursery, a post office, a café and a bakery (which reflected the local shops where Freya lived). Each of the spaces contained real tools and tasks. The children had researched these key areas, created designs, made models and prepared a full simulation of the community in the classroom. In this context, a school newspaper was created and a café menu produced (see the restaurant design brief in Chapter 7) for the restaurant, which the other children in the school could visit.

Figure 10.5 Setting up the classroom to simulate the community: what children value

Technologies education has been shown in this book to be a very active approach to learning. Many technologies activities require additional support as well as additional expertise. This means volunteers are welcome in classrooms and early childhood settings. In Figure 10.6, Krishma has drawn a picture of his mother helping out in the classroom.

Setting up learning environments where volunteers are invited into the classroom requires organisation. The organising infrastructure that could be put in place might feature:

- sending a letter to all families and to the local volunteer groups (e.g. Rotary Club) inviting volunteers

Figure 10.6 Having volunteers to support the technologies program

- putting up a whiteboard at the child pick-up point asking for volunteers, with a roster plan with a permanently marked school calendar on it for parents to record their names
- inviting all families into the classroom in the last hour of each day to support the planned activities
- surveying or interviewing families at the beginning of the year to find out about their special skills and interests, which could be drawn upon
- establishing tinkering or fixing clubs run by volunteers to support the technologies program
- running lunchtime iPad clubs or cooking clubs
- creating design briefs (laminated) with detailed instructions about how volunteers can interact with children to support them, with kits of resources.

PEDAGOGICAL REFLECTION 10.2

Designing learning spaces for technologies education

Consider how you might design the spaces for technologies education in your classroom or early childhood centre. What will be your role in these spaces in your classroom or early childhood centre? Will there be volunteers? How might families and other volunteers be integrated into your classroom or early childhood setting? Draw upon Table 10.4 to support your thinking. Record your ideas.

Table 10.4 Pedagogical critique of technologies education

Collective and open approach to planning	Structured and individual approach to planning
Teacher and children work together in a collaborative manner.	Children work individually.
Teacher introduces design brief with task-specific constraints, but thereafter open-ended (all produced different outcomes).	Teacher gives out design briefs with task-specific brief set.
Children decide as a group what materials/processes they wish to use – not specified.	Materials are specified by the teacher.
Children use the materials to model and create their designs.	Designing is done in advance, on paper.
Teacher supports children in situ, encouraging children to problem-solve in their groups.	There is a high level of teacher input.

When families are included in the program through one or all of the above infrastructures, a great deal of time can be saved and the richness of the technological experience for children can be enhanced.

Designing spaces and interactions for assessment and planning

You will notice in the case examples in this section how teachers design spaces and interactions with children to support the assessment process (Figure 10.7). The examples focus on both the planning and the assessing. As you read them, consider how they have been conceptualised, with assessment *for* learning, assessment *about* learning and assessment *during* learning all featuring.

PEDAGOGICAL REFLECTION 10.3

Designing spaces and interactions – planning and assessing

As you read through the case examples, think about assessment from the perspective of the following dimensions of working and thinking technologically:

- *personal* (how an individual child is experiencing something)
- *interpersonal* (how they are communicating together about something)
- *cultural/contextual* (how the tools or artefacts available shape what might be possible).

Consider how you would need to:

- set up the learning spaces
- consider what types of materials are needed
- plan the interactions you will have (see the previous section for key questions you could consider)
- examine how assessment could be embedded.

Some of the examples are presented briefly and are intended to be discussion starters, while the others are detailed in full so you can see the depth of learning that is possible. Record your ideas about assessment and learning as you read each example.

Figure 10.7 Planning your interactions

Example 1: Sherlock Holmes – identifying needs and opportunities

Figure 10.8 shows an example of a design brief for children auditing their technological world.

> Your role as Sherlock Holmes is to investigate the spaces around your playground and school buildings. Talk to the children and the teachers about how they use the spaces, the objects and the systems (e.g. lunch ordering, library use):
> - Identify any problems.
> - Ask for ideas about solutions – how changes could be made.
> - Ask questions that may help with finding out what could be done – for example, 'What part could be different?', 'Is there someone who might know that we could ask?', 'Have you seen this somewhere else where it worked better?'
> - Ask about what people need, like and don't like.
> - Talk about decisions that might need to be made, such as consulting families, parents and the community or school council.

Figure 10.8 Design brief – auditing our environment

This example is completely open-ended. How might you plan and assess for this design brief? It is probable that you will plan your interactions with the children very carefully, supporting them to think deeply about what they notice about their technological world. You will also need to create a framework for self-evaluation and consider assessment interaction during the design process.

In a self-evaluation framework, do the following:

- Invite children to talk to each other about what they have done and how well (or not) it went.
- Ask the children to talk about what they like or don't like about the objects, systems and environments in the school.
- Discuss how they feel about something, and how satisfied they felt with the result in relation to the initial need that was identified.
- Ask children to comment on the materials and processes used in solving the problem.

Once children have undertaken the environmental audit, they are in a good position to decide about how to solve the problems identified or design the solutions they have imagined, discussed and researched. Assessment interaction can now explore the design dimensions – for instance:

- Children should review their original design and discuss what they would change.

- Talk about design intentions, original needs, users' views, how cost-effective the product or process was, and whether there is a possibility for production (what scale of production might be considered).
- Justify the materials, particularly in relation to local sourcing, resource footprint, sustainability, culture, time constraints, costs and aesthetic value.

In order to move children towards a deeper sense of critique of their environment and their subsequent designed solution, the questions asked by the teacher should also deepen.

Another important aspect is assessment interaction during the design process. Things to think and talk about when designing could include:

- Who needs or wants it?
- What is it needed for? Why do they want it?
- Does the design invite a positive response and interaction possibility – 'come and use me'?
- How has it been made?
- What has it been made from?
- How has it been joined together?
- Could it be used in a range of ways, or only one way?
- Is it safe to use?
- How much did it cost to make?
- How much time did it take to make?

Example 1 featured a lot of planning for the kind of interaction the teacher would have with the children – both for quality learning and for assessment (Fox-Turnbull, 2015).

Example 2: Design briefs for fairy tales and nursery rhymes

Example 2 consists of a series of early childhood design briefs that support a host of technological activities. Engagement in technologies is shown through fairy tales and nursery rhymes (see Figures 10.9–10.12).

'Humpty Dumpty'

Research the different designs and materials used for making walls for Humpty Dumpty. Select the material type and design, and build a wall that will support the weight of a hard-boiled egg.
   Detail the steps needed.
   Select a way to share your work with the class (e.g. slowmation, poster, report).

Figure 10.9 Building a Humpty Dumpty wall

'Hansel and Gretel'

Design and make a gingerbread house.

After receiving some teacher support with different ways to hang doors and windows, design, build and decorate the gingerbread house. Think about the hinge (investigate the types of hinges in your school).

Figure 10.10 Designing a gingerbread house

'Jack and Jill'

After some discussion about how wells work and methods of winding up a bucket, design and build the well. The bucket must be able to hold half a cup of water without leaking.

Think about how you can keep the bucket at the top of the well without it slipping down.

Figure 10.11 Building Jack and Jill's well

'The Three Billy Goats Gruff'

Design something the three billy goats can use to get across the river.

Design and build a bridge that spans 30 centimetres (your ruler length) to support the plastic goats (and the troll). Use a variety of materials to test – straw, paper, icy pole sticks, other materials of your choice.

Download 10.3
Designing elements from stories

Figure 10.12 Designing a new bridge for the Three Billy Goats Gruff

Now consider how the general everyday activities found in an early childhood setting might change as a result of these design briefs. Planning here will focus on the best ways to introduce a design challenge to the children. How might this happen? Would the teacher begin by telling a story or singing a nursery rhyme? What might the teacher say next to engage young children in designing, problem-solving and building with the available materials in the early childhood setting (see also Figure 10.13)?

Example 3: Designing through board games

Example 3 shows the instructions for how to make a board game. These instructions were designed by the children, who also designed and created posters to help others (see Figures 10.14–10.16).

Figure 10.13 What kinds of interactions might you plan when working technologically with infants?

Figure 10.14 How to make a magnetic mouse maze: things you need

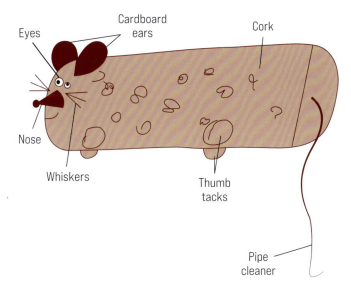

Figure 10.15 Diagram of a magnetic mouse

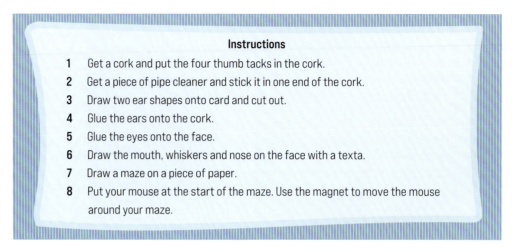

Figure 10.16 How to make a magnetic mouse: instructions

The children also provided details of the game, as shown in Figure 10.17.

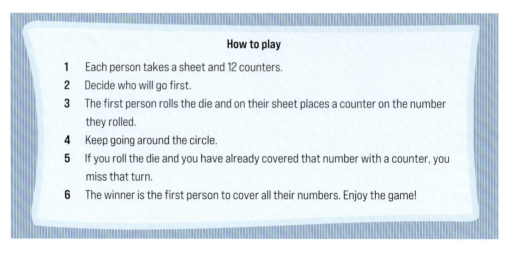

Figure 10.17 How to play the magnetic mouse game

Making board games is a good example of working with different kinds of technologies. Identifying the steps or rules, as well as going through the experience of deciding what makes a board game successful, and preparing posters on this, will support children to make visible the hidden design dimensions of board games. This skill is linked to computational thinking. How might a teacher introduce this idea to children so it is an engaging and relevant experience for them?

Organising learning environments to support creativity and imagination

This section examines four case studies to illustrate how to build into a teaching–learning sequence the ability to assess children's technological capabilities in a meaningful way. The scenarios also demonstrate how to build on children's technological capabilities so their learning opportunities are maximised.

The open-ended case studies are shown below in detail. As you read, note:

- how the children decide on the design brief
- how the open-ended approach allows the teacher to map individual children's capabilities
- what makes the technological task meaningful and relevant to the children, thus stimulating children to work to their potential
- the ways in which the teacher is free to move about and make assessments on individual children's capabilities
- the limited use of materials and minimal preparation
- that the technological experience is designed to extend over time (i.e. two weeks)
- other key learning areas such as literacy and mathematics that are also featured in the units.

The examples shown provide insights into how to organise technological learning environments that allow teachers to make better judgements about children's learning.

Example 1: The Invention Room

Jackie is a teacher of a multi-age group of Year 5/6 children. In developing her technologies program for the term, Jackie decided she wanted to create an integrated curriculum project with the children. She set aside a large space in the classroom that could be used as an Invention Room. She explained her approach:

> We wanted to give the children a space in their classroom where they could do their own thing, a place we had not organised for them. We called this the Invention Room. We have done a lot of talking with the children as a group. We talked about 'What is an invention? What is imagination?' We thought that imagination was a basic idea we had to establish first. We were amazed at some of the concepts the children had.
>
> From there we started to explore the idea of planning from the ideas in their heads. What did it mean? Again, we were delighted at the concepts the children had – drawing a picture, writing or making a model of their ideas. We needed to spend quite a lot of time on the planning process before we went on to the Invention Room.
>
> We sat down together as a group and decided to plan 'What we could do in the Invention Room'. We brainstormed a whole host of ideas – for example, an airport, a police station, a farm. As a result of watching a movie the week before, a common idea emerged. The children wanted to recreate *Willy Wonka and the Chocolate Factory* in the classroom. The children were captivated by the story and decided to make their own chocolates in the Invention Room. The children decided they wished to design their own chocolate recipes, develop a marketing plan, engineer a production and evaluation process and, importantly, project manage the whole event of their chocolate creations.

Example 2: The Imagination Room

In the Imagination Room (see Figure 10.18), Marita provided the children with a completely empty room. She removed all the furniture, equipment and resources from the home room

Figure 10.18 Inside my Imagination Room

(home corner). The children had to think about what they wished to use the room for, and how they could refurnish it based on what they would like the room to be or do for them.

Daisy: It's empty.

Hannah: It's empty – that means nothing's there.

Daisy: It's [furniture] all gone into there. All the home corner is gone – the drawers were here and now they are out there.

Hannah: It's empty, called nothing, not a thing in it.

Cooperative group work was a central part of this technologies unit. In the initial stages of planning for the Imagination Room, the children had to negotiate and compromise. They had to listen and take into account other children's plans and other perspectives of what was going on. It is interesting to note the different strategies the children used.

Lauren: James, do you want to build a jungle?

James: No.

Ellen: Well, yes we are – we want to.

Lauren: Jessica, do you want to build a jungle?

Jessica: Yes.

Lauren: Regan, would you like to build a jungle, and they don't have to.

James: Well we can make the castle. Do you want to make a castle?

Elliot: Yes.

Regan: Yes.

James: Well we can make the castle. See – we need a jungle around the forest with a castle in the middle.

Strategies such as negotiating, mediating, nominating to be a salesperson, confrontation, participation in discussion and seeking support from peers were evident. Marita initially was concerned that the plans were formed on the basis of gender, but as the children moved into the design stage, she noticed their ideas were based more on the interest in the group – for example:

James: In my design no one can escape from the castle (points to drawbridge).

Erin: My trees have string traps in case the people do escape from the castle.

Marita's assessment

The children's designs were quite complex, with interlocking parts of tunnels and turrets, drawbridges and trip wires! In devising their designs, the children drew from previous experiences, understandings and knowledge they had accumulated. They paid incredible attention to design and could explain their design and give valid explanations about certain details, and reasons for the appropriateness and inclusion of design features, as observed:

James: These turrets protect the soldiers.

Lauren: Fibreglass is needed for laying the tiles inside the castles (reflective pause). Actually, fibreglass is dangerous so we should use paper to pretend.

Regan: (referring to drawbridge) Erin and I will make it out of wood and chain … if I can find some at home … cardboard or string will do.

When the children began the making stage, it was interesting to notice that the castle they constructed matched their design perfectly. It was transferred from their imagination to reality. The children worked closely together, and roles were complementary with lots of verbal and non-verbal interaction. They supported and encouraged each other with positive comments such as, 'Hey that looks really good!' Trial and error featured a lot as the children experimented with materials and ideas.

Most surprising was the level of persistence and perseverance given to the task:

James: It keeps falling down (frustrated and angry).

Lauren: We need something to stabilise it.

Together they pulled a playpen into the Imagination Room, then rebuilt the castle walls around it.

The children showed ability to problem-solve and work out design fault, modify their work, and continually reassess and evaluate their work. The children worked together, made informed decisions and were able to combine having fun and working hard to produce a model that they were all excited about and proud of.

All the children involved in the project demonstrated a high level of understanding of the concept of planning and showed their obvious ability to plan technological activities. The children had various experiences to bring to the project that shaped what they did.

Marita reflects on her own learning

What have I learned? I have gained important understanding of technology from a child's perspective. I have a much broader knowledge and awareness of background information about my children because I visited their homes [see Figure 10.19] and found out about what technologies are in their environment and how they engage with them, especially with their understanding about planning. I have also learned that pre-school children can be actively involved in planning for many more projects. As James said, 'You can do anything and everything when you imagine.'

> Questions asked during the home visit and interview:
> - Show and tell me all the things you do at home. We will walk together from room to room as you share.
> - What activities do you like to do and what toys do you like to play with at home – inside and outside?
> - What things do you do or make with your mummy or daddy? Your sisters/brothers?
> - What does your mummy plan or make at home?

Figure 10.19 Home visit – interview questions directed to 4-year-olds

Marita reflects on her role in the Imagination Room

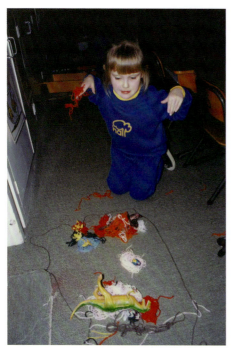

Figure 10.20 Designing our cubbies with string

My role was that of a non-active participant. Through home visits and individual interviews, I was aware of the children's understandings and attitudes towards planning and their ability to organise and be in control of their own lives, so I became the adult who would audio-record their conversations on my smartphone, which I later summarised and wrote on the whiteboard – labelling their design and documents. I listened to their verbal reports and watched them interpret and solve problems. I took digital photographs daily and took notes on their research skills. I observed and followed their design and work from a distance and became one of the many guests invited into their Imagination Room. It was really important to document the children's involvement in the process of 'Investigating and defining, Generating and developing, Producing and implementing, Evaluating, Collaborating and managing' (ACARA, 2023).

Example 3: Imagination in cubby building

Mandy teaches children in their first year of school. After watching the children at playtime spend all their time making cubbies outside, Mandy decided to use this interest to plan a unit of work on cubby building (see Figures 10.20–10.22).

Figure 10.21 Designing our cubbies with straw

Figure 10.22 Sarah's two-storey cubby house made of one box on top of another box

Mandy prepared a blank A3 booklet with a cover that the children used to document their learning each week when they built cubbies. The children's booklet featured an ongoing record of their design and technologies activities over 10 weeks. In addition to documenting what they did in their cubbies or how they made their cubbies each week, the children also made evaluative comments in their booklets:

- *Week 1:* (Inside cubbies made with sheets and chairs) 'I think cubby houses are fun to play in because you can have tea parties in them. Some cubbies have TVs, beds and toys. My cubby house has lots of toys in it. I like playing in my cubby house.'
- *Week 2:* (Inside cubbies made with boxes – children were invited to bring in something from home to play with in the cubby) 'I liked the box cubbies just because they were so high – you could make swimming pools and cars and rainproof the veranda.'
- *Week 3:* (Design your cubby using construction materials and string) 'We made designs of cubbies. I used pop sticks to make my design on the carpet. It was easy to change my mind about how it looked. I could also join my design with Daniel's, so we had a really big design for a cubby. I don't think I could make it. It would take too long.'
- *Week 4:* (Outside cubbies in the sand pit) 'I played with Madison and we made a fairy house. We used a whole heap of sand and some sticks and a fairy car.'
- *Week 5:* (Design and make a model of your own cubby) 'Cubbies are good for kids and good for people with other sisters or brothers. A cubby is made of wood, metal, sheets, table and chairs. I think cubbies are bad because they have no power points.'
- *Week 6:* (Design the smallest cubby you can) 'We made cubbies for our fairies. It was so small we could carry it around. It fitted through all the doorways in the school. I made

a fairy house down at the sand pit. I used pinecones, some twigs, some leaves, wattle and sand. The fairies left some glitter.'
- *Week 7:* (Tree house cubbies) My idea of a cubby house is a tree house in the top of a tree. When I am in my cubby house at night, I look at the stars. I like cubbies because they can be in trees.'

Teacher evaluations

All the children were able to make a plan, drawing on their variety of experiences and depending on their interpretations of their daily lives. The children could easily visualise what they would like to happen and what they would like to make, and saw themselves as a person who could decide and act upon that decision.

Example 4: Cubbies in Years 5 and 6

In this example, Jackie plans and implements a unit of work on cubbies.

She began her unit of work on cubbies by asking the children to reflect on what they knew, felt and liked about cubbies, using a Y chart, as shown in Figure 10.23.

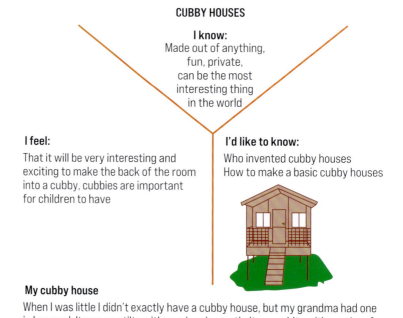

Figure 10.23 Y chart to find out what children already know about cubbies

The children had a lot of questions about cubby houses, such as:

- I'd like to know how to dig a hole for an underground cubby.
- I'd like to know how much underground cubbies cost to build.

- I'd like to know how to build a cubby that stands up properly.
- I'd like to know how big the biggest cubby ever built was.
- I'd like to know how to get running water to a tree house.
- I'd like to know if all kids like cubbies.
- I'd like to know where the first cubby was built.

The children had futuristic ideas about cubbies too:

- In the space age, where would the kids' private space for a cubby be?
- How hard would it be and how much money would it cost to put air into a cubby?

Figure 10.24 shows the work of one child in creating a floor plan for their cubby. As part of their research, the children also interviewed other children about cubbies.

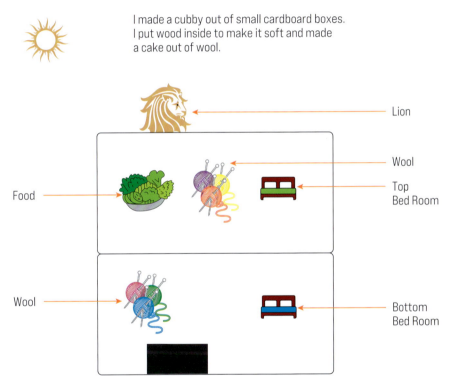

Figure 10.24 Jack's floor plan of a cubby

Figure 10.25 presents the interview questions that were asked of Jessica. The children also created a step-by-step set of instructions for how to build a cubby, as shown in Figure 10.26.

The examples shown in this section illustrate the depth and complexity of a unit of technologies teaching – and the challenges. In responding to the questions at the start of this section, it is clear that the children had a lot of autonomy in relation to the original design brief. The approach was very different from a closed design brief that is intended to be taught in one session.

Figure 10.25 Interview questions

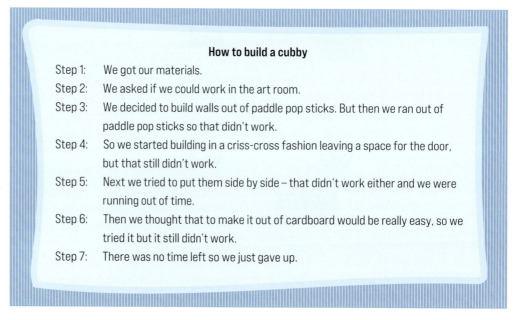

Figure 10.26 How to build a cubby

The open-ended approach allows the teacher to map individual children's capabilities as well as record how the whole group is progressing in their work. In addition, the technological tasks were meaningful and relevant to the children, thus stimulating children to work to their potential. The teacher was not the focus of attention; rather, the emphasis was on the children and what they were trying to achieve as a group. This meant that the teacher was free to move about and make assessments of individual children's capabilities.

The projects also allowed for other key learning areas to be featured in the Technologies unit. The children needed to research for a real purpose, so reading was meaningful and relevant to what they were doing. Making measurements was an important dimension of working technologically, as children designed and prepared models, and created their designs. You would have noted some of these points as you read the scenarios.

PEDAGOGICAL REFLECTION 10.4

Design briefs for longer-term projects

Chapter 2 explored the differences in design briefs. Go back to Chapter 2 and draw from your notes about the advantages and disadvantages of closed and open design briefs. Put these ideas together with what you have gained from thinking about the nature of planning and assessing when a technologies project is created over an extended period. These larger projects provide an opportunity to really learn about what young children can do in technologies education.

Tinkering activities designed to enhance girls' technological capabilities

The under-representation of girls in technologies education continues to be noted (Kim et al., 2021). In this section, we examine how children bring to technological activities not just their prior knowledge and skills, but potentially a gendered perspective. Two scenarios are presented to illustrate the importance of working positively in technologies to support the development of boys' and girls' technologies competence.

Scenario 1: The tinkering table
Context
Twenty-five preschool children were provided with a tinkering table containing screwdrivers, pliers, hammers and saws, and an array of technological artefacts (telephone, keyboard, radio) and containers in which to put dismantled pieces. The teacher thought it was important for the girls to be given opportunities to use tools during free time.

An analysis of what was happening
During free-choice times, there were always at least two boys who stayed and pulled the technological artefacts apart. Each boy remained for at least 15 minutes. Usually one girl would join the group briefly, mostly observing what was occurring before moving on. An example of the conversations held by children around the tinkering table follows:

Sam: I'm going to undo this [keyboard].

Peter: I might undo that one [telephone]. (Sarah and Freya approach the tinkering table.)

Sarah:	They have done a lot! How did you get the telephone out?
Peter:	I didn't, it was already out, and now I am breaking this [backing] off. You're allowed to break it.
Sarah:	So, we are not breaking it, are we? (said with a strong emphasis)
James:	Well, that's a way of breaking it! Yep, you're doing it undone.
Sarah:	Have you done a painting? (addressing Freya who is observing) Come on, you can come with me and do a painting.

Both Sarah and Freya move away to the painting area. The remaining children work on in silence.

In this first scenario, it could be speculated that the girls found the tinkering task destructive because it was considered as breaking the objects apart. Sarah's comments and the girls' subsequent lack of participation would suggest that this was so. Here, the girls tended to observe the boys tinkering, followed by moving off to other play and learning experiences within the preschool.

Scenario 2: A study of clocks

Context

In a Year 2/3 classroom, the children are grouped into self-selected, single-gender groups of two or three. The teacher had planned a 10-week program focusing on how clocks work. The children were asked to pull apart the clocks and ask questions about the technology.

An analysis of what was happening

The girls' conversation concentrates on fixing or constructing. The following transcript illustrates the constructive nature of the technology.

Group A

Andrea:	Well, we're going to make a robot now.
Teacher:	You're going to make a robot now, are you?
Andrea:	Yes, umm …
Helen:	The earrings. (taking another piece from the clock)
Teacher:	How are you going to make it?
Andrea:	I don't know. If you put this thing on here, and then she got this bit and then she was trying to bend this bit …
Helen:	No, she's not in our group. (looking at a child who hovers nearby)
Andrea:	We need to put her ears on.
Helen:	And her earrings.
Samantha:	Ears.
Helen:	Earrings?

Andrea:	Yeah, she can have earrings.
Samantha:	She'll be a rattly tummy.
Andrea:	The arms.
Samantha:	Here are the arms.
Helen:	They look like big dangly earrings.
Andrea:	The arms.
Samantha:	Umm, what were her legs?
Helen:	I know!
Samantha:	And this goes …

Group B

Chris:	We have finished our clock, we are taking apart this radio, we are trying to work out how to take off these screws, so then the teacher comes and unscrews one and then we start, then we take it all out.
Teacher:	What's this here?
Chris:	We don't know, but I just unscrewed that.
Teacher:	What do you think it's for?
Chris:	Oh, that's most of the radio. Look at this. (moves numbers) We are having quite a lot of fun. My little brother thinks these are bombs. (pointing to white cylinder objects inside the radio section) We are going to take these apart and see what we can do with them. I had a radio like this at home and my friend came up, we both like taking apart things, and we made bombs and those can explode.
Teacher:	They can explode?
Chris:	Yeah, we put them on to wires, and put some of that on, and all these little things, and they did explode, we lighted them outside, at night and they really made a big explosion.

In this second scenario, the girls conceptualised the activity as making a robotic construction. They looked at the clock as a source of parts for making a robot, rather than as a clock to be pulled apart and understood. In contrast, the boys had a different conceptual orientation. They were preoccupied with dismantling the clock, to which they brought their previous experiences of pulling apart objects without purpose.

The transcript shows that the boys drew upon their prior experience of dismantling machines. Their frame of reference was geared to the identification of components in the clock radios. Their prior thinking (bombs) in relation to their experience (causing components to explode) meant that they thought differently from what the teacher had intended (examining the inside of a clock).

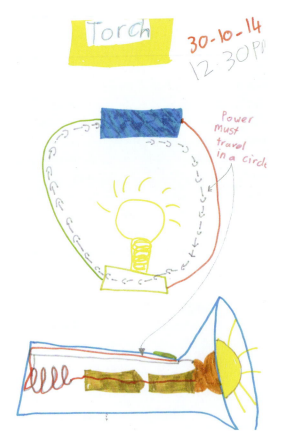

Figure 10.27 Tinkering with torches – what can we learn about how a torch works by pulling it apart?

What can be noticed from the transcripts is that there is a clear difference between the language of the girls' groups and that of the boys' groups. The girls did not use terms that focused on destruction. Similarly, the boys rarely used constructive terms. What is evident is that there is a gendered pattern of language use associated with the children's prior experiences. For the activity on tinkering – something that is popular in primary schools (e.g. see Figure 10.27) – a destructive or constructive orientation was observed for the children in this study (Fleer, 1990).

In this Year 2/3 classroom, the girls appeared to focus on creating, and on helping or relating to people. It would appear that, in the classroom, the activity was reframed (e.g. making a robot) in order to support girls to better understand the destructive task given to them through the tinkering table, where it was expected that the children would pull apart the clocks and clock radios.

The tinkering activity was organised so the children had access to a range of old technological devices, such as old machines and clocks. They also had tools for pulling apart the components (screwdrivers and pliers). The key here was that no teacher support was offered. Consequently, the activity gave the impression that technology was more about things than people. The activity was decontextualised, since no purpose was given. We saw that the children contextualised the activity through linking it to their previous experience. For the boys, it was making bombs and for the girls it was making a robot. The complex nature of the objects to be pulled apart (telephone, clock) meant the particular components that the children had retrieved were not connected with their scientific and technological understandings. This meant that only limited comprehension of what they retrieved was possible. The children were not inspired to ask questions relevant to supporting scientific or technological thinking, or to set up an investigation. As a result, most of what the children did in the classroom and how they talked about the clocks was not directly relevant to the activity set up by the teacher.

PEDAGOGICAL REFLECTION 10.5

Developing girls' technological capabilities

The introduction of the tinkering table in the preschool and the sequence of technological learning over 10 weeks with clocks were designed to enhance girls' technological capabilities. Yet this goal was not achieved. How do you think the teachers could have met this goal? Record your ideas.

The rationale for including tinkering in the classroom focused on giving the children opportunities to see what was inside a range of technologies. In addition, it was deemed important to give children – particularly girls – opportunities to use tools. Finally, the tinkering table was thought to provide an interesting context that would support children to ask scientific or technological questions that could, in turn, drive an investigation. However, the study revealed that the activity actually supported the boys' interests, and the decontextualised nature of the experience meant that prior language and ways of interacting when pulling objects apart were featured, which had not been the desired outcome. The girls were not as readily attracted to the experience and their interest was not maintained.

With the introduction of technologies into schools and preschools, careful thought needs to be given to planning, otherwise masculine constructions of technology may be supported inadvertently. It is important that technologies be introduced in ways that contextualise their value socially.

When technologies education is introduced, much guidance by teachers is needed, otherwise children may react in ways that are not predicted. In the two scenarios shown above, the children's behaviours in relation to the technological artefacts they were exploring reinforced rather than modified gendered interaction. The study found that when a choice of participation was given, girls tended to avoid the activity and took on more of a role of being passive observers. In contrast, the boys actively participated and reconstructed the tinkering contexts in ways that reinforced a destructive orientation. It was also found that, when participation was made compulsory, both girls and boys responded by reframing the task to give it a social context (i.e. robots/bombs). Planning for both boys' and girls' engagement in technologies education is key to developing citizens who have a broad range of technological skills, understandings and competence. Evaluating what happens as a result of that planning ensures that gendered interactions are not reinforced and actively worked against.

Assessing for learning, assessing about learning and assessing during learning are key ideas that support the educator's critical eye on any potential gendered interactions during technologies education. What practical solutions could you come up with to solve the problem identified in the scenarios? How do these ideas sit with what you recorded for Pedagogical Reflection 10.5?

SPOTLIGHT 10.3

Researching gender and technologies – a review of the literature

Sultan, Axell and Hallström (2018) systematically reviewed the literature to: (1) identify the most common descriptions of the relationship between girls and technology; (2) identify how girls' engagement in technology education is described; and (3) identify the type of technology concerned. They examined what is known in relation to children 10 years of age and older. What they found is quite disturbing.

First, they note that terms such as 'negative', 'reluctant', 'insufficient', 'discouraged' and 'lacking' were regularly associated with girls and women in technology. This framing was within a context of describing the under-representation of girls and women in STEM as 'lacking' and 'disconnected' from technology.

Second, their review shows that studies did not discuss girls' engagement in technologies, but rather simplified results as merely a difference in boys' and girls' interests. According to the studies reviewed, 'Girls are considered less interested in technology than boys'. They suggest (Sultan, Axell and Hallström, 2018, p. 236) that 'a traditional view of what technology is – a concept of technology and empirical examples of types of technology with a typical male, nuts and bolts code' – continues to dominate the literature. This suggests that there is still a need for research into gender and technologies, and that this research should be conceptualised as beyond a typical male nuts-and-bolts code.

Spotlight 10.3 focused on children aged 10 years and older. In Spotlight 10.4, the results of two preschool studies are shown. These studies suggest that the gendering of technologies and the lack of opportunities for girls in technologies begin early.

SPOTLIGHT 10.4 Studies of preschool children's play

Chapman (2016) undertook detailed observations of two preschool settings during free play periods, and interviewed the staff about their program and beliefs in relation to typical play behaviours of boys and girls in the different areas of the preschool. She found distinct patterns in choice of activities between the boys and girls. An example of the indoor choices is shown in Table 10.5.

Table 10.5 Frequency of indoor experiences

Areas in the preschool	Boys	Girls
Collage, drawing, painting and other art experiences	15	38
Book corner	3	2
Construction area	30	18
Puzzle shelf/table/mat	5	3
Home corner and dramatic play area	8	11
Role-play	12	0
Sensory play such as sand, water, materials to feel like cloth, etc.	2	27

Source: Adapted from Chapman (2016, p. 1278).

In the second study, undertaken by Hallström, Elvstrand and Hellberg (2015), the researchers specifically note the gendering of technology in free play in Swedish early childhood education. Using digital video to document the play practices of children and the interaction of teachers, they identify some alarming examples of gendered play in the centre. The following scenario is taken from their field notes:

A group of children are playing in the construction room. The room is equipped with different kinds of materials with the purpose of stimulating construction games. Two boys [5-year-olds] are playing with blocks. They are talking with each other and decide to build a tower as high as possible. Amanda [5 years old] is looking at the boys' play but she does not touch or play with the blocks herself. After a while, she starts to serve one of the boys with blocks. For several minutes, the girl is watching the construction play. She never tries to build herself but gives blocks to the boys. (Hallström, Elvstrand and Hellberg, 2015, p. 244)

Hallström, Elvstrand and Hellberg (2015) found the following:

- Children aged 3–8 years reinforce gender differences during free play time when constructing and block building.
- In free play with block building and experimenting, teachers are not gender-conscious.
- During block building and constructing, it is the boys who are most active, while the girls tend to distance themselves. Boys present themselves more confidently and are more eager to try out new things.
- Girls handle technologies in different ways from boys. Girls build with a purpose or make because they need something to support their play. The construction and building actions are thought to be part of creating and being in a social context.
- Boys appear to make the constructing and building the central focus of their activity.
- Helping behaviour of girls is observed.

The last point is captured in the scenario of the field notes, in which a girl starts to serve blocks to one of the boys. This action positions the boy as having agency, and as the person to be leading the block play.

How might these different situations arise and how might girls be given more agency to engage in technologies education?

PEDAGOGICAL REFLECTION 10.6

Changing practices – gender equality: Changing the environment to give technological agency to girls

Using the story of *Princess Smartypants* by Babette Cole (2004), design a technologies program where girls are positioned as powerful, strong and technologically clever and boys as valuing being caring and nurturing. For example, transform the block area into a playworld of the castle where Princess Smartypants lives. Make available to the children the book and the props to role-play during free play time. The availability of role-play resources and a designated space for a particular playworld reposition the block area as something that the girls can powerfully be a part of, and somewhere

where boys can practise being caring and nurturing. Educators can be a part of this playworld, building alongside the children and being aware of and adjusting interactions so they are always respectful. It is in these spaces that challenges arise:

- Do girls feel it is okay to use the block area, and do boys feel it is safe to be playing in the home corner?
- What policies are in place to review spaces, and to make sure all areas are welcoming and inclusive of all children?
- Monitor, and if necessary, change the discourse for equity and opportunity for all children – but given the results shown in long-standing and recent research, this is especially important for girls in technologies.

What other environments might you reconceptualise to provide agency to girls?

Summary

Educators need to focus on identifying what children know and can do in technologies education. It is the progression that is important and not the race to a predetermined end-point. The challenge for educators is to devise assessment techniques that eliminate the need for simultaneous testing of all children. The examples in this chapter provide a starting point for devising appropriate ways to determine children's technological capabilities. Thinking about a range of ways of planning and assessing for children's learning and development in technologies is an important part of being a teacher of technologies. Chapter 11 considers the broad range of pedagogical practices that currently support technologies education in Australia.

Acknowledgements

Special thanks to all the teachers and children who participated in the units of work described here and willingly shared their creative ideas for the purposes of supporting new understandings of technologies education, in particular Prep teacher Mandy and Year 5/6 teacher Jackie, who explored many dimensions of technologies. Acknowledgement is also made of the families at the play centre who agreed to be photographed and filmed undertaking everyday technologies as they played and worked in the centre, and to Bob, Renee and the children who also allowed filming and photographing as they engaged in rich technological activities. Finally, thanks to Yuejiu Wang for support with updating the references for this chapter.

Planning for teaching technologies: Analysing the pedagogical approaches

CHAPTER 11

Introduction

This chapter focuses on the range of pedagogical approaches available for technologies education in schools and early childhood settings. As you read this chapter, consider how the different approaches concentrate learning. What do children gain? What do children miss out on? What is the role of the teacher? Which pedagogical approach suits you best? Why?

Technologies education has evolved in many different ways within and across countries (McLain, 2021) and a range of ways of working technologically in classrooms can be observed (see Figure 11.1). Internationally, great variability exists in relation to curriculum directions, policies, resourcing and histories, resulting in a smorgasbord of teaching approaches across the globe (Williams, 2012). This diversity provides a rich pool of understanding, as researchers and teachers work together to determine the multiple ways in which the two strands of Design and Technologies and Digital Technologies can be enacted in classrooms and early childhood settings. This chapter begins by bringing together all the teaching approaches that featured across the book in a summary table (Table 11.1). This enables discussion of the particular pedagogical features of each approach and reflection on when a particular approach

Figure 11.1 Digital role-playing
Source: Monash University PlayLab and Redeemer Lutheran College.

would best be used. This is followed by details of some of the approaches that were not covered in detail as working examples of the particular pedagogical approach in action. The chapter concludes by inviting you to identify your own personal approach to teaching technologies.

Designing for pedagogical diversity

Although a range of ways of sorting, classifying and naming of technologies education is possible, thought should be directed towards how technologies may be experienced in classrooms or early childhood settings, and what it means when only one way of learning in technology is provided.

Table 11.1 brings together a range of perspectives on Design and Technologies and Digital Technologies education practices as seen within classrooms and early childhood settings in Australia. It shows discrete technology, problem-based technology, interactive simulation technology, symbiotic technology, values-based technology, culturally framed technology and futures technology. The final column contains links back to the chapters in this book, where examples of each pedagogical approach can be found in the detailed case studies or design briefs.

Table 11.1 Different pedagogical approaches to technologies education

Pedagogical approach	Learning focus	Perspective	Pedagogical example and chapter link
Teacher-framed technologies – design technologies	Tightly framed design brief	Teacher-centred	• Making your own popcorn holder to collect free popcorn (Figure 2.9) • Designing, producing and evaluating a greeting card (Figure 2.16) • Designing and comparing musical instruments (Figure 2.18)
Teacher-framed technologies – digital technologies	Tightly framed design brief for supporting computational thinking	Teacher-centred	• Exploring a range of push-and-pull toys, with battery-powered features for programming musical tunes – teacher asks key questions (Chapter 6) • Taking photos and organising systems for efficient sorting and retrieving (Chapter 6) • Using action card games, children act out a sequence of steps (Chapter 6) • Exploring how our bodies move (Chapter 8) • Exploring bridges – which is the strongest (Chapter 8)
Problem-based technology – design technologies	Problem-based design brief	Teacher-set design brief with a lot of child engagement to take the brief and follow own interests	• Making and designing paper planes to transport a doll (Figure 2.26) • Designing new houses for the three little pigs that are 'wolf proof' (Figure 2.22) • Designing and testing paper planes (Figure 2.32) • Designing own French knitting tools and pattern for making soft toys (Figure 7.8) • Designing a kite that can fly in light wind (Figure 2.33)

Table 11.1 (cont.)

Pedagogical approach	Learning focus	Perspective	Pedagogical example and chapter link
			• Conducting a nutritional audit of a favourite takeaway food (Figure 7.15) • Exploring and designing own recipes (Chapter 7) • Building a boat for *Mr Gumpy's Outing* (Burningham, 1970) (Figure 8.24) • Creating an imaginary situation from *Where the Wild Things Are* (Sendak, 2001) (Figure 8.25) • Creating a farmyard, and following the map in *Rosie's Walk* (Hutchins, 1967) (Figure 8.26) • Designing a bus for the song 'The Wheels on the Bus' (Figure 8.27) • Designing a bridge for the song 'London Bridge is Falling Down' (Figure 8.28) • Designing a farm for the song 'Old MacDonald Had a Farm' (Figure 4.8)
Problem-based technology – digital technologies	Problem-based approach to support computational thinking	Teacher-set design brief with a lot of child engagement to take the brief and follow own interests	• The Freddo frog challenge (Figure 6.14) • Exploring robotic toys and programming them to see what they can do (Chapter 6)
Studio-based technology	Open design briefs that feature real work situations, where children set the criteria	Child-centred	• Creating a new superhero character – designing the costume your character will wear (Figure 2.14) • Designing party accessories (Figure 2.13) • Designing and setting up a café (Figure 7.18) • Creating a simulated architect's studio (Figure 4.10) • Designing a new school hat (Figure 2.17) • Surviving in the bush (Figure 2.19) • Using the wooden puppets children have made to design a puppet play for 'Jack and the Beanstalk' (Figure 3.8) • Curating a class art gallery (Chapter 9) • Setting up and managing mini-enterprises (travel agency) (Chapter 9)
STEM-oriented technology	Purpose-oriented pedagogy that integrates technology with another curriculum area	Community-centred	• Investigating and designing a school radio station (Figure 5.5 – literacy and technologies) • Designing a class newspaper (Chapter 9 – literacy and technologies) • Managing a zoo investigation (Chapter 9 – science and technologies)

Table 11.1 (cont.)

Pedagogical approach	Learning focus	Perspective	Pedagogical example and chapter link
Conceptual PlayWorlds/ RealWorlds for technologies	Inquiry-based real-world scenarios and role-plays	Personally meaningful to the child	• Digital Conceptual PlayWorld (Chapter 6) and STEM RealWorld (Chapter 8) summarised as: – Story creates the problem context – Imaginary space is created for role-play – Children jump into the story – Problems arise that need designed solutions – Teachers are in role being characters in the story and helping solve problems
Values-based technology	Socially critical technology	Values-based	• Designing and appraising a range of bags (e.g. handbag, nappy bag, backpack) – examining their purpose, the content and values (Chapter 9) • Using digital tools and recycled materials to design, create and critique from a values perspective your own Christmas card (Table 4.6) • Adopting and caring for a Furby family and their robotic friends (Figure 5.12) • Auditing Santa Claus's gifts (Chapter 5)
Futures technology	Designing for the future	Agency-oriented – building agency within a globally embedded context	Features include openness, richness, fostering collaboration, progression with increasing complexity and sophistication, authenticity, independence, multiple cultural perspectives, building individual and community agency, creativity, and foregrounding of ethics, values and critical technological literacy (see Chapter 3).

ACTIVITY 11.1

Evaluating the different approaches to technologies education

Table 11.1 provides an overview of all of the pedagogical approaches that are presented in this book:
- discrete technologies
- problem-based approach to technologies
- studio based technologies
- STEM-oriented approaches to technologies
- values-based approach to technologies
- futures technologies.

Consider how the different approaches concentrate learning:
- What do children gain?
- What do children miss out on?
- What is the role of the teacher?
- Which pedagogical approach suits you best? Why?

Are there any pedagogical approaches you noticed that connected with you, that you believe could be incorporated into Table 11.1? Examples might include:

- How might a pedagogy of critiquing, as discussed by Keirl (2020), be drawn upon for some/all of the approaches?
- How would you incorporate the concept of disruptive technologies that was discussed by Kafai, Fields and Searle (2014) into one or all of the models of teaching technologies?
- Where would the work by Litts and colleagues (2017) on e-textiles with codeable stitching be placed?
- How might the learning in the Maker Movement presented by van Dijk, Savelsbergh and van der Meij (2020) be realised? To which model of technologies education does this relate?
- Consider the place of the food technologies model by Slatter and France (2018) that was discussed in Chapter 7. Where would this be placed in Table 11.1?

Details of the teaching models discussed throughout this book are outlined briefly below for your easy reference. They elaborate on some of the content summarised in Table 11.1. Some critical questions are posed and some case examples given.

Teacher-framed technologies

Design and Technologies education is frequently presented in classrooms as a discrete learning experience for children. For example, often worksheets present a challenge to children and invite them to come up with a solution, such as folding a paper plane following the design of a predetermined plane. This discretely framed design challenge is often set by the teacher and is usually closed. Chapter 2 discussed open and closed design briefs and critiqued what these approaches meant for children's learning in technologies education.

One advantage of a teacher-framed technologies approach is that it ensures children acquire specific technical skills. Other examples of teacher-framed technology can be found in the popular *Bob the Builder* (BBC Worldwide Ltd, 2000, 2002) magazine series. In Issue 2 of the magazine, young children are given specific instructions on how to build and decorate a toolbox. The value of this type of teacher-framed technology activity is that children can learn to use equipment and tools correctly and achieve success by participating in hands-on activities. Examples of activities that focus children's attention on hammering and carpentry were previously noted in some of the examples of working with wood (see Chapter 9).

One disadvantage of teacher-framed technology is that the design briefs or one-off activities may be disconnected from children's real lives or cultural context.

> ## PEDAGOGICAL REFLECTION 11.1
>
> ### What are the advantages and disadvantages of teacher-framed technologies?
>
> Go back to the notes you made in Chapter 2 and discuss with a peer (or record your thoughts) the main challenges you noted in relation to a closed design brief. When might you use a discrete approach to technologies education? What are the advantages?
>
> Record your ideas. You will return to these at the end of the chapter when you consider how you decided you would plan for or teach technologies education (see Pedagogical Reflection 11.5).

A great deal of research in science education has been directed to inquiry-based learning. Two pedagogical approaches that have emerged from this field of pedagogical study, which are relevant to technologies education, are the problem-based approach to technologies and studio-based approaches to technologies. These two approaches are now discussed.

Problem-based approach to technologies

Problem-based approaches to learning focus on setting up interesting and complex technological problems for children to solve. Although the design briefs are usually set by the teacher, they can also emerge from situations that children and teachers come across in their everyday lives, such as designing a better set of tools for French knitting as explored in Chapter 7, or designing a kite to fly in light wind (Chapter 2).

Problem-based approaches to technologies focus on problem-solving. A lot of trial and error is needed, as might be seen when children make kite models that they progressively test and refine. It is important for children to experience design briefs that have complex problems to solve – problems that are not immediately evident or that require a lot of modelling and designing, testing and evaluating. In this approach, the problem is built into the design brief, and the design brief is relevant and engaging for the children. That is, the problem is something children are really interested in solving. Children's motives for solving the problem are what generate the actions and development in technologies learning and thinking.

Studio-based technologies

Studio-based approaches have featured in practice, and they have a long history. In a studio-based approach, the focus is on some form of working as a professional. As with problem-based approaches, studio-based approaches also focus on a project. The project is usually framed as something for children to make, so they will meet problems that they need to solve – often as a simulation. In this approach, the teacher is likely to set up a more open-ended design challenge, mirroring aspects of the children's or the adults' lives – for example, setting up an invention room in which children can act out being inventors and designers. In these environments, the focus is on the children's interests and experiences, with the teacher supporting the direction they wish to take. Fantasy and creativity often play an important role. This approach was apparent in Chapter 7, where an example of designing and setting up a restaurant was shown, or in Chapter 4, where children worked with an architect. Studio-based approaches to technologies are complex, take a long time to enact and require a great deal of space in the classroom or early childhood setting. The simulations lend themselves well to curriculum integration.

PEDAGOGICAL REFLECTION 11.2

What are the advantages and disadvantages of problem-based and design-based approaches to technologies?

- Can you think of the advantages of problem-based and design-based approaches? What might be the challenges?
- What is the same and what is different about these approaches? How are they different from discrete technology?
- When would you use a problem-based approach and when would you use a studio-based approach?
- Record your ideas. You will return to them at the end of the chapter.

STEM approach to technologies

A STEM approach brings together at least two curriculum areas for a real purpose, integrating learning for children through the technology activities. For example, a STEM approach to science and technology enables children to appreciate that there is a real purpose for making their technological products work effectively. Jane (2008) introduced this approach when she analysed a case study of children exploring their environment through catching and studying small creatures.

The children needed to design effective 'bug catchers' in order to study the creatures. The children put their bug catchers to the test when they used them to catch small animals in the school ground. Their animal houses were tested too, because each one had to contain the animals throughout the short-term study. Towards the end of the unit, the children reflected on the performance of the products they had produced, made realistic appraisals and evaluated the suitability of the materials. Involvement in this unit developed the children's technological knowledge because they were able to suggest improvements in terms of both the design of their products and the types of materials used. The STEM approach is captured in the case example in Figure 11.2.

In this integrated unit, the science and technology were equally valued and the two areas depended on each other (a symbiotic relationship). The technology design brief required the children to design and make a bug catcher to collect small animals and an enclosure to house them while they were being studied as part of their science program. The unit was designed to build on the children's previous experiences of plants in the school environment. Children were given ownership of their work and encouraged to answer their own questions about the animals that interested them.

Science activity about plants

Plant study

1. Select a shrub or tree to study.
2. Are there differently shaped leaves on the plan (adult/juvenile)? Closely examine a leaf from your plant. Consider its shape, size and texture. Why is it this shape? How could the leaf shape help the plant? Think about the advantages.
3. Bark: consider the colour, texture and its function.
4. Research the name of the plant, its origins and its ideal growing conditions (design a possible experiment).

Animals in, on and under your plant

When you start looking for your animals around the tree you have been studying, use your magnifying glass to look at:

- the animal's legs – number of legs: spider (eight), insect (six), slater (?)
- how it moves
- what it looks like.

Design and make

- a device for safely catching a small animal such as a slater (woodlouse)
- a suitable container to house the animal until you finish your study (it will then be returned to its original habitat).

Figure 11.2 Integrating science and technology

STEM PlayWorlds/RealWorlds approaches to technologies

In this book, two examples of Conceptual PlayWorlds were presented. One was oriented to Digital Technologies (Chapter 6) and the other to the contexts of engineering in Technologies and Design (Chapter 8). Both examples were for students in Years 5 and 6. However, the Conceptual PlayWorlds concept has been extensively researched and presented in relation to STEM learning generally for early childhood settings (see Fleer, 2022a), and recently it has started being enthusiastically used in schools as a model of choice for STEM RealWorld scenarios. The characteristics of a Conceptual PlayWorld/RealWorld scenario are as shown in Table 11.2. This is used as a planning pro forma, providing teachers with the areas they need to consider when using this model in their classrooms and centres.

Values-based approach to technologies

Most teachers recognise that technology, and therefore technologies education, are not value-free. Chapter 1 provided a critique on the nature of technologies education. An example of a values-based approach to technologies was shown in Chapter 5, where an audit of the gifts given by Santa Claus was introduced in the context of exploring robotic toys for

Table 11.2 STEM PlayWorlds/RealWorlds

Pedagogical characteristics	Pedagogical practices that are planned
Selecting a story for the Conceptual Playworld/RealWorld	• Context of children • Selecting a story that is enjoyable to children and adults • Building empathy for the characters in the story • A plot that lends itself to introducing a problem situation • Being clear about the concept(s) and its relation to the story and play plot to be developed • Adventures or journeys that spring from the plot (e.g. chapters)
Designing a Conceptual Playworld/RealWorld space	• Finding a space in the classroom/centre/outdoor area suitable for an imaginary Conceptual PlayWorld of the story • Designing opportunities for child-initiated play in ways that develop the play plot further or explore concepts and make them more personally meaningful
Entering and exiting the Conceptual Playworld/RealWorld space	• Plan a routine for entering and existing the Conceptual PlayWorld of the story • Whole group enters and exits the Conceptual Playworld • All the children are in the same imaginary situation • Children choose characters as they enter into the imaginary situation • Teacher is always a character in the story or acting as a human prop (e.g. such as a tree or the Sun)
Planning the play inquiry or problem scenario	• The problem scenario is dramatic and engaging • The problem invites children to investigate solutions to help the play in the Conceptual PlayWorld • Problem scenario is not scripted, but a general idea of the problem is planned • Being clear about the concepts that will be learned from solving the problem situation • Concepts are in service of the children's play
Planning teacher interactions to build conceptual learning in role	• Teachers working in interactional pairs: Teachers are not always the same character. Roles are not scripted • There are different roles teachers can take: Teachers plan their role for the Conceptual PlayWorld to be equally present with the children, or to model practices in role, or to be needing help from the children. Their role can also be together with the child leading (primordial we), where they literally cradle the child or hold their hand and together act out the role or solution • Conceptual intentions are planned: Planning of who will have more knowledge and who will be present with the children to model solving the problem • Creating different spaces/moments/adventures that give opportunities for exploring STEM and social and emotional development

Source: Adapted from Fleer (2021).

digital technologies learning. The complexities of teaching from a values-based approach were considered in Chapter 10, where teachers were invited to consider how they could represent technologies education to their children in ways that encouraged children to consider values and ethics during technologies education. Design technologies from a values-based approach were highlighted by examining a range of different bags.

Each of the design briefs and case examples presented throughout the previous chapters could also be rethought from a values-based approach. In Chapter 1, key concepts were introduced that invited you to consider technologies education from the perspectives of:

- appropriate technologies
- culturally constructed technologies
- sustainable technologies.

PEDAGOGICAL REFLECTION 11.3

Framing teaching from a values-based approach

Go back to the design briefs that you found particularly interesting in the previous chapters and select three of them. How could you plan to teach these from a values-based perspective for students in Years 5 and 6 (Figure 11.3)? What would you need to change? Prepare a design brief so that the project can be taught using a values-based approach.

Figure 11.3 How might you plan a values-based approach in Years 5 and 6?
Source: Monash University PlayLab and Laburnum Primary School.

Document your ideas as a design brief. You will return to these at the end of the chapter.

Examine your notes from Pedagogical Reflection 1.3, where you were asked to consider whether there really were global technologies – that is, universal perspectives. How might you introduce projects and units of work that recognise the cultural nature of technologies so that children can build deeper and richer understandings?

PEDAGOGICAL REFLECTION 11.4

Values-based technologies education

How might you introduce a design-based project or a project that featured the redesigning of the Australian flag? How might you introduce this to children in Year 5? How could you examine issues of colonisation with children? How might you change the design briefs introduced throughout this book in order to begin with a cultural framing for each?

Document your ideas as a design brief. You will return to these concepts at the end of the chapter.

Futures technologies

In total, the diversity of practice in design and technology education has provided the profession with a deep understanding of how learning can be enacted in classrooms. Unfortunately, the practice in classrooms at this stage in the theorisation of technologies education has meant that there is no sophisticated approach to building children's learning in the early years of school and in early childhood settings. Individual teachers, however, have provided rich examples of children engaged in ethically driven, ecologically motivated or culturally sensitive pedagogical approaches.

The first five categories of technologies education detailed in Table 11.1 provide a starting point for making explicit the pedagogical approaches that are possible or enacted daily in Australian classrooms and early childhood centres. Although no category identified and named is exclusive – that is, teachers can construct pedagogy that takes into account both teacher-centred and child-centred practices within one teaching sequence – it is important to analyse and name common practices so that these can be communicated both within the profession and externally to it. Similarly, labels help with the important conceptual work that is still needed in what has been described by many teachers as a 'relatively new field of study' – this being so mainly in the early and primary years of education.

The analysis of existing practice in Australia, as shown in Table 11.1, draws attention to thinking about technologies education in terms of a meta-pedagogy – that is, examining the balance of pedagogy encountered by Australian students in classrooms and early childhood centres. It is important to ensure that teachers examine both the sequential development of technological knowledge and capability in children, and their exposure to higher-order processes in technology and design over the duration of their education. Simply applying one approach, such as tightly framed design challenges devoid of social context, may never give children opportunities for building other ways of thinking in technologies education, such as social, ethical and cultural thinking in relation to technology and design. Similarly, focusing only on social issues may never provide students with the important technical skills needed for realising designs.

Sophisticated pedagogy in design and technologies education is about teachers being thoughtful in the way they teach technology and the balance of approaches they use throughout a school year or within programs for early childhood (AGDE, 2022). This conscious approach to technologies pedagogy is important for building a range of technological capabilities in students if technologies are to move forward into the arena of futures thinking. This orientation was examined in detail in Chapter 3.

Consequently, the final layer of pedagogy and conceptual work in Table 11.1 represents a movement from considering just the artefact to the process of building agency and conscious thinking about values, culture and ethics. For example, learners won't simply make something; instead, they will think about how what they make affects resource use, they may work towards peace (rather than war), and they may consciously think about their role as designers for positive technologies in the context of ecological and political sensitivities. Chapter 4 featured an example of design and technologies in the context of designing cards, where the focus was not on 'making a card' but also what messages the card may give through to how it was made (e.g. recycled paper, fair trade). Chapter 3 focused on designing for preferred futures as a key idea of the technologies curriculum. Thinking and designing for the future are challenging, but young children can and do think about future ideas, as seen in Figure 11.4, where a child has designed a TV bus.

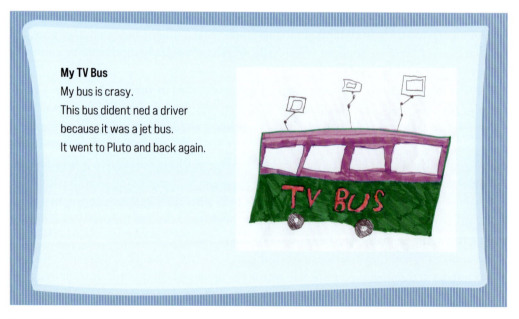

Figure 11.4 A magic bus doesn't need a driver.

Learners will think about what technological experiences and skills they still need in order to work in this way. This not only has the effect of teachers working more consciously in relation to pedagogy and the future (Herro, Visser and Qian, 2021), but also means learners think consciously about the conceptual tools they are developing as a result of technologies education, where they can be designing for their own future.

This chapter discussed a range of pedagogical approaches, revealing that teachers use open and closed design briefs for introducing technologies education to children. Open-ended contexts produce uncertainty and allow for child independence and a diversity of artefacts to be produced, supporting creativity and high-level technological learning (see Chapters 2 and 4). Closed design briefs focus more on technical proficiency and help to build confidence for first-time technologies education teachers and learners. Now return to your response to Pedagogical Reflection 1.7.

PEDAGOGICAL REFLECTION 11.5

Teaching technologies – what are your feelings about teaching the Australian Curriculum: Technologies?

Go back to Pedagogical Reflection 1.7, where you were asked to record what you thought technologies education should involve. How should this learning area be taught to children?

Draw another image of yourself teaching children technologies education. Now look back at the first image you drew for Pedagogical Reflection 1.7.

How have your ideas changed? What image do you now have of yourself as a teacher of technologies? What ideas do you now hold about how to teach this curriculum area? What pedagogical approach to technologies education have you adopted as your central approach to teaching technologies education?

Summary

This chapter has provided an overview of a range of approaches to technologies education. The challenge for the technologies education community is to realise how the pedagogical features shown in column 4 in Table 11.1 give rise to a child's technological agency. An individual's agency (or feeling that they have the power, capacity and skill to act) can only be built at the conscious level.

What is needed is pedagogy that foregrounds agency so children can invent ideas that have not as yet been envisaged, are able to move into paradigms not yet conceptualised, can build globally responsible policies not yet considered and will imagine futures embedded in thoughtful analyses of values and ethics. Through framing technologies education within an agency-oriented approach, new ways of conceptualising pedagogy are possible. These technological thinkers will be the school graduates that society needs to build community capacity for peaceful, harmonious, trusting coexistence in a diverse and multicultural global community. Technologies education that is conceptualised in this way will make a lasting and important contribution to education in Australia.

A final word

From reading and engaging with the ideas presented in this book, you will hopefully have gained an understanding of technologies education and the benefits for children when they have opportunities to participate in technological processes. The many examples included in the book, and in the accompanying online resources, show ways by which you can implement technologies education in classrooms and early childhood settings. Many of the case studies are evidence-based examples of best practice. You are encouraged to participate in research by documenting your own practice, thereby building cases studies to share with colleagues, to present at conferences and as a basis for publications in the future – as you too realise new ways of working in technologies education.

Acknowledgements

Acknowledgement is made of the families at the play centre who agreed to be photographed and filmed undertaking everyday technologies as they played and worked in the centre, and to Bob and the children with whom he worked who were engaged in rich technological activities in their classroom. Thanks to Laburnum Primary School and Redeemer Lutheran Primary School for curriculum development photos taken by Bas Gerald. Finally, thanks to Yuejiu Wang for support with updating the references for this chapter. Australian Research Council Laureate Fellowship Scheme (Grant Number 180100161) funding contributed to the development of open access curriculum materials and research.

References

Allen, P. (1982). *Who Sank the Boat?* Penguin.

Arnott, L. and Yelland, N.J. (2020). Multimodal lifeworlds: Pedagogies for play inquiries and explorations. *Journal of Early Childhood Education Research*, 9(1), 124–46.

Ashdown, S.P. (2013). Not craft, not couture, not 'home sewing': Teaching creative patternmaking to the iPod generation. *International Journal of Fashion Design, Technology and Education*, 6(2), 112–20.

Australian Curriculum, Assessment and Reporting Authority (ACARA) (2015a). *Australian Curriculum: Science F–10*. www.australiancurriculum.edu.au/f-10-curriculum/science

Australian Curriculum, Assessment and Reporting Authority (ACARA) (2015b). *Australian Curriculum: Technologies F–10 (Version 8.4)*. ACARA.

Australian Curriculum, Assessment and Reporting Authority (ACARA) (2023). *Australian Curriculum: Technologies F–10*. https://v9.australiancurriculum.edu.au

Australian Government Department of Education (AGDE) (2022). *Belonging, Being and Becoming: The Early Years Learning Framework for Australia (V2.0)*. Australian Government Department of Education for the Ministerial Council.

Axell, C. and Bjorklund, L. (2018). Teacher students' critical thinking skills: Using the concept of disruptive technologies. In N. Seery, J. Buckley, C. Canty and J. Phelan (eds), *Research and Practice in Technology Education: Perspectives on Human Capacity and Development, 2018 PATT36 Conference Proceedings* (pp. 239–45). Athlone Institute of Technology.

Baker, S.T., Le Courtois, S. and Eberhart, J. (2021). Making space for children's agency with playful learning. *International Journal of Early Years Education*. https://doi.org/10.1080/09669760.2021.1997726

Balme, J., O'Connor, S., Maloney, T.R., Akerman, K., Keaney, B. and Dilkes-Hall, I.E. (2022). Fibre technologies in Indigenous Australia: Evidence from archaeological excavations in the Kimberley region. *Australian Archaeology*. https://doi.org/10.1080/03122417.2022.2054510

Barak, M. (2019). Problem solving. In D. Barlex and J. Williams (eds), *An International Perspective on Pedagogy for Technology Education in Secondary Schools* (pp. 245–65). Springer.

Barlex, D. (2015). Developing a technology curriculum. In P.J. Williams, A. Jones and C. Buntting (eds), *The Future of Technology Education* (pp. 143–68). Springer.

Barlex, D. and Steeg, T. (2018). Maker education in the English context. In N. Seery, J. Buckley, C. Canty and J. Phelan (eds), *Research and Practice in Technology Education: Perspectives on Human Capacity and Development, 2018 PATT36 Conference Proceedings* (pp. 341–6). Athlone Institute of Technology.

Bati, K. (2021). A systematic literature review regarding computational thinking and programming in early childhood education. *Education and Information Technologies*. https://doi.org//10.1007/s10639-021-10700-2

BBC Worldwide Ltd (2000). *Bob the Builder Magazine*, 2, 12–13.

BBC Worldwide Ltd (2002). *Bob the Builder: Bob's Birthday CD Story Book*. Hinkler Books.

Beers, S.Z. (2022). *21st Century Skills: Preparing Students for THEIR Future*. https://cosee.umaine.edu/files/coseeos/21st_century_skills.pdf

Bers, M.U. (2008). *Blocks, Robots and Computers: Learning about Technology in Early Childhood*. Teachers College Press.

Bers, M.U. (2019). Coding as another language: A pedagogical approach for teaching computer science in early childhood. *Journal of Computers in Education*, 6(4), 499–528.

Bers, M., Flannery, L., Kazakoff, R. and Sullivan, A. (2014). Computational thinking and tinkering: Exploration of an early childhood robotics curriculum. *Computers and Education*, 72, 145–57.

Boland, J., Banks, S., Krabbe, R., Lawrence, S., Murray, T., Henning, T. and Vandenberg M. (2022). A COVID-19-era rapid review: Using Zoom and Skype for qualitative group research. *Public Health Research and Practice*, 32(2), e31232112. https://doi.org/10.17061/phrp31232112

Borg, F. and Gericke, N. (2021). Local and global aspects: Teaching social sustainability in Swedish preschools. *Sustainability*, 13(7), 3838.

Brecka, P., Valentová, M. and Lancaric, D. (2022). The implementation of critical thinking development strategies into technology education: The evidence from Slovakia. *Teaching and Teacher Education*, 109, 103555. https://doi.org/10.1016/j.tate.2021.103555

Brown, P. (2018). *The Wild Robot*. Piccadilly Books.

Bryksa, B.C. and Yada, R.Y. (2012). Nanotechnology: The word is new but the concept is old. An overview of the science and technology in food and food products at the nanoscale level. *International Journal of Food Studies*, 1, 188–210.

Buck Institute for Education (n.d.). What is PBL? www.pblworks.org/what-is-pbl/gold-standard-project-design

Burningham, J. (1970). *Mr Gumpy's Outing*. Jonathan Cape.

Busch, G. (2018). How families use video communication technologies during intergenerational Skype sessions. In S.J. Danby, M. Fleer, C. Davidson and M. Hatzingianni (eds), *Digital Childhoods: Technologies and Children's Everyday Lives* (pp. 17–32). Springer.

Carrico, M. and Kim, V. (2014). Expanding zero-waste design practices: A discussion paper. *International Journal of Fashion Design, Technology and Education*, 7(1), 58–64.

Cassidy, T., Grishanov, S. and Hsieh, W.-H. (2008). Yarn CAD simulation for fashion and textile design education. *International Journal of Fashion Design, Technology and Education*, 1(1), 13–21.

Chapman, R. (2016). A case study of gendered play in preschools: How early childhood educators' perceptions of gender influence children's play. *Early Child Development and Care*, 186(8), 1271–84.

Chaudron, S., Marsh, J., Navarette, V.D., Ribbens, W., Mascheroni, G. … Soldatova, G. (2018). Rules of engagement: Family rules on young children's access to and use of technologies. In S.J. Danby, M. Fleer, C. Davidson and M. Hatzingianni (eds), *Digital Childhoods: Technologies and Children's Everyday Lives* (pp. 131–46). Springer.

Chiang, F.-K., Chang, C.-H., Wang, S., Cai, R.-H. and Li, L. (2020). The effect of an interdisciplinary STEM course on children's attitudes of learning and engineering design skills. *International Journal of Technology and Design Education*, 32(1), 55–74.

Chou, P.-N. and Shih, R.-C. (2021). Young kids' basic computational thinking: An analysis on educational robotics without computer. In *International Conference on Innovative Technologies and Learning* (pp. 170–80). Springer.

Cole, B. (2004). *Princess Smartypants*. Picture Puffin.

Compton, V. and Harwood, C. (2003). Enhancing technological practice: An assessment framework for technology education in New Zealand. *International Journal of Technology and Design Education*, 13, 1–26.

Conway, B., Leahy, K. and McMahon, M. (2021). Design education for sustainability: Identifying opportunities in Ireland's second level education system. *Sustainability*, 13(16), 8711.

Cunningham, C.M. and Carlsen, W.S. (2014). Teaching engineering practices. *Journal of Science Teacher Education*, 25, 197–210.

Davidson, C., Danby, S.J., Given, L.M. and Thorpe, K. (2018). Producing contexts for young children's digital technology use: Web searching during adult–child interactions at home and preschool. In S.J. Danby, M. Fleer, C. Davidson and M. Hatzingianni (eds), *Digital Childhoods: Technologies and Children's Everyday Lives* (pp. 65–84). Springer.

de Vries, M.J. (2005). The nature of technological knowledge: Philosophical reflections and educational consequences. *International Journal of Technology and Design Education*, 15, 149–54.

DiFrancesca, D., Lee, C. and McIntyre, E. (2014). Where is the 'E' in STEM for young children? Engineering design education in an elementary teacher preparation program. *Issues in Teacher Education*, 23(1), 49–64.

Doyle, A., Seery, N., Gumaelius, L., Canty, D. and Hartell, E. (2018). Reconceptualising PCK research in D&T education: Proposing a methodological framework. In N. Seery, J. Buckley, C. Canty and J. Phelan (eds), *Research and Practice in Technology Education: Perspectives on Human Capacity and Development, 2018 PATT36 Conference Proceedings* (pp. 363–70). Athlone Institute of Technology.

Dowling, D., Carew, A. and Hadgraft, R. (2015). *Engineering Your Future: An Australasian Guide* (3rd ed.). Wiley.

Dowling, D., Hadgraft, R., Carew, A., McCarthy, T., Hargreaves, D., Baillie, C. and Male, S. (2022). *Engineering Your Future: An Australasian Guide* (4th ed.). Wiley.

Drechsler, W., Natter, M. and Leeflang, S.H. (2013). Improving marketing's contribution to new product development. *Journal of Product Innovation Management*, 30(2), 298–315.

Eastman, P.D. (1960). *Are You My Mother?* Random House.

Ehsan, H., Rehmat, A.P. and Cardella, M.E. (2021). Computational thinking embedded in engineering design: Capturing computational thinking of children in an informal engineering design activity. *International Journal of Technology and Design Education*, 31, 441–64.

Ellen MacArthur Foundation (2017). *A New Textiles Economy: Redesigning Fashion's Future*. www.ellenmacarthurfoundation.org/publications/a-new-textiles-economy-redesigning-fashions-future

Engineers Australia (2010). Our Code of Ethics. www.engineersaustralia.org.au/resource-centre/resource/code-ethics-article

Engineers Australia (2022). *Women in Engineering*. www.engineersaustralia.org.au/sites/default/files/women-in-engineering-report-june-2022.pdf

Engstrom, S. (2018). What technology content and values emerge in the teaching of climate change? In N. Seery, J. Buckley, C. Canty and J. Phelan (eds), *Research and Practice in Technology Education: Perspectives on Human Capacity and Development, 2018 PATT36 Conference Proceedings* (pp. 40–6). Athlone Institute of Technology.

Ethical Fashion Forum (2018). The issues. www.ethicalfashionforum.com/the-issues

Featherston, M. (2014). The designer: Moulded to shape. In D. Whitehouse (ed.), *Mid-century Modern Australian Design* (pp. 144–61). Council of Trustees of the National Gallery of Victoria.

Fleer, M. (1990). Gender issues in early childhood science and technology education in Australia. *International Journal of Science Education*, 12(4), 355–67.

Fleer, M. (2002). Curriculum compartmentalisation: A futures perspective on environmental education. *Environmental Education Research*, 8(2), 137–54.

Fleer, M. (2010). *Early Learning and Development: Cultural–Historical Concepts in Play*. Cambridge University Press.

Fleer, M. (2017). Scientific Playworlds: A model of teaching science in play-based settings. *Research in Science Education*, 49, 1257–78.

Fleer, M. (2018). Digital bridges between home and preschool: Theorising conceptually inclusive practice in digital environments. In S.J. Danby, M. Fleer, C. Davidson and M. Hatzingianni (eds), *Digital Childhoods: Technologies and Children's Everyday Lives* (pp. 33–48). Springer.

Fleer, M. (2021). Conceptual Playworlds: The role of imagination in play and learning. *Early Years*, 41(4), 353–64.

Fleer, M. (2022a). *Working Papers from the Conceptual PlayLab, Monash University*. www.monash.edu/education/research/projects/conceptual-playlab/publications

Fleer, M. (2022b). Engineering PlayWorld – a model of practice to support children to collectively design, imagine and think using engineering concepts. *Research in Science Education*, 52, 583–598.

Forbes, P. (2006). *The Gecko's Foot: How Scientists are Taking a Leaf from Nature's Book*. HarperCollins.

Foster, J. and Yaoyuneyong, G. (2014). Collaborative cross-disciplinary client-based projects: A case study. *International Journal of Fashion Design, Technology and Education*, 7(3), 154–62.

Fox-Turnbull, W. (2015). Conversations to support learning in technology education. In P.J. Williams, A. Jones and C. Buntting (eds), *The Future of Technology Education* (pp. 99–120). Springer.

Fox-Turnbull, W. (2018). Implementing digital technology in the New Zealand curriculum. In N. Seery, J. Buckley, C. Canty and J. Phelan (eds), *Research and Practice in Technology Education: Perspectives on Human Capacity and Development, 2018 PATT36 Conference Proceedings* (pp. 432–40). Athlone Institute of Technology.

Fox-Turnbull, W.H. and Snape, P.M. (2011). Technology teacher education through a constructivist approach. *Design and Technology Education: An International Journal*, 16(2), 45–56. http://jil.lboro.ac.uk/ojs/index.php/DATE/article/view/1625

Freeman, B., Marginson, S. and Tytler, R. (2015) (eds). *The Age of STEM. Educational Policy and Practice Across the World in Science, Technology, Engineering and Mathematics*. Routledge.

Fry, T. (1994). *Remakings: Ecology/Design/Philosophy*. Envirobooks.

García Terceño, E.M., Greca, I.M., Redfors, A. and Fridberg, M. (2021). Implementation of an integrated STEM activity in pre-primary schools [Conference presentation]. *The 11th International Conference on European Transnational Educational (ICEUTE 2020)*. Springer.

Garvis, S. (2018). Digital narratives and young children. In S.J. Danby, M. Fleer, C. Davidson and M. Hatzingianni (eds), *Digital Childhoods: Technologies and Children's Everyday Lives* (pp. 183–96). Springer.

Gates, B. (1996). *The Road Ahead* (rev. ed.). Penguin.

Gilbert, D.J., Lehman Held, M., Ellzey, J.L., Bailey, W.T. and Young, L.B. (2014). Teaching 'community engagement' in engineering education for international development: Integration of an interdisciplinary social work curriculum. *European Journal of Engineering Education*, 40(3), 256–66.

Grobler, R. and Ankiewicz, P. (2021). The viability of diverting from a linear to a parallel approach to the development of PCK in technology teacher education. *International Journal of Technology and Design Education*, 32(2), 1001–21.

Gumbo, M.T. (2015). Indigenous technology in technology education curricula and teaching. In P.J. Williams, A. Jones and C. Buntting (eds), *The Future of Technology Education* (pp. 57–76). Springer.

Gumbo, M.T. (2020). Teaching technology in 'poorly resourced' contexts. In D. Barlex and J. Williams (eds), *An International Perspective on Pedagogy for Technology Education in Secondary Schools* (pp. 283–96). Springer.

Hallström, J., Elvstrand, H. and Hellberg, K. (2015). Gender and technology in free play in Swedish early childhood education. *International Journal of Technology and Design Education*, 25, 137–49.

Hanson, J. and Lucas, B. (2020). Signature pedagogies and Design and Technology: How they can enhance status and improve learning. In D. Barlex and J. Williams (eds), *An International Perspective on Pedagogy for Technology Education in Secondary Schools* (pp. 45–63). Springer.

Harfield, S. (2012). Design problems, satisficing solutions, and the designer as formalizing agent: Revisiting wicked problems. In H. Middleton (ed.), *Explorations of Best Practices in Technology, Design and Engineering Education, vol. 2* (pp. 133–40). Griffith Institute of Educational Research.

Harrison, C. (2009). Assessment for learning: A formative approach to classroom practice. In A. Jones and M. de Vries (eds), *International Handbook of Research and Development in Technology Education* (pp. 449–60). Sense.

Hatzigianni, M., Stevenson, M., Falloon, G., Bower, M. and Forbes, A. (2021). Young children's design thinking skills in makerspaces. *International Journal of Child-Computer Interaction*, 27. https://doi.org/10.1016/j.ijcci.2020.100216

Havenga, M. and Swart, A.J. (2022), Preparing first-year engineering students for cooperation in real-world projects. *European Journal of Engineering Education*, 47(4), 558–76.

Henriksen, D., Creely, E., Henderson, M. and Mishra, P. (2021). Creativity and technology in teaching and learning: A literature review of the uneasy space of implementation. *Educational Technology Research and Development*, 69(4), 2091–108.

Herro, D., Visser, R. and Qian, M. (2021). Teacher educators' perspectives and practices towards the Technology Education Technology Competencies (TETCs). *Technology, Pedagogy and Education*, 30(5), 623–41.

Highfield, K. (2010a). Possibilities and pitfalls of techno-toys and digital play in mathematic learning. In M. Ebbeck and M. Waniganayake (eds), *Play in Early Childhood Education: Learning in Diverse Contexts* (pp. 177–96). Oxford University Press.

Highfield, K. (2010b). Robotic toys as a catalyst for mathematical problem solving. *Australian Primary Mathematics Classroom*, 15(2), 22–7.

Highfield, K., Paciga, K.A. and Donohue, C. (2018). Supporting whole child development in the digital age. In S.J. Danby, M. Fleer, C. Davidson and M. Hatzigianni (eds), *Digital Childhoods: Technologies and Children's Everyday Lives* (pp. 165–82). Springer.

Högsdal, S. and Grundmeier, A.-M. (2021). Integrating design thinking in teacher education: Student teachers develop learning scenarios for elementary schools. *International Journal of Design Education*, 16(1), 1–26.

Howard-Jones, P.A. (2002). A dual-state model of creative cognition for supporting strategies that foster creativity in the classroom. *International Journal of Technology and Design Education*, 12, 215–26.

Hurst, E. (2016). *Imagine a City*. Doubleday.

Hutchins, P. (1967). *Rosie's Walk*. Simon and Schuster.

Hvid Stenalt, M. (2021). Digital student agency: Approaching agency in digital contexts from a critical perspective. *Frontline Learning Research*, 9(3), 52–68.

Isaac, S. (1996). *Intellectual Growth in Young Children*. Schocken Books.

Jane, B. (2008). Spirituality in technology education: Addressing the issue of student disconnectedness. In H. Middleton and M. Pavlova (eds), *Exploring Technology Education: Solutions to Issues in a Globalised World, Vol. 1* (pp. 214–21). Griffith Institute for Educational Research.

Jarvis, T. and Rennie, L. (1994, March). *Children's Perceptions About Technology: An International Comparison*. National Association for Research in Science Teaching.

Johansson, A.-M. (2021). Examining how technology is presented and understood in technology education: A pilot study in a preschool class. *International Journal of Technology and Design Education*, 31(5), 885–900.

Jones, A. and Moreland, J. (2001, 11–14 July). *Frameworks and Cognitive Tools for Enhancing Practising Teachers' Pedagogical Content Knowledge*. Australasian Science Education Research Association Conference.

Jurayeva, Z.I. (2020). Innovational methods of raising the profile of the pedagogical profession. (on the example of a practical subject profile). *International Journal on Integrated Education*, 3(8), 167–73.

Kafai, Y.B., Fields, D.A. and Searle, K.A. (2014). Electronic textiles as disruptive designs: Supporting and challenging maker activities in schools. *Harvard Educational Review*, 84(4), 532–65.

Kalamatianou, M. and Hatzigianni, M. (2018). Teaching visual arts with visual technologies. In S.J. Danby, M. Fleer, C. Davidson and M. Hatzingianni (eds), *Digital Childhoods: Technologies and Children's Everyday Lives* (pp. 197–214). Springer.

Kansou, K., Laurier, W., Charalambides, M.N., Della-Valle, G., Djekic, I., Feyissa, A.H., Marra, F., Thomopoulos, R. and Bredeweg, B. (2022). Food modelling strategies and approaches for knowledge transfer. *Trends in Food Science and Technology*, 120, 363–73.

Katz, L.G. and Chard, S.C. (2000). *Engaging Children's Minds: The Project Approach* (2nd ed.). Ablex.

Kaui, T.M.M., Doria, K., Gomera, K., Kamakau S.M. IV and Waiki, Q. (2018). Developing creativity and imagination in native Hawaiian adolescents. In N. Seery, J. Buckley, C. Canty and J. Phelan (eds), *Research and Practice in Technology Education: Perspectives on Human Capacity and Development, 2018 PATT36 Conference Proceedings* (pp. 207–15). Athlone Institute of Technology.

Keirl, S. (2020). Developing a pedagogy of critiquing as a key dimension of design and technology education. In D. Barlex and J. Williams (eds), *An International Perspective on Pedagogy for Technology Education in Secondary Schools* (pp. 135–49). Springer.

Kervin, L., Verenikina, I. and Rivera, C. (2018). Digital play and learning in the home: Families' perspectives. In S.J. Danby, M. Fleer, C. Davidson and M. Hatzingianni (eds), *Digital Childhoods: Technologies and Children's Everyday Lives* (pp. 117–30). Springer.

Kewalramani, S., Kidman, G. and Palaiologou, I. (2021). Using Artificial Intelligence (AI)-interfaced robotic toys in early childhood settings: A case for children's inquiry literacy. *European Early Childhood Education Research Journal*, 29(5), 652–68,

Kewalramani, S., Palaiologou, I., Dardanou, M., Allen, K.A. and Phillipson, S. (2021). Using robotics toys in early childhood education to support children's social and emotional competencies. *Australasian Journal of Early Childhood*, 46(4), 355–69.

Khoo, E., Merry, R. and Nguyen, N.H. with Bennett, T. and MacMillan, N. (2015). *iPads and opportunities for teaching and learning for young children (iPads n kids)*. Wilf Malcolm Institute of Educational Research, University of Waikato.

Khosronejad, M., Reimann, P. and Markauskaite, L. (2021). 'We are not going to educate people': How students negotiate engineering identities during collaborative problem solving. *European Journal of Engineering Education*, 46(4), 557–74.

Kim, E.H., Flack, C.B., Parham, K. and Wohlstetter, P. (2021). Equity in secondary career and technical education in the United States: A theoretical framework and systematic literature review. *Review of Educational Research*, 91(3), 356–96.

Kimbell, R. (2006). Innovative technological reform. In J.R. Dakers (ed.), *Defining Technological Literacy: Towards an Epistemological Framework* (pp. 159–78). Palgrave Macmillan.

Kimbell, R. (2020). Capability, quality and judgement: Learners' experience of assessment. In D. Barlex and J. Williams (eds), *Pedagogy for Technology Education in Secondary Schools* (pp. 201–17). Springer.

Konca, A.S. and Tantekin Erden, F. (2021). Young children's social interactions with parents during digital activities at home. *Child Indicators Research*, 14(4), 1365–85.

Kopcha, T.J., Ocak, C. and Qian, Y. (2021). Analyzing children's computational thinking through embodied interaction with technology: A multimodal perspective. *Education Technology Research Development*, 69, 1987–2012.

Koutropoulos, A. (2011). Digital natives: Ten years after. *MERLOT Journal of Online Learning and Teaching*, 7(4), 525–38.

Kozulin, A. (1998). *Psychological Tools: A Sociocultural Approach to Education*. Harvard University Press.

Kravtsova, E.E. (2008, 17 December). *Zone of Potential Development and Subject Positioning*. Vygotsky Symposium, Monash University.

Kuperman, A., Aladjem, R. and Mioduser, D. (2018). Kindergarten programming goes mobile. In N. Seery, J. Buckley, C. Canty and J. Phelan (eds), *Research and Practice in Technology Education: Perspectives on Human Capacity and Development, 2018 PATT36 Conference Proceedings* (pp. 81–7). Athlone Institute of Technology.

Kyza, E.A., Georgiou, Y., Agesilaou, A. and Souropetsis, M. (2022). A cross-sectional study investigating primary school children's coding practices and computational thinking using ScratchJr. *Journal of Educational Computing Research*, 60(1), 220–57.

Laidlaw, L., O'Mara, J. and Wong, S.S.H. (2021). 'This is your brain on devices': Media accounts of young children's use of digital technologies and implications for parents and teachers. *Contemporary Issues in Early Childhood*, 22(3), 268–81.

Lavigne, H.J., Lewis-Presser, A. and Rosenfeld, D. (2020). An exploratory approach for investigating the integration of computational thinking and mathematics for preschool children. *Journal of Digital Learning in Teacher Education*, 36(1), 63–77.

Leahy, K. (2018). Multiple design representations to foster idea development. In N. Seery, J. Buckley, C. Canty and J. Phelan (eds), *Research and Practice in Technology Education: Perspectives on Human Capacity and Development, 2018 PATT36 Conference Proceedings* (pp. 475–89). Athlone Institute of Technology.

Leung, C.F. (2000). Assessment for learning: Using SOLO taxonomy to measure design performance of design and technology students. *International Journal of Technology and Design Education*, 10, 149–61.

Lewis, T. (2009). Creativity in technology education: Providing children with glimpses of their inventive potential. *International Journal of Technology and Design Education*, 19, 255–68.

Leyden, F. (2008). Genius bears fruit, *Herald Sun*, 8 March, p. 101.

Ling, L., Yelland, N., Hatzigianni, M. and Dickson-Deane, C. (2022). The use of Internet of Things devices in early childhood education: A systematic review. *Education and Information Technologies*. https://doi.org/10.1007/s10639-021-10872-x

Litts, B.K., Kafai, Y.B., Lui, D.A., Walker, J.T. and Widman, S.A. (2017). Stitching codeable circuits: High school students' learning about circuitry and coding with electronic textiles. *Journal of Science Education and Technology*, 26(5), 494–507.

Lo, C.K. (2021). Design principles for effective teacher professional development in integrated STEM education. *Educational Technology and Society*, 24(4), 136–52. www.proquest.com/docview/2583394834?accountid=12528andpq-origsite=primoandforcedol=true

Ma, Y., Wang, Y., Fleer, M. and Li, L. (2022). Promoting Chinese children's agency in science learning: Conceptual PlayWorld as a new play practice. *Learning, Culture and Social Interaction*, 33, 100614.

Mackey, G. (2014). Valuing agency in young children: Teachers rising to the challenge of sustainability in the Aotearoa New Zealand early childhood context. In J. Davis and S. Elliott (eds), *Research in Early Childhood Education for Sustainability. International Perspectives and Provocations* (pp. 180–93). Routledge.

Mannheimer Zydney, J. and Hooper, S. (2015). Keeping kids safe from a design perspective: Ethical and legal guidelines for designing a video-based app for children. *TechTrends*, 59(2), 40–59.

Mannila, L., Dagiene, V., Demo, B., Grhurina, N., Mirolo, C., Rolandsson, L. and Settle, A. (2014). Computational thinking in K–9 education. In *ITiCSE-WGR 14 Proceedings of the Working Group Reports of the 2014 on Innovation and Technology in Computer Science Education Conference*. http://dx.doi.org/10.1145/2713609.2713610

McLain, M. (2021). Towards a signature pedagogy for design and technology education: A literature review. *International Journal of Technology and Design Education*, 32, 1629–48.

Meinel, C. and Thienen, J.V. (2022). Design thinking – Enabling digital engineering students to be creative and innovate. In *Design Thinking in Education* (pp. 9–23). Springer.

Merinomink™ (2018). Information. www.merinomink.com/Information/56

Middleton, H. (2005). Creative thinking, values and design and technology education. *International Journal of Technology and Design Education*, 15, 61–71.

Miles-Pearson, S. (2020). Exploring food education in the English primary curriculum. In M. Rutland (ed.), *Food Education and Food Technology in School Curricula* (pp. 9–30). Springer.

Miller, M.G. (2014). Intercultural dialogues in early childhood education for sustainability: Embedding Indigenous perspectives. In J. Davis and S. Elliott (eds), *Research in Early Childhood Education for Sustainability: International Perspectives and Provocations* (pp. 63–78). Routledge.

Mills, J.E. and Treagust, D. (2003). Engineering education: Is problem-based or project-based learning the answer. *Australasian Journal of Engineering*, 3. https://webarchive.nla.gov.au/awa/20050127221015/http://pandora.nla.gov.au/pan/10589/20050128-0000/www.aaee.com.au/journal/2003/mills_treagust03.pdf

Milne, L. (2013). Nurturing the designerly thinking and design capabilities of five-year-olds: Technology in the new entrant classroom. *International Journal of Design and Technology*, 23, 349–60.

Milne, L. (2018). Drawings to depict or drawings to explain: A whole-school analysis of children's drawings of bridges. In N. Seery, J. Buckley, C. Canty and J. Phelan (eds), *Research and Practice in Technology Education: Perspectives on Human Capacity and Development, 2018 PATT36 Conference Proceedings* (pp. 498–505). Athlone Institute of Technology.

Milne, L., Chambers, M., Moreland, J. and Jones, A. (2002). Application of an analytical framework to describe young students' learning in technology. *Proceedings of the 2nd Biennial International Conference on Technology Education Research* (pp. 60–9). Centre for Technology Education Research, Griffith University.

Milne, L. and Edwards, R. (2013). Young children's views of the technology process: An exploratory study. *International Journal of Design and Technology*, 23, 11–21.

Monteiro, A.F., Miranda-Pinto, M. and Osório, A.J. (2021). Coding as literacy in preschool: A case study. *Education Sciences*, 11(5), 198.

Moreland, J. and Cowie, B. (2009). Making meaning in primary technology classrooms through assessment for learning. In A. Jones and M. de Vries (eds), *International Handbook of Research and Development in Technology Education* (pp. 461–76). Sense.

Moreland, J., Jones, A. and Chambers, M. (2000, 29 June–1 July). *From Formative to Summative Strategies in Technology Education*. 31st ASERA Conference, Fremantle.

Mosely, G., Harris, J. and Grushka, K. (2021). Design education in schools: An investigation of the Australian Curriculum: Technologies. *International Journal of Technology and Design Education*, 31(4), 677–95.

Mueller, T. (2008). Biomimetics design by nature. *National Geographic*, April, 68–91.

Mukendi, A., Davies, I., Glozer, S. and McDonagh, P. (2020). Sustainable fashion: Current and future research directions. *European Journal of Marketing*, 54(11), 2873–909.

Murphy, G. and Salomone, S. (2013). Using social media to facilitate knowledge transfer in complex engineering environments: A primer for educators. *European Journal of Engineering Education*, 38(1), 70–84.

Nikiforidou, Z. (2018). Digital games in the early childhood classroom: Theoretical and practical considerations. In S.J. Danby, M. Fleer, C. Davidson and M. Hatzingianni (eds), *Digital Childhoods: Technologies and Children's Everyday Lives* (pp. 253–66). Springer.

Nussbaum, M., Barahona, C., Rodriguez, F., Guentulle, V., Lopez, F., Vazquez-Uscanga, E. and Cabezas, V. (2021). Taking critical thinking, creativity and grit online. *Educational Technology Research and Development*, 69(1), 201–6.

O'Connor, A., Seery, N. and Canty, D. (2018). Supporting discourse using technology-mediated communication: The community of inquiry in design and technology education. In N. Seery, J. Buckley, C. Canty and J. Phelan (eds), *Research and Practice in Technology Education: Perspectives on Human Capacity and Development, 2018 PATT36 Conference Proceedings* (pp. 148–55). Athlone Institute of Technology.

Ordaz, M.S., Klapwijk, R. and van Dijk, G. (2018). Supporting learning design language in primary education. In N. Seery, J. Buckley, C. Canty and J. Phelan (eds), *Research and Practice in Technology Education: Perspectives on Human Capacity and Development, 2018 PATT36 Conference Proceedings* (pp. 270–7). Athlone Institute of Technology.

Orzada, B.T. and Cobb, K. (2011). Ethical fashion project: Partnering with industry. *International Journal of Fashion Design, Technology and Education*, 4(3), 173–85.

Owen, D. (2020). Positive ingredients to redefining food education in schools in New South Wales, Australia. In M. Rutland and A. Turner (eds), *Food Education and Food Technology in School Curricula: Contemporary Issues in Technology Education*. Springer.

Owen, S., Davies, S. and Iles, S. (2021). Bridging communities: Developing digital literacies and introducing digital technologies in the Montessori early childhood education classroom. In D. Holloway, M. Willson, K. Murcia, C. Archer and F. Stocco (eds), *Young Children's Rights in a Digital World: Play, Design and Practice* (pp. 133–46). Springer.

Palaiologou, I., Kewalramani, S. and Dardanou, M. (2021). Make-believe play with the Internet of Toys: A case of multimodal playscapes. *British Journal of Educational Technology*, 52, 2100–17.

Papert, S. (1980). *Mind Storms: Children, Computers and Powerful Ideas*. Basic Books.

Parker, L. and King, D. (2008). Life after Pong. *The Age*, 24 April, 29.

Petrina, S. (2019). Philosophy of technology for children and youth (the relationship between philosophy and pedagogy). In D. Barlex and J. Williams (eds), *An International Perspective on Pedagogy for Technology Education in Secondary Schools* (pp. 311–23). Springer.

Plowden Committee (1967). *Children and Their Primary Schools*. Her Majesty's Stationery Office.

Plowman, L. and McPake, J. (2013). Seven myths about young children and technology. *Childhood Education*, January/February, 27–33.

Pomelov, V.B. (2021). The William Heard Kilpatrick's Project Method: On the 150th anniversary of the American educator. *Перспективы науки и образования*, 4, 436–47.

Portz, S.M. (2014). Teaching project management. *Technology and Engineering Teacher,* April, 19–23.

Primary Industries Education Foundation Australia (2015). *Investigating Technologies in Agriculture: An Educational Unit for Primary Schools*. http://primezone.edu.au/resources/pdf/11.%20investigatingtechnologies.pdf

Relkin, E., de Ruiter, L. and Bers, M.U. (2020). *TechCheck:* Development and validation of an unplugged assessment of computational thinking in early childhood education. *Journal of Science Education and Technology*, 29, 482–98.

Robbins, J. and Babaeff, R. (2012). The significance of early childhood teachers' conscious awareness of technology: Australian and Singaporean perspectives. In H. Middleton (ed.), *Explorations of Best Practices in Technology, Design and Engineering Education, Vol. 2* (pp. 84–92). Griffith Institute of Educational Research.

Rogoff, B. (2003). *The Cultural Nature of Human Development*. Oxford University Press.

Roos, C. and Olin-Scheller, C. (2018). Digital participation among children in rural areas. In S.J. Danby, M. Fleer, C. Davidson and M. Hatzingianni (eds), *Digital Childhoods: Technologies and Children's Everyday Lives* (pp. 49–64). Springer.

Rutland, M. (2018). Food education in the school curriculum: A discussion of the issues, influences and pressures on the teaching of food. In N. Seery, J. Buckley, C. Canty and J. Phelan (eds), *Research and Practice in Technology Education: Perspectives on Human Capacity and Development, 2018 PATT36 Conference Proceedings* (pp. 461–7). Athlone Institute of Technology.

Scriven, B., Edwards-Groves, C. and Davidson, C. (2018). A young child's use of multiple technologies in the social organisation of a pretend telephone conversation. In S.J. Danby, M. Fleer, C. Davidson and M. Hatzingianni (eds), *Digital Childhoods. Technologies and Children's Everyday Lives* (pp. 267–84). Springer.

Seemann, K. (2000). Technacy education: Towards holistic pedagogy and epistemology in general and Indigenous/cross-cultural technology education. In *1st Biennial International Conference on Technology Education Research 2000 Proceedings* (pp. 60–74). Griffith University.

Seemann, K. (2003). Innovation through diversity: Beyond the know-how to the know-why and who-with in cross-cultural technology education. In *Proceedings of the American–Australian Technology Education Forum* (pp. 252–61). Technical Foundation of America and the Centre for Technology Education Research, Griffith University.

Seemann, K. (2022). *Technology Genre Theory Video*. Technacy. http://technacy.org/help/technology-genre-video

Seery, N., Buckley, J., Canty, C. and Phelan, J. (eds) (2018). *Research and Practice in Technology Education: Perspectives on Human Capacity and Development, 2018 PATT36 Conference Proceedings*. Athlone Institute of Technology.

Selwyn, N. (2014). Education and 'the digital'. *British Journal of Sociology of Education*, 31(1), 155–64.

Selwyn, N. and Jandrić, P. (2020). Postdigital living in the age of Covid-19: Unsettling what we see as possible. *Postdigital Science and Education*, 2, 989–1005.

Sendak, M. (2001). *Where the Wild Things Are*. Bodley Head.

Shively, K. (2014). Digital progressive learning environments for elementary children. *Curriculum and Teaching Dialogue*, 16(1 & 2), 141–56.

Siegle, D. (2013). iPads: Intuitive technology for 21st-century students. *Gifted Child Today,* April, 146–50.

Siraj-Blatchford, J. (1997). *Learning Technology, Science and Social Justice: An Integrated Approach for 3–13 Year Olds*. Education Now Publishing Cooperative.

Slatter, W. and France, B. (2018). A model for food literacy education. In N. Seery, J. Buckley, C. Canty and J. Phelan (eds), *Research and Practice in Technology Education: Perspectives on Human Capacity and Development, 2018 PATT36 Conference Proceedings* (pp. 453–60). Athlone Institute of Technology.

Soomro, S.A., Casakin, H. and Georgiev, G.V. (2021). Sustainable design and prototyping using digital fabrication tools for education. *Sustainability*, 13, 1196.

Sorrentino, P. (2018). The mystery of the digital natives' existence: Questioning the validity of the Prenskian metaphor. *First Monday*, 23(10). http://dx.doi.org/10.5210/fm.v23i10.9434

Stables, K. (2020). Pedagogies related to teaching and learning designing. In D. Barlex and J. Williams (eds), *An International Perspective on Pedagogy for Technology Education in Secondary Schools* (pp. 99–120). Springer.

Stammes, H., Henze, I., Barendsen, E. and de Vries, M.J. (2021). Teachers noticing chemical thinking while students plan and draw designs. In *Design-Based Concept Learning in Science and Technology Education* (pp. 311–43). Brill.

Steinberg, S. (2021). Family tech talk: 20 questions for you and your kids. www.verizon.com/about/parenting/family-tech-talk-conversation-starters

Stine, M. and Weinberg, E. (2018). *Little Chef*. Pan Macmillan.

Sultan, U.N., Axell, C. and Hallström, J. (2018). Girls' engagement in technology education: A systematic review of the literature. In N. Seery, J. Buckley, C. Canty and J. Phelan (eds), *Research and Practice in Technology Education: Perspectives on Human Capacity and Development, 2018 PATT36 Conference Proceedings* (pp. 231–8). Athlone Institute of Technology.

Svärd, J., Schönborn, K. and Hallström, J. (2018). Connecting authentic innovation activities to the design process. In N. Seery, J. Buckley, D. Canty and J. Phelan (eds), *Research and Practice in Technology Education: Perspectives on Human Capacity and Development, 2018 PATT36 Conference Proceedings* (pp. 216–22). Athlone Institute of Technology.

Svensson, M. and von Otter, A.-M. (2018). Technology teachers' different ways of thinking about sustainable development in technology education. In N. Seery, J. Buckley, C. Canty and J. Phelan (eds), *Research and Practice in Technology Education: Perspectives on Human Capacity and Development, 2018 PATT36 Conference Proceedings* (pp. 33–9). Athlone Institute of Technology.

Tamati, A., Treharne, G.J., Theodore, R., Ratima, M., Hond-Flavell, E., Edwards, W., ... Poulton, R. (2021). He Piki Raukura: Assessing Ao Māori developmental constructs – Part I: Reliability of novel strengths-based measures among preschool Māori children. *New Zealand Journal of Psychology*, 50(2), 22–34.

The Sustainable Angle (2018). Future Fabrics Virtual Expo: About. www.futurefabricsvirtualexpo.com/about

Trystram, G., Broyart, B., Perrot, N. and Trelea, C. (2011). New modelling stakes and tools to face complex food systems. *Proceedings ICEF11* (pp. 321–2).

Tunnicliffe, S.D. (2022). Play and STEM foundations in the earliest years. In S.D. Tunnicliffe and T.J. Kennedy (eds), *Play and STEM Education in the Early Years*. Springer.

Ura, S.K., Stein-Barana, A.C.M. and Munhoz, D.P. (2011). Fashion, paper dolls and multiplicatives. *Mathematics Teaching*, 221, 32–3.

van Dijk, G., Savelsbergh, E. and van der Meij, A. (2020). Maker education: Opportunities and threats for engineering and technology education. In D. Barlex and J. Williams (eds), *An International Perspective on Pedagogy for Technology Education in Secondary Schools* (pp. 83–98). Springer.

Vargo, D., Zhu, L., Benwell, B. and Yan, Z. (2021). Digital technology use during COVID-19 pandemic: A rapid review. *Human Behaviour and Emerging Technologies*, 3(1), 13–24.

von Mengersen, B. and Wilkinson, T. (2020). Pedagogy for understanding the material world. In D. Barlex and J. Williams (eds), *An International Perspective on Pedagogy for Technology Education in Secondary Schools* (pp. 151–75). Springer.

Vygotsky, L.S. (1966). Play and its role in the mental development of the child. *Voprosy psikhologii*, 12(6), 62–76.

Vygotsky, L.S. (1997). The history of the development of higher mental functions. In L.S. Vygotsky, *The Collected Works of L.S. Vygotsky, Vol. 4*, ed. R.W. Rieber, trans. M.H. Hall. Plenum Press.

Vygotsky, L.S. (2004). Imagination and creativity in childhood. *Journal of Russian and East European Psychology*, 42(1), 7–97.

Walker, S., Danby, S.J. and Hatzigianni, M. (2018). Electronic gaming: Associations with self-regulation, emotional difficulties and academic performance. In S.J. Danby, M. Fleer, C. Davidson and M. Hatzingianni (eds), *Digital Childhoods: Technologies and Children's Everyday Lives* (pp. 85–100). Springer.

Wallas, G. (1929). *The Arts of Thought*. Jonathan Cape.

Wang, S.-C., Peck, K.L. and Chern, J.-Y. (2010). Difference in time influencing creativity performance between design and management majors. *International Journal of Technology and Design Education*, 20, 77–93.

Weller, J. (2020). How to write a design brief: Examples and free templates. Smartsheet. www.smartsheet.com/content/design-briefs-templates?s=519andc=29andm=1026anda=597549260762andk=andmtp=andadp=andnet=ganddev=canddevm=andplc=andds_rl=1286294andgclid=Cj0KCQjwz96WBhC8ARIsAATR252X1xabZduHDr0zLr8_9qd6ob_rUAeuVGyZ5rJNX1eSzPBA8DilgDMaAgIIEALw_wcBandgclsrc=aw.ds

Wells, J. and van de Velde, D. (2020). STEM appropriate pedagogy in technology education. In D. Barlex and J. Williams (eds), *An International Perspective on Pedagogy for Technology Education in Secondary Schools*. Springer.

Whitehouse, D. (2014). Design for life: Grant and Mary Featherston. In D. Whitehouse (ed.), *Mid-century Modern Australian Design* (pp. 144–61). Council of Trustees of the National Gallery of Victoria.

Willbold, M. (2019). Social media in education: Can they improve the learning? https://elearningindustry.com/social-media-in-education-improve-learning

Williams, P.J. (2012). Technology teachers PCK: The need for a conceptual revision. In H. Middleton (ed.), *Explorations of Best Practices in Technology, Design and Engineering Education, Vol. 2* (pp. 165–79). Griffith Institute of Educational Research.

Williams, P.J., Jones, A. and Buntting, C. (2015). *The Future of Technology Education*. Springer.

Wing, J. (2008). Computational thinking and thinking about computing. *Philosophical Transactions of the Royal Society A*, 366, 3717–25.

Wolfinbarger, K.G., Shehab, R.L., Trytten, D.A. and Walden, S.E. (2021). The influence of engineering competition team participation on students' leadership identity development. *Journal of Engineering Education*, 110(4), 925–48.

Wong, G.K.-W. and Cheung, H.-Y. (2020). Exploring children's perceptions of developing twenty-first century skills through computational thinking and programming, *Interactive Learning Environments*, 28(4), 438–50.

Wu, Y., Mechael, S.S. and Carmichael, T.B. (2021). Wearable e-textiles using a textile-centric design approach. *Accounts of Chemical Research*, 54(21), 4051–64.

Xu, M., Williams, P.J. and Gu, J. (2021). Developing an instrument for assessing technology teachers' understandings of the nature of technology. *International Journal of Technology and Design Education*. https://doi.org/10.1007/s10798-021-09698-y

Yang, W., Ng, D.T.K. and Gao, H. (2022). Robotic programming versus block play in early childhood education: Effects on computational thinking, sequencing ability, and self-regulation. *British Journal of Educational Technology*. http://doi.org/10.1111/bject.13215

Yelland, N. (2021). STEM ecologies: Productive partnerships supporting transitions from preschool to school growing a generational of new learners. In C. Cohrssen and S. Garvis (eds), *Embedding STEAM in Early Childhood Education and Care*. http://doi.org/10.1007/978-3-030-65624-9_12

Yelland, N. and Waghorn, E. (2020). STEM learning ecologies: Collaborative pedagogies for supporting transitions to school. *International Journal of Early Years Education*. http://doi.org/10.1080/09669760.2020.1863193

Yliverronen, V., Kangas, K. and Rönkkö, M.-L. (2021). Investigative activities as a basis for integrating pre-primary craft. *Technology and Science Education*, 28(2), 173–80. https://journals-stage.oslomet.no/index.php/techneA/article/view/4317

Young, T.C. and Cutter-Mackenzie, A. (2014). An AuSSI early childhood adventure: Early childhood educators and researchers actioning change. In J. Davis and S. Elliott (eds), *Research in Early Childhood Education for Sustainability. International Perspectives and Provocations* (pp. 143–57). Routledge.

Yu, K.-C., Fan, S.-C. and Lin, K.-Y. (2018). Professional development program for teaching engineering-focused curricula in technology education. In N. Seery, J. Buckley, C. Canty and J. Phelan (eds), *Research and Practice in Technology Education: Perspectives on Human Capacity and Development, 2018 PATT36 Conference Proceedings* (pp. 400–10). Athlone Institute of Technology.

Zhao, Y., Llorente, A.M.P. and Gómez, M.C.S. (2021). Digital competence in higher education research: A systematic literature review. *Computers and Education*, 168, 104212.

Zimilies, H. (1987). The Bank Street approach. In J.L. Roopnarine and E. Johnson (eds), *Approaches to Early Childhood Education* (pp. 163–78). Merrill.

Index

Aboriginal and Torres Strait Islander technologies, 13–16, 17
abstraction, 145–6
action card games, 168
activities
   design briefs, 50, 55
   evaluation, 267
   food and fibre production, 174
   food specialisations, 174
   pedagogical approaches, 296
   preferred futures, 77, 80
   sustainable technologies, 21
   technology perceptions, 11, 12
   values-based design, 264
actual zone of development, 265, 266
adhesion technologies, 5–7
affective aspect (assessment), 261
agency, of children, 73, 77, 128, 262, 291–2
agentic approach
   in assessment, 262
   in systems thinking, 20
air transport, 61
Aizenberg, Joanna, 7
Alcorn, Allan, 5
Apple Computers, 4
appropriate technologies, 17–21, 210
apps, 126, 128, 160
architect's studio (role-play), 113–17
art galleries, 244–6
assessable moments, 266
assessment
   affective aspect of, 261
   agentic, 262
   cultural-historical approach, 258, 264
   future-focused approach, 264–5
   in-the-moment, 261
   interaction and, 256–7, 271–6
   learner's experience of, 261–2
   lenses, 258–61, 262–4
   of quality, in technologies education, 268
   personal knowledge and, 257–8
   potentive, 265
   practices, 255–7
   proximal, 265, 266
   spaces for, 271–6
   taxonomy, 257
   technological, 256–7
   types, 255
Atari, 5
Australian Curriculum
   achievement standards, 255
   computational thinking defined, 149

content descriptions, 255
cross-curriculum priorities, 102
Australian Curriculum: Technologies
   achievement standards, 134, 139, 155
   aims, 25–6, 55, 125, 145
   apps, 160
   concepts, 71
   content descriptions, 36–28
   contexts, 8
   creating designed solutions, 100
   creating preferred futures, 78, 79, 82, 119–20
   design briefs, 49
   design decisions, 62
   engineering principles and systems, 204–5, 219
   food specialisations, 173–4, 188
   force, 218
   high technology, 8
   learning area content, 24–6
   materials and technologies specialisations, 204–5, 216, 219, 221
   preferred futures, 72–3
   project management in, 48, 235–6
   project work in, 231
   robots, 161
   website, 27
   Years 5 and 6 band level descriptions, 155
   see also Design and Technologies; Digital Technologies
Australian Curriculum website, 26–7
authentic tasks, 232–3
automation, 146
automobile industry, 22
Autumn, Kellar, 6
axes, 14

bags, 262–4
Barlex, D., 22–3, 42–3
basket construction, 15
biomimetics, 5–7
biomineralisation, 7
bird wings, 62–3
birthday parties, planning for, 196–8
blindness, 7
block coding, 148–9, 154
blocks, 56–9, 111–13, 226–30, 291–2
board games, 274–6
board room, 214
Bob the Builder (magazine), 297
Book Week, 134–9
books, 228, 229
box constructions, 32, 227

boys, play and, 290–2
brain train, 109
bridge-building, 221–6
buddy programs, 236
bug catchers, 299
bush survival, 55

cafés, 194–6, 248
cakes, 172, 188
Canberra, 95
canteens, 194
capability curriculum, 261
card games, 168
care, creating a system of, 139–43
careers, future orientation in, 98
cars, 22
cat cake, 172
catwalk, 46–7, 184–5
cellular phone technology, 7
Centre for Appropriate Technology, 17
chefs, 195
children
   agency of, 73, 77, 262, 291–2
   assessing, 254–67
   conceptualising futures and, 73–6
   as digital natives, 126–7
   drawing skills, 69
   holistic engagement of, 250–1
   need to be tech savvy, 128
   perceptions of technology, 9–13
   teaching technology to, 29
   technological experiences of, 74–6
   technology use, 126
   view of the future, 76–9
chocolate, 188
Christmas, 99–100
class newspapers, 242–4
classroom setting
   bridge-building, 221–6
   changing part of, 269
   computational thinking, 134–9, 147, 155–60
   Conceptual PlayWorld, 155–60, 214–18
   creating designed solutions, 99–102
   design briefs, 60–9
   digital technologies, 160–1, 165
   engineering principles and systems, 214–20, 221–6
   fashion, 185
   fibre production, 185–6
   food specialisations, 192–3, 196–200
   force, 218–20
   Foundation, 139–42
   Foundation to Year 2, 99–102, 198–200

318

kite-making, 66–9
learning environment, 276–85
paper planes, 60–6
planning for preferred futures, 80–6
play as creative design, 113–17
project management, 239–41
STEM (Science, Technology, Engineering and Mathematics), 155–60
technology education integration, 33–42
tinkering activities, 285–9
Year 1, 280–2
Year 3, 185–6
Year 6, 80–2, 160, 184–5, 214–18
Years 1 and 2, 82–6
Years 2 and 3, 239–41, 286–8
Years 3 and 4, 113–17, 134–9, 196–8
Years 5 and 6, 160–1, 194–6, 239–41, 277, 282–3
client-based projects, 181
clocks, 286–8
clotheslines, 107
coding, robots, 153
collaboration, 62–3, 209
collective designing, 108
communication, 27–8
communities
    engagement with, 212–13
    perceptions of technology in, 12
community project approach, 232–6
    history, 231
    holistic engagement through, 250–1
    in a classroom setting, 239–41
    in an early childhood setting, 236–9
community projects
    evaluation, 232, 234, 246
    in a classroom setting, 239–41
    management of, *see* project management
    pedagogy of critiquing in, 233
computational thinking
    coding and, 147
    conceptual framework, 152
    Conceptual PlayWorld, 155–60
    core concepts, 149–52
    defined, 145
    early childhood, 153–4
    historical accounts of, 145–7
    in a classroom setting, 134–9, 147
    in an early childhood setting, 165–70
    parents' views of, 148

progression of, 150
see also programming
computer clubhouses, 124
computers
    Apple, 4
    Microsoft, 5
    simulations using, 146
concept maps, 165
concepts
    contexts and, 21, 23–4
    of technological knowledge, 24
Conceptual PlayWorld
    designing a city, 218
    fashion industry, 184
    food specialisations, 198–9
    for technologies, 296, 300
    healthy eating, 199
    in a classroom setting, 155–60, 184–5, 218
    pedagogical characteristics, 301
    STEM learning, 300
    Wild Robot, The (Peter Brown), 160, 300
consequence thinking, 20
contexts
    concepts and, 21, 23–4
    of designing, 42, 105
contextual assessment lens, 260–1, 262–4
contracts, 234
COVID-19 pandemic, remote schooling, 121
creative design, play as, 111–17
creativity
    collective, 108
    cultural-historical approach, 108
    described, 108
    fostering environments for, 109
    in design and technologies, 102, 107–10
    as job skill, 98
    learning environments supporting, 276–85
    process, 109–10
creatures, lonely, 86–9
critical approach
    engineering principles and, 210
    issues-based, 241
critical thinking, 98
cross-curriculum priorities, 102
cubby building, 280–3
cultural assessment lens, 260–1, 262–4
cultural-historical approach
    to assessment, 258, 264
    to creativity, 108
culture, technology and, 13–17

curriculum documents (general)
    digital technology in, 148
    supporting creativity, 110
    technological concepts in, 24
    see also Australian Curriculum; Australian Curriculum: Technologies
Cutkosky, Mark, 6

damper, 199
data, gathering and analysing, 136–7
de Mestral, George, 6
debates, 163–4
debugging, 158, 166, 167
decisions, design, 62
design(s)
    assessment taxonomy and, 257
    biomimetics and, 5–7
    collective, 108
    contexts, 105
    decisions, 62
    dimensions, 272
    drawing, 114–17
    generating, 42–3, 52–6, 63
    imagination and creativity in, 102
    iterative approach to, 64, 261
    plans for, 117
    skills progression, 69
    technological knowledge and, 22
    values-based, 97, 262–4
Design and Technologies
    classroom integration of, 36
    content structure, 26
    creativity and imagination in, 107–10
    described, 25
    food and fibre production, 6, 173–4, 182, 188
    high technology, 8
    Knowledge and Understanding strand, 79, 204
    Processes and Production Skills strand, 37–8, 61, 63, 66, 67, 232, 236
    project management in, 236
design briefs
    analysing, 51–6
    Australian Curriculum: Technologies, 49
    bush survival, 55
    closed, 44–5, 49–50, 55, 305
    comparing, 48–51
    components, 42
    creating, 55–6
    environmental audit, 272
    evaluating, 43–51
    fairy tales, 83, 228, 273–4
    Furbies, 139–43

design briefs (cont.)
  greeting cards, 52
  hats, 53
  in a classroom setting, 60–9
  in an early childhood setting, 56–9
  kite, 66–9
  for mini-enterprises, 246–7
  musical instruments, 54
  nursery rhymes, 273–4
  open, 45–7, 49–50, 51, 55, 305
  paper planes, 65–6
  programming, 163
  for a puppet play, 83
  songs and, 229
  stories and, 83, 228–9, 273–4
  teacher preparation for, 50
  three little pigs, 57–9
design principles, 207
  engineering, 207–13
design processes
  assessment during, 273
  engineering, 208, 220
  in a classroom setting, 113–17
  in an early childhood centre, 111–13
design questions, 91–3
  ecodesign approach and, 96–8
  framework for stimulating, 96, 101
  of design solutions, 95
  quality, 96–8
design studios, 106
design technologies
  problem-based technology, 294
  teacher-framed technologies, 294
design thinking, 33–42, 110
designer competence, 255
designers, 102–5
development, zones of, 265, 266
diaries, 77, 80, 232
digital design practices, 152
digital documentation, 123
digital entries, 126–7
digital environments, questions about, 92
digital narratives, 126
digital play, 127
digital systems, 137–8
digital technologies
  ethics and, 123–5, 163–4
  in a classroom setting, 160–1, 165
  in everyday life, 121–3
  myths about, 126–8
  place of in community, 125
  problem-based technology, 295
  teacher-framed technologies, 294
  use in the community, 123

Digital Technologies
  content structure, 26
  described, 25
  high technology, 8
  Knowledge and Understanding strand, 129–31, 133, 138, 155
  Processes and Production Skills strand, 28, 39–131, 132, 138
  strands, 129–31
digital tools, 212
digital toys, 139–42, 165–7
  see also robots
disruptive technologies, 97–8, 182
documentation, digital, 123
drawing
  about the future, 76–7, 79–80
  block constructions, 227
  designs on paper, 114–17
  orientation, 57–9, 114
  skills progression, 69, 225–6
  techniques, 116–17
DUPLO blocks, 111–13

early childhood setting
  children's play in, 290–1
  computational thinking, 165–70
  design briefs, 56–9
  fibre production, 187
  materials and technologies specialisations, 226–30
  planning for preferred futures, 74–5, 86–9
  play as creative design, 111–13
  project management, 236–9
  robots, 165–7
  volunteers in, 56
Early Years Learning Framework (EYLF)
  computational thinking, 168–70
  digital technologies in, 168–9
  engaging with, 59
  on digital devices, 129
  Outcome 4, 89, 169
  Outcome 5, 27–8, 99
  play in, 110
  technologies and, 27–9
ecodesign teaching, 96–8, 99–100
eco-development, 17
eggs, 199
Ellen MacArthur Foundation, 181
engineering
  appropriate technologies, 210
  defined, 202
  design principles, 207–13
  design processes and, 208, 220
  engaging girls in, 201
  food, 189
  habits of mind, 207

  problem-based learning in, 209, 210
  as a profession, 201, 202–3, 207, 211
  project-based learning in, 210
  project management in, 235
  sustainability in, 210
engineering principles and systems
  digital tools, 212
  force, 218–20
  in a classroom setting, 213, 218–20
  in curriculum, 204–5
  knowledge associated with, 206
  teaching approaches, 207
engineers, types of, 202–3
Engineers Australia, 203, 212
enterprises (mini), 246–8
environment
  acting for the, 76–9
  auditing the, 272
  community projects, 239–41
  questioning the created, 93–5
environments
  for assessment, 271–6
  for creativity, 109
  for learning, 104–5, 254, 268–70, 276–85
e-textiles, 181–2
ethics
  as assessment dimension, 260
  digital technologies and, 123–5, 163–4
  fashion and, 179–80
evaluation
  of bridge-building unit, 224–5
  of community projects, 232, 234, 246
  of design briefs, 43–51
  of kite designs, 66–9
  of paper plane designs, 66–7
  of self, 272
  of teaching programs, 266–7
exploded plans, 117
exploitation, of poor countries, 17
exploratory activities, 165
extended tasks, 165

fabrics, 179
Fair Labor Association, 179
fairy tales, 82–6, 228, 239, 273–4
family members, as volunteers, 56, 269–70
fashion
  background information, 175–84
  ethics and, 179–80
  in a classroom setting, 184–5
  marketing and, 181

320 INDEX

sustainability and, 177–8, 179, 183–4
Featherston, Grant, 102–3
Featherston, Mary, 102–5
fibre production
　background information on, 175–84
　in a classroom setting, 185–6
　in curriculum, 173–4, 182
　in an early childhood setting, 187
fibres, 180–1
financial reports, 115
finger puppets, 185–6
flight, understanding, 60–9
food
　designing with, 192
　learning about, 190–1
　takeaway, 193
food and fibre production, in curriculum, 188
food engineering, 189
food literacy, 190–1
food politics, 192
food production, in curriculum, 173–4, 182
food specialisations
　background information on, 187–92
　in a classroom setting, 192–3, 196–8, 200
　in curriculum, 188
food technologies, 14, 191–2
force, 218–20
Ford, Henry, 22
formative assessment, 255
Fox-Turnbull, W., 21
Freddo frog challenge, 163
French knitting, 186
frequency-hopping spread spectrum (FHSS), 4
Fuller, Bob, 6
Furbies (toys), 139–42
furniture, 102–3
Future Fabrics Virtual Expo, 182
futures
　assessment focused on, 264–5
　children conceptualising, 73–6
　children's view of, 76–9
　drawing about, 76–7, 79–80
　in a classroom setting, 80–6
　in an early childhood setting, 74–5, 86–9
　orientation, in careers, 98
　preferred, *see* preferred futures
futures technologies, 296, 303–4

games technologies, 5
Gates, Bill, 5
Geckskin, 6
gender
　play and, 290–2
　technology and, 285–90, 291–2
girls
　engineering and, 201
　play and, 290–2
　technology and, 285–9, 290, 291–2
'Goldilocks and the Three Bears', 228
Google Earth, 158
greeting cards, 52
group time, 268
Gumbo, M.T., 14, 15–16, 21

'Hansel and Gretel', 274
Hastings–Monash School–Community Science and Technology Challenge, 10–11
hats, 53
healthy eating, 189, 198–9
hexadecimal code, 158
high technology, 8, 11
Hills Hoist clothesline, 107
Home Economics Institute of Australia (HEIA), 187
home visits, 280
how things work, 10–11
human movement, 218–20
'Humpty Dumpty' (nusery rhyme), 273

icy pole sticks, 114
ideas
　about technology, 22
　of technology, 22
ideas books, 236, 237
imagination
　cultural-historical approach, 108
　defining, 107
　in design and technologies, 102, 107–10
　in play, 110
　learning environments supporting, 276–85
Imagination Room, 277–80
Imagine a City (Elise Hurst), 214
Indigenous technologies, 13–16, 17, 21
infants, 27–9
information technology, 5
inquiry-based approaches, 298–9
interaction, 127, 128, 256–7, 271–6, 285–9
interpersonal assessment lens, 259–60

interviews, 80–2, 236, 237, 280
Invention Room, 277
inventions, 107–8
investigating and producing, 60–2
investigation booklets, 222–4
iPad, 126, 166

'Jack and Jill' (nursery rhyme), 274
'Jack and the Beanstalk', 82–6, 239
Jarvis, T., 9
jigsaw approach (patterns), 178
job skills, 98
Jobs, Steve, 4

Kim, Sangbae, 6
Kinderbot, 166
kite-making, 66–9
knitting, 185–6
knowledge, engineering, 206
Knowledge and Understanding (curriculum strand)
　data representation, 131, 138
　Digital Technologies, 129–31
　privacy and security, 133
　teaching ideas, 131
　technologies and society, 79
Kravtsova, E.E., 265

Lamarr, Hedy, 4, 61
language, gendered patterns of, 288
Lapland, 16
learning areas, combining, 227
learning environments, 104–5, 254, 268–70, 276–85
learning planning, in technologies,
lens technologies, 7
life-cycle analysis, 20, 183
'London Bridge is Falling Down', 229

Maker Movement/Education, 129
manufacturing, 22
marketing, 181
materials
　analysis approach to, 20
　engineering, 208, 216
materials and technologies specialisations
　bridge-building, 221–6
　in a classroom setting, 221–6
　in curriculum, 204–5, 221
　in an early childhood setting, 229
　Years 1 to 4, 221–6
mazes, 148, 166–7
Merinomink™, 180–1
Microsoft, 5
mind maps, 197, 216, 218, 219
mini-enterprises, 246–8

INDEX 321

mobile phone technology, 7
model boats, 213
model-making, 75, 113–17, 225
motivation, for learning, 220
Mr Grumpy's Outing (John Burningham), 228
multiplicative thinking, 178
musical instruments, 54

nanotechnology, 189
NASA, 6
New Zealand, curriculum in, 148
newsletters, 32
newspapers, 196, 242–4
nursery rhymes, 273–4
nutritional audits, 193

observation, drawing from direct, 116
'Old MacDonald Had a Farm', 111–13
oral planning, 75

paper dolls, 178–9
paper planes, 60–6
Parker, Andrew, 7
pattern-making, 176, 177, 178
pedagogical approaches, to technologies education, 294–6
pedagogies
  for technologies education, 269, 270
  of critiquing, 90, 208, 233
  of materiality, 183–4
  of the studio, 106
  signature, 105
personal assessment lens, 259
perspectives, 262–4
photographs, 10, 168
plan-view orientation (drawing), 57–9, 114
planning
  Conceptual PlayWorld, 157–8
  for a birthday party, 196–8
  for preferred futures, 74–5, 80–2, 86–9
  for student interaction, 271–6
  for technologies learning, home experiences featuring, 74–6
plants (science activity), 300
play
  as creative design, 111–17
  as design thinking foundation, 110
  digital, 127
  engineering principles and, 229
  gender and, 290–1

  indoor, 290
  plans for, 229
  technologies integrated into, 28
playgrounds, 220
Pong (video game), 5
popcorn holders (design brief), 44–5, 49–50
possum fur, 180–1
potential zone of development, 265
potentive assessments, 265
preferred futures (concept), 72–3
  in a classroom setting, 80–6
  in curriculum, 78, 79, 82, 119–20
  in an early childhood setting, 74–5, 86–9
  teaching, 73, 78
Prensky, Marc, 126
preschool-aged children, 27–9
Princess Smartypants (Babette Cole), 291
problem-based approaches, 294, 295, 298
problem-based learning, 209, 210
problem-solving
  computational thinking and, 145–6
  design solutions and, 96–7
problem zones, 96
process diaries, 232
Processes and Production Skills (curriculum strand)
  classroom integration of, 33–5, 36
  collaborating and managing, 67
  content descriptions, 36–28
  Digital Technologies, 129–31
  evaluating, 66, 138
  generating and designing, 63
  investigating and defining, 61
  privacy and security, 132, 138
  producing and implementing, 66
professions, 8, 160, 184, 201, 237–9
programming, 160–1, 166–7
  see also computational thinking
progress, technology and, 11
project-based learning, 209–10
project management, 235–6
  art galleries, 244–6
  class newspapers, 242–4
  in a classroom setting, 239–41
  in curriculum, 48, 235–6
  in an early childhood setting, 236–9
  mini-enterprises, 246–8
  progression in, 241–2
projects
  client-based, 181
  in curriculum, 231
  see also community projects

proximal assessments, 265, 266
proximal zone of development, 265, 266
puppets, 82–6, 185–6

questions, 10–11, 18, 80–2, 94, 165
  see also design questions

radio signals, 4
radio stations, 134–9
radios, 136
recipes, 172, 188–9, 199–200
recycling thinking, 12, 20
reflection, student, 261
reindeer herding, 16
Rennie, L., 9
reports, 68, 238
resources, for technology education, 14
restaurants, 194
robots
  classifying, 165
  coding, 153
  Conceptual PlayWorld, 153, 160
  debates around, 163–4
  Furbies, 139–42
  in a classroom setting, 160–1, 165
  investigation of, 93
  programming, 160–1, 166–7
Rogoff, Barbara, 258
role-play, 113–17, 291–2
Rosie's Walk (Pat Hutchins), 228

'S' approach (design), 42
satisficing zones, 96
school canteens, 194
science activities, 248, 299
scrambled eggs, 199
ScratchJr, 147, 148–9, 150–1, 154
screen time, 127
Seemann, Kurt, 13
self-evaluation, 272
sewing, 176–7
signature pedagogies, 105
skills, job, 98
Skype, 127
snowmobiles, 16
social embeddedness, of technologies, 13–16
social interactions, 127
social media, 211–12, 216
social value, of technology, 11–13
sociocultural approach (assessment), 258, 264
songs, 229
Star Tracker App, 154
steel axes, 14

322   INDEX

STEM (Science, Technology, Engineering and Mathematics), 2, 3, 5, 289
  in the classroom, 214–18
STEM-oriented approaches, 295, 299
STEM RealWorlds, 300
Stickybot, 6
storyboarding, 187
structured tasks, 165
studio-based approaches, 295, 298–9
studios, design, 106
summative assessment, 255
superhero catwalk (design brief), 46–7
sustainability, 188, 196
  creativity for, 108
  fashion and, 177–8, 179, 183–4
  in a classroom setting, 115
  in engineering, 210
Sustainability (cross-curriculum priority), 102
sustainable technologies, 17–21
Sydney, 95
systems thinking, 20, 77, 134–9

tacit knowledge, 211
takeaway food, 193
teacher-framed technologies, 294, 297–8
teachers
  design brief preparation by, 50
  on sustainable technologies, 19
  on teaching technology, 23, 29
  on technology, 2
teaching approaches, to technologies education, 294–305
technacy, 13–16
technologies education
  changes in, 29
  content knowledge, 21–7, 256
  pedagogical approaches to, 294–305
  pedagogical critique of, 270

question types supporting, 94
resources available for, 14
social embeddedness in, 13–16
technologists, 3–8
technology/ies
  children and, 9–13, 74–6, 126
  community project approach in, 232–6
  cultural dimensions, 13–17
  disruptive, 97–8, 182
  domination of, 127–8
  food, *see* food technologies
  high, 8, 11
  issues-based approach to, 241
  people behind, 3–8
  professions and, 8
  social interactions and, 127
  society and, 79
  teacher reflections on, 2
technology transfer, 16–17
techno-toys, 165–7
  see also robots
tessellations, 178
theatre, block area as, 227, 228
'Three Billy Goats Gruff', 274
three-dimensional planning, 75
three little pigs, 57–9
tinkering activities, 285–9
tinkering club, 10–11
tinkering tables, 136, 285–6
toddlers, 27–9, 111–13, 167–70
touchscreen interfaces, 126
toys, 129, 139–42, 165–8
  see also robots
TPACK (Technological Pedagogical Content Knowledge), 24
travel agencies, 247
two-dimensional planning, 75

Unifix® Cubes, 114

values
  as assessment dimension, 260
  in design, 97, 262–4

values-based approaches, 296, 300–3
Velcro®, 6
verbs, 218
video games technologies, 5
visual documentation, 124
volunteers, 56, 250, 269–70
Vygotsky, L.S., 107, 108, 110, 265

wall charts, 33–5
wardrobe wonders (design brief), 45–7, 49–50
waste reduction, 177–8
'The Wheels on the Bus' (song), 229
Where the Wild Things Are (Maurice Sendak), 228
whirlybird pattern, 62
Who Sank the Boat? (Pamela Allen), 228
wicked problems, 97
Wild Robot, The (Peter Brown), 97, 160
Williams, John, 23–4
windmills, 219, 220
Wing, Jeanette, 145–7
wireless technology, 4
wish lists, 236, 237
women, in engineering, 203
wood working, 239
Wooranna Park Primary School, 104
Wozniak, Steve, 4
writing, in design and technologies, 64

Y charts, 161, 282
yarn, 180–1
YarnCAD, 180–1

zero-waste design practices, 177–8
zones of development, 265, 266
zoo investigations, 248
Zulu Mama Chair, 15